Private Charity and Public Inquiry

PRIVATE CHARITY
AND PUBLIC INQUIRY

A History of the Filer and Peterson

Commissions

Eleanor L. Brilliant

Indiana University Press

Bloomington and Indianapolis

This book is a publication of

Indiana University Press
601 North Morton Street
Bloomington, Indiana 47404-3797 USA

www.indiana.edu/~iupress

Telephone orders 800-842-6796
Fax orders 812-855-7931
Orders by email iuporder@indiana.edu

The paper used in this publication meets the minimum
requirements of American National Standard for Information
Sciences—Permanence of Paper for Printed Library
Materials, ANSI Z39.48-1984.

Manufactured in the United States of America

Library of Congress Cataloging-in-Publication Data

Brilliant, Eleanor L.
Private charity and public inquiry : a history of the Filer and Peterson commissions/
Eleanor L. Brilliant.
p. cm. — (Philanthropic studies)
Includes bibliographical references and index.
ISBN 0-253-33751-8 (cl : alk. paper)
1. Commission on Private Philanthropy and Public Needs. 2. Commission on
Foundations and Private Philanthropy. 3. Charities—United States. 4.
Endowments—United States. 5. Tax exemption—United States. 6.
Corporations—Charitable contributions—United States. I. Title. II. Series.
HV91.B693 2000
361.7′632′0973—dc21
00-039647

1 2 3 4 5   05 04 03 02 01 00

To my parents,
Joseph and Leah Luria

Contents

10

Filer Commission Follow-Up: Missed Opportunities and
Emergent New Groups *126*

11

Lessons from the Past and Issues for the Future *144*

Preface

The origins of this book in a sense date back to the spring of 1976, when I attended my first United Way conference in Boston, and left the conference bearing two volumes, one, *Giving in America* (the Report of the Commission on Private Philanthropy and Public Needs) and the other, "Private Philanthropy: Vital and Innovative or Passive and Irrelevant," written by the Donee Group in response to *Giving in America*. I kept the reports for many years, without attaching great significance to them. Although I realized from discussions at the Boston Conference that the reports were considered important, I must confess to a limited understanding of that importance. I had just begun to work in the field of philanthropy, and at the time I was focused more narrowly on United Way issues.

Over a decade later, when I started my book about the United Way (*The United Way: Dilemmas of Organized Charity*), I went to my bookshelves and revisited the work of the Commission on Private Philanthropy and Public Needs. By then the Commission was more widely known as the Filer Commission (in reference to its chairman, John H. Filer, Chief Executive Officer of Aetna Life & Casualty), and I had more knowledge about its context. By then there was also a growing group of scholars and practitioners concerned about the role of the third sector at the end of the twentieth century. Both the Filer Commission and its predecessor, the Commission on Foundations and Private Philanthropy (known as the Peterson Commission, after its Chairman Peter G. Peterson, Chief Executive Officer of Bell & Howell), were now of interest. Although the Peterson Commission has received less attention in recent years, it helped shape events leading up to, and including, the work of the Filer Commission.

Both the Filer and Peterson commissions had discrete endings, leaving files to be disposed of. After the establishment of the Independent Sector, the papers of the Filer and the Peterson Commission were moved to that new organization for safe keeping. In 1992 Independent Sector transferred these papers to the Indiana University Center for Philanthropy and they became part of the Archive Collections of the Indiana University–Purdue University Library in Indianapolis. In the spring of 1992, I was pleased to be selected for the study and publication of the work of the Peterson and Filer Commissions; I was also given funding for the research from both Independent Sector and the Indiana University Center on Philanthropy. Indeed, without their support, this book would not have been possible.

In carrying out my research, I have relied extensively on the primary materials found in the Filer and Peterson Commission Archives in Indianapolis. Since John D. Rockefeller 3rd's role was fundamental to the formation and work of the two commissions, I have also worked frequently at the Rockefeller Family Archives of the Rockefeller Archives Center at Pocantico Hills, which contains numerous important related primary documents. I was also able to use government documents of the period (congressional hearings, reports and so forth) from the library of my own institution, Rutgers University. Most of all I was fortunate in being able to interview more than fifty people, some more than once, who had been involved with the work of one or both of the commissions, or who had special knowledge of them; thus I could put together living sources to back up the primary materials in the Archives.

While I was working on this study John Filer died, and, later, Gabriel Rudney; their presence at the end is sorely missed. John D. Rockefeller 3rd died in 1978; regrettably, I never met him. Peter Peterson remains very much a public figure, but with the passage of time, many other individuals who participated in the two commissions are no longer active in public life.

I am indebted to far too many people to thank them all by name. However, some individuals have been so important to my efforts that they merit particular acknowledgment. Among this group are Eric Pomeroy, former Director of the Archives at the Indiana University Library in Indianapolis, Janet Huettner, librarian, and three research assistants, Delynn Cravens, David Kauffman, and Tony Lentych at the Indiana University Center on Philanthropy. At the Rockefeller Archives Center, I was welcomed by the Director, Darwin Stapleton, and Archivist Tom Rosenthal provided invaluable expertise and assistance in locating key documents. A special note of thanks is due to Virginia Hodgkinson and E. B. "Burt" Knauft for starting me on this path, and to other members of an advisory committee that gave me early comments on Filer Commission Research; other members of the Committee included Elizabeth Boris, Charles T. Clotfelter, Stanley Katz, John Simon, and Carl Milofsky. I have also benefitted from the wisdom of Squire Bozorth, Harvey Dale, Philip Temple, and other attorneys who gave advice on particular matters of fact and law.

I want to thank Mary Edna Davidson, Dean of the Rutgers University School of Social Work, for her support, and also to acknowledge the assistance provided me with government documents by Mary Fetzer of Alexander Library. Librarian Ellen Gilbert gave frequent assistance with extraordinary competence and cheer. Two other individuals helped facilitate what used to be called typing of the manuscript, Sandy Greene and Pat Applebaum.

Special appreciation goes to Dwight Burlingame, for his faith and patience throughout this process. I also want to thank Robert Payton, who has somehow always been in the wings, and express appreciation to the very helpful editors at the Indiana University Press.

A number of people read chapters of the manuscript, including the late Elinor Barber, Daniel Halperin, and my husband, Richard Brilliant, who read it all. I am grateful to them for insightful comments. The analysis that follows is my own, but I am indebted to these individuals for their assistance. I also want to thank the many people who participated in the events described, and who left behind the records of their struggles along with their achievements.

A Note on Archival Sources

Two primary archival sources have been used throughout this manuscript: The Peterson Commission and Filer Commission Archives in the library of Indiana University, Purdue University at Indianapolis (IUPUI), and the collections related to John D. Rockefeller 3rd and the Council on Foundations at the Rockefeller Archive Center at Pocantico Hills, Tarrytown, New York.

Because these archival sources are referred to frequently, for simplicity I have used the following system respectively for each of them:

For the Peterson and Filer commissions archives, after the name of the specific document, the citation form used is: IUPUI, Box number (referring to the Box number), and then the specific Folder (File) number, for example, IUPUI, Box 2, 3. For the Rockefeller Archives, after the name of the specific document, the first reference is to the Rockefeller Archive Center, then to the collection (e.g., Rockefeller Family Archives, or Council on Foundations—COF); then the Record Group, followed by the Series (and Sub-series if there is one); the Box—number or name—and the Folder (File) name or number. Thus, for example, RAC, RFA, RG3, JDR Conf.: Philanthropy.

Special Note: Toward the end of my research in the Rockefeller Archives (late 1996), the Archives began a total reorganization of the JDR 3rd collection and related materials. It was not possible at that point to change my citations, and a reader who refers to the original documents at the Rockefeller Archives now will have to have help in locating the sources under the new classification system. In 1999 the IUPUI University Library, Special Collections and Archives, reorganized the Peterson and Filer Commissions Collections; therefore researchers will also need to have help with references that I have made to these Collections as originally organized.

Private Charity and Public Inquiry

1

Introduction

It is a distinguishing mark of our national character that we acknowledge
both a private and a public responsibility to meet the needs of our society.
To the fulfillment of this responsibility philanthropy is nothing less than
essential. . . .

[A]re we in philanthropy meeting our opportunities in today's rapidly
changing society?

If I had to answer yes or no, my answer would be no. . . . Because I believe
philanthropy generally is not attuned to the tempo of the times: it is not
giving due attention to society's new and unmet needs.

To accomplish this, I submit it is essential that we display a greater readiness
to venture, to take risks, to dare.

—John D. Rockefeller 3rd (1964)

Two Commissions

In the 1960s a great transformation occurred in American life. There were
new conceptualizations of civil rights and social justice, along with serious
challenges to basic social, political, and economic institutions in American society. The War on Poverty and a host of other social programs of the Kennedy-
Johnson administrations encompassed significant changes in the perception of
emergent groups, democratic institutions, and the construct of an evolving welfare state. In addition, during this period Americans were forced to confront
problematic international situations—first the Vietnam War and then the oil
embargo—which resulted in deteriorating economic conditions; by the mid-
1970s, matters of political integrity marred the image of the United States and
affected national morale. Although it might seem paradoxical, in the midst of
these tumultuous times, the United States Congress also took time to focus on
the nature of philanthropic activity in our country, and in particular on the issue
of charitable giving through foundations; and major tax reform legislation was
passed.

In these turbulent years John D. Rockefeller 3rd, eldest son of John D. Rockefeller, Jr. and namesake of the famous industrialist and philanthropist John D. Rockefeller, was quietly and carefully seeking ways to participate meaningfully in the process of social change around him, while at the same time fulfilling his responsibilities as a member of the Rockefeller family. The events surrounding the passage of the Tax Reform Act of 1969 gave him an opportunity to take actions which would have an impact on the charitable world and on the future of foundations in this country. Thus, in the late 1960s and early 1970s John D. Rockefeller 3rd initiated two private commissions whose purpose was to influence public policy regarding foundations and philanthropy. Ultimately the two commissions also left an important heritage for scholars and activists interested in the future of American civil society.

Through a combination of personal and institutional factors, John D. Rockefeller 3rd became a leader in the defense of voluntarism and philanthropic activity in a troubled period.[1] In front of Congressional Committees and in behind-the-scenes activity he urged the value of philanthropy and charitable institutions, even while he recognized the need for some key reforms. In 1969 and again in 1973 Rockefeller was instrumental in creating two national commissions whose efforts were dedicated to safeguarding the role of philanthropy. The first of these formal efforts was the Commission on Foundations and Private Philanthropy (1969–70), chaired by Peter G. Peterson and referred to as the Peterson Commission; the second and more widely known was the Commission on Private Philanthropy and Public Needs (1973–1977), dubbed the Filer Commission because its chairman was John H. Filer.[2] Although it was the first commission—the Peterson Commission—that was created to deal with threats to philanthropy posed by the Tax Reform Act of 1969, it was the second—the Filer Commission—which is credited with helping to promulgate the name and conscious identity of a "Third Sector"—separate from business and government, and composed of the numerous nonprofit organizations that embody the range of philanthropic and voluntary activity in the United States.[3]

This book is concerned with the history of these two commissions, the individuals who were involved with them, their plans and aspirations, and their eventual successes and failures. In telling their story I will focus on the underlying issues that affected the initial formation of both the Peterson and Filer Commissions, analyze their basic differences and commonalities, and consider the implications of the actions of the two commissions for public policy in our country.

My analysis in this book is intended to move beyond the commissions to exploration of their meaning for American society more broadly. I argue that their activities have significance beyond their own immediate context because of what they reveal about fundamental aspects of voluntarism and philanthropy, and because of the issues they raise about the development of social policy in this country generally—with particular attention to the role of powerful individuals and the intersection between public and private interests in policy making. The argument also includes consideration of the reasons why JDR 3rd wanted to create the two commissions and why the concept of "commission" might have special meaning for members of the Rockefeller family and individuals connected to them. Finally, the argument will address the heritage these commissions left behind in light of issues facing the philanthropic arena at the end of the 20th century.

This chapter begins with a discussion of some basic issues which define the general context for the efforts of the two commissions.

The Context: Voluntarism and Philanthropy

Voluntary activity has been a part of American life since the earliest days of the American colonies, when settlers had to rely on some degree of mutual support as they faced the harsh climate and unprecedented difficulties of their new situation. Although the exact scope of early voluntarism and its relationship to the developing role of government may be debatable, few would seriously challenge the words of the famous French traveler who in the 1830s described Americans as constantly forming associations and as using voluntary action to achieve purposes which elsewhere were performed by government or royalty:

> Americans of all ages, all conditions and all dispositions constantly form associations. They have not only commercial and manufacturing companies in which all take part, but associations of a thousand other kinds, religious, moral, serious, futile, general or restricted, enormous or diminutive. . . . Wherever at the head of some new undertaking you see the government in France, or a man of rank in England, in the United States, you will be sure to find an association.[4]

These familiar words by Alexis de Tocqueville have become a part of American mythology and are still recognized as representing a valued truth about the American character.

In contrast to voluntarism, philanthropy and charitable activity have a more ambiguous place in the theoretical construct of modern American society. Philanthropic activities and the giving of money may have been essential to the support of American voluntarism as it developed after the turn of the 19th century, but this historic context and particular socioeconomic framework have also resulted in charitable activities being construed as antithetical to the structure of an institutionalized welfare state. The notion of philanthropic foundations in particular has been connected to ideas of capitalism, ruthless actions by captains of industry, and the tradition of "robber barons" with excessive economic power.[5] Philanthropy has been viewed negatively because it is associated with the philosophies of Social Darwinism and *noblesse oblige,* with their implication that the fittest not only survive but prosper. In this regard, the first John D. Rockefeller was perhaps the most notorious and most frequently reviled of the original great industrialists, but he was not alone. Still, in his own time, Rockefeller's practices in building up the Standard Oil empire were considered to be monopolistic, and his philanthropic activities, like those of J. P. Morgan and Andrew Carnegie, were perceived as self-serving and opportunistic. Although justified in the name of God, these activities were nonetheless seen as the way rich people in effect redeemed their names for posterity.

Foundations started by these famous millionaires, and others such as the Lilly Endowment, the Kellogg Foundation, or later the Ford Foundation (1936), were connected to business wealth, and they have never enjoyed an easy place in American society. The events in this book in fact constitute what might be considered the third attack on powerful foundations in American life. The first focused on the Rockefeller Foundation, and arose out of federally authorized investigations of industrial power during the Progressive Era; concern centered on what was considered tainted money and excessive concentrations of industrial wealth. But as we shall see below, opposition to foundation power emerged in subsequent years from groups with differing ideological viewpoints. Thus, the second notable attack occurred amid the repressive conservatism of the McCarthy era (1952–54). The third such attack emerged in the reform era of the 1960s and continued through the early 1970s, and is a fundamental part of the story in this book.

Although foundations have been subject to the most continuous criticism, over time other forms of charitable activity have also suffered from a less than favorable reputation. Indeed, in the late 19th century the prestigious Charity Organization Society, considered to be dominated by a Social Darwinist philosophy, was ridiculed for having "scrimped and iced, in the name of a cautious, statistical Christ."[6] Federated fund-raising organizations, which developed around the same time as the early Rockefeller and Carnegie foundations, have also been criticized frequently for being tools of business interests, or for not meeting the true needs of their communities.[7] And at the end of the 20th century, debate about the role of private charity in a high-tech modern world continued. Questions have been raised from both ends of the political spectrum about the value of philanthropy and the connected issues of tax forgiveness, accountability, and private inurement, as well as about the relationship between the three formal institutional arenas of our society: business, government, and the voluntary sector. Thus, a fourth, more inclusive attack on philanthropic institutions was led by conservatives in the 1990s. This necessitated concerted counter action by leaders of the third sector; it is discussed in the final chapter.

Nonprofit Institutions: Scope and Tax Benefits

Despite the constancy of these difficult questions, voluntary activity undeniably remains a fundamental aspect of American life. In recent years our model of voluntarism has even become an inspiration for the idea of civil society in other countries around the world, including those of eastern and central Europe.[8] It is widely recognized that the character of American democracy has been shaped by the existence of a whole host of groups, organizations, and formal institutions that have developed under "voluntary auspices."[9] Moreover, these organizations of the American third sector, these voluntary, nonprofit organizations, have received the blessings of public policy through tax preferences provided under American laws since the initiation of this country's formal tax codes.[10]

Tax-exempt organizations in the United States may generally be divided into two groups: those nonprofit organizations that enjoy forgiveness for various federal, state and local taxes relating to property, purchases, and income from their activities; and a second group (defined under the 501 (c)(3) category of the U.S. tax code) which are considered to have specific charitable purposes, and therefore to warrant an additional second, or "double," benefit under our federal tax laws.[11] This second group includes most of the organizations that the general public usually associates with the idea of voluntarism. These organizations have enjoyed a second tax benefit since the ratification of the Sixteenth Amendment and the passage of the War Revenue Act of 1917, which established the principle that contributions to these organizations may (under defined circumstances) be deducted from calculations of taxable income by the donors.[12] This "tax deductibility" is allowed because these organizations are expected to carry out significant charitable activities in the public interest. Organizations awarded this second benefit of charitable deductibility include smaller single purpose organizations, self-help groups, and religious organizations, as well as more formal, complex health and welfare organizations created to serve emerging needs of the people of an industrialized country. Included also are educational and cultural institutions such as museums, universities, and foundations.

In the past hundred years the number and extent of voluntary charitable institutions has expanded and assumed increasing importance in the daily life of Americans. These organizations have received support from business as well as from the donations of countless individuals, including individuals not counted among the wealthiest members of our society. They have also frequently received government support, but until the mid-1960s these funds were derived primarily from local or state government. Such local support has continued even though, after the Great Depression, federal responsibility for the American welfare state developed extensively under the New Deal programs of President Roosevelt. However, our welfare state has characteristically been a reluctant one, and accordingly in the mid-1960s the paradigm was modified again through greatly expanded use of nongovernmental organizations for public purposes. Thus the number of nonprofit organizations in our country increased dramatically by the end of the next decade.[13] The impact of this change is reflected in the events discussed below.

Models of Decision Making and Policy Discourse

American democracy can be viewed as an essentially contested idea; it is connected to unresolved empirical questions about how decisions are made in such a large and diffuse society. Certainly the question of who rules America, and how we are governed, is constantly debated by concerned citizens as well as by scholars and academics. Since policy making is a subset of decision making, in the process of the debate a myriad of explanatory models for policy formulation in the United States have been explicated and argued by social scientists and social philosophers. In the period of the two commissions, during the 1960s and 1970s, two contrasting views of public decision making were given particular saliency: the construct of pluralism, on the one hand, and the opposing notion of an elite ruling class with dominant power, on the other.[14] While there is some justification for each of these positions, they involved different value systems that had real consequences for subsequent actions. In this vein, in the activist 1960s there was particular support for the argument that public decision making was dominated by members of an "establishment" group who came from the same universities and interacted extensively in social and business settings, as well as in the halls of Congress. In popular literature of the time, the Rockefeller family was specifically named as a prime example of this phenomenon.[15] In the 1960s this model seemed to explain a great deal of American life, and indeed it still has robust explanatory power. By extension, for example, the existence of a powerful ruling elite, posited in this approach, also explains why individuals and groups who are disadvantaged economically and socially in our society are disadvantaged politically as well.

On the other hand, belief in a pluralistic model of American society has also been widely held by the general public—and by scholars—since the time when it was articulated by de Tocqueville, if not before. Proponents of this view point to the extensive numbers and wide varieties of voluntary organizations in the American polity as proof that many group interests are represented and actively involved in a democratically based civil society, both at the community and national level. Implicit in this formulation is the fundamental belief that most groups in American society have a chance to be part of the decision making process, and in effect do so in various arenas.[16] Closely related to this view, but separated by its driving normative aspect and more progressive ideology, is the position that true democracy must be based on widespread public participation, by individuals as well as by interest groups they form.[17] However, the problem of true participation is complicated by vast differences in wealth and access, and is exacerbated in a high-technology age when expert knowledge and specialized advice have critical importance for decision makers.[18] Indeed, the history of the Peterson and Filer Commissions provides additional evidence of the importance that technical expertise assumes for government decision making.

This brief recapitulation of two contrasting public policy models highlights issues of decision making and policy formulation at the national level in our country with regard to philanthropic institutions and tax policy. To what degree is there differential access to policy makers, and to the policy making process, and how can new and emerging groups, or disadvantaged groups, gain such access? These questions are fundamental to the analysis of the two commissions under consideration here.

Also significant for the analysis that follows is another conceptual approach to public policy analysis, where attention is focused on the *nature of the policy making* that occurs rather than on the question of *who* is included. In this view questions about decision making focus on the type of decisions being made and the kind of decision making that occurs. The emphasis of this second approach is on the degree to which decisions are cut from a whole new cloth, and the extent, both in depth and breadth, of change which can—or should—be anticipated.

At one end of the continuum, scholars have posited the concept of incremental change[19] in a democratic model of decision making that has been described as disjointed incrementalism.[20] Adherents of incrementalism view the policy process through a highly political lens, including evidence of congressional decision making and federal budgetary processes. Moreover, this view is frequently contrasted with more normative, or prescriptive, views of decision making as a rational process. Emphasis in this latter approach is on data gathering, factual analysis, and consideration of a variety of feasible alternatives, along with extensive cost-benefit analysis.[21] However, attempts to impose such a model of decision making on the regular political process inevitably reveal the difficulties of implementing truly objective, rational modes of decision making in real-life contexts.[22] Nevertheless, as the case studies in this book demonstrate, even incremental policy making may utilize rational or comprehensive analytic techniques as part of decision making processes. In fact, that is one of the justifications for using technical experts as advisors to governmental agencies making policy choices.

Despite well articulated social science models and intelligent debate about how public policy is formulated, understanding of decision making processes in the complex American state remains elusive. In this regard, the history of the Peterson and Filer Commissions provides an in-depth picture of concentrated efforts to influence public decision making, as well as a paradigmatic critique of the idea of American pluralism. Here we see groups of private, concerned individuals, beginning with John D. Rockefeller 3rd, coming together to focus on public policy issues with determination to have an impact on the formulation of public policy in matters related to their own financial or charitable interests. Thus the ability of these groups, enabled as commissions, to cross private lines and to influence public decisions reflects the nature of an imperfect American pluralism, and sheds light on the way that major institutions of the American government (particularly the Congress and the President) intersect with private interests. In effect, these studies illustrate the functioning of a powerful policy network which included representatives of private wealth, professional expertise, public officials, and business interests.[23]

Finally, the story of these commissions and their contexts also helps to illuminate the nature of discourse involved in policy making in our country. Indeed, it will be shown how deliberations of the two commissions inevitably touched on key dilemmas of American public policy beyond their original intentions. Among the critical issues that emerged in the discussions of the two commissions were questions which have concerned Congress and the public since the earliest days of foundation-building:

1. How can the public be assured that the economic power which is vested in "private" foundations will not remain in control of a small group of individuals in perpetuity?

2. How can the public interest be protected in the use of funds that are concentrated in private instruments defined in public law and that enjoy tax

protection at all levels of government (federal, state, and local)? To what extent do such tax "shelters" interfere with the realization of an equitable tax code?

3. How, if at all, should the law distinguish between service-providing organizations that are recipients of funds from foundations, and the foundations, endowed with funds from individual or corporate sources, that are created for the purpose of supporting activities of such beneficiary organizations or groups?

4. Should money shielded from public taxes through "special" preferences, such as the charitable deduction, be construed as private or public? And if it is judged to be public, can there be any meaning to the concept of private philanthropy?

5. What would be an appropriate relationship between the three sectors— private for-profit, government, and nonprofit—in meeting public needs? Indeed, can such a relationship be prescribed?

The next chapter will develop these questions further and will provide a framework for understanding why—in a highly cathected environment—a member of the Rockefeller family would consider taking the initiative in developing two public policy oriented commissions. Chapter 2 will set the stage for analysis of the later events and outcomes of the Filer and Peterson Commissions.

2

Point and Counterpoint

Emergent Questions about Philanthropy

The funds of these foundations are largely invested in securities of corporations dominant in American industry. . . . The policies of these foundations must inevitably be colored, if not controlled, to conform to the policies of such corporations.

—*Final Report of the Commission on Industrial Relations* (1915)

Mr. Keele (General Counsel): Mr. Rockefeller, over the years that you have been interested in the Foundation, from your conversations with your father, have you . . . detected any apprehension or fear personally or on the part of your father that the Rockefeller Foundation or foundations in general were giving support to projects which might tend to undermine the capitalistic system?
Mr. John D. Rockefeller, 3rd: I have not, sir.

—*Hearings* of the Select Committee on Tax-Exempt Foundations, 1952

Americans provide support for organized charity through preferences embedded in the federal tax code, but they do not do so without second thoughts. Indeed, their ambivalence about charitable institutions erupts from time to time in front-page headlines about philanthropic issues or the role of philanthropy in American life. In this sense, the attacks on foundations in the late 1960s, which are the focus of this book, are part of a historical pattern of Congressional concern about the institutions of organized charity, and even more specifically, about some perceived leaders of the field—the major American foundations. Thus, as noted in the previous chapter, the attacks at the end of the 1960s had been preceded by two earlier investigations of foundations. The first was in the Progressive Era when the United States Commission on Industrial Relations uncovered the close connection between industry and foundation development; the next occurred in the reactionary mood of the 1950s when foundations were criticized for what were viewed as "suspect" liberal ideologies.

In these first two Congressionally authorized inquiries, members of the Rockefeller family, and their philanthropic activity, came under special scrutiny; this continued even after the 1950s when the limelight began to be shared with other members of the growing foundation field. But the two initial investigations remained a significant part of the institutionalized memory of the Rockefeller family in subsequent years—and through the period of our primary interest (1960–1978). In addition, the Congressional inquiries of the 1950s had a strong impact on other philanthropists as well. Both of these early investigations therefore provide an important background for the later story of the Peterson and Filer commissions.

The Walsh Commission

The U.S. Commission on Industrial Relations, also referred to as the Walsh Commission because of its Chairman, Frank P. Walsh, was created by an act of Congress on August 23, 1912.[1] The impetus for the commission was a specific incident—the bombing of the *Los Angeles Times* building almost two years before—but, in light of the increasing labor unrest in the country, the commission was given a broad mandate to consider industrial and management issues.[2] Membership on the commission included representatives from the three groups affected by these issues: management, labor, and the public. It was granted two years to do its work; it was also given subpoena powers and what was, for the time, a large sum of money to enable it to hold hearings and carry out its inquiry.[3] After more open conflict erupted in the coal mines of Colorado, a subcommittee of the House Committee on Mines and Mining was also involved in similar investigations, but it was claimed that the lines of inquiry had a somewhat different focus.[4] In any case, the Walsh Commission actually began its inquiry under President Woodrow Wilson, after strikes had erupted in the Southern Colorado mines in September 1913.[5]

Matters escalated further when, on April 20, 1914, workers of the Colorado Fuel and Iron Company (CFI) and their families were attacked by state militia in the tiny "hamlet of Ludlow." What came to be known as "the Ludlow massacre" involved forty fatalities, including the tragic deaths of eleven children and two women. These deaths became a rallying cry against the mine managers and owners.[6] Among these owners was John D. Rockefeller Sr., who had a large block of shares of the CFI, while his son, John D. "Junior," served as his representative on the CFI Board.[7] The Rockefellers insisted that they had given over operations of the mines to the managers; nevertheless, after the Ludlow violence, they were directly identified with the struggles in Colorado, and both Rockefellers, but particularly Junior, became targets of public outrage and investigation. Junior appeared once before the Congressional investigating committee under Representative Martin Foster (April 6, 1914) and twice before the Walsh Commission (in New York in January, and in Washington in the spring of 1915). By then the commission had subpoenaed Rockefeller papers, including correspondence in which JDR Junior had expressed approval of harsh treatment of mine workers. In the Washington questioning in May, Junior was given a much rougher time by Commissioner Walsh.[8]

JDR Senior and Junior were strongly affected by the negative publicity they suffered in this period. By spring of 1914 Junior was already seeking counsel from new advisors, starting with the soft-spoken but acute Southerner Ivy Lee, who became his effective public relations buffer. Under continued pressure about poor labor relations, Junior also hired MacKenzie King to head a project on industrial relations for the Rockefeller Foundation. This resulted in a plan for a company union in the Colorado mines, and also led to increased suspicion about the ways in which the Rockefeller Foundation was used, and could be used, for industrial purposes.[9]

Despite his intensive investigations, Walsh did not achieve consensus in his commission, and majority and minority reports were issued together. The principal final report was a minority report written by Basil M. Manly, Director of Research and Investigation; it was signed by Walsh and three of the pro-labor commission members. This report discussed many problems related to abusive industrial practices and corporate power, singling out the Rockefellers for particular attention. The Walsh Report included condemnation of the vast fortunes of the Rockefellers and other powerful business interests.[10] When it was released, its conclusions were criticized, and Walsh was soundly rebuked in the *New York Times* for being an excessive ideologue.[11] Several months later Congress refused to provide resources for continuation of the commission as it had been constituted. Meanwhile, in December 1915, the Colorado strike was settled; a trip by Junior to Colorado in October was said to have helped reduce tensions with the miners.[12] Later when America entered World War I, President Wilson asked Frank Walsh to co-chair the War Labor Board with William Howard Taft.[13]

The Walsh Commission raised troublesome questions about the concentration of wealth and industrial power in American society, and made many suggestions about improving industrial relations and working conditions. It also tied industrial wealth to the creation of foundations.[14] Although the final report clearly targeted the Rockefeller "group of foundations," it included a number of general recommendations: (1) that foundations with multipurpose functions and funds of over $1 million should be required to have a federal charter;[15] (2) there should be limitations on the accumulation of funds by foundations, and at the same time also limits on the expenditures of such funds in a ten-year period; (3) foundations should make open reports to the "proper government officials"; (4) there should be "provision by Congress for the through investigation by a special Committee or commission, of all endowed institutions with significant property or income"; (5) the federal government should counter the influence of these foundations by appropriations in support of its own activities in the field of education and social services.[16]

At the time, these recommendations did not receive wide acceptance, and were not among the parts of the report most seriously considered by Congress. Still, the recommendations and the issues raised were apparently not entirely forgotten. Indeed, in many respects, the same issues resurfaced in the 1950s and even more emphatically in the 1960s Congressional inquiry into foundations. In the event, the Rockefeller family appeared to have learned from the past: they would never again be unprepared to deal with public opinion, and they would take measures to avoid unpleasant publicity. As we shall discover below, their efforts have frequently, although not always, paid off. But others involved in the foundation world were less vigilant.

Cox and Reece: Congressional Committees in the McCarthy Era

Periodic outbreaks of public concern about the Rockefellers and the philanthropic activity of the wealthy elite reflect both the ambivalent feelings, and the fascination, that Americans have for the rich and the powerful. The public has given particular attention to the Rockefeller family because of its industrial past and because throughout the 20th century it has remained among the richest and most influential of American families. However, it was already signaled in 1915, and by the 1950s it became evident, that for Congress and for many others the use of foundations as a protection for individual family and corporate fortunes was a more generalized, growing problem.[17] Thus, in the outbreak of Congressional investigations in the early 1950s, questions were raised about the involvement of tax-exempt organizations and businesses more broadly. Most dramatically, in the mid-1950s the primary attack came from conservative forces on the right, now worried that powerful foundations were giving their money in support of anti-American, pro-communist causes. This attack, surprisingly, happened in a prosperous and relatively quiescent time when a spirit of optimism generally prevailed in the United States.

As a whole, the early 1950s in this country were marked by a belief in the inevitable successes of democratic capitalism.[18] But concomitantly, the period was characterized by a pervasive fear of communism. Beginning with the Truman administration after World War II and accelerating in the Eisenhower years of the 1950s, cold war politics and opposition to communism became a fact of American life; in the early years of that decade, the country was also fighting a real war against communism in Korea.

In this period a virulent anti-communist rhetoric emerged in the Congress. It was in this environment, in July 1951, that the first of two select subcommittees of the Congress was proposed for the purpose of investigating suspected anti-American activities by leading, well-respected foundations. Included in the inquiry were the Carnegie Corporation, the Rockefeller Foundation, the Guggenheim Foundation, and the Rosenwald Fund.[19] Under the chairmanship of Congressman E. Eugene Cox (Democrat, Georgia) the Select Committee to Investigate Foundations and Comparable Organizations (established in April 1952) heard testimony from representatives of the leading foundations. Consequently in 1952 the third John Rockefeller, JDR 3rd, as Chairman of the Rockefeller Foundation, was called to Congress to defend his family and his family's most sacred institution. This time the Foundation's president, Dean Rusk, also testified, along with other professional representatives of the foundation world. Foundation professionals later described the process as thorough and fair, on the whole.[20]

In the end, in fact, the Cox Committee's bark proved worse than its bite. Although the Committee found some abuses in grantmaking, overall it absolved the foundations of intentional "wrong doing" and, after six months of hearings, issued a report which stated:

> The committee believes that on balance the record of the foundations is good. . . . While unwilling to say the foundations are blameless, the committee believes they were guilty principally of indulging the same gullibility which infected far too many of our loyal and patriotic citizens and that the mistakes they made are unlikely to be repeated. The committee does not want to imply that errors of judgment constitute malfeasance.[21]

However, matters did not rest there. Claiming that the Cox Committee had too short a time to do its work well, in early 1953 Representative B. Carroll Reece (Republican, Tennessee) obtained Congressional approval (and some appropriations) for continuation of its work.[22] Among the areas investigated by this Special Committee to Investigate Tax-Exempt Foundations and Comparable Organizations (the Reece Committee) was the extensive support provided by the Carnegie Endowment for Gunnar Myrdal's study of the Negro in America, *An American Dilemma*,[23] and that of the Rockefeller Foundation for the work of Dr. Alfred Kinsey (Indiana University) on American sexual behavior. The Rocke-

feller Foundation funded Dr. Kinsey's studies, beginning in 1941, and his best-
selling *Sexual Behavior in the Human Male* (1948) raised the level of national
attention to American sexual mores.[24] Congressman Reece apparently was particularly disturbed because he believed that tax-subsidized money provided by
the Rockefeller Foundation enabled Kinsey to disseminate findings that under-
mined important moral and cultural values of American society.

In carrying out its investigation the Reece Committee asked no foundation
representatives to testify; statements were taken from staff members, technical
experts in the government, and five general witnesses not connected with foundations.[25] In the end the proceedings were riddled by strife, and the Committee
faced open opposition from one of its own members, Representative Wayne
Hays (Democrat, Ohio) whom conservatives labeled a liberal "New Deal"
Democrat.[26] Given the dissension, the majority report was not unanimously
accepted by the Committee and had very little impact in Congress.

The questioning of foundation activity by two special committees of Congress took place in the context of the hysterical, anti-communist investigatory activities of other Congressional committees chaired by Senator Joseph
McCarthy (Wisconsin) and the similarly driven Senator from Nevada, Patrick
A. McCarran.[27] Thus the attacks on foundations certainly had profoundly ideological motivations, but they were also tied to core issues of the American political economy and the nature of national public support for private charitable
activity. Those who viewed tax forgiveness through the devices of the charitable deduction and tax-exempt status for charities as essentially a public sub-
sidy found particular reason to be concerned about the stewardship of such
money. Questions were primarily directed at foundations, rather than other
kinds of tax-exempt organizations, such as direct service (family) agencies,
schools, or museums, because disbursal of the accumulated wealth connected
to foundations was subject to less direct public observation. In addition, the
foundation structure seemed to enable a relatively small group of individuals,
extensively linked through membership on foundation boards and related institutions, or even one major donor, to use vast resources for influencing public
policy in our country and abroad.[28]

In the period of prosperity following World War II, and with high tax rates
connected to the Korean War effort (1950–53) encouraging their establishment,
the number of foundations had begun to mushroom. Most notably the numbers
of family foundations with significant holdings in related businesses had increased considerably.[29] Concern about the implications of this growth for the
future was stated expressly in discussions about the purposes of the Reece Committee.[30] Arguably the attitudes expressed by members of both the Reece and
Cox committees also reflected the American tradition of distrust of wealthy,

primarily eastern, elite leadership. Indeed, the Cox Committee explicitly recommended that the foundations try to broaden their boards to include individuals from outside the East Coast, notwithstanding the fact that, in comparison
with the Reece Committee, members of the Cox Committee seemed more accepting of elite establishment leadership. In effect, this suspicion of the hege-
mony of the eastern "establishment" joined with the fear of anti-American con-
spiracies that emerged in the Congress—despite the fact that given the nature
of the groups involved, the charge of communism might have seemed absurd.
Indeed the quoted exchange with John Rockefeller (in the Epigraph) would suggest this. Nevertheless, prominent individuals and "suspect" institutions once
funded by the Rockefeller Foundation were harmed in the process.[31]

In addition to particular ideological concerns, however, a fundamental,
long range question about the national interest in philanthropic institutions was
raised in the charges to the Cox and Reece committees. Thus, in the Resolution
(adopted April 4, 1952) that created the first (Cox) Select Committee to Investigate Foundations, the Committee stated that it was

> authorized and directed to conduct a full and complete investigation and
> study of educational and philanthropic foundations and other compara-
> ble organizations which are exempt from federal income taxation to de-
> termine which such foundations and organizations are using their re-
> sources for the purposes for which they were established and especially
> to determine which foundations and organizations are using their re-
> sources for un-American and subversive activities or for purposes not in
> the interest or tradition of the United States.[32]

The Committee's investigatory charge was clearly built on the implicit assumption that certain kinds of organizations which enjoy tax benefits (i.e., educational, philanthropic) should be held publicly accountable for carrying out
activities in the public interest. However, as it turned out, Committee members
seemed to consider accountability particularly problematic in the case of foundations, for all the reasons already mentioned. Indeed, in what was the first
statutory distinction between publicly supported charitable organizations and
others which were not so defined, Congress had already passed a law a decade
earlier (1943) requiring only certain exempt organizations to file annual information returns; in effect, these were the foundations. Churches, certain other
religious and educational groups, and *"other publicly supported organizations"*
(i.e., those who get support from widespread donations) had been *explicitly excluded* from this requirement (emphasis added).[33] Apparently at that time Congress was seeking information to determine the need for additional legislative
restrictions on charitable organizations. But the 1943 legislation indicated the

need for giving special attention to organizations protected from public exposure by virtue of the private source of their funding. Consistent with this concern, the Cox Committee had also determined that

> So far as we can ascertain there is little basis for the belief expressed in some quarters that foundation funds are being diverted from their intended use. There have been instances of such diversion but we believe that the criticism is unwarranted in the main. . . . *The committee believes that public accounting would go far toward eliminating such abuses.*[34] (Emphasis added)

The Cox Committee report concluded with a suggestion that specific tax issues remained to be explored which they considered would be more appropriately handled by the Internal Revenue Service (disclosure and accountability) or the House Ways and Means Committee (corporation control and tax avoidance).

The Cox Committee proposed an Act for increasing foundation accountability which was not adopted, but in fact similar provisions for public disclosure of information through the tax returns of exempt organizations had already been authorized in the Revenue Act of 1950.[35] Still, despite the requirement to file annual IRS reports, foundations were amazingly reluctant to do so.

In regard to accountability and public information the Cox Committee stated explicitly that it "was unable to obtain an Executive order which would have permitted an examination of the returns required of tax-exempt organizations." Major issues passed to the House Ways and Means Committee were defined by questions 11 and 12 in the report: (11) Are foundations being used as a device by which the control of great corporations are [sic] kept within the family of the foundation's founder or creator? (12) To what extent are foundations being used as a device for tax avoidance and tax evasion?[36] Thus, concerns of the Cox Committee influenced the revamping of the Internal Revenue Code in the Tax Reform Act of 1954, which included a new codification of the policies regarding tax-exempt organizations. Ultimately, however, some of the bigger questions of accountability remained, and were to be part of the later discussions of the 1960s and 1970s regarding tax policies and American foundations. A brief review of policies concerning tax exemption prior to the reform era of the 1960s will help the reader to understand these later developments.

Tax Policy and American Foundations

To begin with, U.S. tax policy has been described as a compilation of complex provisions and regulations, piled on top of each other without any intentional overall plan. This unsystematic development includes provisions that have had a direct impact on the history of tax-exempt organizations as well.[37] As a whole the development of American tax policy, like the formulations of the American budget, reflects incrementalism in policy making—with the President, the Congress, contextual factors (like the economy), and administrative and judicial bodies all influencing the shape of policy at any given moment. Moreover, tax policy in this country is not just a federal matter; a variety of state and local tax policies are also part of the legal parameters for tax-exempt activity.[38] Despite these complexities, identifiable values and conditions have certainly affected the way that the law of tax-exempt organizations has been formulated since its initial development in the late nineteenth century.

Tax exemption in the United States is determined by local and state laws, by federal statutes, and by judicial decisions. In this country foundations also may be formed either as trusts or corporations.[39] However, like other nonprofit entities, they are most frequently created under state corporate law; under these laws they have been consistently distinguished from profit-making corporations because of their presumed public purposes. From the colonial period on, they have generally been granted state and local tax benefits. Thus, even though there is great variation in law and practice among the states, for the most part nonprofit organizations, and particularly the large subset of charitable organizations of concern here, are in some degree exempt from local property taxes, state income taxes, sales taxes, estate taxes, and other miscellaneous taxes, as well as from national income taxes.[40]

Although a limited form of national income tax had been enacted long before then (in connection with the Civil War), 1894 is considered a watershed year in the conceptualization of federal income tax policy.[41] In that year inclusive income tax legislation was passed by Congress for the first time. However, the 1894 Act was ruled unconstitutional (Pollock v. Farmers' Loan and Trust Company, 1895), and it was not until the Sixteenth Amendment to the Constitution was ratified by the states (February 3, 1913) that a federal income tax was firmly established.[42] The Revenue Act of 1913 marked the beginning of what has been called "constitutional" income taxes at the federal level. This legislation, like the earlier unsuccessful Act of 1894, included a provision that excluded from taxation certain kinds of organizations that were determined to be in the public interest (religious, charitable, educational, and scientific).[43]

Second, in its general parameters the American definition of tax-exempt charitable activity draws upon British legal tradition, including reference to the purposes of charitable trusts described in the Preamble to the Elizabethan Poor Law of 1601. The Preamble referred to these purposes as some for relief of aged, impotent and poor people, some for maintenance of sick and maimed soldiers, and mariners, schools of learning, free schools, and scholars in universities, some for repair of bridges, ports, havens, causeways, churches, seabanks and highways, some for education and preferment of orphans, some for or towards relief, stock or maintenance or houses of correction, some for marriages of poor maids, some for supportation, aid and help of young tradesman, handicraftsmen and persons decayed, and others for relief or redemption of prisoners or captives, and for aid or ease of any poor inhabitants concerning payments of fifteens, setting out of soldiers and other taxes.[44]

In the original delineation of tax-exempt organizations in the Corporation Excise Tax Act of 1909, the earlier English enumeration of tax-exempt activities was consolidated into three main categories: religious, charitable, and educational.[45] However, in the income tax legislation finally passed in 1913 a fourth category was added, scientific.[46] In common parlance the listed categories belong to a larger tax-exempt group which is often characterized in its entirety as "charitable" because of its relationship to the charitable deduction. Nevertheless the question of what is meant by "charitable" specifically, as opposed to the other categories in this list, has remained an unresolved issue in the United States. If "charitable" includes all of them, why are some of them differentiated and named separately? And if "charitable" is not all-inclusive, instead of using the common law tradition, should we be employing the more narrow definition of charity generally used in everyday language (i.e., to help the poor and needy), as critics of current practices often argue?[47] In the broader view of charity America again follows British precedents: in 1891 a famous legal decision by Lord McNaughten (and still often quoted) stated unequivocally that

> charity in its legal sense comprises four principal divisions: trusts for relief of poverty; trusts for the advancement of education; trusts for the advancement of religion; and trusts for other purposes beneficial to the community, not falling under any of the preceding heads. . . . The trusts last referred to *are not the less charitable in the eye of the law, because incidentally they benefit the rich as well as the poor, as indeed, every charity that deserves the name must do either directly or indirectly.*[48] (Emphasis added)

Third, the concept of a charitable tax privilege passed from a focus on the organization's taxpaying status to consideration of the donors' income taxes.[49] Thus, in 1917 when personal income taxes were increased to pay for World War I, Congress also authorized the deduction of contributions made by individual taxpayers to "corporations or associations operated exclusively for religious, scientific, or educational purposes" with a limited "maximum of 15% of the taxpayer's net income computed without the benefit of the charitable deduction."[50] By 1918 "prevention of cruelty to children or animals" had been included among the tax-exempt provisions and in 1921 "literary" became another listed purpose, thus demonstrating once again the mutable nature of the definition of "charitable purposes." Well into the 1960s American law treated the charitable deduction with favor and protected the exemption of philanthropic organizations.[51] Congress generally increased the amounts of individual tax deductions available over the years, even while subjecting some activities to additional scrutiny.[52] In this vein, in 1918 Congress authorized deductions from estate taxes for charitable transfers;[53] gift tax deductions soon followed but were not finalized until 1932.[54] Nonetheless, some members of Congress continued to perceive the charitable tax deduction as providing more benefits for the rich than it did for the American public.

Fourth, although foundation activity (as distinct from that of other exempt direct service organizations) had been scrutinized as early as the Progressive Era, the initial conceptualization of tax-exempt organizations did not distinguish foundations from other charities. This was rectified in the Revenue Act of 1921 which explicitly expanded the class of permissible donees to include any "community chest, fund, or foundation, organized and operated exclusively for religious, charitable, scientific, literary, or educational purposes."[55]

With the minor exception noted above, for the first half of the 20th century federal tax laws really did not distinguish materially between service-providing charitable organizations, like museums or hospitals, and private intermediary organizations, like foundations, whose main purpose was funding the activities of others. Charitable entities were all grouped together both in reference to their organizational exemption from income tax and with regard to the tax deductibility of gifts to them. The one exception was the 1943 provision for annual information to be provided by the group of non–publicly funded organizations, which apparently was not rigidly enforced. However, undeniably by the early 1950s a sense of distinction between foundations (that is, private charities) and publicly supported charities had begun to emerge.

Tax Exemption and the Public Interest

Tax exemption and tax deductions for charitable gifts are based on a distinction between activities dedicated to making profits and those that are presumed to be devoted to the public welfare. Indeed, although Congressional discussions have on the whole not attempted precise definitions of the nature of this public good, this basis for tax exemption is stated in numerous places as the core rationale for tax forgiveness for charitable organizations.[56] For example, a House Ways and Means Committee Report relating to the Revenue Act of 1938 stated that

> The exemption from taxation of money or property devoted to charitable or other purposes is based upon the theory that the Government is compensated for the loss of revenue by its relief from financial burden which would otherwise have to be met by appropriations from public funds, and by the benefits resulting from the promotion of the general welfare.[57]

Unlike most of the Acts passed by Congress in the preceding decades, which had tended to broaden the scope of tax-exempt activities, the 1938 Revenue Act contained a defined limitation on the deductions of charitable contributions by corporations and individual taxpayers, restricting them "to contributions made to domestic institutions." Given the financial condition of the United States in the years of the Great Depression, limiting the charitable tax deduction to organizations operating in this country was certainly understandable.[58] It also reflected President Roosevelt's evident reluctance to reduce tax revenues needed by the government. In this vein, in 1935 Roosevelt had actively opposed legislation to provide tax incentives for corporate giving, but after intensive lobbying, the law—which allowed corporations a charitable deduction of up to five percent of their net profits—was passed over his objections, and probably contributed to the need for restrictions in the 1938 Act.[59] In any case, although corporations have never averaged close to the allowable five percent contribution, the 1935 law established an important legal principle.

Charities, Profits, and Business

Corporations may make tax-deductible contributions to tax-exempt organizations, and they may, under defined circumstances, count contributions to good works in the community as part of their operating expenses; they may also create their own foundations. However, the Internal Revenue Code and state statutes have generally attempted to maintain a distinction between business activity and nonprofit purposes. Still, as the history of criticism of the Rockefeller Foundation and other foundations indicates, the distinction between business and charitable organizations has never been complete. Indeed, according to Marion Fremont-Smith, before 1950 it was not uncommon for tax-exempt organizations to benefit from "feeder corporations"—that is "enterprises owned by exempt organizations that did not dispense any charity but merely produced income for the parent charity."[60]

Fremont-Smith suggests that before the 1950s this practice was utilized more by other types of charitable institutions than by foundations. A number of court decisions indicate that there was uncertainty about the status of this situation in this period,[61] with possibly the best known case being that involving the gift of a spaghetti factory to the New York University Law School. Prior to the passage of the 1950 Revenue Act, and in fact during the Congressional hearings on it, a Tax Court had ruled that the Mueller Macaroni Company was not exempt from taxation, even though other cases around that time had granted such exemption on grounds that the "destination of income" for charitable purposes was the determining factor.[62]

Given the variety of interpretations on this issue, Congress attempted to remove the uncertainty about the relationship of business activity to charitable organizations. The Revenue Act of 1950 in effect defined charitable status as limited only to organizations which were organized and operated primarily for "exempt" purposes (as already discussed above). The House Ways and Means Committee argued against granting exemption to business and trade organizations which were "feeders" of funds for nonprofit organizations, apparently out of concern that this allowed for unfair competition with other small businesses that did not enjoy such tax exemption.[63] Although often the matter was interpreted pragmatically, the Revenue Act of 1950 also specified that any income that exempt organizations derived from unrelated business activity would thereafter be subject to taxation.

Tax-exempt activity is supposed to realize public good, not private gain. Consequently, prohibition against private gain for "interested individuals" was included in the concept of charitable activity in the formulation of the federal Corporation Excise Tax Law in 1909. The same prohibition against private inurement was built in to the definition of tax-exempt organizations in the 1913 Revenue Law, and has remained a fundamental prerequisite for charitable, tax-exempt status under the law. Benefits accruing to individuals through the use of private foundations are subject to scrutiny under this criteria and the related criterion of public benefit.

In another effort to curb abuses from excessive holding of wealth by families and small groups of interested individuals, the Revenue Act of 1950 included provisions which required foundations to make "reasonable payouts" of funds annually to grantees and recipients. The Revenue Act of 1950 denied tax exemption on income of a foundation for "a taxable year in which accumulation out of income was 'unreasonable in amount or duration.' "[64] Reasonable payout was never precisely defined, and in the next decade the only time that "unreasonableness" was used exclusively as the basis for an unfavorable ruling was in the situation of the Danforth Foundation. In 1962 it was revealed that the foundation's tax-exempt status had been revoked for several years, based on transgressions in the early 1950s.[65] In any case, after the passage of the Revenue Act of 1950 there was an articulated legislative doctrine against excessive private asset accumulation and other fiscal abuses by foundations, and this was joined to the idea of defined public purposes to which such money should be dedicated.[66]

The major revision of the Internal Revenue Code (IRC) in 1954 incorporated provisions from the 1950 Tax Act relating to tax-exempt organizations and, as a whole, reaffirmed the American public policy commitment to charitable giving. The 1954 Internal Revenue Code still included liberal charitable deductions for higher income taxpayers, and also gave birth to the 501(c)(3) number classification which is often used as a substitute term for "charities."[67] However, in the revised code of 1954, Congress also moved toward some delineation of two charity "worlds"—the first consisting of private foundations, and the second of groups that were defined as *not* private foundations.[68] The revised IRC added a differentiation in the amount that could be deducted for gifts to some entities in the group of charities that were formerly covered in Section 101—now Section 501(c)(3) of the IRC. Under the new code taxpayers could deduct up to 20 percent of their adjusted gross income for contributions to all Section 501(c)(3) organizations, but an additional 10 percent was allowed for contributions to "churches, schools, hospitals, certain medical research organizations, and certain organizations affiliated with state colleges and universities."[69] Some limitations on political activities of tax-exempt organizations were also incorporated in the 1954 Internal Revenue Code.[70]

Overall, although Congress was already beginning to articulate concern about the special nature of foundations, the Internal Revenue Code at this point did not treat private foundations as a totally distinct category from that of more broad-based public charities. This distinction was not fully developed until the 1969 Tax Reform Act—after a turbulent period in which foundations once again became the focus of public attack and intensive Congressional investigations. This story unfolds in the following chapters.

3

Leading to Reform

Patman, Treasury, and Congress

The Chairman (Wright Patman): In your view, should foundations [sic] loans
of money or other property to, and purchase, sale, exchange and lease
transactions with donors, related persons, controlled businesses and their
employees and foundation trustees and directors, be prohibited as a
condition to continued tax exemption for the future?

Mr. Harding (Acting Commissioner, IRS): That is a tax policy question,
Mr. Chairman.

—Patman Hearings of 1964

There is nothing sinister in so arranging one's affairs as to keep taxes as low
as possible. Everybody does so, rich or poor, and all do it right. Nobody
owes any public duty to pay more than the law demands. . . . To demand
more in the name of morals is mere cant.

—Justice Learned Hand, *Commissioner v. Newman,*
159 F. 2d 848 (1947)

Leading to Tax Reform

The opening gambit in the third round of Congressional investigations of
American foundations was made in a speech entitled, "A Fresh Look at Tax-
Exempt Foundations," in the House of Representatives on May 2, 1961, by
Wright Patman, Congressman from Texas. Patman's main theme was the "dis-
proportionately rapid growth" of foundations—a point which he would develop more fully in later communications.[1] His tone at this point was relatively
mild, but it was just the beginning of a campaign that he would thereafter pursue relentlessly.[2] Indeed, in 1961 Patman was winding up for the start of a cru-
sade against foundation abuses which by the end of the decade would end in
significant action by the Congress.

24

Congressman Patman's warning about the problems of tax-exempt foundations occurred in the days of a new administration in Washington but did not appear to be directly connected to mainstream events or the agenda of President Kennedy. The country in general had not yet begun the questioning of fundamental institutions that was so characteristic of the late 1960s. The shock of the Sputnik launching by the Russians (1957) and a subsequent recession (1957–58) had not greatly diminished the level of American optimism.[3] In this period of "grand expectations" the idea of poverty amidst plenty or the suffering of particular groups (such as urban minorities or the rural poor) still had little salience.[4]

The passage into the 1960s, however, contained the seeds of reform that would lead to dramatic changes by the end of the decade.[5] Even though there was no great suffering like that of the 1930s, at the closing of the Eisenhower years (1959–60) attention was turning toward internal problems facing the country, including pockets of poverty and economic inequality.[6] Tax issues and fiscal policies were discussed in the late 1950s, even after the major 1954 revisions of the tax code. Yet despite concerns about the strength of the economy, the Eisenhower administration had not pushed for further changes in tax policy, so this remained an issue for the 1960s.[7] President Eisenhower apparently believed that with relatively low unemployment in the country, it was better to reduce the federal deficit and maintain higher tax rates against inflation.[8] Thus high taxes continued, while compensatory tradeoffs made the higher taxes more palatable to special interests, particularly rich individuals and powerful business groups.

In January 1961, five months before Patman's first speech about the proliferation of foundations, a Democratic President had come into office. John F. Kennedy named Douglas Dillon as head of the Treasury Department, and, perhaps even more significant in the long run, he put Harvard professor Stanley Surrey, an expert on tax policy, into a leading position in the same department. The appointment of Dillon, a banker and a Republican, was considered balance for Surrey, who had well defined, progressive views about tax policy. His opinions about the need to curb tax exemptions were already well known.[9] Indeed, newspapers reported that Surrey was controversial and unlikely to be accepted by Congress without the appointment of a more conservative Secretary of the Treasury.[10]

Changes in the executive branch of government were of course watched by the Rockefeller family as well as the foundation world generally. In addition, the Rockefellers paid close attention to Congressmen who were influential in the key committees determining tax policy—the Senate Finance Committee, the Joint Committee on Internal Revenue Taxation, and the House Ways and

Means Committee. JDR 3rd and the Rockefeller family had contacts with Senator Richard Byrd (Chair of the Senate Finance Committee), Senator Russell Long (a powerful member of the Committee), and Representative Wilbur Mills, Chair of the Ways and Means Committee, among others.[11] But the interest of Representative Patman in philanthropic foundations appeared to emerge out of nowhere, with an agenda that was particular and self-driven. These early Patman events seemed to be almost serendipitous, challenges for which no one in the foundation world was prepared.[12]

However, as we shall see, there were good reasons why the attack came from the Chair of the House Committee on Banking and Small Business. The Patman investigation was really another in the series of sporadic but significant challenges that had occurred intermittently in 1914–15, 1948, and 1951–54.[13] In fact despite the continuous encouragement of philanthropy in American tax laws, ever since the earliest foundations were formed, a corresponding contrapuntal note of alarm had frequently been sounded from both the left and the right, in Congress and elsewhere. It was echoed in the limitations on business-related activities of foundations of the Revenue Act of 1950 and Congressional discussions of the 1950s.[14] However, in 1961 questions about the financial power of foundations were linked more aggressively to broader concerns about inequities in our tax system and the accelerated erosion of progressivity in the tax base. Moreover, these concerns were beginning to spread beyond the halls of Congress.[15]

Equity, Progressivity, and Tax Loopholes

We have already noted that in the first half of the twentieth century, American tax law incorporated a general bias in favor of philanthropic giving, through a variety of deductions from income taxes, estate taxes, and gift taxes for this purpose.[16] War-related corporate income taxes and excise tax rate increases were extended beyond 1951, but Congress also enacted additional provisions for dividend credits and exclusions, retirement income credits, and accelerated depreciation.[17] Despite Presidential rhetoric, in the mid-1950s there was only a slight overall reduction in the tax base, and most of the resulting tax cuts were in targeted benefits for particular groups.[18] As Wilbur Mills and others have pointed out, tax policies are fairly obscure matters not readily understood by non-experts, and the special provisions incorporated in the tax code in these years added greatly to its complexity. In any case the public seemed to have become accustomed to high taxes after the Korean War (1950–53) and World War II before that. Nevertheless, the progressive nature of our tax system was being weakened by Congressional actions as the numbers of tax exemptions, or what were coming to be labeled "tax loopholes," increased in those years.[19] In 1958 small businesses were given an estimated $260 million in tax relief.[20]

The 1954 Revenue Act reorganized the tax code, but at the same time included provisions which allowed businesses, and particularly oil companies, to reap higher profits through "paper" allowances for depletion of resources such as oil and coal.[21] As noted already, the Act also increased incentives (or preferences) for charitable giving, including the unlimited charitable deduction for the very rich.[22] Thus benefits to business, stockholders, and wealthy donors were granted even while Congressional committees were looking into the supposed anti-American activities of the foundations that they supported. For the most part the concerns raised in Congress by the investigations of the 1950s had concerned foundations only, and not broader notions of voluntarism or other charitable activities. Pluralism was in vogue with American social scientists and political leaders, and charitable nonprofit groups were part of this concept. Leaders in the foundation world, including JDR 3rd, also naturally embraced the idea of pluralism.[23] They did so even while the reality of American life was certainly that of a very imperfect pluralism in which different groups had unequal access to the decision making process, and the rich and well-connected had far greater access to the halls of power.[24] In this regard it is worth noting that after the election in the fall of 1960, President-elect Kennedy was said to have "raided" the board of the Rockefeller Foundation for members of his administration.[25]

Given the conditions of the economy and permissive tax policies, foundations grew in number in this period and the value of their assets increased. Fueled by high tax rates, large business profits, and generous charitable deductions, by 1960 American foundations were reported as having assets of $11.5 billion. It was estimated that their numbers were growing by about 1,200 annually.[26] In a recessionary year this reported growth became an issue when concern about inequities in the tax code was connected to a search for additional federal revenues. Major tax reform had been resisted by Eisenhower, but as the time for a national election drew closer, Congress gave more attention to this issue. Even before Wright Patman's initial gambit in 1961, a series of panel discussions on income tax revisions were held in the House Ways and Means Committee (1959), and they included a panel on tax-exempt organizations. Although one expert on foundation law later suggested that the Ways and Means Committee discussions were not directed at immediate changes in tax law, at the very least they seemed to be setting the stage for future developments after the elections.[27] Meanwhile, in this same period, pressure was still being exerted in Congress (House and Senate) to pass tax bills with benefits for specific individuals or groups, and in fact, even for the interests of one family—that is, the Rockefellers. It will therefore be helpful to catch up with developments in the Rockefeller family in the years leading to these events.

The Rockefellers and New Philanthropic Concerns

The years between 1952 and the early 1960s were a time of transformation for the entire "third" generation of Rockefellers, the generation known as "the brothers." In this period the wealth of the Rockefeller family continued to grow, and it was said that in 1957 (just three years before his death) the richest man in America was John D. Rockefeller, Junior. However, this would have been hard to substantiate, since Junior had been busy giving his money away in large doses, and at his death he reportedly left only $150,000 in taxable assets.[28] In these years the various interests and career directions of the five Rockefeller brothers, John, Nelson, Winthrop, Laurance, and David (as well as their less involved sister, Abby ["Babs"]) became more fully identified; members of "the third generation" began to carve out separate public and private identities. Thereafter it would be possible to characterize the brothers more concisely: John as the family's leader in philanthropy; Nelson as a politician; Winthrop as Governor of Arkansas; Laurance as an environmentalist and business entrepreneur; and David as a banker.[29]

Despite these neat characterizations, however, the alleged separateness of the Rockefeller pursuits could be questioned. As critics have pointed out, there seemed to have always been considerable intermingling of the family interests in business, politics, and even philanthropy. Thus, gifts of Standard Oil of New Jersey and Standard Oil of Ohio initially were a large part of the assets of the Rockefeller Foundation (RF) when John Rockefeller (Senior) established it in 1913. Appreciation of the value of those stocks, and profits enabled by the generous oil depletion allowances passed by Congress, subsequently greatly increased the value of the holdings of the RF as well as other family-dominated foundations, and this was certainly a way of avoiding both claims of monopolistic controls and corporate taxes for the Rockefeller interests.[30] Later when the brothers formed the Rockefeller Brothers Fund (RBF) with gifts of their own (1940), its worth and significance were considerably augmented by Junior through his gift to the brothers ($52 million) in 1952, and with additional gifts of stock at the end of his life.[31] On this basis in 1960 the RBF was listed as having total assets of $116,173,369, much of it in shares of Standard Oil.[32] In this period the Rockefeller Foundation suffered internal conflict between staff and directors, including efforts to resist direct family influence on project selection.[33] However, at this time the brothers were able to maintain far more

active involvement in the Rockefeller Brothers Fund, and used the RBF for realizing their own pet projects.

In these years Rockefeller contributions also provided significant support
and guidance to large-scale cultural developments such as Lincoln Center and
Colonial Williamsburg. These projects were presumably philanthropic, but the
reality was complicated. Certainly the Lincoln Center development had a positive impact on real estate values in the area, and questions were later raised
about the tax status of Colonial Williamsburg.[34]

In 1952 conflict between JDR 3rd and his father reportedly erupted over
the purposes and development of Colonial Williamsburg, resulting in JDR 3rd's
resignation from direct involvement in Williamsburg. This apparently permitted
him greater freedom in setting his own directions in philanthropy,[35] including
the Japan Society. JDR 3rd had been President of the RBF since its inception,
but now (1952) he became Chairman of the Board of the family's most prestigious charity, the Rockefeller Foundation.[36] He had been passed over for this
position earlier with the selection of John Foster Dulles in 1949 (Secretary of
State in 1952) when the argument was made that it would appear to give the
family too much control of the foundation if a Rockefeller became Chairman.
Certainly by the end of the 1950s JDR 3rd had begun to assume the philanthropic mantle of his father and grandfather. However, it was less clear what
was to be his role as head of the family office as office affairs became more
complicated and family interests were diversified.[37]

After the death of his father in 1960, JDR 3rd gave even more attention to
philanthropy. In addition to his three identified fields of interest—population
control, Asia, and the arts—he developed an interest in general philanthropy.[38]
While he later became known for having a broad vision about philanthropy in
the modern world, JDR was from the start also forced to be concerned about
the consequences of tax policy for himself and the family. Thus it was not accidental that two commissions sponsored by him would become deeply en-
meshed in technical matters of tax policy that had significance for the Rockefellers, as well as for other wealthy philanthropists.

By the end of 1952 JDR 3rd was Chairman of the Rockefeller Foundation,
and as a consequence of the Cox and Reece Committee investigations he personally experienced the animus directed against large foundations and the individuals with whom they were connected. In 1954 he wrote the introduction
to the formal statement that Dean Rusk was submitting on behalf of the RF to
the Reece Committee; in that year he also established a Policy and Planning
Committee to advise him on a variety of tax matters as well as philanthropy.[39]
In its initial period, in addition to JDR personal staff "associates" Don McLean
and Ed Young, this group included Frank Jamieson, Dana Creel, and, notably,

the Rockefeller family tax lawyer and confidant, John Lockwood. Dean Rusk, President of the foundation, was not a member.

Given the Congressional climate in the 1950s, it is not surprising that during those years other groups with similar interests also began to form. Among them were the New York Foundation Luncheon Group of which F. Emerson Andrews was a member, and by the end of the decade, also the broader, national 501(c)(3) group, which had members from a variety of charitable organizations, and which included prominent tax attorneys.[40] In addition to the spate of books which had started to emerge about philanthropy and foundations, seminars and workshops on tax-related issues were now also being held on a regular basis by academic institutions, such as New York University. In this period the Ford Foundation also sponsored seminars on legal research in philanthropy, with professors of trust, estate, and tax law, as well as F. Emerson Andrews.[41]

Foundations were coming of age, although their confidence may have been mixed with a touch of wariness. As Dean Rusk expressed it, after the turbulent events of the mid-1950s:

> I do not believe that foundations and their trustees have been intimidated by the events of the past two years. And I have no doubt but that ten or twenty years hence, whenever the next round of investigation comes, we shall have an interesting list of controversial items for consideration. Just which they shall be, we have no way of knowing, for that will depend upon the predilections of the investigator.[42]

Rusk was to appear prescient when the next full-scale Congressional investigation of foundations began in 1961, even earlier than anticipated. As Rusk had suggested, at the beginning the inquiry did appear to be very much dependent upon the predilections of one investigator; however, a variety of factors subsequently helped shape the direction of the investigations.

Rockefeller Bills

Congressional attacks in the 1960s emerged from the efforts of one individual, Wright Patman, Democratic Congressman from Texas. Patman, an old-style populist, was chair of the House Select Committee on Small Business when he first raised the questions that developed into a full-scale attack on the foundations. Patman had proven credentials as a populist; he was well known for his anti-bank, anti–big business, anti-elitist, and pro–the "little man" stance. In this capacity he was concerned not only about the abuses of many foundations, but also with their large-scale concentration of wealth and power and their intermingling of business and philanthropic interests. As it was to turn out, he was also concerned about the role of the IRS and its capacity for monitoring the activities of private foundations and other tax-exempt entities.

Patman had unusual methods of working, but he was certainly not alone in his awareness of abuses in foundation practices. Congressional concern was also growing about increased inequities in the tax structure and the growth in business holdings sheltered through foundations.[43] This was happening while there was still pressure to insure the continuation of the charitable deductions enjoyed by the very rich. Indeed in the period 1958 through 1962 a number of specific bills concerning the charitable deduction even had the Rockefeller imprimatur on them, reminiscent of the early days when John D. promoted federal incorporation of his foundation. In this context the attitudes of Congress toward foundations were of particular concern to Rockefeller lawyers and those associates with defined responsibilities for protecting family affairs.

Activities of these family attorneys reflected shared interests of the brothers with regard to taxes. Thus following the 1958 legislation, F. Roberts Blair and others wrote a series of memoranda to Laurance Rockefeller and brother John concerning the unlimited deduction for charitable contributions.[44] The memos about legislation in 1959–1960 differed only slightly in their basic thrust: they dealt with different amendments and bills which would in effect loosen conditions for the unlimited deduction by requiring fewer years of high giving (that is, contributions of 90 percent of adjusted gross income) or by making the qualifications effective retroactively (to 1957). In this context a Rockefeller-supported version of the initial bill (H.R. 6799) was eventually passed, and a Secretary to the Chairman of the Senate Finance Committee wrote to tell JDR the news.[45] In the end, however, President Eisenhower vetoed the proposed bill on June 3, 1960, stating in his veto message that he would be willing to sign similar new legislation "providing it applied only prospectively and were truly designed to encourage substitute gifts to educational institutions and other recognized public charities."[46]

The message was clear—what were coming to be seen as "private" foundations were being disadvantaged in comparison with other "public" charities. Still Blair continued his efforts, and wrote JDR and Laurance again concerning H.R. 6352, a proposal for "Unlimited Deduction Averaging." In this memorandum he also provided guidelines to follow in lobbying for passage of the bill in the Congress (naming and commenting on individuals on the appropriate committees).[47] The bill was finally reported on favorably by the Ways and Means Committee in May 1961, but was not passed by the Congress that year.

Protectors of the Rockefeller interests were undeniably inventive. This is clearly demonstrated in another series of memoranda from Blair to JDR about bills and amendments relating to the 30 percent charitable contributions limitation. In this regard specific tailoring of some amendments was ingenious, and arguably also had public merit: for example, on July 21, 1961, H.R. 2244, a bill concerning "Limitations on Deductions in Case of Contributions by Individuals for Benefit of Churches, Educational Organizations, and Hospitals." In committee the title was amended to match a change in the bill allowing "contributions to a foundation that's purpose is to pay over net yearly earnings to those organizations" to qualify for the extra 10 percent deduction, along with publicly supported charities. Conceivably contributions to Williamsburg and other education-related projects of the Rockefeller family would thereby be included, although the application actually depended upon further interpretation by the IRS.

On September 6, 1961, Blair wrote to JDR concerning amendments to H.R. 2244 which would be proposed by Senator Jacob Javits (New York) so as to broaden the 10 percent additional deduction for contributions (the one instituted in the 1954 Code) to include symphony orchestras and operas, in addition to museums and libraries. Though not stated explicitly, it was evident that passage of "the So-called Keogh Bill" would be of benefit to donors to Lincoln Center, as well as New York City. The *New York Times* recognized this potential,[48] but matters were still at an impasse the next fall (September 21, 1962), when Don McLean wrote again to tell JDR 3rd that they were still "trying to see if legislation could go through" to permit the 30 percent deduction for cultural centers.[49] However, on that same day Stanley Surrey asked for a postponement of this legislation so that it could be given further consideration at a subsequent time in connection with a larger tax bill. Arguments about philanthropic giving were about to shift location.

Patman's Crusade

The number and extent of the bills presented by Rockefeller representatives and attorneys in this period would have been enough to raise questions about the selective nature of tax benefits enjoyed by rich philanthropists. Moreover Congress had a longstanding interest in the business relationships of foundations, which if anything seemed to be expanding. Notably also in January of that year David Rockefeller had become Chairman of Chase Manhattan Bank. Furthermore, in the recessionary climate of 1961–1962, others in the Kennedy administration (such as Surrey) as well as members of Congress, including Wilbur Mills, were concerned about increasing revenues and reforming taxes. However, given the relationship enjoyed by the Rockefellers with key members of the Senate Finance Committee and House Ways and Means Committee, and the multiple policy responsibilities of those committees, it might have seemed difficult initially to locate a debate about foundations inside those committees.[50]

Patman had previous experience as a prosecuting attorney, which made him seem the right person for the job that he undertook. He began immediately with his own survey of a substantial group (546 in all) of foundations and charitable trusts, and with a staff dedicated to getting the answers. Thereafter, despite his reputedly gentle manner, for a period of almost ten years he was dogged in his pursuit of information and persistent in his investigations. Thus, his first speech on May 2, 1961 was followed in rapid succession by two stronger speeches in the House (May 3, "Power and Influence of Large Foundations"; May 4, "Foundations Fail to Give Adequate Financial Reports" and by a longer (largely statistical) item in the *Congressional Record* (May 8, "IRS Needs Sharper Tools"). On August 7, as his survey was progressing, he gave a speech entitled "Lid Lifted on Information about Tax-Exempt Foundations." While events moved rapidly, however, questions were raised about the way that Patman was carrying out his inquiry; as early as September 6, 1961 Representative Thomas B. Curtis openly questioned the propriety of Patman's letters of inquiry to the foundations, and later a member of his own subcommittee objected to his procedures.[51]

Patman resigned from the chairmanship of the Select Committee on Banking and Small Business to head a new subcommittee of the Select Committee, Subcommittee No.1 on Foundations. On January 18, 1962 he obtained authorization for this subcommittee to "conduct studies and hold hearings of the impact of tax-exempt foundations and charitable trusts on small business," and he obtained subpoena power for these activities. In the next decade he issued a series of interim reports or "installments" based on his findings. The first "Interim Report" was issued in December 1962, a second installment in October 1963, a third in March 1964, and thereafter installments were more intermittent—in April 1967, March 1968, with the seventh (and final) installment on June 30, 1969. Content from these interim reports was also reproduced in the *Congressional Record,* and thereby disseminated widely.[52] In addition Patman's subcommittee held hearings in the summer of 1964 and in the fall of 1967, and Patman himself was the opening witness in the later hearings on tax revision held by the House Ways and Means Committee (1969).

The foundation community was at first cautious in its reaction. However, by 1968 Manning Pattillo, President of the Foundation Center, reported that Patman's attacks "have been roundly condemned by foundation administrators and trustees" while "uncritically reported in the popular press."[53] Patman was criticized for operating as an individual detective rather than through committee process, and it was true that he called no foundation witnesses in his 1964 hearings. His numbers were challenged for being carelessly arrived at, particularly for the aggregate number of 45,124 foundations, as well as figures relating to particular foundations.[54] However, even Patman critics recognized that aggregate numbers were problematic in large part because of difficulties in defining the term "foundation" and the undifferentiated manner in which the IRS collected data about tax-exempt organizations generally.[55]

Despite his praise for the work of his chief of staff, H. A. Olsher, Patman's survey was certainly not scientific; moreover, at some points he focused on particular foundations such as the Baird Foundations (second report)[56] or the Americans Building Constitutionally (1967 Hearings), which had particularly abusive practices.[57] Nonetheless, at a time when little information was available, the compendium of reports as a whole, with their vast tables and data obtained by subpoena, provided a great deal of information about the wealth of the great foundations including assets, liabilities, and interactions among financial transactions.[58] In addition the reports also served to draw attention to possible foundation abuses.

The Rockefeller family was apparently not supposed to be immune from these investigations. In fact, a good part of the transmittal letter of Patman's first interim report highlights Rockefeller interests:

> The forerunner of modern antitrust enforcement was the successful prosecution in 1907 of the Rockefeller-controlled monopoly, Standard Oil Co. As a result, competition was restored . . . by the creation of a number of oil companies; e.g., Standard Oil Co. (New Jersey), Standard Oil Co. (Kentucky) et al. . . . .
>
> It is a well known fact that the Rockefeller family controls Standard Oil Co. (New Jersey), and the Rockefeller-controlled foundations own a substantial part of the corporation. At the close of 1960, 7 Rockefeller-controlled foundations owned 7,891,567 shares of common stock of Standard Oil of New Jersey with a market value of $324,946,110. The same 7 foundations owned 602,127 shares of the common stock of Socony Mobil Oil Co. with a market value of $423,610,770. Two Rockefeller foundations owned 306,013 shares of Continental Oil capital stock with a market value of $17,060,224 . . . ; 4 Rockefeller foundations owned 468,135 shares of Ohio Oil common stock with a market value of $17,998,495; 5 Rockefeller foundations owned 1,256,305 shares of the common stock of Standard Oil Co. of Indiana with a market value of $59,736,991; and the Rockefeller Foundation, itself, owned 100,000 shares of the capital stock of Union Tank Car Co. with a market value of $3,100,000.
>
> If Standard Oil Co. (New Jersey) were to attain substantial ownership in its competitors [*sic*], it would certainly tend to eliminate competition

and again tend toward monopoly, and engage the Department of Justice in inquiry.

The use of a subterfuge—in the form of Rockefeller controlled foundations—in effect produces the same result as if Standard Oil Co. (New Jersey) owned substantial stock interest in Continental Oil, Ohio Oil, Standard Oil Co. (Indiana), et al.[59]

This last paragraph would suggest that even a powerful family that liked privacy could have their affairs publicly exposed. However, the Rockefellers actually seemed to suffer little direct damage from the Patman inquiries, and made no public protests. The Rockefeller Foundation did make a disclaimer in the *New York Times* about a mistake Patman made in reporting a figure for accumulated income, a mistake that according to Andrews came from a misreading of a photocopy of the figures.[60] And in the end the Rockefeller family was certainly spared the more concentrated focus given to other families like the Du Ponts or the Bairds, perhaps because their affairs were in better order. Indeed, in that regard, in connection with proposed tax legislation of 1964, Chauncey Belknap asked:

> Would not the Rockefeller Foundation be rendering a better service if it maintains a big degree of independence from possibly entangling alliances . . . when the new legislation will be pending?
> This would leave the Rockefeller Foundation officers free to consult with their opposite numbers in other foundations, as was done with the Cox Committee and Reece Committee investigations. It would also have the greater advantage of leaving the Rockefeller Foundation officers free, if they chose, to express opinions which representatives of other foundations could not . . . because of the vulnerability of their own records.[61]

Meanwhile in the period from 1961 to 1965 a variety of tax initiatives were pushed by other forces within the administration and Congress. To begin with, in 1962 after a recession and downturn in the market, President Kennedy proposed tax reductions to business in the hope of assuring a recovery from the recession.[62] Some minor adjustments in taxes were made that year in favor of business, but major tax adjustments were deferred.[63] Discussions of the proposed tax bill in 1963 suggested that Wilbur Mills and the Treasury Department wanted tax reform and reduced public expenditures in 1964. However, Mills was a consummate politician who recognized reality. His language in introducing the Tax Bill testified to his ability to reframe issues:

> The route I prefer is the tax reduction road which gives us a higher level of economic activity and a bigger more prosperous and more efficient economy with a larger and larger share of the enlarged activity initiative in the private sector of the economy.[64]

Subsequently the final tax bill as enacted contained a "huge reduction" in individual and corporate income taxes and had eliminated most of the proposed reforms. The Senate had considered eliminating the unlimited charitable deduction entirely; but in the end Mills helped to ensure a compromise that protected "operating foundations," which from the definition used would seem to cover some of the Rockefeller causes, including Colonial Williamsburg.[65] Also of significance in an election year, after the tax cuts went into effect the economy expanded sharply.[66]

While Patman's work was underway, there were parallel administration efforts to ensure greater accountability on the part of tax-exempt organizations and foundations. On December 29, 1962, just two days before Patman's transmittal of his first interim report, the Treasury Department announced that "it had statutory authority to disclose to the public all information required on Form 990A with the exception of the names of contributors."[67] In 1963, the Treasury Department was also authorized by Congress to conduct a study of foundations, and in conjunction with this study in 1963 Secretary Dillon appointed an Informal Advisory Committee on Foundations, staffed by Surrey, and "composed of reputable and responsible individuals associated with foundations on a full time basis."[68] Among them was F. E. Andrews of the Foundation Library Center.[69]

It was probably not a pure coincidence that in the Transmittal Letter of the "Second Installment" (October 16, 1963), around the time of the Advisory Committee's formation, Patman had pointed out the omissions of Treasury. Indeed, Patman had spoken scathingly of the Department:

> Ours is a fact finding study, and a call for action because the program and action has not come—as it should have come—from the Treasury Department. . . .
>
> It is evident that nonfeasance on the part of Treasury officials has fostered tax-free commercial activities, violations of law and Treasury regulations, and tax avoidance through the device of foundations. Unquestionably, the Treasury's indefensible apathy and its archaic procedures have encouraged certain owners and foundations to exploit their tax-exempt status for personal gain and for the benefit of others with whom they are affiliated through stockholdings . . . and other financial relations and transactions.[70]

It therefore should not have seemed surprising that in its 1964 hearings the Subcommittee on Foundations heard testimony only from a few officials of the Treasury Department and the Securities and Exchange Commission. In his statement before the Committee Secretary Dillon of Treasury was somewhat defensive, although he reported that the IRS had stepped up its program for auditing exempt returns from 2000 (1963) to 10,000 (1964), and indicated that they were still working on new tax legislation.[71] Nevertheless, in connection with the testimony of the Acting Commissioner of the IRS (Bertram M. Harding) before the Subcommittee, Chairman Patman recorded a litany of the sins and failures of omission on the part of the IRS, and in general pursued the attack on the foundations and their supposed monitor, the IRS, vigorously throughout the 1964 hearings.[72]

Treasury Responds

The Patman investigations raised serious questions about tax benefits, foundation abuses, and ineffective monitoring by the IRS that would not go away; they consequently became catalysts for action in other arenas. Patman's investigatory style may have been unorthodox, but the message certainly reverberated—and, in the end, the Treasury Department had to respond. Finally, in 1965 (after the Presidential elections) Treasury issued its much anticipated report. Like Patman's opening in 1961, it began in a relatively unalarming tone:

> The Department's investigation has revealed that the preponderant number of private foundations perform their functions without tax abuse. However, its study has also produced evidence of serious faults among a minority of such organizations. . . .
> Private philanthropy plays a special and vital role in our society. Beyond providing for areas into which government cannot or should not advance (such as religion), private philanthropic organizations can be uniquely qualified to initiate thought and action, experiment with new and untried ventures, dissent from prevailing attitudes, and act quickly and flexibly. Private foundations have an important part in this work.[73]

Although the Treasury *Report* found little evidence that foundation holdings had become a large part of the national economy, it did identify six major problem areas for which it also proposed solutions. Briefly listed, their recommendations included:

1. Prohibitions on self-dealing by foundations.
2. Strengthening limitations on excessive accumulation of income and assets, by requirements for spending income (or absent that) some portion of assets.
3. Additional restrictions with regard to involvement by foundations in business.
4. Denial of income tax deductions for gifts of stock or other prop-

erty closely controlled by the donor until the foundation disposes of that asset, or the asset is devoted to active charitable operations.

5. Severe restrictions on financial transactions unrelated to charitable functions such as loans, or speculative trading.

6. Need to broaden foundation management, with the recommendation that after the first 25 years donors and related parties would not constitute more than 25 percent of the foundation's governing body.

Treasury also requested that "affected foundations" submit their own views and potential problems in writing to the Department; these replies were published in two large volumes. However, according to Andrews, the Foundation Library Center was "extremely busy" in the period following issuance of the *Report* and consequently took no position on any of the recommendations. Andrews expressed his own opinion in a "pamphlet" which was distributed in the foundation community, reporting that he found the *Report* to be generally "able, judicious, and . . . worthy of serious consideration." However, he suggested that both the requirement to reduce "speedily" to 20 percent stock holdings of any business, and the restriction to 25 percent donee membership on foundation boards, would be impossible for company-sponsored foundations and difficult for others. He also criticized some of the figures in the report and apparently roused the ire of Patman and Olsher with his comments.[74]

In the next few years no major action was actually taken on the Treasury recommendations. Patman continued with his specialized reports, including the one already mentioned on ABC. But the country seemed to have more pressing problems to deal with. In these years poverty was "rediscovered," and after Kennedy's death, in the years between 1963 and 1967, President Johnson and the Congress were involved in passage of an ambitious program which included civil rights legislation, legislation implementing the War on Poverty, Medicaid and Medicare, and new social service provisions of the Social Security Act. At the same time, the war in Vietnam began to escalate, and by the summer of 1967 there was considerable civil unrest and urban rioting in the country. In the next years, these problems increased making it more difficult to go back to business as usual. However, when Congress returned again to the idea of tax reform, recommendations of the Treasury Report became an important part of the discussions. These ideas consequently will be considered again in the next two chapters, in connection with the Tax Reform Act of 1969 and the Peterson Commission.

4

The Gathering Storm

Later this year, I shall present to Congress a major program of tax reform.
This broad program will reexamine tax rates and the definitions of the
income tax base. It will be aimed at simplification of the tax structure, the
equal treatment of equally situated persons, and the strengthening of
incentives for individual effort and productive investment.

—John F. Kennedy, Economic Message, 1962

There is no evidence that the Congress will reverse its historical attitude
favoring philanthropy in general. Nevertheless the investigations of
tax-exempt foundations and the concrete provisions of the 1964 Revenue
Act point toward a greater indulgence of the "publicly supported" charitable
organizations over the so-called private foundation that is new to the federal
government as well as of the laws of any of the states.

—Marion Fremont-Smith, 1965

The trouble with the Treasury people under Mr. Surrey's leadership is that
they do not believe in the foundation field.

—John Lockwood, Memorandum to JDR 3rd, 1967

The 1964 Revenue Act

Shortly after Lyndon Baynes Johnson took office as President he signed a tax
bill whose major outlines were in place before President John F. Kennedy
was assassinated. The Revenue Act of 1964 was certainly not a tax reform act;
and its passage had only been assured after President Johnson promised reduced federal spending in his January budget message.[1] For even though President Kennedy had proclaimed the necessity of tax reform, and despite Wright
Patman's continued highlighting of the abusive nature of charitable "tax shelters" afforded businesses and the rich, tax reform remained elusive. Indeed, in
the recessionary period of 1962 Kennedy had included accelerated depreciation allowances and tax credits for investment in equipment by business in his
legislative proposals on revenue matters.[2] Kennedy had faced international

39

problems (Cuba, Vietnam) and with an election year coming up he needed the support of big business. So it was hardly surprising that the bill which emerged in late 1963 was less a tax reform bill than a tax reduction document[3]—even though originally both the President and Wilbur Mills seemed to want tax reform.[4]

In the spring of 1963 the House had been working on the administration-initiated bill which included measures affecting tax preferences, deductions, and the treatment of capital gains at death. Initially Mills and the Treasury supported structural tax reform, but, as the process unfolded, reforms were deleted by Congress and reduced revenues appeared more certain.[5] This process, like others in the Ways and Means Committee in those years, reflected the style of the Chairman, Wilbur Mills. Mills was an astute politician, and above all a consensus builder. In developing legislation, he negotiated both publicly and privately, shifting gears when necessary,[6] and by this means validated his reputation for assuring that bills from the House Ways and Means Committee would generally pass successfully through Congress. This helps explain why there were so many concessions in tax policies in the early 1960s and why significant tax reform was so slow in coming.

In the Ways and Means Committee tradeoffs were made in the administration bill to make it more acceptable to the majority of members of both the House and Senate. Even before Kennedy was killed in November 1963, the bill which Johnson would sign (February 1964) differed greatly from the one originally proposed. The Revenue Act finally passed would result in reduced taxes with projections of reduced federal revenues and at the same time an anticipated budget deficit of $5 billion. "Compensatory finance" had by now replaced the idea of balanced budgets as American economic doctrine. In effect business and other "special" interests had prevailed.

During the discussions in Congress the unlimited charitable deduction had been seriously threatened, but it had not in fact been eliminated in the new Revenue Act. Among notable reforms that had failed was a proposal by Senator Albert Gore, liberal New Deal Democrat from Tennessee. Gore had suggested an amendment that would have limited the charitable deduction, making it applicable only for gifts to churches, schools, or other organizations with contributions from the "general public." But in the end gifts to this group were allowed to enjoy a 30 percent maximum charitable deduction, as compared to 20 percent for what were increasingly being delineated as "private" foundations.

Still, as Wilbur Mills later reported, House members on the Joint Committee on Internal Revenue Taxation were able to arrange for the larger deduction to be available to "two additional types of organizations that might be classed as private foundations"—"operating" charities and private foundations that in a short period (three years) expend or use such charitable deductions directly for active charitable purposes.[7] In line with the incremental manner of American politics there were tax gains for a variety of others as well, and individual income tax rates were reduced generally. Rates for individuals in the lowest bracket were also cut from 20 percent to 14 percent. It was anticipated that taxpayers overall would be saved $9.1 billion in 1964, and economic prosperity was promised.[8] As expected, after the 1964 tax cut there was considerable expansion of the economy, although the improvement apparently began even before the Act went into effect.[9]

Tax Reform Talk Continues

President Kennedy had preached tax reform and had placed a controversial person in an important policy position in the Treasury Department,[10] but he had also brought Douglas Dillon and other eastern establishment individuals into his administration.[11] Thus there were significant people in the administration who were likely to be sympathetic to Rockefeller concerns about philanthropic institutions,[12] and, at the same time, ever-attentive tax attorneys also were protecting the family's interests in charitable deductions.[13] Furthermore, in what might have been a fortunate coincidence, around the time that Patman's report, with its exposure of Rockefeller family holdings, was being released,[14] John's son Jay Rockefeller went to Washington looking for a job. He ended up as a special assistant to Sargent Shriver, head of the Peace Corps and brother-in-law of the President; thus, he was in effect inside the Kennedy administration.[15] But after Lyndon Johnson became President the situation became more uncertain. Now the government was headed by a Texan, a Southwesterner, who was more astute at handling Congress and also more driven in his implementation of government programs.

After Kennedy's assassination, Patman's pursuit of foundation abuses continued and even accelerated. On the eve of the upcoming presidential elections, in August of 1964, he held formal hearings on the problems of the accountability of private foundations.[16] In the fall Johnson won a landslide victory over Republican Barry Goldwater, and thereafter there were some changes in the Cabinet; in March 1965 Treasury Secretary Dillon left office. At this point foundation officials and the Rockefellers might well have worried about facing a less responsive administration, at least in regard to Treasury policy.[17]

JDR 3rd Prepares

After events in Congress quieted down in the mid-1950s,[18] JDR 3rd appeared to devote his primary attention to his special interests (Asia, art, and population concerns) and to the major project of Lincoln Center. This changed with Junior's death in 1960. In this period the Rockefellers had initially relied on attorneys to protect their philanthropic interests. However, with increasing heat in Congress, the family recognized the need for more attention to Washington. For, despite the brave face put on the matter, once Patman had explicated the figures about the Rockefeller investments and their foundations in his 1962 report, family sensitivities had to be aroused. And in some respects their concerns were now shared by other leading foundations.

With Surrey's establishment in Treasury, and Patman's investigatory efforts, it had become apparent to astute observers of the Washington tax scene that the situation on Capitol Hill was extremely volatile. The National Democratic Party Platform in 1960 had already embodied notions of tax reform, although the examples cited (inequitable depreciation allowances, special consideration for recipients of dividend income, and deductions for extravagant "business expenses") did not refer specifically to charitable deductions or foundation abuses.[19] The same omission was essentially true of a earlier article written by the Chair of the House Ways and Means Committee.[20] Still there remained the possibility that tax reform would also affect the charitable deduction.

After the election in November 1964, when Johnson began to realize the liberal domestic program that Kennedy had only conceptualized, government spending was expected to increase. Thus the ideological commitment to tax reform might well be invigorated by the demand for new revenues. Furthermore, by 1964 there were also signs that tax reform would be connected to philanthropic affairs. The Treasury Department was already at work (if slowly) on a study of private foundations, and in that same year Patman had stepped up his activities in the Congress. Around this time the Committee on Charitable Organizations of the National Association of Attorneys General held a Seminar on the supervision of Charities, with representative of the Treasury Department and the IRS discussing cooperation between the states and federal agencies. The IRS also made its first significant effort to create a national registry of tax-exempt organizations linked to a new electronic data processing system.[21] Meanwhile the rumblings about charitable abuses would not go away, and only a month after Johnson's election success, a headline in the *New York Times* proclaimed aggressively "$10 Billion given to Charity in US: Questionable Philanthropies Collect Estimated Total of $300 Million a Year."[22]

There was still little unity in the foundation world, and essentially no communication between the big and well-established foundations and the many thousands of smaller ones. In these years most private foundations were at best only loosely affiliated through associations like the Foundation Library Center or the Council on Foundations, and there was certainly difference of opinion on how to deal with events in Washington.[23] Among the unresolved issues was the question of how much to recognize the legitimate criticism of real abuse by some foundations and therefore the need for more institutionalized systems of philanthropic accountability—in contrast with the desire to protect the privileges and privacy which foundations and charities generally enjoyed.

In this context an idea that had emerged in the Rockefeller family offices appeared particularly judicious. The public defender role in relation to philanthropy seemed to be a good position for JDR, now the titular head of the family. In a sense this was a revisiting of the Rockefeller public image story—with parallels to John D. and Junior after the various earlier investigations of 1913–1915. Given the career lines of his brothers, the bearer of the "John D." name was really the most suitable member of the family for this role, even though Laurance and Nelson, as well as David, at various times were engaged in philanthropic matters. In any case it was becoming increasingly evident that it was important to separate lobbying about philanthropy from any apparent connection to the family's business activities or personal entrepreneurial interests, or—what could perhaps be more difficult—from Nelson's politics.[24]

In the next decade JDR's diaries would record numerous visits to high-ranking politicians involved with tax policy. Considering their connection to the family foundations and their vast holdings in real estate and securities, the other brothers also had a stake in the outcome of tax legislation and would be likely to know many of the key actors in Washington. Indeed, this was an issue at a meeting of JDR with Don McLean, of JDR's staff, and Wes Vernon, a family tax lawyer, when strategy regarding the Gore Amendment was discussed. Referring to this meeting in his diary, JDR stated, "It was agreed that David was the best man to talk with Mills as he already knew him."[25]

Nevertheless, around this time considerable attention was being given to enhancing JDR's role in philanthropy. A file document dated November 14, 1963 had already presented a view of what JDR's "new" role might be. Entitled "John D. Rockefeller 3rd as Spokesman for Private Philanthropy," it seems to have been an early guideline for an expanded concept of JDR as philanthropic visionary, prepared by Earl Newsome, head of a public relations firm of the same name.[26]

The document of November 14 counsels that in order "to qualify for this role" JDR "must add to his own views an understanding of others and then reach an enlightened synthesis which will be his own opinion but developed in the light of the experience of others." To do this it is urged that he see and talk to persons with a "great diversity of views," and a number of people are mentioned for this purpose. Newsome's subsequent letter (November 18) suggests additional names. Interestingly, the document of November 14 begins, "If

John is to qualify himself for this role . . . " and thereafter consistently refers to "John" in the third person as though it was written for someone else to discuss with John, rather than directly for JDR himself.

The argument about developing John's role is summarized in the concluding paragraph, which refers to a continuing process and a series of meetings with significant individuals by which "John can not only enrich his understanding but reveal himself to many important people as a man who is exceptionally knowledgeable in the field of private philanthropy and determined to make a contribution." One more point is noteworthy in light of the future; Newsome suggests that JDR's "conclusions may be presented in the form of important speeches but also articles and even a book" and that he might want to "draw public attention" to significant developments in the United States and overseas.

As tax reform concerns were intensifying again in the spring of 1964, the idea of JDR's leadership role in philanthropy was further developed. A memorandum to JDR from staff member Don McLean begins with a general argument that is in effect a justification for the need for John Rockefeller to take an active role in dealing with the Washington attacks on foundations. McLean points out that one Treasury official had told him that " 'Foundation' has come to be a dirty word around here." In this paper McLean mentions a variety of factors that may be influencing this attitude, including Patman's speeches, suspicions on the part of "many people who live outside of the large foundation centers" about foundations as a tax avoidance device, and even the use of foundations for political purposes. In that regard he specifically names H. L. Hunt's use of resources for defeating members of Congress.[27]

McLean is careful, if not cautious, in framing the issue, as evidenced by his wording of the basic question, "is [there] anything which can be done or should be done in this state of affairs, having in mind the stake the Rockefeller family has in maintaining the integrity of the foundation concept[?]"[28] Any doubt about the intent of these words is immediately clarified in the next section of the memorandum, which begins: "We agree that you should not sit idly by in what appears to be a deteriorating situation and that several steps can be taken." The rest of the document lays out the steps to be taken by JDR, which in their essentials were: a critical first step of self-analysis and self-education; and thereafter (after defining the problem, identifying allied concerns, and heading off misconceptions) to "*approach the problem on three separate fronts— Washington, other foundations*, and the *public at large* . . . broadly outlined" (underlining added on the document with what appear to be marginalia of JDR 3rd). In regard to Washington, the Treasury Advisory Group of foundations [*sic*] is explicitly mentioned as are members of the Ways and Means Committee and the Senate Finance Committee who are defined as "generally cordial and receptive to your approaches."[29] Specific names are not mentioned in regard to the point about other foundations; emphasis is on developing a set of principles (for ethical behavior) which would be adaptable to both the few large and numerous other smaller foundations. Less detail is given about the approach to the public.

Next Steps: JDR 3rd Takes Action

No matter how the role was created, it was well tailored for the man. In a major speech delivered on October 3, 1964 at the inaugural dinner of the Federation of Jewish Philanthropies of New York John Rockefeller spoke with enthusiasm of his faith in philanthropy.[30] Portions of his speech are quoted extensively here because of its significance in presenting JDR's ideas as he was beginning his public career as philanthropic spokesman:

> I would like to talk about philanthropy broadly, and to suggest that we take a fresh look at the responsibilities as well as opportunities that philanthropy is facing in our modern world. Review seems necessary because our society is in a state of awesome change—change that increases our responsibilities to our fellow men even while it broadens our opportunities to serve them.
> At the outset, let me affirm my personal faith in private philanthropy as a unique feature and a vital strength of American society.

JDR's remarks were amplified further in a slightly different vein, and in a direction which seemed to reflect a new kind of vision:

> The fact that organized charity has come to a half-century milestone in an age of unprecedented change makes this time doubly appropriate for a stock-taking, for a candid reappraisal of our work. . . .
> I believe that philanthropy generally is not attuned to the tempo of the times: it is not giving due attention to society's new and unmet needs.
> . . .
> I further submit that if we are to be able to venture, we must be more willing to turn over to government a greater share of the burden of support of the tried and proven. . . .
> I submit also that we should be prepared to think of government as a partner in those areas where it shares the burden of support.

Finally, JDR came to a point which may have been either surprising or controversial to many, but was certainly the major thrust of his speech:

I suggest that the philanthropic foundations—already now ["now" added in pencil] associated in a common purpose—should also associate themselves in fact. An important start has been made. Already existing are the Foundation Library Center, the Council on Foundations, and the National Information Bureau. What I have in mind is an association with wider membership and more comprehensive objectives which can gain the active support of foundations generally.

The association I visualize would be a positive force encouraging its members, each in its own way, to play a more active role in meeting the needs of our society.

Three themes emerge from this speech: (1) that JDR did indeed value philanthropy and envision it as a critical aspect of American democracy; (2) that despite his belief in philanthropic institutions, he felt foundations were failing to meet the current needs of society; and (3) that he recognized the need for some new kind of association to bring the foundations together to ensure that they become more effective in meeting the needs of modern society. The first two themes had in fact already appeared in the documents related to the new role for JDR; the third represents a different kind of thrust for a Rockefeller. This new thrust seems to derive at least partly from discussions that Rockefeller had with Patman and his staff during this period.

During the winter of 1963–1964 JDR and John Lockwood had met several times with H. A. Olsher, Patman's chief staff person. In more than one of these meetings, Olsher had asked their opinion of Patman's proposal for an independent agency, separate from Treasury and the IRS, which would have responsibility for regulation and oversight of foundations, and which could even receive some support from the foundations. In Rockefeller's words, "His suggestion was, of course, motivated by the fact that he feels the Treasury does such a poor job in carrying out its responsibilities to check on foundations."[31] JDR and Lockwood apparently pointed out their strong "reservations." In his diary Rockefeller cites three concerns: first, that most of the abuses by foundations related to tax issues and would properly be the responsibility of Treasury; second, the majority of personal foundations operated within state boundaries so perhaps would not fall under federal regulation; and finally, "A new body might be given broad authority and responsibility . . . substantially beyond what we consider to be necessary." In any case Rockefeller made it clear that on the one hand Lockwood and he considered the "freedom and independence of foundations" to be critical, and on the other hand he was convinced that Olsher wanted foundations to be required to pay taxes.

Almost immediately after JDR's speech in the fall of 1964, it became apparent that there would be opposition to his idea of a new association of foundations. In fact, there was even opposition within the Rockefeller group itself. This was evident in the communication to JDR 3rd from Chauncey Belknap, attorney for the Rockefeller Fund, in which Belknap asked: "Would not the Rockefeller Foundation be rendering a greater public service if it maintains a big degree of independence from possibly entangling alliances during these coming months when the new legislation will be pending?" Belknap argued for a path similar to that taken during the Cox Committee and Reece Committee hearings and that would leave Rockefeller officers free and more able to "take positions which representatives of other foundations could not . . . because of the vulnerability of their own records."[32]

In the meantime, however, JDR continued to take steps to enlarge his foundation-related activities. In this period he added to his staff Ray Lamontagne, a Peace Corps friend of his son Jay, who was described as having an intelligent and fresh approach.[33] Although Lamontagne was hired primarily for work in the population field he soon had other responsibilities related to JDR's idea for a new association of foundations. In this pursuit JDR, McLean, and Lamontagne met with John Gardner, who, as President of the Carnegie Corporation of New York, headed one of the large and prestigious foundations essential to the realization of such an association. The meeting was followed in a few weeks by a letter to Dr. Gardner from Lamontagne (November 18, 1964) with an enclosed memorandum outlining some views on the "Proposed Association of Foundations." In line with JDR's earlier speech before the Jewish Federation of New York, the memorandum mentions the need for communication between foundations, and for standards to promote public accountability. Consideration was given to a list of other organizations that might fill this role, in particular the newly renamed Council on Foundations.[34] Finally, the accompanying letter refers to Gardner's offer to help with the names of other contacts, and leaves open the door to further exploration. However, by the end of December 1964, John Gardner had been named Secretary of Health, Education and Welfare and was on his way to Washington.

JDR 3rd as Lobbyist

As already noted, the JDR 3rd diaries and other documents in the Rockefeller Archives indicate that throughout the next decade JDR talked with administration officials about a variety of philanthropy-related matters, including his own special interests in population control and the arts. As foundations were becoming a "hot" concern, JDR also met with political leaders to urge tax support for philanthropy. Thus, in February 1964 JDR met with Douglas Dillon and discussed the Gore Amendment to the 1964 Revenue Act. As proposed the amendment would have eliminated contributions to all private foundations for purposes of calculating the unlimited charitable deduction. In his telephone diary JDR noted that when he met with Dillon he had not fully appreciated the importance of this issue—if not changed in the Joint Committee on Taxation (later renamed Joint Committee on Internal Revenue Taxation), the proposal could have endangered both Colonial Williamsburg and Lincoln Center, at the very least—nor had he understood the role of Stanley Surrey (presumably in relation to eliminating tax incentives); he also suggested the need to see Representative Mills.[35]

A memorandum in the JDR philanthropy files suggests increased attention to briefing JDR after this meeting. The subject of the memo is "Briefing Paper for Meetings with Russell Billis Long and Wilbur Daigh Mills on June 17, 1965." Mills was of course Chair of the House Ways and Means Committee (where tax legislation initiated) and Long was an important Democrat in the Senate—at that time, the second ranking member on both the Senate Finance Committee and the Joint Committee, where any tax bill was subject to intensive review.[36] It might have been assumed that JDR already had knowledge of their activities and background. However, the briefing memorandum suggests that there was some doubt about the depth of this knowledge. Thus the memorandum was divided into three major sections: I. Biographical Data (about Long and Mills); II. Prospective Legislation Affecting Charitable Giving; and III. Known Attitudes of General Interest. Thus, JDR's staff was now carefully briefing him for his advocacy activities, in the same manner as they might do for any novice lobbyist.

Although JDR had separated himself from active participation in the affairs of Colonial Williamsburg in the 1950s, after his father's death he was to become involved on a different level. The tax status of Colonial Williamsburg was apparently somewhat anomalous, and became particularly precarious after passage of the 1964 Revenue Act. In fact Wilbur Mills had named this as one of the institutions whose status would remain uncertain for some time, until IRS rulings and regulations could be further clarified.[37]

At about this time, in a rather technical document addressed to JDR, Chauncey Belknap explained some of the complications of federal sanctions relating to tax exemption violations, as well as issues concerning fiduciary responsibilities of trustees of charities. The major point of the document is an argument for legislation that would regulate fiduciary obligations of trustees and directors of charitable foundations and trusts at the state level, with particular focus on legislation in New York state. This document was actually a precursor of the argument for reliance on state oversight of charities that the Rockefellers were later to expand during the hearings in connection with the 1969 Tax Reform Act.[38] In addition the document recommends the formation of a state commission to review legislation related to trustee responsibility and standards for trusts and incorporated charities. An accompanying memorandum from Ray Lamontagne, however, indicates that there may have been different opinions among Rockefeller advisors on some of the issues raised by Belknap.

Patman, Treasury, and the IRS

The themes of tax reform and abuses by foundations continued through the 1960s, highlighted by the Treasury Report of 1965 and, thereafter, the Tax Reform Act of 1969. However, by 1964 another related but separate theme was also raised by Congressman Patman: the activities and role of the IRS itself. This issue finally surfaced dramatically during the long-awaited hearings of the Patman Committee in the summer of 1964.[39]

The 1964 Hearings of the Subcommittee No. 1 on Foundations, of the Select Committee on Small Business, were held in seven sessions that stretched over the summer from July 21 to September 4.[40] As F. Emerson Andrews pointed out, no foundation representatives were present; the witnesses were all government officials. Andrews's description of the accusatory tone of the hearings is generally confirmed in their published text. Much of the testimony presented in the record comes from Patman and his assistant, H. A. Olsher; there is only sporadic involvement of other committee members; and questions put to the witnesses were frequently in a "leading" form.

Andrews had reported that "[t]he Hearings opened on 21 July to a full room, with some spectators standing."[41] After the Chairman's opening paper came Treasury Secretary Dillon's prepared statement, in which he praised the "value of foundations in a pluralistic society," and suggested that the Treasury study of foundations would be completed by the end of the year. He stated that the auditing program of the Internal Revenue Service had been stepped up and he reminded the Committee that Congress had not always provided sufficient support either for Treasury's recommended policies or activities.

On July 22, Mortimer M. Caplin, former Commissioner of Internal Revenue, testified "as a private citizen." He responded to Patman's "severe criticism of the Internal Revenue Service" with a memorandum that outlined the ways that the IRS had augmented its procedures in terms of exempt organizations, personnel training, field audits, and operations of an Exempt Organization Council.[42] When asked, he also suggested a number of possible tax reforms related to foundations. The next day, Manuel F. Cohen, Acting Chairman of the Securities and Exchange Commission, gave his testimony on the stockholdings of 11 large foundations; it was sharply criticized by Patman.

After some weeks of recess, the hearings resumed with Bertrand M. Harding, Acting Commissioner of the IRS, as chief witness. During this session, considerable attention was given to the relationship between J. M. Kaplan, former president of the Welch Grape Juice Company, and the J. M. Kaplan Fund of New York. Based on apparent stock manipulations, the local District Director had recommended (1957) that the tax exemption of the fund be revoked. The recommendation had been reversed, but the fund was currently under investigation again; however, this had been delayed. The reason for the delay was discussed in a private conference with Patman during the session. It was revealed in the next session on August 31, when Patman, reporting on information from Mitchell Rogovin, assistant to the Commissioner, dropped what Andrews referred to as a "bombshell": the J. M. Kaplan Fund had been serving as "a conduit for channeling funds" for the CIA. This was the reason for the lack of action on the part of the IRS. Patman was asked not to discuss the matter for the public record.[43]

Although apparently persons "close to the foundation field" had known about the CIA's use of foundations as coverup for their work abroad, it was not until Patman's disclosures that the matter became public knowledge. Even then, after private conferences with Patman, the story was dropped. However, the hearings of 1964 continued and early in September Patman again called Harding as a witness. On the last session, September 4, Patman listed in detail eighteen deficiencies of the service, and concluded, "This is the most impressive record of do-nothing that I have seen in my 36 years of Congress. When it comes to the proper policing of tax exempt foundations, the IRS appears to be totally impaled in the quicksands of absolute inertia."[44]

In March 1967 the story about the J. M. Kaplan Fund appeared in *Ramparts* magazine. The following fall Patman continued his questions about the effectiveness of the IRS in another set of hearings. On November 15 the Chairman called the Treasury Secretary, now Henry H. Fowler, as a witness. Once again Patman introduced a prepared statement (including the same eighteen allegations listed in 1964), and once again he castigated the Internal Revenue Service for its sluggishness. Fowler responded more forcefully than Harding.[45] He cited the four-year extensive study by the Treasury, noting Treasury had concluded that although there were certainly abuses that needed correction, on the whole the abuses did not outweigh the benefits to society from private foundations. His testimony was followed the next day by the appearance of Sheldon Cohen, the Commissioner of Internal Revenue, with Stanley Surrey, the Assistant Secretary of the Treasury. Cohen stated that between 1964 and 1967, the IRS had greatly expanded its review of tax-exempt organizations; they had screened a total of 500,000 such organizations and audited 47,754. The great majority of these organizations, including private foundations, were found to be in compliance with the tax laws.[46] In this session Patman also raised questions about the ABC Foundation, a foundation which had been the target of his investigation in previous hearings. Cohen and Surrey supplied a great deal of information, but also pointed out that ABC was under investigation. In his review of Patman's activities, Andrews notes that the IRS investigation of ABC had begun eight months before the Patman interrogation (October 1967), and that by 1968 ABC trustees were under indictment in California.[47]

From Reports to Action

Despite all the general criticism of foundations, and the revelation of notable abuses by particular foundations, foundations on the whole apparently flourished in the 1960s.[48] Even after the Treasury Report on Foundations was delivered to Congress on February 2, 1965, and despite a spate of books about inequitable tax privileges and problems with philanthropy, foundations seemed to weather the storm. A generally favorable economic climate (including moderate inflation) and tax shelters for appreciated assets ensured foundation growth in number and financial worth. Thus the estimated value of their assets was $11.5 billion in 1960; 14.5 billion in 1964; and 20.5 billion in 1968; and the number of foundations was reported as increasing from 15,000 (1964) to 22,000 (1968).[49] The number of tax-exempt organizations also grew in this period, with the help of federal dollars for new programs and services in the nonprofit sector.[50]

By 1968, however, the war in Vietnam was escalating, and the issue of needed revenues became more salient. Indeed, in his sixth Report Installment Patman made an impassioned—if somewhat irrational—argument about taking massive sums from private foundations in order to pay for the costs of Vietnam. In this period the country was also in shock after the shootings of Martin Luther King (April 5, 1968) and Robert Kennedy (June 4, 1968), and there was widespread urban unrest. National budget deficits and inflation loomed large as increased costs of social programs (e.g., housing, welfare, Medicaid, and Medicare) were added to rising military expenditures. It therefore became easier for Treasury and the Congress (with a more committed Wilbur Mills) to take a harder line on tax reform; the notion of tax expenditures also became more salable. Under that concept, charitable deductions represented a loss of taxpayer dollars and a "cost" to the government. Concomitantly, there was even more interest in ensuring that money "sheltered" in private foundations would be used for public good and not for private profit of the donor.

In that mood, and armed with the Treasury Report, Mills opened hearings on a tax reform bill. The first speaker was Wright Patman, who laid matters on the line:

> Today I shall introduce a bill to end a gross inequity which the Country and its citizens can no longer afford: the tax-exempt status of the so-called privately controlled charitable foundations, and their propensity for domination of business and accumulation of wealth.
>
> Put most bluntly, philanthropy—one of mankind's more noble instincts—has been perverted into a vehicle for institutionalizing deliberate evasion of fiscal and moral responsibility to the nation.
>
> This has been accomplished by tax immunities granted by the U.S. Congress.[51]

The Tax Act would eventually cover far more than the privileges of philanthropic institutions and donors, but even so one point was clear. The foundations should be alert: their world was about to change.

5

In Whose Interest?

SENATOR RUSSELL LONG: If a Senator thinks he has had lobbying in this
foundation provision, he should have served on the Finance Committee.
We have had contacts with the truly first-class people in this country, . . .
some of the most powerful and influential people in this country, who
had not even deigned to pay attention to the Finance Committee for a
great number of years.
SENATOR ALBERT GORE: Perhaps the Senator can give me a little credit for that.

—Proceedings and Debates of the 91st Congress, December 1969

If your report does nothing else, I think that it could make a major
contribution by accumulating and presenting for Congress and the public
something of the total record of Good Deeds which America's foundations
can legitimately claim to have performed.

—Bayless Manning (Dean of the Stanford Law School)
to Peter Peterson, September 1969

The Treasury Department Report on Private Foundations had been delivered
to Congress in February 1965 without specific legislative proposals. It was
to be nearly five years before the Tax Reform Act of 1969 dealt with its key
recommendations. The delay occurred despite the fact that President Johnson
urged action to correct "certain abuses in the tax-exempt privileges enjoyed by
private foundations" in his Budget Message of January 25, 1965,[1] and called
for action on the Treasury Recommendations in his Economic Report the following year (January 27, 1966). During that time the Treasury Department had
also requested comments on its report. These were received over a period of
several months and published at the end of 1965.[2] However, in the months
following the issuance of the report the country experienced a series of shocks:
Malcolm X, a noted black leader, was killed in February, and the following
summer the Watts riots erupted. It was hardly surprising that immediate action
was not taken on the Treasury Department Report.[3]

In general, concern for tax equity was eclipsed by other social and economic considerations in this period. Initially the 1964 Tax Act was followed by

continued prosperity and expansion of the economy, and with only mild inflation, Johnson did not push actively for a tax increase after his inauguration in 1965.[4] A revenue bill (HR 13103) intended to help solve the balance of payments deficit was changed by Congress into a grab-bag of tax breaks for a multitude of individuals and organizations, and included a proposal for a check-off for funds to help Presidential candidates. Although this provision was delayed until after the next election, the bill passed in December 1966 still offered so many goodies that it was dubbed the "Christmas tree bill."[5] However, by the following year inflationary pressures increased and the need for additional revenue for the war in Vietnam forced Johnson to ask for a surtax on middle and upper incomes. With business and banking support garnered by Secretary of Treasury Fowler, P.L. 90-364 was finally enacted with the surtax on June 28, 1968.[6]

During this period Assistant Secretary of Treasury Surrey continued to press his case against tax preferences—his more pejorative label for tax incentives—and there were continuous Congressional efforts to eliminate the unlimited charitable deduction along with other tax reforms. Nonetheless neither the full attention of the President nor Congress as a whole was focused on tax reform; the House Ways and Means Committee in particular was busy with the burgeoning amount of legislation sought by President Johnson for his Great Society program.[7] Major laws on Education and Civil Rights and the Economic Opportunity Act (the "War on Poverty") had already been enacted in 1964. After the Watts riots a Voters' Rights Act was also passed to ensure black voters greater access to the voting booth. In 1965, over the opposition of the American Medical Association, and with great assistance from Wilbur Mills, sweeping changes were made in health care through Medicare (for the elderly) and Medicaid (for the poor). Model Cities legislation passed in 1966; and new provisions for AFDC (welfare) recipients were incorporated in the Social Security Amendments of 1967.[8]

Action and Inaction on the Foundation Front

This mass of social legislation helped to expand the voluntary sector, as numbers of tax-exempt organizations were created to carry out new programs and government support of such activities increased.[9] In these years a Democratic majority in Congress continued to support innovative social programs. However, by 1967 Wilbur Mills was complaining about excessive federal spending, budget deficits, and developing inflation, and he wanted increased revenues as well as reduced expenditures. The one-year surtax passed by Congress in June 1968 was expected to raise $10.9 billion in revenues and was accompanied by a Senate-initiated cut in expenditures, which was rumored to have been arranged with Mills's approval.[10] Significantly, attached to the Revenue and Expenditure Bill signed by Johnson on June 28 was an amendment requiring the President to submit a comprehensive tax reform proposal to Congress by December 31, 1968. By then, of course, Johnson, who had already created his own foundations, would be on his way out of office.[11] In any case, as Johnson's term drew to a close, the delay in tax reform was mandated to come to an end; but Johnson still refused to submit legislative proposals.

Meanwhile, Patman's efforts had continued, if somewhat sporadically, with the issuance of two more reports in 1966 and 1968, and through his 1967 hearings. It was said that Patman came out from under wraps with the departure of Johnson, but the fact was that his Select Committee on Foundations had only investigatory power and could not initiate legislation.[12] Nonetheless, Patman had made the most of what he had in his attack on the foundations. Thus, in his 1967 hearings, Patman had directed his attention to another significant problem—the question of IRS effectiveness in monitoring tax-exempt organizations. In this regard two notable events had been reported by the press during these years. The first was the incident concerning the status of the Sierra Club in 1966, and the second was an article in *Ramparts* magazine which revived the story of the CIA involvement in foundation activity just before the 1967 hearings.[13] Both had to do with political activity; but apparently the IRS was not even-handed in its treatment. It had covered up for the CIA, while it pursued the Sierra Club's lobbying activities, so that it lost its 501(c)(3) status.[14]

On the whole at this point the foundation community was still watching warily but without mobilizing a strong counterattack. In any case there was no one foundation community, and certainly no one voice that could speak for all the foundations, even the large ones. This had been evident in the individualized responses to the 1965 Treasury Report, where many of the big foundations (Lilly Endowment, Ford, and Carnegie) made it clear that abuses discussed in the Treasury Report did not relate to *them,* but otherwise had hardly presented a strong common argument.[15] The Rockefeller Foundation and Rockefeller Brothers Fund had also presented separate statements, expressing their own particular preference for a state role in oversight of foundation activity.[16]

Certainly major differences existed in the size, location, and purposes of individual foundations, and the few associations of philanthropies that existed were not a unifying force. The Council on Foundations primarily served the smaller foundations, and the Foundation Center was essentially an information service. The National Council on Philanthropy could not do it, and the National Information Bureau apparently had little relationship with the foundations.[17] There were other related informal groups, including the broader

501(c)(3) group, but there was no unified foundation voice.[18] And as we have already seen, when JDR proposed the formation of an association of foundations, among the first to oppose the idea was the staff of the Rockefeller Foundation itself.

JDR's Group on Philanthropic Issues

During this period JDR continued to give his personal attention to philanthropic matters, in the particular and in the larger sense. He had limited success with President Johnson in regard to establishment of a Presidential Commission on Population,[19] and was also actively involved in fund raising efforts for Lincoln Center, where he still served as Chairman.[20] JDR was also briefed by family attorneys, staff of the various Rockefeller philanthropies, and his own office staff for his meetings with officials in Washington. And, in addition, he began holding more meetings with what was soon to be dubbed the "Informal Advisory Group on Philanthropy." Although the attendance varied, in 1967–68 key advisors in this group included Dana Creel (head of the RBF), Datus Smith (personal staff), and John Lockwood (family attorney), as well as an outsider, William Warren, Dean of the Columbia Law School. Warren's involvement with JDR is interesting in light of the ongoing negotiations between the Rockefeller family and Columbia University with regard to their properties in Rockefeller Center in those years. It was Warren who in January 1968 went with JDR to meet with Wilbur Mills, and who composed the follow-up memorandum for Rockefeller to send to Mills about continuing problems facing the charitable deduction and the status of Colonial Williamsburg.[21] Matters considered by the Rockefeller group varied somewhat in focus, but discussions generally seemed to revolve around three main concerns: (1) the unlimited charitable deduction and the tax exempt status of philanthropic organizations; (2) questions about foundation-related activities and the nature of the broader philanthropic field; (3) distinctions between improving regulation over abuses of individual foundations and more federal control over the foundation field as a whole.

Meanwhile by 1966 Douglas Dillon had left Treasury, and as the budget deficit mounted and the need to seek additional revenues became more urgent, Surrey began to have more success in pushing his tax expenditure concept.[22] In fact Surrey was soon to have a great victory: Treasury presented a report on tax expenditures as part of its analysis for the President's Budget Proposal for fiscal 1968.[23] In this context, on February 2, 1967, John Lockwood wrote to JDR about the position the Rockefeller Brothers Fund had taken in regard to proposals that Treasury was planning to present to Ways and Means. As it had done in response to the Treasury Report, the RBF urged more reliance on state regulation and supervision of charitable organizations, within federal standards, but with less federal control and oversight. In his memorandum Lockwood also noted that Marion Fremont-Smith's book (which suggested an important role for the states) had been published;[24] he also reported that Creel, Warren, and Lockwood had met with a group of Treasury officials and the chief of staff of the Joint Committee on Internal Revenue Taxation, Laurence Woodworth. In addition, the Attorney General of New York (serving in the administration of Nelson Rockefeller) was now proposing new state legislation concerning tax-exempt organizations.[25]

Shortly thereafter, on February 8, JDR met with the Secretary of Treasury, now Henry A. Fowler, to address the question of "our concern at Treasury's seemingly limited approach to philanthropy"; he also talked about the impact of changes concerning the unlimited deduction which complicated his family's "philanthropy efforts." JDR believed that his meeting with Fowler had gone well.[26] However, the tax expenditure concept continued to gain credibility in the administration, and the possibility of Treasury-initiated tax reforms remained. Consequently, in September JDR discussed matters with some family advisors—John Lockwood, Howard Bolton, Dana Creel, Richardson Dilworth, and Robert Douglass; they agreed that he should see Mr. Fowler again.[27] When they met with Fowler on October 12, Jerome Kurtz, Fowler's chief counsel for tax legislation (and assistant to Stanley Surrey) was present. In his diary JDR reported that Kurtz had a "rather negative attitude" and that this meeting was "less productive as we got into technical points concerning the Treasury's recommendations in regard to which I was less at home."[28]

By early 1968 the idea of tax preference had gained formal status, and tax reform legislation, including matters affecting foundation control, was more likely. Consequently JDR became involved in a series of strategy discussions with his own advisors and with Congressional leaders whom he hoped to influence. Warren and he had already met with Mills in January, and on May 9 they met with Russell Long, now Senate Majority Whip as well as Chairman of the Senate Finance Committee. At this meeting he notes that Senator Long mentioned "several abuses of which he was aware" and suggested that the foundations "should be self policing if they were concerned about what Congress might do." He also suggested that it might be useful for JDR to help inform some of the members of his committee, particularly Senator Abraham Ribicoff (Democrat, Connecticut).[29]

The issue of self-policing was discussed in a follow-up meeting with Creel, Lockwood, Smith, and Warren. JDR described "an interesting and constructive discussion" which ended with "agreeing to invite John McCloy, Doug Dillon and Freddy Sheffield (Chairman of Carnegie Corporation) . . . to explore the

matter further." The invitations were accepted, and the group met to discuss
Senator Long's suggestion of self-policing. In his report on the meeting, JDR
wrote:

> This encourages me to pick up again our own idea that there should be
> a stronger organization within the foundation field which could exert
> leadership on the foundations and also represent them in Washington and
> in the states in regard to legislation concerning foundations.[30]

At that meeting the group agreed to talk with Alan Pifer, President of the
Carnegie Corporation, "who also, from a recent speech, seems to be thinking
in the same direction."

Pifer joined JDR and the advisory group (Lockwood, Smith, Warren, and
Phillips) for lunch on September 12, and they discussed the "problem of the
future of philanthropy in this country with particular reference to foundations."
In his diary JDR notes that Pifer proposed the idea of a commission of "distinguished, mostly nonfoundation individuals to make a survey of the field of philanthropy" which would presumably be "appointed and supported by several
foundations."[31] A more formal record of the September 12 meeting of the Informal Philanthropy Committee indicates more fully that Pifer thought the commission "might study the problems confronting private philanthropy and recommend possible solutions to these problems." "An important aspect of the
commission's task would be to consider whether a permanent organization that
might serve as a 'public conscience' over the entire area of private philanthropy
should be created. Pifer apparently believed that few positive results had come
from Congressional investigations of foundations, but an independent investigation by prestigious private citizens could help to set standards and guidelines
for action.[32]

The Rockefeller philanthropy group believed that the need for regulations
to control abuses by some foundations was distinct from the related concerns
about Treasury (tax) policies more broadly. As part of an effort to keep these
separate, the possibility of self-policing by the foundations was undeniably ap-
pealing. The question of an independent agency of government to watch over
philanthropic activity, raised earlier by Patman's chief staff person, H. A. Olsher,
was certainly not given serious consideration by the Rockefeller group. It had
also been specifically rejected in the Treasury Report (under Secretary Dillon)
which stated explicitly: "The Treasury Department does not . . . recommend
that any separate Federal regulatory agency be created to supervise foundations. Rather, the Department is of the view that the effort should be made to
frame the tax laws themselves to curb abuses."[33]

In response to the still worrisome possibility of more federal regulation,

Rockefeller advisors had been exploring two different, but congruent, options: first was the idea of self-policing by the foundations themselves; and the second was the idea originally put forward by the Rockefeller Foundation—that there should be more state-level accountability. Pifer's idea for a full-blown commission to study the philanthropic field suggested another direction. Already on May 24 Datus Smith had discussed the exciting speech that Pifer had just given about the need for some new "mechanism" which would serve as "a kind of collective conscience" for the foundations. By early September members of JDR's staff had begun exploring ideas for both an "initial conference and possible forms for a permanent organization that might arise from such a conference," and they talked with Alan Pifer about it even before the group meeting of September 12.[34]

On September 30, 1968, the group, now called the "future of philanthropy group," met again in JDR's office, with a new member, Oscar Ruebhausen, Chairman of the Russell Sage Foundation. Prior to this meeting JDR sent a memorandum to the group about the scope of the proposed commission, suggesting that it might "include the field of philanthropy in general, though with special attention to foundations." Questions were included, ranging from "What is the role of private philanthropy?" to "What methods of self-policing of foundations might be effective?" Also discussed was the sponsorship of such a commission. The memorandum included a preliminary list of possible foundation sponsors, and a reference to outside sponsorship (such as the White House or Congress), which had been discussed at the previous meeting, but apparently was now being reconsidered negatively by several individuals.[35]

At the September 30 meeting more names were reviewed for participation in the group, but a tone of caution prevailed. The chairman of the Ford Foundation (Julius Stratton) was to be invited and Kingman Brewster, President of Yale, would be approached informally by JDR. Stratton showed some interest, but Brewster never became directly involved with the informal Rockefeller group or the subsequent Peterson Commission. However, as we shall see in later chapters, Brewster did subsequently take independent, and related, action focused on the nonprofit sector.

The idea of a commission gained momentum in September and October 1968, although possibly not as fast as JDR would have liked. A series of memoranda considering the concept of the commission, and questions it might address, were discussed in meetings of JDR's Informal Philanthropy Group. However, just as too many cooks spoil the broth, too many advisors may cause problems. In any case, there was by no means general agreement even among this small group, and Dana Creel, for example, proposed that a commission pursue a more sweeping consideration of the role of philanthropy, while Alan

Pifer proposed more focus on "the role of the general purpose foundation" (by which he apparently meant large foundations like Carnegie). JDR suggested a compromise, with a charge to study the "entire field of private philanthropy," to be broken down for operational purposes into "three or four subcommissions, each to concentrate on a particular aspect of private philanthropy."[36]

In this same meeting on October 14 "considerable attention was devoted to identifying a possible commission chairman and members." An initial list was considerably revised, but it was also noted "that the names thus far suggested were short on labor, female, religious and minority group representation." More names were needed, and might come from people who were leaving Washington after the current election. Among the people mentioned for Chairman, Bill Moyers (editor of *Newsday,* and connected to the Democratic administration) and Peter Peterson (CEO of Bell and Howell, and known to JDR through his connection to his son Jay's father-in-law, Senator Charles Percy) "seemed more generally acceptable." Gus Levy (Gustave Lehmann Levy, investment banker and treasurer of Lincoln Center), and Thomas Watson (Chief Executive of IBM) were to be invited to attend the next meeting; however, they never did actually participate.

In any case, Russell A. Phillips subsequently sent JDR a copy of a draft statement developed with Dana Creel, which he had revised by making the tone more positive and eliminating references to abuses by foundations. Still included in this "Draft Prospectus for Line of Inquiry for Proposed Commission on Philanthropy" was an all-encompassing first paragraph which, in keeping with JDR's own views, began, "A salient characteristic of our history is the pluralistic approach with which Americans have confronted problems and needs," and went on to connect the idea of pluralism with the existence of foundations and institutions of the nonprofit sector.[37]

Although at the end of October it seemed as if a commission of public citizens might soon be launched, by early December this was less certain. On December 6 Datus Smith gave JDR a new draft statement on the commission, written by Russ Phillips, and "reflecting the combined ideas of Dana, Alan, Oscar, and Russ; and incidentally having my endorsement also."[38] The new proposal slowed down the notion of a full-blown commission, and suggested a new model, based on the formation of a "steering committee . . . of a representative selection of officers from general-purpose private foundations and persons prominent in the areas of corporate philanthropy and church philanthropy. . . . The committee would be chaired by a person of national stature but without ties to any private foundations, and he essentially would work with a project director identifying problems about private philanthropy and gathering information and opinions about these problems." Only after the "relevant material is assimilated" would a commission be convened, and then "[t]he project chairman would probably be the commission chairman." The project would apparently be largely financed by private foundations, but this was not to be considered sponsorship by the foundations. This same approach is summarized in a file note about a meeting of Pifer, Ruebhausen, Phillips, and Smith on December 9, 1968.

What happened between October 30 and December 9? For one thing, there had been a national election and Richard Milhous Nixon would be taking office in January 1969. Although Nixon was believed to be committed to the voluntary sector, it was not clear what this would mean to the foundations and proposals for tax reform. Possibly there may have been concern about any obvious connection that a commission would have to a member of the Rockefeller family, in light of past ill-feeling between Nixon and Nelson Rockefeller, and a wait-and-see strategy seemed advisable. In addition, lobbying and political activity by tax-exempt organizations was emerging as a salient issue in Washington and a commission could easily be viewed as lobbying activity by the foundations.

In fact, by then the Sierra Club's tax status had been changed to a 501(c)(4) classification after the IRS determined that the club's legislative activities "went well beyond any permissible limits of such endeavors for income tax purposes" (that is for a 501[3] organization). In addition CIA involvement with the National Student Association had been uncovered and the IRS and Treasury, as well as members of Congress, were forced to recognize that political activities were carried out by foundations, including the powerful Ford Foundation. Meanwhile the lobbying activities of the Carnegie Corporation in support of the National Urban Coalition were also receiving press attention. This group had recently been started by John Gardner, former President of Carnegie; and a *New York Times* dispatch of December 5, 1968 had drawn attention to the fact that one of its major objectives was "to organize a massive lobbying effort to obtain the legislation that the coalition considers essential for the cities."[39] Thus caution in regard to advocacy activities by a foundation-related group might well have seemed advisable—particularly to Alan Pifer, now head of Carnegie.

The Commission Gets Underway

In January 1969 as Nixon assumed the Presidency, the issue of tax reform could not be avoided. The federal government had ended its 1967–1968 fiscal year with a deficit of $25.4 billion, a sum which coincidentally was not far from the amount of the total estimated assets of all foundations in the United

States.[40] Moreover, provisions inserted in the 1968 tax act had required that the outgoing administration submit tax reform proposals by December 31,[41] so that now, with Johnson, who perhaps had his own reasons for holding back reform, leaving office, the show would begin, in fact sooner than anticipated by the philanthropic leadership.[42] On January 17, outgoing Treasury Secretary Joseph W. Barr (in the Johnson administration only a month) took a parting shot at America's millionaires and warned of a "taxpayer's revolt." Barr made headlines when he said that in a recent year 155 American citizens with incomes of over $200,000 paid no federal income tax and that 21 other individuals with incomes of over $1 million also paid no taxes.[43] Then on January 25 Wilbur Mills announced that foundations would be the first order of business when hearings on tax reform started in February.

Rockefeller mobilized quickly. By February he had recruited Peter "Pete" Peterson,[44] and on March 4 the informal committee on philanthropy met "for the purpose of providing Mr. [Peter] Peterson an opportunity to discuss . . . the possibility of his assuming the chairmanship of the philanthropy commission."[45] At the meeting Rockefeller stressed that hearings in the House Committee on Ways and Means "added a new sense of urgency" to the creation of the commission and initiation of a study. JDR noted that he had mentioned the commission idea in his appearance before the House Committee (on February 27), and that the Committee asked that the commission provide its recommendations to Ways and Means in a timely fashion.

In his comments to the informal philanthropy group Peter Peterson stated clearly that the new commission should be totally independent of "the foundation orbit," in fact as well as appearance. He believed the commission had to be composed of private persons not directly involved with foundations, it had to set its own agenda, and that funding should come from a variety of "assorted sources." Moreover, the commission "should frankly acknowledge that there are some troublesome questions." In discussions about the budget, Alan Pifer suggested that $200,000 seemed an appropriate amount, although Peterson (who apparently intended to run a tight ship) thought the cost could be held to about $90,000.[46] In recognition of the importance of the political situation, the group agreed that it would be desirable to obtain a letter indicating that Mills had requested the establishment of the commission; perhaps Mills might even want Senator Long and Treasury Secretary Kennedy to join him in making the request.

At this meeting the list of names for possible commission members was reviewed, as well as a list of questions which had already been raised by the group. It was proposed that a report be ready that summer in time to influence

Congressional bills on foundation matters, even if it was not final. Peterson ended the meeting with a request that each organization represented there send him suggestions for commission membership, funding, staff, and agenda within a week.

By March 5 Rockefeller had replied to Peterson's request in considerable detail. He referred to a meeting with Wilbur Mills the next day in Washington, and said he would make the point that discussions about forming a commission had begun at least six months prior to this time. In connection with possible commission membership, JDR sent a very long list of names, suggesting for special consideration C. Douglas Dillon, Patricia Harris, Father Theodore Hesburgh, Robert A. Lovett, Bill Moyers, John J. McCloy, and Cyrus R. Vance. He also submitted names for staff positions.[47] Ultimately, one of those highlighted for "special consideration" (Patricia Harris, a black woman and respected attorney) and several people from JDR's long list became members; none of the staff were selected. Indeed when Peterson accepted the chairmanship he made it plain that he would choose his own staff.[48]

The Commission at Work

By mid-April the Peterson Commission was officially named the Commission on Foundations and Private Philanthropy. Articles about the commission appeared in the *New York Times* on April 13 and on April 20; the first was based on a press release from JDR's office on April 12, the second on a press release from Peterson himself.[49] By that time Rockefeller had met with Wilbur Mills, but the *New York Times* article reported only that Mills had been "recently informed of the establishment of the citizens' committee . . . proposed by Mr. Rockefeller in testimony on Feb. 27." No claim was made that Mills supported the commission, and the newspaper reported that the Chairman of the Ways and Means Committee "was not available for comment."

Including Peterson, the Commission on Foundations and Private Philanthropy ultimately had 16 members, including several African Americans, two women, and representatives from unions, universities, and a leading art gallery. No foundation representatives were on the commission.[50] With the exception of one individual (Fritz Heimann), all five staff members were Chicago based, all were attorneys, and all were known to Peterson himself. The Staff Executive Director was Everett L. Hollis, an attorney from Chicago.

In its final report the commission stated that a workplan had been drawn up as early as April 14.[51] However, the first official meeting of the Peterson Commission was actually held on May 21, 1969 at Peterson's home in Winnetka, Illinois. Peterson introduced members of the staff and also mentioned that an additional person, Dr. Franklin Long, had accepted commission membership. He noted that Hermon "Dutch" Smith was serving as Treasurer for the commission, and that he and Smith were seeking funds from 500 major corporations as well as individuals.[52] Although he had previously taken steps to have the commission incorporated as a charitable organization in the state of Illinois, Peterson now suggested that the group should not seek a ruling for tax-exempt status as a 501(c)(3) organization.[53] Since lobbying and political activity by tax-exempt organizations had emerged as one of the key issues in discussions on Capitol Hill, it seemed advisable for the commission to avoid any possible questions about the appropriateness of its own activities. Peterson certainly anticipated that he and his staff would be in close contact with Congress and the administration, and the commission would also be keeping "appropriate officials informed" about its work.[54]

At this first meeting there was considerable discussion of the "Major Areas of Inquiry" paper distributed in advance. A revised draft of this outline included these major topic headings:

    I. Foundation funding of political social action and other controversial activities
    II. Allocation of foundation resources in a changing society
    III. Evaluation of foundations as "philanthropic middlemen"
    IV. Relations between donors and their foundations
    V. Evaluation of tax incentive system
    VI. Governmental and other forms of supervision
    VII. Other studies

The last topic included three sub-issues relating to the dimensions of U.S. philanthropy, the relation between individual philanthropy and foundation programs, and the notable contributions made by foundations. In this regard, after reading the outline sent him, JDR had characteristically suggested that Peterson should "encourage the Commission to approach its assignment in terms of philanthropy as a whole" since foundations were only a "segment" of the philanthropic field.[55]

Each of the first six major areas of inquiry included specific issues to be addressed, as well as work projects that would be needed. But the projects were presented in general terms, for example, a survey "of existing and proposed legal restrictions on foundation activities" without details about how or when it would be done. The commissioners were outspoken even while groping for an approach to their work, and they requested that a more orderly method of procedure be developed before the next meeting. It was also suggested that the issues should be framed in a more positive tone, and the need for more fact gathering was emphasized.

Various approaches were discussed, including a model in-depth study of one foundation, proposed by staff member Everett Hollis. Another staff member suggested that the next meeting should start with a factual presentation on the background and types of foundations, followed by a panel presentation of "knowledgeable individuals" from both "activist" and "non activist" foundations. Peterson emphasized that the commission "should seek to complete its study by December 1, 1969." Thus a compressed timetable was agreed to, with six meetings of two days each to be held every month (except July) between June and November, when in order to discuss the final report, there would be an extra meeting. (This later was changed; no full commission meetings were held in November, and two meetings were planned for October.)[56]

A draft of the commission's "operating plan" (apparently not distributed to commissioners) noted that "the principal contribution which the commission can make will be to develop and articulate policy judgments and recommendations on a limited number of basic policy issues affecting foundations." Methods of working were to include liaison with Congress (primarily staff), and development of issues, through "(a) background papers, (b) panel discussion, (c) written expressions of views, and (d) interviews. The final report would be of moderate length; there would be no interim reports; and background papers by leading experts would not be published. Essentially, the commission would attempt to act in this fast-track style; however, the lack of available data necessitated late changes in the research agenda and also contributed to delays in the final report.[57]

A major aspect of the commission's work consisted of the monthly meetings with panel discussions on key topics. There was no difficulty in securing appropriate experts. Among the insightful as well as controversial individuals who met with the commission were McGeorge Bundy, President of the Ford Foundation; John Simon (a young maverick and expert on foundation law); Marion Fremont-Smith; and Stanley Surrey.

In a sense the tone for the entire effort was set at the June meeting of the commission, which was something of a marathon. The first morning was devoted to presentations on: (1) the role of philanthropy including foundations in American society; (2) the history of Congressional concern about foundations; and (3) the relationship between government and foundation activities.[58] The two days included three more panel discussions of four speakers each and an executive committee meeting over lunch. In keeping with the commitment to hear diverse viewpoints, panelists included foundation executives, academic experts, and activists. Among the speakers was Vernon Jordan, Director of the

Voter Education Project, Southern Regional Council (Atlanta). This project was among those whose political overtones were questioned by some members of Congress; but it was later accepted as a nonpartisan protection of civil rights.[59]

Membership on the commission was a learning experience for many of those who came to the meetings. Commissioners had, after all, been selected deliberately to be outside of the foundation loop, although some—like Sheldon Cohen, former IRS commissioner, Edward Levi, president of a preeminent tax-exempt organization (the University of Chicago), and Thomas Curtis (former Congressman and member of Ways and Means)—had highly relevant expertise. Attendance on the whole was markedly uneven. Few members attended regularly and staff played a key role throughout. In the end a fair amount of data was gathered. However, given the magnitude of the task, it is not surprising that there were apparently also methodological problems with some of the original studies.[60] Evidently some of the staff were learning too, and the idea of using the model in-depth study of one foundation was dropped. In any case, the final report included the following studies as Appendixes: Survey of Distinguished Citizens, Survey of Chicago Philanthropic Organizations, and Survey of Foundations. Two additional papers by outside experts were also added as appendixes: "Philanthropy and the Economy" by Mary Hamilton, and "Enlightened Self-interest and Corporate Philanthropy," by William J. Baumol.

Congressional Action and Reaction to It

While the commission was meeting, events on the Hill of course did not stop, even if that might have been desired by both JDR and Peterson. Although the Tax Reform Bill was intended to cover items other than foundations and philanthropy, the hearings on HR 13270 began in February with the first topic, Tax-exempt Foundations.[61] Testimony on this topic was in essence to be a response to the prior recommendations of the 1965 Treasury Report; as noted above, the first witness was Wright Patman, who presented "for the record" data on the Ford and Rockefeller foundations as well as other material. He also asked for a 20 percent tax on all foundation assets.[62]

The foundation community as a whole was still watching without evident alarm. A few months before the Ways and Means Committee Hearings began, the Council on Foundations had published F. Emerson Andrews's assessment of the Patman Committee attack on foundations, stressing the weaknesses of Patman's inquiry. Now, early in February, David Freeman, President of the Council on Foundations, sent a memorandum about the hearings to members of the Council, saying that he was requesting the opportunity to testify about activities of the Council. He indicated that some individual foundation representatives would also be appearing before the Committee. Freeman described the "just-released 1968 tax reform package" as an 'orphan'; it was not endorsed by the Johnson administration and was unlikely to be pushed by President Nixon because in relation to private foundations it was "basically a restatement of the 1965 [Treasury] report." In this mode Freeman predicted that the hearings on foundations would "probably only last a week."

Given the problem of delineating precisely what was considered a foundation and the extensive nature of related issues, the exact length of time devoted to foundation issues may be debated.[63] But discussion of "tax-exempt organizations" and issues related to the Treasury Report (on foundations) were held on February 18, 19, 20, 21, 24, 25, 26, and 27. The discussions became the first 1,732 pages of the large printed volumes of hearings transcripts.[64]

Among the first witnesses to appear before the House Ways and Means Committee were representatives of the Rockefeller interests, including J. George Harrar (Rockefeller Foundation) and Dana Creel (Rockefeller Brothers Fund), as well as McGeorge Bundy, President of the Ford Foundation. Altogether a great number of foundations of diverse sizes, purposes, and locations would testify individually, as well as representatives of the few associated groups like the Council on Foundations and the Foundation Center. On the whole, in their testimony speakers representing large foundations, and the Foundation Center, appeared to accept the need to curb abuses and insure greater accountability by providing more information and issuance of annual reports (Pifer, Merrimon Cuninggim, Harrar and Creel, and Manning Pattillo). But McGeorge Bundy's presentation was more problematic, since committee members were concerned about the Ford Foundation's ownership of company stock as well as its politically suspect grantmaking. Other foundations including Kellogg, Kresge, Duke, and the Lilly Endowment also had problems with their intertwined business relationships.[65] There remained different voices even among the big foundations. Harrar and Creel were still urging accountability largely through state regulation; Pifer and Cuninggim recognized the need for controlling abuses but expressed great concern over any threats to foundation independence. And interestingly, in his own statement, McGeorge Bundy expressed doubts about both the capacity for self-monitoring by foundations and the efficacy of state monitoring.[66]

Foundation watchers from the outside also had opinions about the direction matters were taking. An article in *Science* stated that "Congress cannot be said to be hostile to the foundations" but nonetheless suggested that "the era of what amounted to self-regulation for the foundations is probably over." Although Patman's suggestion for heavy taxation (20 percent) did not seem worthy of serious attention, *Science* noted that a new note was sounded with the move to legislative action. The article continued:

> What is also new this year is that not only are the business activities of foundations and the sharp practices of a few of them in question, but major foundations are also being criticized for political and social action. The dramatic high point of last week's hearings unquestionably came with the testimony of McGeorge Bundy.[67]

Still, the author thought Bundy had been a "formidable, unapologetic witness" and that he had been handled more gently than others who had appeared before the committee. Other viewers interpreted matters differently, and some newspapers suggested that Bundy's testimony had been highly inflammatory.[68]

Another event may have contributed to the mood of Congress at this time. On February 27, John D. Rockefeller 3rd had also testified before Ways and Means. In his testimony, JDR made a point that he apparently considered significant, stating that although he "qualified for the unlimited deduction privilege during every year since 1961" he had "deliberately paid a tax of between five and ten percent" of adjusted gross income each year.[69] Rockefeller later sent the Committee a letter explaining more carefully what he meant—that no one should be able to completely avoid paying taxes, and therefore an amount (20 percent) should in every case be required even for those who benefitted from the unlimited tax deduction.[70] But in the meantime, although he seemed to be treated rather benevolently by the Committee, JDR undoubtedly added fuel to the fire created by McGeorge Bundy. In any case, on February 28 the *Wall Street Journal* reported that complaints were pouring in to Congress about the privileges enjoyed by the foundations and their rich sponsors. The *Journal* noted that there were "marked changes," as "Congress suddenly . . . turned against private, tax-exempt foundations."[71] By now private foundations were clearly identified as a separate group, different from other 501(c)(3) charitable organizations, and worthy of suspicion.[72]

In this climate tax reform moved forward. A House Bill (HR 13270) went to the Senate in late summer—without an official report from the Peterson Commission, and with more punitive provisions than had been expected. Senate Finance Committee Hearings were now scheduled for early September; before then Peterson met with Treasury officials—presumably to discuss the commission's preliminary findings but undoubtedly also to attempt to influence their deliberations.[73] This was around the time that the Treasury Department was completing a new Technical Memorandum to accompany the bill to the Senate Finance Committee.[74]

Meanwhile, Peterson Commission staff were still gathering data, and commission members were thrashing out major issues that confronted Congress. Although not every point was resolved to everyone's satisfaction, there had been lively, and lengthy, discussions of issues such as an appropriate payout rate for foundations and the question of political advocacy by foundations. Separately there had also been communication with key individuals in Treasury and on the Hill while the commission report was being pulled together.[75] By October therefore Peterson apparently felt ready, or at least obliged politically, to testify at the Senate hearings. Thus on October 22, he appeared as a witness before the Senate Finance Committee. In doing so, he made it evident that the commission was not the creature of the foundations and represented an independent voice. However, Peterson was in close communication with JDR's office, and certainly the commission's approach was consistent with JDR's expressed interest in the whole philanthropic field, beyond just tax issues. Indeed, Peterson's testimony seemed in some ways as closely related to concerns of the recipients of foundation monies as to those of the donors. The record of correspondence between staff and some beneficiary institutions, such as universities and research institutes, and the membership on the commission, also reflects this.[76]

By now the foundations had also been forced to get their own act together. In the press release announcing its hearings, the Senate Finance Committee had urged groups, including foundations, to present consolidated testimony in order to avoid excessive repetition. Consequently, an ad hoc "coordinated foundation testimony group" was created to insure that there would be more unified foundation and foundation-related presentations.[77] Although all foundations may not have been in accord on all matters under discussion, particular institutions could certainly agree on some key issues. Thus the new group arranged to present their testimony in panel form around critical topics. And the Foundation Center subsequently circulated the testimony in a paperback volume.[78]

In forming the coordinated testimony group, the foundations also brought in some allied beneficiary institutions, primarily from the field of higher education, to help strengthen their case. But overall this remained only another in the series of ad hoc groups formed in response to outside pressure, without the status of a permanent coordinating body. In a separate but related move, around this time the Council on Foundations, the Foundation Center, and the National Council on Philanthropy came together out of a sense of urgency to create "an agency to set and maintain standards of operation for foundations and to sanction them in the event of unremedied abuses." According to the *New York Times,* the "initial work on the self-policing agency was done by a six-member committee headed by Mr. Pattillo."[79] Presumably such a group would be concerned with prevention of abuses in the major areas of Treasury concern—self dealing, low payouts, business holdings, and lack of accountability, and might possibly satisfy Congressional demand for more oversight of advocacy activities. However, it would not prove easy to form such an organization; there were too many different concerns and interests to represent, and in fact there was still a real reluctance to be coordinated.

6

Law and Regulation

In all likelihood the most attractive feature of the use of a foundation is that
it enables the donor, at least in some measure, "to have his cake and eat it
too." He obtains a tax deduction at the time he makes a donation to the
foundation; yet he can still exercise a substantial measure of control over
the assets which he has donated to the foundation. The point is, of course,
of particular importance when the asset contributed . . . is stock in
family-controlled or otherwise-closely-held business.
—Peter G. Peterson, testimony before the Senate Finance Committee,
October 22, 1969

Mr. President, the real essence of this debate is that this is not a tax reform
question but rather a sociological decision for the Nation.
—Senator Jacob R. Javits, Senate Discussions on the Tax Reform Act,
December 1969

From Treasury Report to House Bill

In the spring of 1969 the Ways and Means Committee moved rapidly on the
tax bill which, by August 1, was approved by the House and named the Tax
Reform Act of 1969. Under the rules adopted by the House, HR 13270 had been
subject to only a brief discussion on the floor, no amendments were permitted,
and the whole procedure took only six hours.[1] Moreover, it appeared that an
accelerated schedule of review was likely to continue in the Senate. Consequently, although four weeks of hearings were scheduled to begin there in September, it was now expected that action on the Tax Reform Act could be completed in the fall.

The bill passed by the House was harsher in its provisions than the recommendations of the original 1965 Treasury Report. This was due largely to controversy in the Committee on Ways and Means around the troublesome matters
of foundation lobbying and political activism. Under the existing Internal Revenue Code, substantial amounts of such activity by 501(c)(3) organizations, in-

cluding foundations, was already prohibited. However, during the hearings in the Ways and Means Committee it became apparent that small individual foundations, as well as powerful foundations like Ford, often ignored existing limitations on political action. Indeed Congressman John Rooney, Democrat from Brooklyn, engaged the attention of the House Ways and Means Committee when he discussed the way his opponent, Henry Richmond, had used the Richmond Foundation in the election campaign against Rooney. Thus, although neither had been included in the original 1965 Treasury Report, both tighter regulation of political activity and fiscal "penalties" on foundations (a 7.5 percent tax on income) were now incorporated in the House tax bill.

The bill that went from the House to the Senate embodied a broad sweep of reforms affecting individual and corporate taxes, as well as the practices of foundations, and was altogether a major tax reform effort. According to the *New York Times* there had been an agreement between Wilbur Mills and Treasury officials about these proposals,[2] and furthermore the passage from Treasury through Congress occurred during an unusual combination of circumstances—the war in Vietnam and the restless mood of the country—which together highlighted the need for tax reform and new revenues. In this climate, the idea of tax preferences pushed by former Assistant Treasury Secretary Surrey gained credibility. Furthermore, Mills apparently had great confidence in Laurence N. Woodworth, Chief Counsel of the Joint Committee on Taxation, who had worked closely with Surrey on the tax reform proposals. The importance of Woodworth's role was well known and understood also by John Rockefeller.[3]

Given the scale of its recommended changes, HR 13270 went through Congress fairly rapidly. However, Treasury proposals presented to the House in January 1969 not only incorporated suggestions of the original 1965 Treasury Report but also were based on studies that Treasury officials had worked on since at least early spring of 1967. In fact it seems that a large number of economists and attorneys had been deeply involved in preparation of Treasury's proposals considerably before they were sent to Congress.[4] Thus any haste evidenced in the process was presumably related to the required submission of the proposals at the end of the Johnson administration[5] and the realization that, with the arrival of a new President, the proposals would be "orphans" at risk.[6]

The Tax Reform Studies and Proposals of the Treasury Department were introduced with a statement by Henry H. Fowler, Secretary of Treasury, dated December 11, 1968, but were transmitted by his successor, Secretary Joseph W. Barr, to the incoming Secretary-Designate (for the Nixon administration), David M. Kennedy, on January 17, 1969.[7] The accompanying letter from Barr suggests that these were not presented as proposals of President Johnson, but were "Studies and Proposals" which had been reviewed earlier by Secretary Fowler "prior to his leaving office." The significance of this strategy may be apparent in the next steps of the proposal's trajectory. In a cosigned letter to David Kennedy, Wilbur Mills and Russell Long requested that Kennedy forward the Studies and Proposals to each of their committees, and in his follow-up transmittal letter on January 29, Secretary of Treasury Kennedy refers to "our understanding," apparently regarding their routing. He mentions the fact that the studies and proposals originated during the Johnson admimistration but also indicates that he is now transmitting the proposals to the House Committee on Ways and Means.[8] Consequently these proposals satisfied the mandate for a tax reform initiative by the end of 1968; but they came to Congress via the Treasury Secretary in the Nixon administration; in any case, they were not endorsed by President Johnson.

Whatever the somewhat strange pathway of the tax reform proposals, Treasury's initial intentions seem clear. As stated in Fowler's introductory Statement to the document:

> We present to the Congress proposals for comprehensive reforms of the Internal Revenue Code of 1954. This program contains proposals for tax reform developed by the Treasury Department over more than 2 years and meets the request of the Congress in Section 110 of the Revenue and Control Act of 1968. . . .
>
> The proposals recommended have been framed to provide a fair and orderly transition in those cases where individuals and businesses have made their arrangements based on existing law. We do not intend to have the harsh impact of abrupt changes. On the other hand, we do not want to be frozen into the status quo where it causes special inequities or preferences.
>
> Tax Reform here is used to mean structural tax reform—revision of those provisions of our law which shape the tax structure through defining the taxable base, rates of tax, and the administrative requirements of reporting and payment.[9]

Included among the two dozen major ways Treasury proposed for addressing inequities in the tax code were several that were likely to have an impact on the charitable deductions, primarily for the rich: capital gains would be taxed on property before it passed to any heirs, making *inter vivos* gifts more desirable; and a unified estate and gift tax provision would lower estate taxes, while eliminating some tax avoidance routes; there was a disallowance of contributions that totaled less than 3 percent of a taxpayer's adjusted gross income;[10] and there were also procedures to insure that no one could avoid paying a minimum income tax.[11] At the lower end of the income scale, there was an increase in the non-itemized deduction for those defined as poor under federal guidelines, which would almost entirely eliminate them from the tax rolls; and at the high end, the elimination of the unlimited charitable deduction some of the rich enjoyed was meant to insure that everyone would pay some taxes.

In line with Surrey's views, the suggested Treasury program was directed at eliminating many of the tax preferences which favored the rich, while at the same time including a lower basic (structured) tax rate for middle and upper income individuals. Overall the tax code was expected to move toward being "fair and equitable" and also would provide additional relief for the poor.[12] Although recommendations concerning basic tax rates or permissible deductions were likely to affect 501(c)(3) organizations generally, and not just private foundations, Treasury included provisions aimed specifically at the latter group. In line with the 1965 Treasury Report these included tighter restrictions regarding self-dealing by foundations and related individuals, control of businesses by foundations, income distribution requirements, and recommendations relating to diversifying board management, as well as insuring greater accountability and more available information.

HR 13270 and New Proposals

As we have seen, while few foundation officials were happy with most of the proposed reforms, many of the more established foundations, such as Ford, Rockefeller, and Carnegie, recognized some need to address real abuses in the foundation world. Although the provisions suggested by Treasury concerned abuses by what were considered a small group of foundations, most of the larger, more prestigious foundations were reluctant to openly oppose them. This applied even to some measures they were not enthusiastic about, such as those affecting foundation control of company stock.[13] However, after the House hearings in February, the proposed tax reform changed in tone. The next set of Treasury recommendations, presented under the auspices of the Nixon administration on April 22, 1969, for the first time included a total limitation on foundation programs concerning political activity, even if "educational."[14] In addition, although Stanley Surrey was no longer in Treasury, there was an indication of continued pressure from the administration, not only for increased equity in the tax code, but specifically for raising revenues through the elimination of tax preferences benefitting the rich—including depletion allowances, charitable deductions, and favorable treatment of capital gains and appreciation. Thus Nixon's message to Congress on tax reform had stated, "Reform of our Federal income tax system is long overdue. Special preferences in the law permit far too many Americans to pay less than their fair share of taxes. Too many other Americans bear too much of the tax burden."[15]

When HR 13270 emerged from the House in August, it still contained elements from the original Treasury proposals at the end of the Johnson administration. But it was new, more onerous, provisions regarding foundations that drew the attention of foundation watchers and the philanthropic community. Foundation leaders now recognized that they were facing a new degree of crisis, both from restrictions in Title I which concerned foundations, and from other provisions of the Act which eliminated tax "loopholes" that had benefitted foundations and charities in the past.[16]

Among the provisions in HR 13270 that were particularly disturbing to the foundations were the proposed 7.5 percent tax on their investment income, stricter delineation of permissible activities in relation to lobbying and political activities, and penalties for foundation officers who knowingly allowed their foundations to engage in any prohibited activities under the new law.

These provisions not only had practical ramifications for the foundations but they touched on core aspects of foundation ideology. To begin with, a tax was for the first time to be imposed generally on organizations whose very essence had been defined over the years as enjoying a tax-exempt privilege; not unnaturally this seemed like an opening effort to end the whole notion of tax exemption. Secondly, increased prohibitions on lobbying and legislative activity attacked the essential construct of the charitable world as a free space for dialogue and advocacy. This was serious because although 501(c)(3) organizations had been limited since the 1930s with regard to dedicating "substantial" amounts of resources to such activities, they were able to support these activities without excessive restrictions. Now there was to be an absolute prohibition on lobbying activity by foundations themselves, and defined limits on support they could provide to grantees for such previously accepted political activities as voter registration, as well as for individual grants.[17] And finally, enforcing penalties on individuals connected with foundations, rather than on the entity as a whole, would remove vital protections for individuals in taking creative and courageous positions. Consequently foundations would be in a weaker position than other classes of organizations, including other philanthropic organizations as well as corporations whose board members enjoyed a degree of personal immunity from liability for organization actions.

In addition, Title I of HR 13270 concretized the concept in the 1965 Treasury Report that there was a major distinction between public charities under the 501(c)(3) section of the Internal Revenue Code and the group designated as private foundations. This group of private foundations was now to be even more definitively distinguished from the other 501(c)(3) "public charities" for whom donors were able to receive a 30 percent tax deduction.[18] And it was this group—distinct from public charities or even the group now defined as operating foundations—that was the target of Congressional anger, and was subject to what the foundation world considered particularly oppressive changes.[19] In effect, separate provisions against private foundations reflected public and Congressional sentiment against foundations that abused their power politically, concomitantly with a preference for the role of direct-spending charities that visibly provide services (i.e., museums, libraries, universities). It seems also to have reflected the response of Congress to the widespread unrest of the late 1960s and the distrust of all institutions, including those of the rich who used them to escape taxes.

In this regard, there were other—clearly revenue producing—aspects of the bill that were likely to have severe negative effects on donations to major "public charities" as well as foundations. One of the most significant was the proposed tax on appreciated values of donated property, including tangible personal property such as works of art or books as well as stocks and bonds; and also eliminating deductions on gifts of original works of art by an artist or copyrights held by original authors which would produce ordinary income if sold.[20] In effect, this would have included Johnson's donated papers. This provision was to apply to all 501(c)(3) organizations. Thus the so-called "public charities," like most museums and universities, or service-providing organizations,[21] were in jeopardy along with the private foundations—even though their situations were not identical. All charities, and certainly foundations, would suffer from taxing capital gains on gifts of stocks and bonds (whose dollar value had in fact increased greatly overall in the preceding decade);[22] while museums were among the groups most likely to suffer particularly from taxes on donations of tangible personal property, specifically on great works of art, such as paintings and sculptures with increased values.[23] This must have suggested to the rest of the 501(c)(3) group of exempt organizations that their fate was in fact linked to the foundation world even though their needs were not entirely coterminous. Indeed this argument was made by Peterson in the Senate hearings, when he pointed out that foundations had to make greater payouts in order to meet the vast needs of institutions like hospitals and universities.[24] Peterson also argued against proposed "restrictions on appreciated property to foundations" (that is, the taxation of capital gains on donated property) because it would affect the incentive for contributions by large donors to foundations.[25]

While the House was preparing HR 13270 a parallel event occurred in the Senate that reflected the general tone of this period, and must have caused discomfort to the more elitist foundations, members of the Peterson Commission, the Rockefeller family, and some 501(c)(3) "public" charities. In June hearings were held on S. 2075, a bill to "deny tax-exempt status to private foundations and organizations engaging in improper transactions with certain Government officials and former Government officials and to impose a tax of 100 percent on income received by such officials and former officials from such foundations and organizations."[26] Although the most obvious target for the bill was the kind of grants Ford had given to members of the Kennedy administration after Bobby Kennedy's death, the requirement of two years' distance from government for involvement could also have been problematic for many of the most prestigious foundations, including Ford and Rockefeller, as well as for some museums or universities. Conceivably it might have affected former Treasury officials with tax-exempt organizations among their clients. The bill had scare value, but was clearly contrary to accepted practice. In the end, somewhat less draconian limitations on payments to government officials were incorporated in the final Tax Reform Act.

From House to Senate: Peterson Emerges

During the spring and summer of 1969, while HR 13270 was progressing from the House to the Senate, the Peterson Commission met monthly. It heard from experts, and debated vigorously—with the participation of high-powered staff—on the major policy issues that had emerged in connection with the House bill. Despite the initial outlines of the original workplan, commission staff were now also busy developing studies that were to be a source of data for the commission's report and recommendations.

The original expectation expressed in the workplan had not proved to be realistic. The workplan had stated: "The Commission does not expect to engage in any extensive fact-finding activities. Very extensive data about foundations and their activities are available from both public and private sources."[27] With regard to these words, Peterson was later to say in his statement to the Senate Finance Committee, "No commission ever started its inquiries upon a more erroneous assumption."[28] In addition to studies that were contracted out to consultants and research groups, staff was now also reviewing a number of 990 forms which foundations prepared for the IRS and which were made available for commission analysis. This point was made, although perhaps somewhat exaggeratedly, by Senator Percy in his testimony before the Senate Finance Committee:

> I do not know of anyone who has ever gone in and analyzed all the 990 forms for the year 1968 except the Peterson Commission. They have pulled every single 990 form that has been filed. They have now a team of professional interviewers going out to their offices. . . . But until such time as we have this body of facts put together, I do not see how we can

possibly legislate and start to destroy these foundations, before we know what they are doing.[29]

If Percy knew about the work of the commission, the commission was also informed about events on Capitol Hill. It seems highly unlikely that it was pure coincidence that in September, less than a week before Wright Patman formally introduced his bill to establish a "Private Foundation Control Commission" to regulate private foundations,[30] the commission meeting dedicated considerable attention to the issue of the IRS, government regulation, and alternative mechanisms for oversight and supervision of foundations. However, interestingly, this appears to be one of the critical areas in which there was divided opinion on the commission, with the discussion being inconclusive on all the major aspects of the issue: what would be the scope of an alternative group (i.e., regulatory, standard setting, voluntary, or mandatory); the auspices of the group (private, semi-public, or governmental); who the members would be and how they would be chosen (e.g., by government, from government or private groups); and the ratio of private-public representatives overall.[31] Again, ideological views of the proper role for state and voluntary action inevitably affected decision making on concrete proposals.

In the meantime hearings on HR 13270 in the Senate Finance Committee finally began early in September. Treasury also sent their Technical Memorandum on the bill to the Senate in this period, including among other things a modification of the complex formula for assuring that a minimum tax be paid by all, through a combination of Limitations on Tax Preferences (LTPs) and controlled Allocations on Deductions (AOD).[32] In its essence, overall the Treasury Department Memorandum of September 30 offered some gentler alternatives to the harshest measures of the House bill, but still penalized foundations in comparison with public charities. Among the suggested changes that would most affect charities and the Rockefeller family were the following: (1) some clarification on the definition of political activities; (2) the suggested 7.5 percent tax on foundation income was too high and should be changed to a 2 percent supervisory tax—it should also be counted as part of the 5 percent mandatory payout by foundations; (3) liberalization of charitable deduction provisions concerning estates and charitable trusts; and (4) somewhat more liberal provisions regarding gifts of appreciated property as well as in applying the maximum 50 percent of allowable deductions. The report also noted that IRS clarification of the 501(c)(3) status of hospitals was expected soon.

In any case, after a short delay the Finance Committee resumed hearings on October 6, 7, and 8, including the testimony from the Coordinated Foundation Testimony Group, and concluding on October 22 with Peterson's testimony. However, in the process some additional alarms were sounded. For one thing, as the bill was being drafted, Senator Albert Gore (Tennessee) argued forcibly for a 40-year limit on the life of all foundations, and this provision was included in the final mock-up of the Senate bill. Gore, with his populist views and New Deal vision of government responsibility, wanted more tax relief for the poor and considered foundations an "abomination"; he argued that this provision would prevent a massive accumulation of wealth, and in essence force foundations to spend their money in a timely fashion on the charities for whom they were actually created. Gore expressed his position bluntly in the Senate Finance Committee Hearings:

> We are subsidizing bogus, phoney charities. . . . [O]nce an organization has achieved tax-exempt status there is no Federal Agency adequately equipped for regulation, supervision, record keeping or knowledge of what happens. Under our present law, the organization enjoys that status forever.[33]

Gore's proposal was not entirely new, since the idea of a limit on the life of foundations had been suggested before, but coming at this time it received considerable attention, and its proposed inclusion in the Senate version of HR 13270 sent an alarming signal to foundation watchers.[34]

By the time Peterson made his presentation to the Finance Committee, it was evident that the foundations' attackers were more numerous and more vocal than their defenders. In fact it appeared that most Congressional constituents were probably more concerned about other features of the Tax Reform Bill than with the plight of foundations.[35] Meanwhile Patman was still trying to keep a fire lit under the need for regulating foundations, and had also testified before the Senate Finance Committee, chaired by Russell Long. Long's position on foundations was not entirely clear; although a Democrat, he was certainly a conservative. He might have been willing to protect tax support of foundations, but he argued for the 40-year limit on the floor of the Senate. For many liberal Senate Democrats, other social welfare and business-related provisions of the bill might could have had more salience than those relating to foundations. However, the protection of major educational and cultural institutions was a different matter.[36] In any case, with a few exceptions such as Charles Percy and Jacob Javits, Republicans would be unlikely to enter the fray in support of a group that they considered politically suspect. In general, with regard to the role of foundations, the terms *liberal* and *conservative* seemed to mean very little.

This was the context in which Peterson came to testify before the Senate Finance Committee. He had previously met with Treasury officials privately, but this was a new public role. Still, he seemed ready for it, thanks to both his personal style and good staff preparation.[37] In his testimony Peterson presented new material derived from the preliminary findings of studies being carried out under the auspices of his commission:[38] a variety of charts and figures concerning assets of foundations and the nature of their allocations; attitudes of rich donors toward giving and, in particular, the negative impact that the House bill (if enacted) would have on their giving; and an analysis of abuses uncovered with the assistance of CPAs who had access to the tax reports of charitable organizations.[39] Two of Peterson's statistics were later frequently cited: only 12 percent of foundations surveyed reported giving innovative, experimental, or "out of the ordinary" grants in the previous three years; and less than 1 percent of respondents replied yes to the question, "Have any of the projects supported by your foundation's grants or gifts in the past three years been considered controversial or particularly unpopular?"[40] However, what Peterson did not emphasize was revealed in further analysis of the data in the report: if the figures were disaggregated to consider responses by size of foundation, it became evident that for the group of larger foundations, the percent supporting controversial grants actually increased to 38 percent.[41]

In general Peterson seemed to be treated with respect by the Finance Committee, and particularly by Republican members. (He himself was a staunch Republican.) He was given a full day to present his testimony. Chairman Long made it evident that he was hoping for confidential testimony from Peterson. However, this suggestion was rejected openly by one Committee member, John J. Williams (Delaware), who although a Republican was reportedly an ally of Senator Gore on foundation matters. Gore was apparently not receptive to the presentation. In any case, in the late afternoon, before only a few members of the Committee (Gore was absent), Peterson concluded his presentation. In the end two of the Republican senators on the Committee, Paul J. Fannin (Arizona) and Jack Miller (Iowa), thanked Peterson effusively, with Fannin stating: "Mr. Peterson, I want to commend you for your performance. When we talk about the performance factor, we would certainly give you a high grade in your performance here today and for the work that you and your Commission has been doing preparing this information."[42]

Nonetheless Peterson's testimony was not unproblematic. To begin with, he had apparently annoyed some of the Committee, including Gore and possibly even the Chairman, with his businesslike presentation style.[43] He had come, in good corporate tradition, well armed with slides and charts prepared by the staff, illustrating early findings from the commission studies. In the official record Gore's rather sarcastic teasing ("I am having difficulty seeing the label on this projector. Is that a Kodak or Bell and Howell?") and his impatience with

Peterson's long justification of the commission's credentials was evident.[44] In addition, even though he seemed to have been well prepared by staff, Peterson was hardly hesitant in reminding the Committee that he was neither a tax expert nor a philanthropy expert; indeed during his testimony he gave incorrect information about the United Givers Fund.[45]

Overall, Peterson's presentation and preliminary recommendations were interspersed with disclaimers about his lack of expertise on some critical issues related to the bill. Peterson also repeatedly stressed the lack of data on foundations generally. He highlighted the specific need for more information on the incentives for charitable contribution, beyond those of tax deductions for the rich, as well as objective knowledge about the contributions of foundation activities. Such an appraisal he considered one of the "world's most difficult tasks."[46] Based on the commission's survey of 85 wealthy donors, however, Peterson emphasized that the bill as now written would be likely to result in drastically reduced charitable contributions by the rich as well as a decrease in the formation of new foundations.[47] Among reforms supported by the commission, Peterson mentioned elimination of self dealing and related financial abuses by some foundations; foundation spending of money for purposes that were not charitable (such as corporate charity that was really a business expense); and most significantly the need for a higher payout rate to charities, based on a better return on investments. He argued strongly against provisions in the House bill which would result in taxing capital gains on appreciated property going to charity, and also against the limitations on foundation control of business stocks.

In his testimony Peterson presented facts suggesting the inadequacy of both state oversight of foundations (only 8 percent of foundations audited by the states in the past three years), and IRS oversight (only 34 percent of returns audited in the past three years).[48] Despite the fact that there had been mixed opinions about this in commission discussion, and indeed in the Rockefeller camp, Peterson emphatically denied the value of self-regulation, and proposed that a special fund be set aside to insure that over the next years the auditing of the foundations by the IRS would be 100 percent (i.e., all foundations would be audited by the end of that period). His final recommendation was for the creation of a "quasi-governmental" Philanthropic Advisory Board, with members perhaps appointed by the President and approved by the Senate. This recommendation was more finely delineated here than the divided opinion of commission members would have justified at that time. In fact, both of these last points differed from a draft of staff recommendations, in which the idea of the board was presented with unresolved options and the IRS was rejected as the appropriate oversight agency for tax-exempt organizations.[49] It should be noted also that although much fuss was made over the recommendation for a 6–8 percent payout figure which Peterson presented in the discussion with the Finance Committee, Peterson was careful to say that no specific payout rate figure should actually be included in the Act, but that within some established guidelines, considerable flexibility of interpretation should be given to Treasury.[50]

Although the commission's recommendations already appeared to be well articulated in Peterson's statement, most had not yet been fully accepted by the commissioners. Peterson was presenting his opinion considerably ahead of the commission members' approval of the final report. He had handled this by seeking some preliminary general consensus on key issues among the members present at the early October meeting and through consideration of various issues during the summer. In his presentation, however, Peterson undoubtedly gave his own cast in framing the recommendations.

The commission's final report was drafted by both staff and consultants; it was written under the direction of Wineberg, but with considerable material from the various consultants. Nonetheless, as the Preface suggests, the report bore the heavy imprint of Peterson. There were a few dissenting notes, including one strong comment from Lane Kirkland, but generally the report was presented as a consensus document. Overall the report was not an encomium to foundations, although it recognized their importance to American society. Peterson's views on this matter are indicated in a memorandum from Peterson to Wineberg (December 1970) in which he states his dissatisfaction with a nearly final draft of the report as being "too favorable to the foundations."[51] We will consider the commission's final recommendations in the next chapter.

The Senate and the Final Bill

After years of placating powerful interests in business and philanthropy, the Congress was finally taking serious steps toward tax reform. As a whole the Tax Reform Act really did attempt to make structural reforms in the tax code. There was an effort to come to grips with two opposing features of American tax law: a structural determination of the basic aspects of taxable income including the general tax rate; and targeted incentives (preferences) to achieve specified social and political objectives. These two principles while separate are obviously also interactive, and together they determine the overall equity of the tax code. In this connection, personal correspondence between JDR 3rd and Wilbur Mills indicates that Rockefeller was unhappy with the extent of the reforms that Mills and his Committee proposed in the spring of 1969.[52]

In the end HR 13270, like all tax-related bills, when it emerged from the

House, represented compromises between competing interests. Although the House proposals came down slightly on the side of tax equity and a more progressive tax code, a lowered maximum basic tax rate (70% to 65%) would also benefit higher income individuals. However, President Nixon had already announced the need for producing higher revenues in the tax bill. Therefore, while the bill promised tax relief for low and moderate income individuals as well as those in high income brackets, it also included revenue-producing proposals, such as reduction in the amount of accelerated depreciation on real estate, minor adjustments in previously untaxed capital gains, the repeal of investment credit, and also taxation of state and local bonds, as well as six months' extension of a (now) 5% surcharge on income.[53] Furthermore, the House bill required minimum tax payments by everyone; this was done by reductions in tax preferences and allowable allocations in the deductions for high income individuals. In addition, earlier Treasury proposals that might have democratized charitable giving were not included in the final bill, such as permitting a separate charitable deduction to non-itemizers (generally lower income individuals) who took the standard deduction. Moreover, the standard deduction would be increased over three years; a change that was beneficial to people with lower incomes, but not necessarily helpful to charitable organizations.

When HR 13270 came to the Senate, however, surprising things happened. That venerable group operated under different rules than the House, where Wilbur Mills essentially assured the passage of bills originating in his Committee. As we have already shown, the call for hearings by the Senate Finance Committee included the proviso that testimony be consolidated. This was supposedly to avoid the extensive, and seemingly endless, barrage of testimony and formal statements by interest groups typical of hearings in the House Ways and Means Committee.[54]

Nevertheless, as Senator Long himself described it, in the Executive Sessions of the Senate Finance Committee discussing the bill, a total of 457 motions were made on specific proposals. Most of these were in response to particular interests wanting changes that would accommodate their special concerns. It was during the mockup of the bill by the Senate Finance Committee that Senator Gore, who also proposed increases for social security and tax relief for the poor, suggested the ultimate measure that would insure adequate payout of foundation income and assets. This was the proposal to mandate a maximum life of 40 years to foundations, after which the foundation would have to go out of business.[55] This amendment was, however, knocked out of the bill during its debates on the floor of the Senate.[56]

In the Senate Finance Committee stricter regulation and controls supposedly applied in procedural matters, but they did not apply on the floor of the

Senate itself.[57] In fact, the Senate as a body operated under rules which allowed for a more open procedure than the House, permitting more debate and amendments to be presented from the floor. The impact of this open debate on the floor was evident in the variety and numbers of amendments to HR 13270 that were proposed there and even ultimately accepted.

One of the interesting proposals from the Senate floor was made by Senator Jacob Javits. His amendment called for the establishment of a public body, separate from the IRS, in the form of a commission with oversight power over foundations. The debate around the discussion suggested that Javits was interested in postponing final resolution of the proposed legislation (or at least of certain aspects of it); but in the end he was apparently willing to trade off consideration of specific aspects relating to foundations in his effort to create a public body focused on foundations.[58] Considering that Javits was a Republican Senator from New York, it might not be unreasonable to assume that there was some Rockefeller consideration in his actions. (Indeed when JDR 3rd gave his testimony before the Committee, and Javits came to "visit," Long specifically recognized a connection between them.)[59] However, as Javits feared, his amendment did not survive final decision making in the Conference Committee.

The 40-year life for foundations proposed by Senator Gore was obviously a serious threat to foundation officials, although even Gore must have realized that his amendment was a long shot.[60] Nonetheless, in the climate of the times, it was not impossible that it would pass. In this regard Peterson's proposals for a mandated high payout rate related to income and asset return offered a distracting alternative. Peterson was adamant that a high payout rate, based on an appropriate investment performance by foundations, should be possible. Even if the rate varied over the years, it was important that foundations would not only have to secure a suitable return on their money, but that they actually would have to pay out these monies for charitable use each year. Peterson's suggestion would avoid excessive accumulation of wealth by foundations and therefore also could serve to "avert the severe decree" proposed by Senator Gore.

This payout proposal, which received some press attention at the time, has been highlighted in discussions of the Peterson Commission since then.[61] What has often been less understood was that the high payout rate was presented in terms of an objective, and determination of the required payout rate for any given year was to be a discretionary power of the Treasury Department. There was some question whether Congress would cede such a broad power, and the final Tax Reform Act included both a formula and a range of numbers.[62] Moreover, along with Treasury's original intent to make drastic reforms happen incrementally, the minimum investment payout rate (established at 6 percent) was to be phased in for private foundations *formed before May 27, 1969* (many of whose major assets were the stock of one company, like Kellogg) and would "not apply to such organization(s) until taxable years beginning after 1971." Even then, the 6 percent minimum payout was not to be fully effective. The payout would be phased in beginning with a 4½ percent rate in 1972, increasing to 5 percent in 1973, 5½ percent in 1974, and only reaching 6 percent in 1975.[63]

The Final Act and the Final Report

In presenting the Senate Finance Committee version of HR 13270 to the whole Senate, Senator Long noted that "this bill emphasizes equity" and invoked Joe Barr's words about millionaires escaping taxation.[64] He urged "the distinguished members of the Senate to view the bill as a whole," presumably in an effort to avoid the kind of ideological argument or constituency-driven add-ons that might bog down its passage. And in fact, as he also pointed out (surprisingly), the Finance Committee had heard 300 witnesses in 23 days, with the result that the bill had become even more complicated. What had emerged from the House as 368 pages of bewildering complexity was now 585 pages that were certainly not simpler. During the final discussion on the Senate floor some critical changes were also made, but the debate did not keep the bill from moving quickly to the Conference Committee.

On December 30, 1969 President Richard Milhous Nixon signed the Tax Reform Act of 1969. Nixon had threatened to veto the Senate version of HR 13270 because he had feared the inflationary effect of the Senate bill, which would have diluted some revenue producing provisions. But he was apparently relieved by the Conference version of HR 13270 which by now included considerable input from administration-selected Treasury officials (such as Assistant Secretary for Tax Policy Edwin S. Cohen) working with Congressional representatives.

Ultimately the final bill that emerged from Conference and was signed into law presented some compromises between the House and the Senate versions.[65] Approximately one-fourth of the total Act reportedly contained provisions that materially affected private foundations and other tax-exempt organizations.[66] Altogether a large number (111 in all) of the Senate versions of provisions in the bill were used as alternatives to the House versions. Nonetheless, overall the bill reflected much of the original intent of Wilbur Mills and Treasury officials under Johnson, particularly in regard to controlling foundation abuses. Some tradeoffs had been made by the Conference Committee, which was chaired at this time by Mills himself.[67] In the final Act some of the more controversial provisions concerning tax preferences, such as taxes on state and municipal bonds, or taxing the appreciated value on donated personal property to all charitable (501 [c] [3]) organizations, had been eliminated or modified.[68] There were also relaxed timetables for such changes as eliminating the unlimited charitable deduction or requiring the higher payout rate by foundations. However, many of the tougher new regulations affecting foundations and their donors remained, and a 4 percent excise tax (separate from the high payout requirement) was passed as an audit "fee" (a tax by another name) to insure that the IRS was able to carry out future audits of private foundations.

Moreover, despite all the debate, discussion, and negotiations (or perhaps because of them), in the end there remained considerable ambiguity surrounding many of the key provisions affecting foundations. There were certainly definitional questions about the distinctions between public charities, private foundations, and operating foundations, as well as issues to resolve about permissible lobbying and political activities. Overall, in fact, the Tax Reform Act was now recognizably so complicated that, as one author put it, "it is sometimes called the 'Lawyers and Accountants' Relief Act' and it still needs clarification in Treasury rulings and court decisions."[69] The final assessment was therefore yet to come. And concomitantly so were the conclusions of the Peterson Commission Report, which was not yet published when the Tax Reform Act was signed into law. Peterson had written JDR that he thought it wiser to wait until after the passage of the Act to issue his report, and, with Rockefeller's concurrence, the final bound volume was not issued until December 1970.

7

The Peterson Commission

A Summation

To sum up: Foundations have encountered criticism from virtually the entire
political spectrum. They have been an easy and convenient target for
politicians who, in order to prove their zeal as guardians of the Republic,
need a "threat" or a "conspiracy" to "expose."

There is an ironic element in all of this which cannot be overstated. It is that
despite the fears voiced about the imperial foundations . . . the foundations
are ill prepared to defend themselves under attack. Unlike operating
charities, they have no ready-made constituencies—no alumni . . .
no parishioners . . . no out-patients. . . .

Their constituency is in a sense an abstraction called "the public interest."
—The Peterson Report, 1970

By the time that the Peterson Commission Report was actually published, the Tax Reform Act had already been the law of the land for over six months.[1] Congress and the public were moving on to other matters. Certainly the final report made no front page headlines, and the Peterson Commission itself seemed to end more with a whimper than a bang.[2] Thus there remained the big question of whether the commission's efforts had made a difference, with evidently mixed opinions on this subject.[3] However, given the complexities of the issues the commission addressed, the question really needs to be reframed and parsed into smaller parts: that is, to whom (if anyone) did the commission make a difference? And in what manner? Answers to these questions begin with a brief recapitulation of the commission's purpose and constituencies.

Commission Purpose and Origins

The Peterson Commission's connection to John Rockefeller gave it a good heritage, and associated it—even if loosely—with his special attention. It had developed after all out of discussions by JDR 3rd's "Informal Advisory Group on Philanthropy"; this somewhat changing group contained a core of "inside" Rockefeller advisors with a mix of commitments that seemed about equally composed of personal concern for the role of JDR 3rd, Rockefeller family philanthropy, and other family interests more inclusively. Overtly, of course, the Rockefeller advisors shared major concerns of the "outside" group members about general issues of philanthropy, and particularly the status of foundations.[4] In any case the legal and fiscal implications of tax policies being discussed in Washington during these years (1965–1968) was a common underlying theme for the group, along with worries about Congressional hostility toward foundations, epitomized by the almost continuous attacks by Congressman Wright Patman, from 1961 on. Nonetheless, although the advisory group discussed the formation of a commission for over a year, it remained ambivalent about the essence of its task or the precise structure to be used.

Thus although Rockefeller advisors were watching the Washington scene closely, and JDR himself was lobbying on matters relating to philanthropy and population control, there was no agreement about group action.[5] However, in February 1969 what had been a darkening cloud became a storm that moved from an investigatory committee (the Subcommittee on Foundations and Tax-Exempt Organizations of the House Committee on Banking and Currency) to the powerful House Ways and Means Committee, which had legislative power over revenue and tax matters. Treasury's recommendations for tax reform were passing to the House Ways and Means Committee and hearings on them were scheduled for mid-February; serious tax reform became a real possibility.[6] At this point JDR talked with Peter Peterson about chairmanship of the new commission.

Whatever mixed motives were originally involved, there can be little doubt that as constituted in the spring of 1969 the commission's primary purpose was to head off disastrous legislation by Congress. Despite Peterson's and JDR 3rd's rhetoric about perceiving the commission's task more broadly in terms of the value of philanthropy in American society, practicality—indeed necessity—determined that the commission's activities would be essentially defensive and centered around protection of big donors as well as large foundations. This became even more so when the initial Treasury focus (from the 1965 Treasury Report) on controlling foundation abuses was joined by what could be defined as a broader Patman/Surrey position.[7] Legislative discussion thereafter moved rapidly beyond correcting particular abuses, to more general concern about the use of foundations as both (inequitable) tax shelters for the rich and the means by which "dangerous" concentrations of wealth could be amassed and perpetuated.[8] Consequently, despite the gloss put upon it by Rockefeller and

Peterson, the commission's initial task undeniably involved trying to avert the severe decree for a small group of wealthy philanthropists and major foundations. This was so although the initial language of a draft document expressed the purpose of the commission more diplomatically:

> The purpose of the National Commission on Philanthropic Foundations [*sic*] is to make an objective appraisal of the role and operation of foundations in American society. . . .
>
> It is anticipated that the primary function of the Commission will be to formulate judgments on the principal policy questions which are raised by the role of foundations in our society, by their structure and operation, and by the system of government incentives and government supervision of foundations.[9]

There were some difficulties related to the stated commitment of "an objective appraisal . . . of foundations." As noted in chapter 5, in order to avoid the charge of being a tool of the foundation world, and to insure the appearance—and perhaps ultimately the reality—of independence from foundation influences, Peterson deliberately chose not to have members of the foundation group serve on his commission and also not to seek financial support from them. In addition the decision was made not to seek status as a 501 (c)(3) (charitable) organization in order to avoid any possibility of questions about lobbying activities by the commission. Its proclaimed independence, however, had some costs as well as benefits. For example, it was able to avoid dealing directly with competing needs of certain possible constituencies (such as the Council on Foundations or the larger establishment foundations), but in the end could be criticized for not responding to their issues more definitively. In addition, as we have already suggested above, the commission itself was vulnerable to influence from other interest groups including the universities in particular—with whom some commission members had close ties.[10]

The commission appeared to have trouble raising adequate funds and was said to be short of money even as the report went to press.[11] Indeed, it was claimed that no widespread constituency emerged to underwrite its efforts on behalf of the foundations, and Peterson himself pointed out how badly the commission missed foundation support.[12] As was later suggested, difficulty in raising funds was undoubtedly also connected to the lack of tax deductibility for contributions to the commission.[13] This difficulty would in fact have provided further evidence for Peterson's own arguments about the impact of tax incentives on philanthropic contributions.[14] However, despite protests to the contrary, later evidence indicates that the commission actually ended with a small surplus of funds.[15]

The Commission Report

Product and Process

By the fall of 1969, after HR 13270 moved to the Senate, it became apparent that tax legislation would be passed before the end of the year. Certainly Congress and the Treasury wanted tax reform and President Nixon wanted revenues that such legislation might produce.[16] In this period Peterson was evidently talking with administration officials, as well as with some Congressional leaders, and he had the opportunity to observe personally the pressure to move the bill forward; participants in discussions of the commission also suggested an urgency about the debates in the Senate Finance Committee. However, although he mobilized an "interim report"—complete with graphic findings—for presentation to the Finance Committee in October 1969, as noted above, Peterson decided, with the concurrence of the Rockefeller office, not to publish the final report until after passage of the Tax Reform Act. The justification given was that this would prevent premature issuing of the report before the bugs were all worked out; it would also permit the final report to respond to issues which were raised by provisions of the Act. Meanwhile reference to the pending report was used by Senator Percy in efforts to defer action in the Senate. However, in the end it was not possible to muster sufficient support for preventing passage of the bill by the Senate.[17]

Peterson's testimony in effect became an interim report, but it was apparently not widely circulated.[18] The final report, published in late 1970 by the University of Chicago, was to be distributed to an impressive list of decision makers that included the President and the Congress.[19] The title, *Foundations, Private Giving, and Public Policy (Report and Recommendations of the Commission on Foundations and Private Philanthropy)*, reflected its overall content, and in using the terms public and private hinted at the ambiguities involved in discussion of the public/private nature of foundations and philanthropic giving.

The book contained 278 pages of text and appendixes. The main corpus is divided into three sections: Part One: Private Philanthropy; Part Two: Foundations; and Part Three: Recommendations.[20] In addition, appendixes contained descriptions of the surveys carried out, and tables of their findings, as well as two essays about philanthropy—"Philanthropy and the Economy" by Mary Hamilton and "Enlightened Self-Interest and Corporate Philanthropy" by William J. Baumol. Hamilton presented evidence about a downward trend in giving as a percentage of income in most income groups, and reported an apparent increased importance in contributions from large donors—which could be considered arguments in support of protecting tax incentives for those donors.[21] However, while both essays contain some interesting data, they seem like afterthoughts utilized as "quickie" fill-ins for identified gaps in the commission argument. In this regard, moreover, it should be noted that commission efforts to have a number of papers written by experts (inside and outside of the commission) had been embarrassingly unsuccessful; experts met readily with the commission, but many individuals declined to present written materials, probably largely because of the commission's short time schedule, as well as a lack of available funding.[22] There may also have been an "intellectual" bias against using papers from the foundation world. According to Emerson Andrews, a paper he prepared at the request of the Peterson Commission was not acknowledged; he suggested that this experience was shared by other persons solicited by "this hurried and harried commission."[23]

Various memoranda and drafts of the Peterson Report in the commission archives indicate that there were many modifications in the tone and style of sections of the report, but that from October 1969 to the time the book actually went to press in August 1970 (with a few minor additions still needed) there was relatively little substantive change in its main argument. The basic thrust of the recommendations was also maintained although some adjustments were made to insure that the recommendations reflected passage of the Tax Reform Act. Arguments in agreement or disagreement with key provisions of the act were included and there was some clarification of positions such as that concerning the role of the IRS.[24] The final report was written after staff drafts were reviewed by commission members, consultants, and outside experts, but with few exceptions (Edward Levi, and two dissenters: Lane Kirkland and J. Paul Austin) commission members did not get deeply involved in writing or reviewing sections of the report.[25] Peterson, however, while asking the staff to draw up parts of the report, offered a number of critiques or presented staff with material or ideas from others whom he consulted, apparently bypassing the staff at times.[26] In the process he utilized outside sources to carry out the surveys, and also brought in a professional editor to work on style and consistency of format. In the end, some of the "purple prose" that was noted by readers of early drafts was removed.[27]

Recommendations

The commission report promoted the value of philanthropy for our country, and advocated specifically for the important role of foundations in supporting vital social welfare activities as well as cultural and educational institutions. In doing so, the report relied heavily on self-reported projections of future needs by recipients of philanthropic funds, for which it was criticized. Indeed, in his dissenting note to the report, Lane Kirkland highlighted the self-serving articulation of a "crisis" in philanthropic funding. He also demurred generally in regard to what he considered to be an apologia for foundations, and questioned the report's position about "the democratization" of tax incentives to support them. Perhaps then it is not totally coincidental that quotations of attitudes toward foundations which are drawn from the survey material include a large number of union leaders.[28] On the whole, despite the original commitment to a policy focus for the commission, as much exhortation as tight analysis is incorporated in the narrative of the final report.[29]

Although the report supported philanthropy, it was still rather critical of foundations, with regard particularly to their innovativeness and fiscal effectiveness. It stated sharply:

> While the public record of foundations stresses continuing bold, venture-some leaps into the future, a more complete picture would include a rather pervasive passivity, and a sluggishness that marks not only their financial investments and payout to charity but also the quality of grant making of most American foundations.[30]

However, while the report posited that foundations and government had overlapping functions, it also said: "We believe that foundations can in fact do a number of things better than government agencies."[31] It then presented a list of "Recommendations to Foundations"—before getting to recommendations concerning government and foundations. The report's recommendations to foundations were mixed with descriptions of the special quality of foundations: articulation and implementation of a unique role in experimentation; increased controversial activities and specialized programs; the filling of niches and flexibility in response to emerging needs.[32]

While the report encouraged self-evaluation it also suggested that, in the absence of external constituencies, foundations should involve the public more in evaluation efforts. In addition, the commission urged foundations to improve planning and staff resources, monitor and evaluate their grants better, increase representation of diverse groups on their boards, and in general communicate better with the public.[33] Like Peterson's testimony before the Senate Finance Committee, the final report highlighted the need for better data about foundations, and gave special attention to the need for higher payouts to recipients as well as to the need for a strong organization which would improve performance and broaden understanding of foundations.[34]

The commission report specifically addressed provisions of the new Tax Reform Act which affected foundations and philanthropic giving. In this regard, it highlighted and criticized these major pieces of the legislation: (1) excessive sanctions against foundations that violated key provisions of the act (such as self-dealing or programmatic violations); (2) the 4 percent excise tax imposed on investment income; and (3) codification of legal distinctions between private foundations and other charities which made private foundations into "third class charities"; for example, the greater percentage of charitable deduction allowed other charities, the more favorable handling of appreciation of property, and mandated restrictions on holdings of "control" stock of businesses.[35] The report considered these provisions to be disincentives to giving that would result in a decrease in the creation of new foundations. But they could also have a deleterious affect on activities of some of the large existing foundations as well as those of the Rockefeller family.[36] While recognizing the legitimacy of limitations on certain kinds of political activity by foundations (i.e., support of candidates or grass roots lobbying), the report also urged the IRS to use caution (i.e., "narrowness") in determining regulations and interpretation of provisions relating to provisions of the Act affecting public policy/legislative activity by foundations.[37]

On the whole, the assessment of the Tax Reform Act in the commission report is, not surprisingly, consistent with Peterson's statement before the Senate Finance Committee. Peterson's own views were particularly evident in his emphatic discussion of the payout rate; the commission's recommendation on this matter was similar to but not exactly the same as the payout rate finally incorporated in the Tax Reform Act. However, the report argued that although the difference (between the Act and the report) was largely in the system of calculation, and apparently a small amount, this was "not a trifling matter."[38] In addition, the report continued the argument against a fixed life-term for foundations (even though this had been eliminated from the final version of the bill), which suggests that these two issues were perceived to be interrelated. In any case, the commission report, like the Act itself, included operating expenses in calculating the amount of payout. Thus although emphasis on a high payout was in keeping with Peterson's belief in the need for businesslike returns on foundation investments, it furthered the protection of the charitable deduction, without being as onerous as it might have appeared. It was surely to this effect that Douglas Dillon (former Secretary of Treasury under President Kennedy) was referring when he wrote John Rockefeller that

> the iniquitous allocation of deductions provision [in the original House Bill] would have dealt a death blow to private charity . . . in this country. And under pressure Congress *found an entirely different way to get at sheltered income, a way that will not do any harm to charitable giving.*[39] (Emphasis added)

The report also came out in favor of more open disclosure and more moni-toring of foundation activity.[40] In commission discussions there had been some feeling that the IRS might not be the place for supervising philanthropic activity, but the report suggested that in the short run this should not be changed. Rec-ognizing a difference between short and long range policy concerns, the report specifically recommended that the so-called 4 percent "audit" tax be utilized to help insure that every foundation was actually audited by the IRS in the next three years.[41] The report also called for the formation of a permanent national Advisory Board on Philanthropic Policy.

Among the recommendations that seemed most significant to Peterson, some commission members, and John Rockefeller was the one concerning the Advisory Board on Philanthropic Policy. Accordingly Peterson promoted this idea in discussions with George Shultz and other members of the Nixon ad-ministration.[42] Although this was one of the areas of difference among mem-bers of the commission as well as staff—with regard to the public nature of the proposed Advisory Board and specifically to the inclusion of "public" (i.e., gov-ernment) representatives on it—there was clearly a claque in favor of creating some form of permanent national advisory group.[43] The structure, purpose, and composition of the new Board were loosely delineated in the report, but plainly the Board was intended to take on some functions that might be performed better outside of the IRS.

Although the possibility of a federal charter was mentioned, and despite its policy-related agenda, the Board was to "be as independent of government as possible."[44] The original idea of four public members (two each from the Sen-ate and House) had now been rejected in favor of all private citizens. However, members were "preferably" to be appointed by the President and confirmed by the Senate; it was to have "certain governmental powers," including particu-larly the power to obtain information from private organizations and govern-ment agencies—read subpoena power—which Peterson had greatly missed in carrying out his commission's work.[45] The Advisory Board was clearly meant to provide a venue for obtaining information about philanthropy, evaluating the effectiveness of regulations concerning charitable organizations, and insuring adequate discussion of larger policy issues. It was not to be limited to concern with foundations only but to encompass "all philanthropy"; it would therefore include all 501(c)(3) public charities and "recipient" groups. In many respects the Advisory Board seemed to be modeled after the Charity Commission for England and Wales; but it also fit in with the common American practice in the 1960s of using governmental advisory groups to help with the process of public policy formulation.[46]

What Benefit?

One leading commission staff member, Fritz Heimann, later stated that when it was finally issued, the report "aroused all the interest of a review of last year's fashion."[47] If this is so, was the commission's work a totally wasted effort? In the same collection of essays concerned with the effects of the Tax Reform Act of 1969, another staff member (writing in the early 1970s) seems to imply that it might have been, since he is not even sure whether or not the Tax Reform Act itself had been worth all the fuss.[48] Some key players, however, believed the commission had played a significant role and done exactly what it was supposed to do—help prevent the most draconian aspects of legislation affecting foundations and philanthropic giving. In that regard, Douglas Dillon presented his own opinion that JDR in creating the commission had in fact saved the day for foundations; JDR himself was apparently convinced the commission had influenced the outcome of the final bill.[49]

If the commission had any impact on the shape of the Tax Reform Act, it certainly had to have occurred through political discourse in the months from April through December 1969, rather than through the final publication of 1970. It was undoubtedly by means of more elusive but careful networking with powerful decision makers that the commission's influence was realized. This included meetings of commission staff with Congressional and Treasury Staff, but more significantly, Congressional awareness of the commission's report, and Peterson's meetings with members of the administration and Treasury. In addition to the personal connections that Peterson and Rockefeller had with Senator Charles Percy and other members of Congress, assistance was provided by former Congressman Thomas Curtis and the former Commissioner of the Internal Revenue Service, Sheldon Cohen, with regard to major issues and key individuals to be reached.[50] In this connection, work on the commission had an impact on at least two careers. Most notably, Pete Peterson, who began as a bright young man in his early 40s, with little experience of the Washington scene, by February 1971 had been appointed Assistant to the President (Nixon) for International Economic Affairs, and in 1972 became Secretary of Commerce in Nixon's Cabinet. And John Labovitz, who was just out of law school, accepted a position in 1970 as a member of JDR's staff in Room 5600, and by 1974 was a staff member of the Congressional Judiciary Committee involved in impeachment hearings against President Nixon.[51]

On the whole the commission helped fill a gap in the political arena: it served as a group whose expertise and report-in-the making could be flaunted in front of the Senate Finance Committee and utilized behind the scenes with members of the administration and Congress. Although it cannot be proven beyond a shadow of a doubt, the fact that many of the measures most disturbing to foundations and big givers were modified or delayed in the final version of the Bill may have been at least partially due to the commission's existence. Certainly deletion of the Gore Amendment on the floor of the Senate was largely due to Senator Percy's efforts; he was connected to both Peterson and Rockefeller. It is also true, however, that Peterson did not favor two features of the Tax Reform Act which were in line with Treasury's earlier positions, and which survived the final Conference Committee discussions: limitations on foundation ownership of control stock, and the less favorable treatment of charitable contributions to private foundations. Despite mixed opinion on the commission about tax incentives, the report seems to have followed the Rockefeller position, and suggested the need for further consideration of this issue. Regarding the issue of control stock the commission's recommendations were consistent with those of big donors and some of the larger foundations—such as Kellogg and Pew—as well as possibly some smaller emerging foundations. But the commission could not prevail against Treasury and Congress on this matter.[52]

When all was said and done, there was far from total consensus in the foundation community regarding Peterson Commission recommendations. Many foundations were upset about the high percent payout recommendation and probably did not like the commission's emphasis on public disclosure and increased IRS auditing. [53] Nor was there a large ground swell of support for a quasi-governmental body with oversight of the charitable sector. Thus while increased payouts, stepped-up audits, and the idea of oversight from a governmental advisory board might have been acceptable to members of the Rockefeller group, individuals in the Council on Foundations and the Foundation Center were still discussing the idea of a self-policing private organization composed primarily of foundation members (and not a quasi-public body). As could have been expected, even before the Peterson Commission Report was published, Dana Creel, President of the Rockefeller Brothers Fund, said that he was not sure that self-policing would be effective and he could not endorse the idea.[54]

In summary the Peterson Commission's appearance of neutrality was certainly of some value in influencing the final outcome of the struggles of 1969. It afforded a balance to the more obvious advocacy efforts of the foundation group that presented arguments to the Senate Finance Committee. Still, as we have seen, not all of the battles were won. At least one observer of the foundation world later implied that the most serious loss in the long run might have been the failure to gain adequate support either in Congress or in the administration for the establishment of "the Commission's most important idea"—an Advisory Board on Philanthropy (or indeed an American Charity Commission).[55] Others, like Merrimon Cuninggim, worried about the potential threat of limiting "any attempt" at influencing legislation through the general public (i.e., grass roots lobbying)[56] or were concerned about the idea of a tax (the 4 percent tax on investments) which challenged the essential concept of the tax-exempt charitable organization. Efforts to view this as a payment for audits by the IRS were not successful, and this provision cast a shadow over the foundation world.[57]

In the aftermath of the Tax Reform Act, some observers said that the massive tax reform legislation might have been averted if the IRS had enforced the existing laws on open disclosure, adequate payout, and self-dealing,[58] or if the foundation world had paid attention to the 1965 Treasury Report and attempted to put its own house in order. It is certainly true that as a whole, foundations did not react to the early warnings; they could not unify around the need for corrective action such as self-policing, and were arrogant in response to the Patman charges, as well as to the issues raised in the House Ways and Means Committee in 1969.[59] With hindsight it seemed possible that earlier cooperation among the foundations, and particularly the larger among them, might have enabled them to head off the legislation, particularly if, as suggested later, the foundations could have organized their own constituency groups.[60] However, foundations—big and small—had many enemies and few friends: they tended to operate in secret (only a very small percent produced annual reports); they antagonized strong constituency groups (e.g., Albert Shanker and the teachers' union in New York City); small businesses considered them unfair competition because they were able to shelter certain business transactions from taxes;[61] and politicians resented their use as a cover for political action.[62]

Finally, if the foundations represented a public interest with no identified constituency group, filling in for that group could well be defined as the role of the Peterson Commission. In effect that seems to have been the function that Peter Peterson and John Rockefeller believed should be filled by a permanent nationally recognized quasi-public Commission on Philanthropy, which would have incorporated the interests of the donor foundations along with those of the larger 501(c)(3) community of recipient organizations and public charities.[63] In this event a permanent group might have been able to undo some of the damage that had been done when the delineated "private foundations" were separated from the rest of the more-favored charitable world. Furthermore, such a permanent Board could have pursued the policy agenda and issues not addressed by the Peterson Commission. In the end, however, President Nixon gave Peterson a job and Rockefeller a Population Commission, but did not respond to their entreaties for the establishment of an Advisory Board on Philanthropic Policy.[64]

8

After the Tax Reform Act

Emergence of a New Commission

The worst harm that tax on investment income would do [is that] it would
for the first time breach the principle of total exemption from income tax of
charitable organizations, a principle which has been basic to our social
system and served the nation well since a constitutionally based income tax
was introduced in 1913.
A second disturbing theme of the legislative proceedings in Washington
has been the assertion that foundation income is really public money,
because it is itself tax exempt and because it derives from . . . gifts which
offer donors tax advantages.
—Alan Pifer, 1970

First Steps

The Tax Reform Act of 1969 was law, but matters in the charitable world
were far from settled by the early 1970s. To begin with there were problems
in interpreting the complex ideas embedded in the legislation. In addition there
remained questions about the timing for implementation of particular sections
of the Act and the concomitant need for regulations to be promulgated for this
implementation. Moreover, although the foundations had begun to recognize
the need to work together, there were still differences about what this would
mean in practice.

Many of the provisions of the Act were scheduled to slide into effect over
a period of several years. Among these was the change from the unlimited
charitable deduction to a maximum permissible deduction which would go
down to only 50 percent after 1974.[1] However, this would affect only the few
who met the criteria; for most wealthy donors, their allowable charitable deduction actually increased to 50 percent immediately after passage of the Act.

The controversial 6 percent payout rate also had two different schedules of implementation: for foundations established before May 26, 1969, it would be phased in gradually only after 1971, and would not reach 6 percent for three more years.[2] But for newer foundations, the high payout rate would start in 1970. Other parts of the statute were expected to take effect immediately but were nonetheless still subject to development of specific regulations, including those concerning lobbying and political activity.[3] There also remained questions for many organizations about their status as private foundations and the new ramifications of this status.[4]

Thus the year 1970 was viewed as a time of transition by the charity world; uncertainty prevailed and it was hard to do business as usual. Moreover, although many of the larger, more prestigious foundations had taken the position originally that the bill under discussion had very little to do with them, by the time the Act was passed that idea had been proven to be an illusion. The massive scope of the legislation, both in fiscal and programmatic matters, meant that every charitable organization would be forced to ask the question: How does this affect our organization? This was particularly so for any organization that had questions about whether it was to be considered a private foundation under the new law. For although the impact of the law would be different for different foundations, it could hardly be "none at all." By way of example, in what might have been considered a shocker, the prestigious Ford Foundation reported that it would be delayed in its grant-making that year. They were concerned that their procedures might not meet the requirements of accountability under the new statute, either because they had been designated to individuals or groups, or because they had purposes that were questionable under the new law.[5] Even such a well-established institution as the Frick Collection worried about its status and considered the advisability of asking for contributions from the public.[6]

Evidently radial waves from the Tax Act were not affected by size differences. On the one end there was a significant increase in the number of small foundations that merged into community foundations.[7] And on the other end, the Rockefellers, who certainly had always operated with the best of legal advice, were facing new issues in regard to the way that they ran their family office and their multiple charitable foundations.[8]

On the whole, in the first year after the passage of the Act, foundations were still trying to figure out what it meant to come under the new legal classification of "private foundation," in regard to both program and fiscal issues.[9] It was, in any case, evident that of the three categories which were possible—public charity (regular 501[c][3] organizations), private foundation (as defined under the new Section 509 of the IRC), or the special group of private operating foundations—the designation "private foundation" was the most onerous category. Thus, with no new major legislation expected that year, and some concern about lobbying limits, the foundations' primary contacts with Washington turned around legal advice and rulings from the IRS in regard to their status. However, this was not the same for Peterson and his staff. Although the recommendations of the Commission Report were not published officially, they had been conceptualized. And with the looser, non-charitable status of his commission, Peterson had no reason to worry about lobbying government officials on any of the commission's proposals, including establishment of the Committee on Tax Incentives or the Advisory Board on Philanthropic Policy.[10]

Meanwhile, in early 1970, JDR's principal staff person for philanthropic matters suggested caution in regard to public officials and actions in Washington.[11] That spring Rockefeller also resigned as Chairman of Lincoln Center, and, not too long after that, gave up leadership of the Rockefeller Foundation. For a brief time, JDR appeared to focus more on writing his book and working on some of his other interests, like population issues and the Asia Society, as well as an emerging one—the youth revolution.[12]

By early 1970 the Treasury Department had begun to write regulations which could solve problems of interpretation and speed up implementation of the new law.[13] However, although some rapid decisions were made initially, by 1972 many were not yet definite, and there were still provisional regulations out for public review and comment.[14] Interpreting the results of the Act became a growing business. There were papers and conferences which served as forums for the various views of tax lawyers, accountants, economists, and representatives of the Treasury Department.[15] Despite the continued state of confusion, a verdict was soon reached; the word spread that on the whole the tax reform act was not as bad as expected and many foundation representatives were saying they could live with it.[16] Still, as anticipated, foundation expenditures increased, along with the use of expert lawyers and accountants; one source estimated the cost of legal and accounting fees between 1968 and 1970 rose overall by 100 percent.[17] Small foundations without staff had particular difficulty handling administrative matters, which undoubtedly helped them accelerate decisions to join community foundations in this period. Even the venerable Ford Foundation hired specialized staff to deal with emerging procedural matters. However, it was still too early to know for sure if there was excessive concern on the part of the foundations, or whether President Nixon was correct when, in signing the tax bill, he said, "The real harm was psychological not substantive."[18]

A Coordinating Body

In this turbulent climate the question of whether the foundations could agree on some kind of coordinating body remained to be determined, and the issue of its functions and membership assumed additional importance. On these matters there was divided opinion. In January the group led by Manning Pattillo of the Foundation Center was still putting forth the idea of a fully foundation-dominated standard setting group, although apparently others, like Dana Creel (executive of the RBF), believed that in the aftermath of the Tax Reform Act that idea had lost some of its utility.[19] At the other end, the Peterson Report had opted for some kind of quasi-governmental (or public-private) board that would be policy oriented and represent the public interest which they believed was encompassed by foundations and the charitable sector. The need for a more inclusive approach certainly was arguable in light of the lessons from the 1969 Hearings and passage of the Tax Reform Act, and such an organization could avoid characterization as a lobbying group.

Although there was no unity among the foundations about the nature of a new organization, the need to create a different approach was recognized. Thus early in 1970 another committee was formed. Initially named the Committee on the Foundation Field, it was authorized by the Boards of Directors of the principal groups that had developed the proposal to which Dana Creel had objected in January—the Council on Foundations (COF), the Foundation Center, and the National Council on Philanthropy (NCOP). However, it had a new cast of characters and was structured differently. Indeed, the Committee Report contained a clear disclaimer: members were serving as individuals and not as representatives of their organizations. Referred to as the Gardner Committee, it was chaired by John Gardner, who was now head of the Urban Coalition; its members included Merrimon Cuninggim (Vice-Chairman); A. A. (Al) Hechman, Dr. James A. (Dolph) Norton, and Dean Don K. Price. As a sign that something new was intended, it was staffed by Robert W. Scrivner, on loan from the Rockefeller Brothers Fund.[20] Peter Peterson was not part of the group, and indeed apparently was not at first informed about its activities.[21]

By April 15, 1970, the committee had issued its report. Among its key recommendations was that a new organization be formed which would combine the major functions of the COF and the Foundation Center. The organization was to be called the American Council on Foundations; it would have a liaison with the NCOP which however was expected (because of its mixed constituency groups of donors and donees) to remain a separate entity. The Board of the new organization would encompass broader representation than that initially proposed for Pattillo's standard-setting group. Eleven of the 21 Board members of the new American Council were to be nominated by the various foundation groups, now formally classified into Four Sections as follows: Community Foundations; Company Foundations; General and Special Purpose Foundations—Trustee Administered; and finally, General and Special Purpose Foundations—Administered by Professional Staff.[22] Twelve directors were to be "selected at large," with perhaps one-third of these coming from outside the foundation field.

The structure of the new organization, and its name, seemed to incorporate lessons learned from the 1969 debacle: that if the foundations lacked a constituency, many of the other charities—those defined as public 501(c)(3) organizations—did not, and moreover they had a national, not just an eastern, image. In fact, in the 1969 hearings it had become apparent that some well established "public charities" not only had their own organizational supports (such as alumni or members) but were part of nationwide coordinating groups, like the American Association of Independent College and University Presidents, the Council for Financial Aid to Education, the American Symphony Orchestra League, or the United Funds and Councils of America. Indeed the latter organization served as an umbrella organization for many organizations that also had their own nationwide groups, like the Boy Scouts of America, the Mental Health Association, or United Cerebral Palsy. These "charities" had roots in communities where prominent local citizens and businessmen sat on their Boards, and they also had a nationwide presence.[23] Universities, of course, could pull upon the emotions of loyal alumni as well as testimony by academic leaders with national prominence, and attorneys were key members of the emerging 501(c)(3) group.[24]

Thus, in addition to their reputed openness, based on funding sources and concept, many of the public charities had defined constituencies which enabled them to reach Congressional representatives from multiple vantage points across the country. As we have seen in the case of John Rockefeller himself, this group also had the support of people who might be considered in the foundation field, but who at the same time had particular favorite charities of their own, such as the Asia Society, Princeton University, or the Museum of Modern Art.[25] A new organization like the American Council on Foundations could presumably create a nationwide presence that would allow foundations to emulate the kind of Congressional influence mobilized by well-established 501(c)(3) charities during the critical period of the late 1960s.

Although the sponsoring groups were primarily New York based, at least one foundation leader apparently thought it important that Peterson be apprised of the events that were happening there.[26] Consequently as a result of

Alan Pifer's intervention, a draft of the Peterson Commission Report's chapter about an Advisory Board on Philanthropic Policy was forwarded to the Gardner group.[27] Pifer wrote Peterson that the chapter was "excellent" and did not "conflict at all with anything in the Gardner Report." However, a comparison of the commission's recommendations with those of the "Gardner Report" verifies that there were significant differences. Even though the Peterson Report waffled somewhat on the quasi-private nature of the Advisory Board, and the Board included only "private citizen" members, the commission-recommended Advisory Board was evidently designed to be more public (appointed by the President, ratified by the Senate) as well as to fulfill a more public policy function than the totally private-sponsored organization of the Gardner Report.[28]

In this regard, and with JDR's support, Peterson continued talking with the Nixon administration throughout 1970, until he actually moved into the administration.[29] Meanwhile, the Gardner Implementation Committee did not lead to the kind of umbrella organization that seemed to have been intended originally; instead, in the end, a variety of organizational efforts were initiated in the nonprofit arena. These included the United Way–dominated Coalition for Public Good through Private Initiatives[30] and Common Cause, a social action, lobbying organization, classified under the Internal Revenue Code as a 501(c)(4) organization, and founded by John Gardner himself in late 1970. In fact, it was to be another two years before the idea of a policy-oriented national commission actually resurfaced concretely. And this would once again happen under the aegis of action initiated by John Rockefeller.

Effects of the Act, 1970–1973

In regard to the situation as the Act was passed, one observer wrote: "Early in 1970, foundations, notably the bigger ones, appeared to be more influential than ever before, an impression strengthened by the movement between government and private philanthropy of such dignitaries as McGeorge Bundy, Dean Rusk, John W. Gardner, . . . [and] Roger W. Wilkins." However, the author apparently wrote this before fully digesting the message of the 1969 Tax Reform Act, since he also said, "There may still be need for further debate in Congress" with reference to "the alarming acceleration of foundation assets."[31]

For a time the impact of the Tax Reform Act on foundations and charities remained indeterminate and was widely debated. Among the more positive positions, there were many who believed that the foundations had learned a valuable lesson through necessary self-awareness, and had come out stronger. Perhaps somewhat in keeping with the foundation tradition of smiling while in pain, shortly after the passage of the Act Manning Pattillo was quoted as saying,

"It could have been much worse."[32] By 1973 one observer of the scene was writing, "The prevailing view was reported to be that of Merrimon Cuninggim . . . who said that the law 'has not hurt foundations as much as they expected it would, and it has not hurt them much. Both.'"[33] This did not, however, prevent the well-respected Cuninggim from also presenting the view that "foundations are in serious trouble"; they were said to be "under fire" and "to have lost public confidence."[34] Perhaps a Peterson Commission staffer, John Labovitz, put it correctly when he said that "the consensus among major foundations ultimately came to be that parts of the law were beneficial. . . . Parts of it atrocious." [35] Still among those who continued to be pessimistic about the effects of the Act was John Simon, Professor of Law at Yale and an expert on foundations, who quipped, "The bell may have faintly tolled for the private foundation; it is now to be found only in captivity and there are strong doubts about its ability to reproduce."[36]

Given the expected phase-in of the Act's provisions, it is not surprising that in the first few years it was difficult to find hard evidence about its impact on philanthropy activity, and particularly on philanthropic contributions. Gradually, however, some data began to emerge, although not all of it was consistent. According to the *New York Times,* by the spring of 1972, there was "no significant impact on the kinds of programs supported by major foundations." However, there was a sizable increase in the foundations' administrative costs, and there was also a substantial gain in revenues of the federal government. Foundations that had been truly tax exempt before the Act subsequently paid $45 million on investment income from January 1970 to February 1972, and were expected to continue paying at least $35 million a year.[37] John Simon (as his often-repeated quote above suggests) claimed that the birth and death rates of foundations did change in those years; based on a study of 12 states he found that in 1972 126 foundations were established, and 605 terminated, in comparison to a period just before 1969 when 1,228 foundations were established, and only 71 terminated.[38] Although recognizing the argument about the birth and death rate of foundations, in a study done for the American Bar Association John Labovitz was more hesitant about overall effects of the Tax Reform Act, and deplored the lack of accurate or consistent data on philanthropic giving and foundations. However, based on interviews and available data, Labovitz did suggest two major conclusions: first (and in the short run) the Act had probably reinforced the tendency on the part of many foundations "to make grants primarily to well-established charities" and for traditional purposes; and second (and in the long run) the 6 percent payout requirement might well increase foundation distributions for a time, but ultimately (without major new infusion of capital) would result in a declining rate of foundation growth.[39]

In any case there was evidence that in this period philanthropic support for charity was declining in importance relative to government support, and that individual contributions were decreasing as a share of total income. A study of private giving by an economist presented data indicating that in the 12 year period from 1960 to 1972, private philanthropy's share of the American economy experienced "considerable shrinkage," going from a high of 1.98 percent in 1960 to 1.76 percent in 1972. If inflation were taken into account, by 1972 the percentage was even lower (1.54 percent).[40] The picture remained somewhat muddy; charitable contributions also rose in absolute dollars in those years. Moreover, declining percentages of individual income donated to charity were part of a continuing trend that had begun before the Act passed. According to Edwin Cohen, Under Secretary of the Treasury, the percentage of adjusted gross income given to charity had declined from 3.53 percent in 1962 to 3.13 percent in 1966, 3.02 percent in 1968, and 2.82 percent in 1970.[41] On the other hand the amounts of grant funds given out by foundations in this period increased considerably, rising from $1,250,000,000 (1966) to $2,500,000,000 (1971).[42] However, in light of the phasing-in of the higher payout amounts, the exact impact of the Tax Reform Act was difficult to determine.

Some results of the new Act were less ambiguous. After the favored status given community foundations as public charities under the Tax Reform Act, their estimated assets grew by 30 percent in 1972, and another estimated 10 percent in 1973. Much of this was reported to have come from the termination of small private foundations. In addition, Labovitz (1974) found that increased administrative costs resulting from the new requirement of "expenditure responsibility" were particularly true for medium-sized foundations. Smaller foundations apparently did less (or were considering termination), and large foundations could more readily absorb new procedures. However, middle-sized foundations, with some rudiments of program, tended to become more "formal" in their practices.[43]

Meanwhile it was reported that Treasury was drafting regulations that could be lived with. Cuninggim noted specifically the restrained view of the Treasury Department with regard to public policy activities by foundations.[44] Fritz Heimann, former senior staff member of the Peterson Commission, also stated that Treasury has drafted "fairly reasonable regulations interpreting the statutory restrictions on legislative activities." However, Heimann urged that this reasonableness "should not divert attention from the inherent unsoundness of the restrictions."[45] In fact, with the increased pace of auditing of foundations by the IRS, the situation became more difficult politically. For if Treasury Department officials were restrained in drafting regulations, the IRS was evidently not immune from political pressure. Reported abuse by IRS staff against liberal organizations that the President viewed as problematic now emerged as a significant issue. In October 1970 the IRS announced that it had "temporarily suspended the issuance of rulings on claims for tax exempt status by 'public interest law firms' and other organizations which litigate or support litigation for what they determine to be the public good in some chosen area of national interest such as preservation of the environment."[46] In this period also there were other reports about the IRS "cracking down" on nonprofit groups advocating views that differed with those of the administration.[47]

For their part, the foundations did not always demonstrate great effort in complying with some of the new public disclosure requirements of the law. Cuninggim, certainly a part of the foundation group, almost seemed to be damning by faint praise when he indicated that there was an increase in the number of annual (or biennial) reports issued, from 140 in 1968 to 200 in 1972.[48] Richard Magat, a well-known foundation maven, reported that in responding to the requirement to publicize availability of their IRS forms, most foundations initially placed notices in such obscure professional journals as the *New York Law Journal* where few of the general public would be likely to see them. On the other hand, there was evidence that before long the foundation community was making more of an effort to insure wider dissemination through the *New York Times.*[49]

Next Steps Again (What to Do?)

There were problems, but despite the doomsayers no major fiscal crises erupted in the philanthropic world at the beginning of the 1970s, either among the charitable recipient organizations or the foundations. There were, however, constant skirmishes in Congress, and questions about what the regulations would finally mean in regard to program and finances. Looming ahead for some of the very rich was the final reduction of the charitable deduction to a 50 percent maximum and unsettled questions about the classification and tax status of some of their philanthropic activity. Even more problematic for most foundations were the 6 percent payout and the 4 percent audit fee, as well as questions about permissible program activities. There was frequent communication among the foundations and from the Council on Foundations on these issues.[50] But still no strong new organization emerged from the foundation field to deal with its public image or to help unite the private foundations closely with public charities.

In March 1970 President Nixon created the Commission on Population Growth and the American Future and appointed John Rockefeller to be the Chair, and the following November he established a National Center on Voluntary Action.[51] Nonetheless, the administration did not move to create either the tax incentive advisory committee to Treasury or the independent public commission on philanthropic policy requested by Peterson and Rockefeller. There appears to have been good reason. In this period internal administrative advisory groups were being subjected to considerable scrutiny by Congress, and on December 9, 1970 a report was issued that criticized government commissions as a kind of fifth branch of government.[52]

Meanwhile, the critical problem highlighted by the Peterson Commission was still not being addressed—that is, the presumed financial crisis of charitable organizations in the next decade. As the Commission Report suggested, provisions in the Tax Reform Act were likely to seriously undermine incentives for private giving. In the wings, moreover, was the growing dependence of charitable institutions on public dollars (at a time when government expenditures were generally increasing), and by 1971, the complication of economic pressures from a recession facing the country. With its little Appendix about corporate giving, the Peterson Report had also tried to highlight another—unrealized—source of funds: the large corporations that either directly or though their foundations gave far less than the 5 percent of profits permissible under the law.[53] Peterson had some direct experience in this regard: his commission had little success in raising funds from business, even with the help of Datus Smith and John Rockefeller himself.

In this context, and around the same time that the Gardner group was attempting to create a new philanthropic coordinating group, Datus Smith proposed to JDR that he form a "corporate commission . . . similar to the Peterson Commission."[54] Rockefeller's Lincoln Center experience would theoretically have prepared him well for pulling together a business commission, and such a group would not be subject to questions about lobbying.[55] A business commission could help engage public consciousness of the issues before the charitable world, as well as encourage corporate leaders themselves to increase business giving to philanthropic causes. However, the business group was slow in developing. Certainly by all accounts Rockefeller was not at his best in meetings with corporate leaders; but even Peterson had not been able to promote business interest in the philanthropic question.[56] And of course under the informal rules of the "house," David Rockefeller—who might have been more easily able to pull off a business-led commission—could not be involved, at least partly because it was brother John's business.[57]

By the spring of 1970, even while a corporate commission was being considered, John Rockefeller was back in Washington. There were questions about the new directions and regulations being promulgated under the tax law, and entries in JDR's diary reveal that he was again engaged directly in the Washington scene. On April 28 he met with "Messrs. Lockwood, Creel, Bolton, Smith and Leonard Silverstein to discuss my breakfast meeting this coming Thursday with Laurence N. Woodworth." JDR notes that Mr. Silverstein, of the firm of Silverstein and Mullens in Washington, "has been advising us for a number of months now concerning the *philanthropy hearings*" (emphasis in original) and their aftermath.[58] However, in his talk with Woodworth two days later, Woodworth indicated that there was unlikely to be any Congressional consideration of foundation issues for "a maximum of two or three years."[59] Woodworth also apparently suggested that the foundations "were over-reacting to the new legislation" which he thought they should take in stride since "the books were closed."[60] He also mentioned that "Treasury might be glad to talk with foundations in regard to the regulations being drawn up to clarify the recent law." It now appeared that this would cause no difficulty since he would be educating them on matters relating to their own particular needs—which was permissible under the new law.

Throughout this period, various groups, including the Gardner Committee, continued to discuss how they might best create a unified effort in regard to future changes affecting the foundation field. A lawyer's group was also working to insure that there was a solid front in regard to the new regulations.[61] And meanwhile, in October 1971, Rockefeller, in a certain sense a self-appointed emissary, met again with Laurence Woodworth. In this meeting Woodworth revived the idea of an informal advisory "group from the foundation field."[62] On the same day JDR also met with John Connally, Secretary of the Treasury, because of his (Rockefeller's) concern "*that the Administration is not giving support to philanthropy or expressed more broadly, private initiative.*"[63] This was also around the time that Wright Patman was completing a report about the 15 largest foundations, which would of course include Rockefeller enterprises.[64] By 1972 an election year was underway, and declared Democratic hopefuls George McGovern and George Wallace (like Patman, a populist) began to focus attention on the issue of inequity in the tax laws. But the President and Wilbur Mills were indecisive on their positions on tax reform legislation, although Nixon generally remained opposed to it.[65] In any case, talks continued within the Rockefeller group and with officials in Washington, without any firm sense about the direction for action.

Meanwhile the interim time period described by Woodworth was coming to an end, and implementation of some of the more onerous features of the tax act were about to go into effect. Nixon won the election and a few weeks later the *New York Times* reported that tax reform "would be slower in coming and less sweeping than had generally been expected earlier."[66] However, it appeared that there might be some new legislation in 1973,[67] and the Senate

Finance Committee had created a new Subcommittee on Foundations. Consequently JDR and his advisors began to move faster in the creation of a new body. At first this was conceptualized as a Committee on Tax Incentives which was to be advisory to Wilbur Mills.[68] But as tax reform moved forward in Congress, the idea of creating a citizens' commission on philanthropy took on greater urgency in Rockefeller quarters.

By early 1973, and after the election of a Democratic-controlled congress, hearings on tax revision were to begin—with consideration of eliminating "various tax preferences."[69] In the context of increasing inflationary pressures in the country (and in the charitable arena), Congress began discussing unresolved issues of importance to rich donors: equity in estate and gift taxes, capital gains, and accelerated depreciation. The older established foundations that had escaped for a while were now also facing higher payout rates, and the 50 percent maximum charitable deduction was to become effective at the end of 1974. There was also the issue of the 4 percent "excise tax" which remained a philosophical affront to the foundations, as well as a potential loss of income to their recipient "charitable" organizations.[70]

Now, even before a commission was officially formed, the informal 501(c)(3) group, with assistance from the Rockefeller "office," commissioned a study by Martin Feldstein (Professor of Economics at Harvard University) on the question of tax incentives.[71] Around this time Rockefeller and his advisors also began looking for a chairman of the proposed new commission. By the end of July 1973 they had found him: he was John Filer, Chief Executive Officer of the Aetna Life and Casualty Company in Hartford, Connecticut. Filer came with good recommendations and corporate qualifications; like Pete Peterson, he was also not very well known nationally, and was not part of the foundation crowd. Flattered to be asked, he agreed to chair the new commission.

9

The Filer Commission in Action

There is a preponderant view in America that a large majority of the
foundations are not sensitive to the basic gut concerns of the country.

—Reverend Leon Sullivan, Commissioner, 1975

1973 may be the year of the most serious challenges ever made against the
charitable tax deduction for the support of philanthropic constitutions.
Political, social and economic pressures are building to an extent that
Congress will not be able to ignore tax reform or review during the
1973 session.

—American College Public Relations Association, 1972

It is because of the importance of foundations to American society that
this subcommittee has been formed. The human needs which gave rise to
many foundations in the past will increase, rather than diminish, in the
coming years.

—Senator Vance Hartke, Subcommittee on Foundations,
U.S. Senate Committee on Finance, 1973

The Commission Begins

In July 1973 when the phone call came from John D. Rockefeller 3rd, John
Filer was in his office in Hartford, Connecticut and his attention was on the
Aetna Life and Casualty Company. In reflecting on this later, Filer suggested he
was amused by the fact that after the phone rang, his secretary said to him
without any particular emphasis: "There's a John Rockefeller on the phone for
you. Do you know him?"[1] Nevertheless, Filer's credentials had been reviewed
by the Rockefeller staff before JDR spoke with him,[2] and later, Rockefeller staff
members met with Filer before he met with the Commission. For his part, Filer
certainly appreciated JDR's status, and when JDR offered to come to Hartford
for their meeting, Filer replied that it was no trouble for him to go to New York;
on July 30 he did so.

Filer was the Chief Executive Officer of a major insurance company; consequently he certainly had concern about quality of life issues in his headquarters area.[3] More significantly perhaps for his commission role, he had been a State Senator (Republican) and he knew national politicians like Abraham Ribicoff, the Democratic Senator from Connecticut. Filer was a businessman and an attorney; he was described as articulate as well as handsome.[4] However he was not deeply involved in philanthropic issues, and as it was to turn out, he did not evidence the same desire to control the formation of the commission and selection of personnel that characterized Pete Peterson's early efforts. Indeed, Filer concurred from the start with the selection of the chief staff person for the commission being done by JDR's staff and the Rockefeller office. Their choice was, not surprisingly, the Washington tax attorney Leonard Silverstein, on whose legal expertise the Rockefellers had increasingly come to rely in the aftermath of the 1969 Tax Reform Act. Silverstein also had vast experience of the Washington scene, where he moved easily among Congressmen and Congressional staff. He was well acquainted with Laurence Woodworth and was actively involved with the attorneys' group concerned with tax matters and philanthropy.

Silverstein, already serving as a Rockefeller attorney in Washington, had been identified as the chief of staff for the commission prior to Filer's arrival on the scene, and was accepted by Filer thereafter. However, Filer subsequently also chose an Aetna employee, E. B. (Burt) Knauft, to serve as his own staff representative and liaison to the commission.[5] While the dominant staff presence would ultimately be Silverstein, who was to be invaluable in helping the commission get through difficult times ahead, Knauft also was to have a key role as liaison between Filer (after all a busy executive) and the various members of the commission, as well as with other individuals, including the Rockefeller staff. Moreover, although Silverstein's personality and know-how were vital in shaping the commission's efforts, many other voices would also be heard during the deliberations of a diverse membership and constantly expanding advisory group.

The Filer Commission was formed in a transition period which followed a year's ups and downs in regard to proposed legislation on taxation. Among the more salient issues to emerge during this period was the question of lobbying by 501(c)(3) organizations, which was under review in the federal courts as well as by Congress.[6] With the election year over, it was also reported that Mills would be more responsive to Congressional requests for increased tax revenues and greater equity in tax provisions. Around that time a spate of bills emerging in the Congress had potential consequences for the charitable deduction and other financial interests of the Rockefeller family. And on October 1, 1973 a newly activated Senate committee, the Subcommittee on Foundations of the Senate Finance Committee, was to hold two days of panel discussions "designed to present a full and objective review of the role of private foundations to today's society and a review of the impact of the charitable provisions of the Tax Reform Act of 1969 on the support and operations of private foundations."[7] Stock values were down and oil prices rising, so there was increased foundation concern about the 6 percent payout rate which was to come into effect in 1974, while the charitable world generally worried about the "idea of placing a floor under charitable contributions deductibility."[8]

The way that matters were organized in October suggests that the foundations and the Rockefeller group had learned from the experiences of the Tax Reform Act of 1969. In this context the memory of the Peterson Commission also remained and surfaced in the Hearings of the Subcommittee on Foundations of the Senate Finance Committee. [9] In any case the initial panel that appeared before the Senate subcommittee included several foundation officials not associated directly with the "eastern establishment" and no individuals representing the Rockefellers; in addition McGeorge Bundy did not appear as the primary representative of the Ford Foundation.[10]

From its initiation the Filer Commission showed much more of a public presence than its predecessor had. Certainly more effective groundwork was done with leaders in the Senate (Russell Long) and the House (Wilbur Mills) as well as with Treasury officials, and particularly William Simon, at that time (1973) serving as Deputy Secretary of Treasury. As already noted, these preliminary efforts by JDR and his staff were rewarded: to begin with, Wilbur Mills had endorsed the commission idea in a letter to JDR, in which he also connected JDR "officially" with Laurence Woodworth, chief of staff for the Joint Committee on Internal Revenue Taxation of the Congress.[11] Furthermore, there was the invaluable connection to the Treasury Department, where, also through the good offices of Silverstein, Rockefeller succeeded in getting the imprimatur of William Simon, and thereby Treasury, in the establishment of the commission. Later the Treasury department would provide assistance in other ways, including the release of a Treasury official to serve as director of research for the commission. This appointment in particular appeared to set the stage for a true private-public partnership, and possibly even official status, for the commission's efforts.

In this matter as well as other personnel matters Filer showed that he was open to advice and consultation from the Rockefeller office. Indeed, in addition to accepting Silverstein as the chief staff person, Filer asked for assistance in selecting members of the commission and was prepared to accept people from the Rockefeller list. Nevertheless he added at least three of his own personal choices: Walter J. McNerney, President of the Blue Cross Association (Chicago); Jon O. Newman, Judge of the U.S. District Court (Hartford); and David Truman, President of Mount Holyoke College (South Hadley, Massachusetts); all of them

were to be active participants in the commission's work.[12] A suggestion made
to Silverstein by President Nixon was also accepted: Max Fisher, a supporter of
the Republican party, joined the commission. He too participated actively.[13]

Although some attention was given to the question of inclusiveness in the
initial formation of the commission, membership was subsequently to become
a problematic issue. Some of the first individuals who were asked to serve
turned down the invitation, and the final complement of commissioners was
not actually in place until long after the first meeting. Two of the women seem
to have been added later, and one woman who was on an early list apparently
never attended a meeting. In the end, the commission was considerably larger
than the Peterson Commission had been, and ultimately more representative of
diverse viewpoints. However, this diversity was to cause difficulties.[14]

In addition to John Filer, and not counting staff, the final membership consisted of 26 persons from a variety of arenas, including a judge, several civic
leaders and academics, a union representative, business leaders, and one professional foundation official (Alan Pifer). Many commissioners were also involved in leadership activity in museums, symphonies, and other charitable
organizations. Of the group, two were black men, one a black woman, and one
a Hispanic woman.[15] In addition to Marian Whitman, the woman who disap-
peared from view early on, another commissioner resigned before the report
was printed. He was Leo Perlis, a member of the national AFL-CIO staff, and he
was not listed in the final report, *Giving in America.*[16]

Membership on the "advisory committee" to the commission had started
with a few experts on tax law and philanthropic matters, but by early 1974 the
group had increased greatly in size and more consultants were also being hired
in a variety of capacities. Counting the two lists of staff/consultants and the
expanded advisory committee membership, 120 individuals were eventually
listed in the commission's final report, in addition to Silverstein and those serving on the commission itself. The expanded list included individuals who wrote
research papers for the commission, and also reflected an effort to deal with
lack of clarity around the roles of some participants in commission work. However, only a few of these individuals were women or members of minority
groups.[17]

Commission Work: The First Meeting

The first official meeting of the Filer Commission was held in Washington,
D.C. on October 31, 1973. By then Filer had not only met with JDR but had
also been briefed by members of the Rockefeller staff. Silverstein and Howard
Bolton (a Rockefeller family attorney from Milbank Tweed) came to Hartford to

meet with Filer on October 5; and in addition Filer went to see Porter McKeever and Elizabeth McCormack only a few days after that (on October 10).[18] McCormack and McKeever would represent JDR's views on philanthropy to the commission. McCormack (who was in the process of leaving her position as President of Manhattanville College in Purchase, New York) was later listed as a commission member; McKeever was described as a "special consultant."

Despite its high-powered initiation, at the October commission meeting only 12 members were present, including the Chairman.[19] The meeting began in the morning with a brief recapitulation of the origins of the commission, and thereafter seemed carefully structured to set the agenda for the year. Silverstein was introduced by the Chairman (Filer) and it was noted that Silverstein had assembled a group of "technical experts" (attorneys, economists, government officials, law professors, and "others academically concerned with private philanthropy") to serve as a "resource" for the commission.[20] The topics that were to be covered included: Objectives (of the commission); General discussion of private philanthropy (with an emphasis on the need for an objective study of the subject); Community analysis (in relation to views of philanthropy); Decision-making power; Discussion of outline of issues; Impact of funding sources on politics; The federal tax system; Alternative to the tax system. It was also "generally agreed that the commission's focus should be limited to organizations which are tax exempt under section 501(c)(3) of the Internal Revenue Code." Specifically, this meant that the commission would discuss the larger category of organizations that enjoy the double tax benefit and are able to receive tax-free donations; deliberations would not just be concerned with foundation issues. Moreover, groups categorized under other 501(c) categories or political in nature, such as associations or political parties, could be excluded from the discussion.[21]

In the brief history of the commission's origins presented at the October 31 meeting, JDR's role was mentioned, as well as the interest of Treasury and Congress. Indeed, over lunch that first day, Deputy Treasury Secretary Simon addressed the commission and affirmed both his personal interest and that of Treasury Secretary George Shultz in facilitating the work of the commission.[22] Although Laurence Woodworth could not attend, he sent another person to represent the Joint Committee staff. After lunch, the commission touched on such technical matters as the status of the commission, finances, and research projects, before returning to more substantive topics related to the nature of private philanthropy. In this discussion expectations about Treasury cooperation with "information" and current tax issues were also mentioned. Two particular research projects were described: already underway was a study of wealthy contributors by the Survey Research Center (SRC) at the University of

Michigan; another was a proposed study of the effect of tax incentives on corporate contributions. The study by the Survey Research Center faced potential complications because it required information that would have to be provided by the IRS.[23]

Despite a meticulous enumeration of a range of subjects, the real agenda for the commission from the start centered around tax-related matters. Signals that tax matters would be a primary focus predated Filer's arrival on the scene. The choice of Silverstein as lead staff and the timing of the commission reinforced this emphasis; the commission's formation had been accelerated after reports about the likelihood that Mills would lead an effort in Congress to tighten tax provisions that had ramifications for charitable giving.[24] This emphasis was apparent in JDR's discussions with Mills, Simon, and Long, and manifest in the evident pains taken to insure their support for the new commission. Now also JDR's initially proposed Committee on Tax Incentives was shifted into an advisory committee for the commission.

At the first meeting of the Filer Commission possibilities for research on taxation and philanthropic giving were discussed, but nevertheless there appears to have been no mention of the new study by Martin Feldstein, a Harvard economist, on "tax policy and its effect on charitable contributions." This might seem surprising since Feldstein's efforts were already known to the Council on Foundations and were receiving support from David Rockefeller and the 501(c)(3) group.[25] Evidently once again, the Rockefeller brothers' interests were overlapping but not necessarily conjoined. However, before long these studies were to come under the research wing of the Filer Commission and would be influential on the discussion and recommendations of the commission.

The Filer Commission concluded its first official day with an agreement that fewer, longer meetings were preferable to frequent short ones, and with a decision that its next meeting (in early January 1974) would focus on the tax system and analysis of voluntary philanthropic organizations. Before the next meeting commissioners would be sent background materials about the tax system and a bibliography of "appropriate" readings in the "field of philanthropy." Although matters of tax and philanthropy had been defined as critical issues for deliberation, by the time of the first meeting it had become evident that a major tax reform bill would not go through Congress in 1973. Thus at this point there was actually some confusion and uncertainty about the role of the commission.

The Year Ahead: Political Context

It was originally intended that the commission would meet regularly until its work was completed, which Filer expected would happen around the end of the summer of 1974.[26] In this period some major research would be undertaken or digested, with direction and expertise enhanced by the advisory group of experts: the commission would then debate the critical issues before drawing up its recommendations. The next meeting in early January 1974 was designed to be an important step in that process. Stanley Surrey and Boris Bittker were invited together to discuss tax policy and charitable contributions.

It would be hard to imagine a more interesting first step. At that time Surrey was back at Harvard, and Bittker was at Yale Law School, so both were academic attorneys in the field of tax policy and both held strong convictions on tax matters. They were almost diametrically opposed in their views on the subject and indeed Bittker had just given a negative review of a book by Surrey in the *New York Times.* Thus, the issues were laid out clearly in the interchange, and the discussion was intense, although, not surprisingly, it did not lead to any resolution.

However, what happened after this meeting seems proof of the famous dictum that "the best laid plans of mice and men often go awry."[27] Instead of moving rapidly forward in the next months, there was apparently a marked hiatus in commission deliberations between January 1974 and fall 1974. There is no evidence of full commission meetings until after the summer, although some activity did take place on the part of the staff, the consultants, and the Advisory Committee. A research committee met at least once, in February 1974, and possibly again later that spring.[28] Records in the commission archives (at Indiana University) suggest that there may have been meetings in October and November 1974, but there appear to be no transcripts, minutes, or summaries of those meetings; there is somewhat more evidence of a meeting on September 20.[29] In effect there is no detailed record of significant commission deliberations between the preceding January and January 1975. By then Gerald Ford was President and Nelson Rockefeller was Vice President, and the climate in Washington and the nation had changed. And by that time there was also more serious consideration of tax legislation in Congress. This legislation had been initiated by President Ford immediately after he took office in October.

Between the summer of 1973, when Filer met with Rockefeller, and the end of 1974, the American political environment suffered severe shocks. Several of the nation's leading political figures were toppled from power and replaced. One of these events affected the Committee on Ways and Means. In October 1974 Wilbur Mills was charged with disorderly conduct and drunken driving; in the car with him when he was stopped was an Argentinean strip-tease dancer, Fanne Foxe.[30] After another similar incident, Mills resigned as Chairman of the House Ways and Means Committee in December, and Al Ullman (Democrat, Oregon) became Acting Chairman. Thus the commission was forced to deal with new leadership in the House Ways and Means Committee.

In this period reforms were instituted in the rules by which Congress operated. The Ways and Means Committee would increase from 25 to 37 members, but was expected to lose some of its power; the legislative process would be more open. With increased use of subcommittees, power was to become more diffuse and staff expertise would be more important in the decision-making process.[31]

Meanwhile dramatic events were unfolding in the Offices of the President and Vice-President of the United States. The 1972 break-in at the headquarters of the Democratic party (the Watergate Building) by agents of the Committee to Reelect the President (CREEP) developed into a major news story.[32] In an apparently unrelated event, after a negotiated settlement with federal officials, in October 1973 Vice-President Spiro Agnew was forced to resign on serious charges concerning tax evasion and bribery while in office. And on December 13 Gerald Ford was named Vice President to replace the deposed Agnew.

Only a few months later tax evasion charges were raised against President Nixon himself. Nixon was accused of having underpaid his income taxes and of having backdated donations of his personal papers in 1969 so as to meet required eligibility dates for charitable deductions under the Tax Reform Act.[33] Around the same time, revelations from the White House tapes led to further investigation of the administration's illegal activities. Eventually these investigations resulted in three articles of impeachment against the President. On August 8, 1974 Nixon publicly announced his resignation, and the following day Gerald R. Ford became President of the United States.

During this period the actions of another Rockefeller became front page news. On December 18, 1973 Nelson Rockefeller resigned formally from the governorship of New York State, ostensibly to put his full effort into leadership of his Commission on Critical Choices of Americans. This was after already undertaking the chairmanship of President Nixon's National Commission on Water Quality in 1972. Nelson Rockefeller's new Commission on Critical Choices had started as a state-level activity but he had apparently convinced Nixon that it should have national status. Although he was less successful in obtaining financial support for the commission from the Senate Appropriations Committee, Nelson was back in the national arena.[34] And when Nelson was quiet during the Watergate hearings, it was assumed that he was trying to protect his political future.

Later when Gerald Ford offered him the nomination for Vice President, Nelson Rockefeller accepted, even though in the past he had never seemed to want this position. He accepted the offer quickly on August 9, although he was not actually sworn into office until December 19, 1974. In the interim, extensive hearings on his nomination were held, first in the Senate and then in the House Judiciary Committee. Initially the Senate hearings seemed to go well; however, by mid-September more information was uncovered by the FBI and the IRS, and when the hearings resumed, they were more difficult. By the end of the House hearings in December, problems in Nelson's financial affairs were evident, and it appeared that he too had omitted paying some required income taxes. The family was embarrassed by public exposure of family affairs, but in the end Nelson Rockefeller became Vice-President.[35]

Given the sensitivity of the commission to nuances in the political environment, and its concern with matters of tax policy, it seems reasonable to assume that the events in Washington affected commission members and staff, even if no direct causal relationship can be established.[36] Still, some activity did continue throughout 1974. In the spring, papers were filed with the government to insure that the Filer Commission would continue as a private, nonprofit, tax-exempt organization, eligible also to receive tax deductible contributions. Interestingly the name of the commission as it appeared on the Certification of Tax Exemption (filed May 5 and approved May 15, 1974) was now different, and broader in scope, from that which appeared in the original incorporation papers of August 1973. In that earlier time, it was simply "the Commission on Private Philanthropy," but by May 1974 it was the Commission on Private Philanthropy and Public *Needs* (emphasis added) as it had been in a February press release about a new Director of Research for the Commission.[37]

After the January 1974 meeting, the commission seemed to modify its structure and its way of doing business. Notably, its research focus was enlarged and began to receive more attention; early in February 1974 it was announced that Gabriel Rudney had been given leave from his position as Assistant Director of the Treasury Department's Office of Tax Analysis to become Director of Research for the "Citizens' Commission on Private Philanthropy and Public Needs."[38] Meanwhile Congressional hearings began that month on windfall and excess profit taxes, and debate continued about what "substantial lobbying" actually amounted to. This matter would certainly be of importance to the Filer Commission, because its own role and formal status as a private 501(c)(3) organization had not yet been formalized, and because its constituency groups would also be concerned about this issue.

Efforts to achieve statutory clarification in regard to the term "substantial lobbying" had been ongoing in Congress since Senator Edmund Muskie (Democrat, Maine) had initiated them in 1972, but they were beginning to take a different form. A specific formula for defining substantiality was now proposed by the new Chairman of the Ways and Means Committee, Al Ullman. The Tax Reform Act of 1974 would have contained a kind of complex formula for determining substantiality, but it "died aborning" in the House Ways and Means Committee. However, as it was to turn out, Ullman's concept was kept alive and in fact resurfaced as part of tax legislation passed in 1976.[39]

Although there are gaps in the written record of commission actions during 1974, the commission's deliberations would certainly have been affected by the deep drop in the stock market in the spring of that year. Nonetheless, evidently both fund raising and the research agenda continued. Fund raising activity was organized and propelled by two experts in this area: Philip Klutznick, a commissioner, and Jack Schwartz, from the American Association of Fund Raising Counsel (AAFRC), who was brought in by Klutznick. On May 15, 1974 a special fund raising luncheon was hosted by JDR in New York City.[40] To prepare for this important occasion, a Case Statement in brochure format was put together in some haste by Knauft and Silverstein.[41] As listed therein, purposes of the commission turned out to be considerably broader than those in the original incorporation papers, and in addition to questions about tax incentives, they now included these searching questions:

> Should society continue to encourage the formation and support of private organizations and institutions as a major means of satisfying our public needs?

> Would the fabric of American society be altered if government replaced the private initiative and effort which traditionally defined and met our public needs?

> What is the appropriate relationship between government and private society in harnessing national resources of creative initiative, energy and money to define and meet our public needs?

> Are society's resources devoted to satisfying community needs being appropriately allocated among the many purposes, organizations and institutions which depend on private support?

These were far-reaching questions, but they seemed in keeping with JDR's own expressed interests, as well as Filer's general views.[42] Moreover, they set the tone for an enlarged research agenda, and they would in any case avoid the charge that the commission's goals were narrowly delineated to further the purposes of particular members of the foundation community. In the next months, additional experts from a range of disciplines were hired as consultants or contracted with for individual research programs. The staff, principally Silverstein and Rudney, maintained contact with these consultants, and on January 9, 1975 a meeting of the Advisory Committee was also held.

By this time the commission's efforts were revitalized. A neatly compiled list of topics suggests that "certain tax related issues" formed the substance of its meetings in the winter and early spring of 1975. Specifically, deliberations were said to have focused on: "Oversight Agency (January 13–14); Charitable

Deduction Generally" and "Donor Control in Foundations" (February 5–7); "Uniform Accounting," "Religious Reporting," "Oversight Agency," "Extending Charitable Deduction to Non-Itemizers," "Appreciated Property," and "Foundation Governance and Donor Control" (March 10–11); and finally "Lobbying Restrictions and Corporate Giving" (April 7–8, 1975).[43] Experts and consultants were involved in the discussion and the transcripts show that there was indeed lively discussion of the issues. Efforts were made frequently by the Chairman to arrive at consensus on key points,[44] but there was so little consistency in attendance, and the discussion was often so free-ranging, that it seems unlikely that most commissioners would have been strongly committed to the outcomes of many of the discussions.

Consensus became even more complicated in early spring 1975 after the Filer Commission faced another major challenge from outside. A new group had entered the picture and they began raising questions about the content of the research agenda, as well as about the structure and functioning of the commission. At a meeting with commission members in March, this "outside" group expressed great concern about the scope of the commission's research as well as the way it was going about its business. This "pick-up" group, soon dubbed the "Donee Group," emerged after the publication of an article challenging the commission's membership appeared in the *Grantsmanship Center News* in January 1975.[45] The group was initially led by the same person who wrote that article, the well-known Washingtonian Pablo Eisenberg. Its members were to have considerable influence on the commission's activities.

The Research Agenda

While the report was being written, Gabriel Rudney was carrying out a campaign to collect the research papers; in the end 91 papers were received. Most of these were later published in the five volumes of *Research Papers* of the commission.[46] After protests from the Donee Group and questions raised by some commission members, additional research papers were added, but the focus of the commissioned research clearly remained centered on the interface between philanthropy and tax policies. Oversight for this work was essentially the responsibility of Rudney, although a small informal research subcommittee was created (Elizabeth McCormack, John Musser, and Walter McNerney, Chair). Most papers were published with only a little editing, but several were apparently edited heavily. Few papers were rejected, perhaps because to do so would have been politically difficult.[47]

The compilation of research on the whole succeeded in presenting and analyzing new data related to philanthropy, and a number of significant papers discussed tax policies and tax incentives specifically.[48] Given the interests of both Silverstein and Rudney, considerable attention was paid to the econometric studies and modeling of tax incentives that were carried out by Martin Feldstein.[49] Ralph Nelson, Gabriel Rudney, and Burton Weisbrod were among the economists who presented new analyses of the field of philanthropy that had not been available or readily accessible previously.[50] A few historical papers were included and there were also discussions on specific issues by individual attorneys, such as Lawrence Stone and Paul McDaniel, as well as by groups in law firms, like the article by David Ginsburg, Lee Marks, and Ronald Wertheim.[51] Although the majority of the papers were from attorneys and economists, there were also contributions from social scientists and academics, like Paul Ylvisaker and Adam Yarmolinsky, from social welfare experts like Wilbur Cohen, and from practitioner groups such as the Associated Councils of the Arts.[52] The papers ranged in quality and point of view; many were highly insightful, and others were case studies, with more limited scope and data.[53] Volume V was essentially dedicated to the question of accountability and oversight of the voluntary sector.[54]

Working with the proposed researchers was not always easy, and despite requests (or warnings) not to do so, some authors disseminated their work before the commission had issued its own report.[55] A variety of arrangements were also utilized to insure that there would be original and valuable research for the commission. Authors were paid, but apparently at different rates, with some authors or larger studies being paid more.[56] In the end, as a result of the influence of the Donee Group, and with the support of John Filer and John Rockefeller, there were a number of diverse or dissenting papers added to the initial research agenda. Among these were several dealing with minority group interests as well as controversial papers that subsequently attracted attention, including "Who's Funding the Woman's Movement?" by Mary Jean Tully; "Public Needs, Public Policy and Philanthropy" by Thomas R. Asher; and an insightful paper by David Horton Smith, "The Role of the United Way in Philanthropy."[57]

Process and Product: The Report

While the research papers were being compiled and the commission was meeting, the writing of the report was already underway. Indeed chapter drafts were circulated by early spring 1975 and a full hearing on the draft was held by the commission in June. The Donee Group also had access to drafts of the report: By summer completion of the report was a matter of concern and in the fall the matter of timing became important. A date was set; the presentation would be to Congress, as well as at a press conference in Washington on December 2, 1975. Presumably Filer wanted to bring matters to a close, and he now had other matters on his mind.[58] Furthermore this was also the time in which tax legislation was being heatedly debated in the House, and voting was about to take place on amendments that would tighten tax loopholes, including an increase on the minimum tax on preference income (related to capital gains taxation and suggesting echoes of 1969). Significantly, starting in 1975 tax expenditures were to be listed as part of the United States budget document, and this would include charitable deductions among the preference amounts to be exposed.[59]

In the six months preceding publication of the report there had been considerable concern about the product of the Filer Commission and what substantive conclusions could be reached. It was evident that the research findings would not be fully digested in time for the report, and as was to become even more apparent later, no real consensus had been reached on most of the issues. Thus writing the report had presented something of a challenge. The task had been given to Wade Greene, a freelance writer who had been selected by JDR and his staff based on their experience with Greene at a population conference in Bucharest. Greene was considered a good writer, but he was also more liberal than many commissioners and he was not very well versed on the technical issues addressed in some of the research.[60]

In the end it would be hard to claim that the final report, *Giving in America,* was an orderly outcome of discussions of the research carried out for the Filer Commission; it certainly was not. Yet it would not be quite accurate either to say that the report was entirely serendipitous, or created without awareness of the commission's research or diverse points of view debated by the expert advisors and commission members. The truth was somewhere in between—the report was difficult to write because there were in fact differences of opinion on the commission, as well as differential understanding of the issues, and varying amounts of involvement in commission deliberations. Evidently many of the references to particular research papers were added to chapters after initial drafts had been completed, and moreover in regard to decisions about content, institutional loyalties and personal viewpoints on fundamental matters had proved hard to change. However, since no one seemed satisfied with the outcome, it could be argued that a compromise position had actually been reached.

In any case, when the final report was printed, 25 pages out of a 220-page text were devoted to comments and dissents, from both the left and the right.

It will be recalled that a union leader had already resigned from the commission because of disagreement with the report and its recommendations. Still, as the following comments suggest, some commissioners continued to have strong feelings about the process and the product:

> The Commission on Private Philanthropy and Public Needs is itself a prime example of institutional philanthropy's neglect of women, only four out of 28 Commission members have been women and only eight out of the Commission's 118 advisers have been women. No study was prepared on women.[61]

Altogether there were several pages of comments by this group of women, including an emphatic expression of their belief that private philanthropy can only fulfill its role in American society if "it is willing to listen to the advocates of social change, that is those who are articulating public needs from the point of view of those in need."[62]

On the other side, conservative commissioners, including Max Fisher, Lester Crown, Raymond Gallagher, Philip Klutznick, and Ralph Lazarus were equally dissatisfied. This may be seen in the following excerpt from their extensive comments:

> The writing of the text of the report does not do justice to the substance of the Commission's discussion, nor to its conclusions. . . . The report is excessively a defensive response to a series of alleged criticisms of philanthropy. . . . Another defect in the Report is the distortion of the concepts of "equity" and "democracy" applied to philanthropy by the "wealthy." The fact that the wealthy make the largest gifts and have the freedom to decide the object of their gifts, is referred to as inequitable and undemocratic. . . . Yet . . . givers should be able to designate the purposes and objects of their gifts.[63]

Thus, dissatisfaction with the content remained—despite the fact that the report was supposed to have been presented for discussion by the whole commission in June 1975. Moreover, as the report was being completed, a commission subcommittee had been designated to work with Wade Greene in an "oversight" capacity. The committee had included commission stalwarts David Truman and Jon Newman, as well as Burt Knauft and Porter McKeever. While Newman remained involved, McKeever and Knauft in the end seemed to play an increasingly active role. As drafts of the report were circulating, portions had also been modified as a result of suggestions from various commissioners as well as from Filer and Rockefeller. Nevertheless as the report and its recommendations were being finalized, Rockefeller and his staff apparently still had concerns about the final product. Consequently Elizabeth McCormack and Porter McKeever met alone with John Filer for an urgent discussion.[64] It was later reported that the only way to insure issuing a report of the whole commission was by allowing dissenting comments to be included prominently.[65]

In any case, the Donee Group prepared a dissenting report, "Private Philanthropy: Vital and Innovative or Passive and Irrelevant." Their report was separate from, and in some ways parallel to, *Giving in America;* but it was written with commission funding, and it was also widely distributed. In addition, it was to be included later in the commission's published *Research Papers.* Finally, the Donee Group was to be a significant factor in events that followed the issuance of the Filer Commission Report.

10

Filer Commission Follow-Up

Missed Opportunities and Emergent New Groups

At the same time that the charitable deduction is being challenged philosophically, it is being eroded, in very concrete terms, by liberalizations of the standard deduction, the income tax provision that allows taxpayers to deduct a set amount or a proportion of their income in lieu of taking specific, itemized deductions.

—Filer Commission Report, 1975

It is worth remembering that the tax and financial matters which occupied so much of the Commission's time and resources were not ends in themselves, but merely means to achieve policy goals. We regret that the Commission too often failed to recognize that it was dealing with public policy issues affecting the lives of real people.

—Donee Group Report, 1975

Regardless of how the pie is sliced, there is no question that grants made directly for social change or to assist the powerless are dwarfed by the massive philanthropic contributions made annually in support of education, the arts, health services and the like.

—Sarah Carey, in *Research Papers,* 1977

The Commission Report

On December 2, 1975 the Filer Commission Report was presented officially —first in the Congressional offices of the Ways and Means Committee chair, Al Ullman, and then, in the best of political traditions, later on the same day at the Washington Press Club. John Filer made the formal presentation with two short speeches; and William Simon and John Rockefeller participated in the ceremonies with a statement that stressed the idea of an ongoing Congressionally established commission. Leonard Silverstein and Gabe Rudney were present as well as other commission members and consultants. Members of the Donee Group participated, and Pablo Eisenberg presented their report.[1]

Despite the luster of the group, the event did not get front-page headlines after the press conference, and John Rockefeller was reported to have been disappointed with the amount of attention it received.[2] In any case, the President was in China and it was also reported that the story had been leaked earlier to the press from San Francisco.[3] Interestingly, an earlier article in the *Wall Street Journal* on November 26 totally omitted any reference to one of the report's principal recommendations—a permanent advisory commission on the nonprofit sector—and in an article in the *New York Times* Eileen Shanahan mentioned the proposed permanent national commission only briefly, in the context of the objection to it by Leo Perlis (the union representative who had resigned from the commission). In general the Shanahan article featured the dissenting Donee Group, while the article in the *Journal* emphasized the pedestrian nature of the report and noted that the liberals on the commission seemed to have been out-talked by the conservatives, and in particular by Max Fisher, who was characterized as a big supporter of President Ford.[4]

The *Wall Street Journal* article stated that two factual findings dominated the Filer Commission conclusions: the first was that the nonprofit sector was "in 'Acute Crisis' financially" and the second was that "income classes differ markedly In what they give to"—upper-bracket Individuals give more to education, hospitals, and culture while lower-income individuals tend to favor churches and religious causes. In fact the first point was made in the report, but was only partially true: it was essentially religious groups that were suffering from declining revenues; other groups apparently were still benefitting from big gifts or government support.[5] On the other hand, while actually not a primary point of emphasis in *Giving in America,* the second concern was a part of commission discussions, and the significance of these findings was not lost in the *Journal's* analysis. Modifications in tax incentives would indeed affect who gets what, and once again, the major institutional bodies (museums, universities, hospitals) would be likely to have the most to lose from changes in the tax laws, and particularly from any changes in the rules that allowed gifts of appreciated property (stocks, works of art, etc.) to charitable organizations (other than foundations) to be deducted from the donor's income at their appreciated value.[6]

The appreciation issue was particularly problematic. Beyond the analysis in the newspaper, it was clear to analysts of tax policy, and to most commissioners, that the tax code permitted the donor of appreciated property to gain twice: first, he avoided a capital gains tax on property which had increased in value; second, he gained from the large deduction from income based on the total appreciated value. Thus, even presumably liberal commissioners had to recognize the special benefit that this policy afforded wealthy donors. In fact, the issues of equity involved in this situation were debated at length by the commission, while they were at the same time also under Congressional scrutiny in hearings on what would eventually become the Tax Reform Act of 1976.[7] In this context some commissioners argued strongly that resolution of this issue could not relate to the charitable gift alone, since it was inextricably bound to more systematic revision of the tax code related to treatment of capital gains and gift and estate taxes.[8] In the end, perhaps not surprisingly, the commission report came out generally in support of the status quo with regard to charitable bequests, stating explicitly "that the charitable bequest deduction be retained in its present form."[9] More broadly, while recognizing some problems that needed correction, the Filer Commission Report declared that "the charitable deduction should be retained and added onto rather than replaced by another form of governmental encouragement in giving."[10] The commission affirmed the basic rationale of the deduction, that giving should not be taxed because it does not enrich the donor. Meanwhile the Congress was still attempting to enact some reforms in the House tax bill.[11]

In the context of inequitable benefits to rich donors, and concomitant inequality among recipient organizations, some Filer Commission members, as well as the Donee Group, had pushed for a tax credit to replace or augment the existing system. To encourage low-income donors to give more, either a tax credit or an additional deduction (over the standard deduction) for non-itemizers seemed acceptable. However, with a tax credit actual tax payments would be reduced by some percentage (up to 100 percent) of the actual amount of the contribution and consequently a donor would benefit directly from lower taxes. In the discussions some commissioners, including Elizabeth McCormack, supported the idea of a tax credit and argued that it could represent a dramatic breakthrough in the democratization of philanthropy—but while it was in fact recommended in the final Donee Group Report, the tax credit was rejected by more cautious members of the commission, who seemed afraid that such a change in the tax code might open up a Pandora's box. Other experts also argued that either of these changes could result in a serious loss of tax revenues and would not be welcomed by the Treasury Department.[12] Ultimately the commission did recommend two changes to benefit lower-income donors: (1) a separate charitable deduction for those who took the standard deduction and (2) a two-tier special double deduction by which donors with incomes below $15,000 would get a double reduction from taxable income, and families with incomes between $15,000 and 30,000 annually would receive a 150 percent deduction.[13]

In the end, despite the fact that a report was published, the commission did not appear to have really reached consensus on most issues, although there had been some effort to capture an informal sense of agreement during the meetings.[14] A plenary meeting of the commission to approve the final report was planned for mid-June 1975, but it is not clear that it actually took place.[15] Indeed it seems as though most feedback on the document, including recommendations, occurred through mail and phone calls, plus a few small group meetings.[16] In any case, between the voices of the Donee Group and the resistance of the conservatives to any suggestion about flaws in the philanthropic system, it was hardly surprising that the Filer Commission did not reach a true consensus. Consequently its process violated one of the cardinal rules for commissions: to be effective, commissions are supposed to achieve some kind of unanimity in their conclusions.[17] However, the staff (Rudney and Silverstein in particular) were probably more concerned about influencing tax policy through expert documentation than in achieving true consensus.

Although the Filer Commission had a long afterlife, the report itself had not accomplished what JDR 3rd was said to have most wanted from it—to present a bright new vision of philanthropy's role in meeting social needs and also innovative recommendations for increasing charitable giving.[18] In this framework a critical part of his intention was to promote greater contributions from the corporate community, as well as broadening the contribution base from lower-income givers. However, as it turned out, the first idea was not popular with businessmen and some members of the commission. And although he had better luck with the second issue, the report's recommendations were probably still not as dramatic as JDR would have liked them to be. In any case, the commission debated several options for broadening the donor base, but in the end came out more cautiously for charitable deductions for non-itemizers and increased deductions for low and moderate income donors.[19] The report was also criticized for not having given enough attention to the enormous role of government funding of the voluntary sector.

Altogether the commission came up with 19 recommendations in its report, divided into three main areas: (I) Broadening the Base of Philanthropy; (II) Improving the Philanthropic Process; and (III) A Permanent Commission. Under the first area was the concept of "broadening the contributions base" through tax specific recommendations and increased corporate giving; under the second were matters of accessibility and public visibility, minimizing self-benefitting, and loosening limitations on lobbying by nonprofit organizations, other than foundations; and the third was the proposed quasi-public commission on the nonprofit sector.[20] Several recommendations, such as "broadening the boards and staffs of nonprofits," and increasing the actual amount of corporate giving, were of a more "hortatory nature," but most required Congressional action.[21] Only two recommendations were specifically focused on foundations; one asked for a new category of "independent" foundations, and the other recommended a flat 5 percent payout rate. In addition, foundations were explicitly excluded from a recommended loosening of restrictions on lobbying activity.[22]

As a whole the recommendations were described as addressing "the third sector." However, probably most recommendations could be defined more accurately as focusing on the "charitable" part of the third sector, either through their regulatory intent or in relation to motivations for giving. Two key words in the report were in fact "incentives" (to giving) and "accountability"; and for a group concerned about the voluntary sector, the report gave considerable attention to regulation. In addition there was of course the key notion of a permanent, national commission on nonprofit organizations which was aimed at increasing the legitimacy of the sector.[23] Notably, despite the recommendation for a quasi-public commission and strong feelings against the IRS in commission discussions, the report also included a strong statement in favor of keeping oversight and monitoring of nonprofit activity in the IRS. In this regard it should be remembered that the IRS was after all located within the Treasury Department, and Treasury was a supporter of the commission's efforts. Moreover, several of the recommendations would require IRS action or cooperation.[24]

Of all the commission recommendations, among those most worked over was the proposal for an ongoing "independent" commission for the nonprofit sector. Adam Yarmolinsky and Marion Fremont-Smith, both located in Boston, revised and rewrote the proposals for such an entity many times and still were unable to reach a resolution that was satisfactory to everyone.[25] The major problem was the nature of auspices: some commissioners were convinced that, like the Charity Commission for England and Wales, a future commission had to have a degree of public authority, through approval of the President and Congress;[26] others were equally adamant that such a commission had to be established under private auspices, in addition to being funded totally from the private sector. The question of auspices also affected its relation to the IRS; if the permanent commission were public, its functions might be perceived as overlapping or duplicating those of the IRS.

Some drafts defining the auspices of the permanent commission demonstrate painful efforts to walk a careful line on this issue, and there also seems to have been some fear that if a new commission took over IRS functions it would increase regulation of the sector.[27] Details about how many members there would be, or exactly who would appoint them, were also discussed and modified within the rubric of the bigger public-private question.[28] In the end the recommendation was for a quasi-public organization, grounded in Congressional authority, with approximately 50 percent of the members being Presidential appointees (12 out of 20–25 members) and the others privately selected. It would be somehow funded with private money. (The problem of public or private dominance was partially obscured by ambiguity about the size of the group.) Moreover, in a manner similar to the Peterson Commission actions, along the way, draft legislation was prepared for the national commission.[29] The permanent commission was not defined as a monitoring body, and indeed the commission report also included a role for the states in regulating intra-state charitable solicitations. Still the recommendation for a permanent commission aroused concern among some commissioners who were interested in promoting voluntary auspices for any coordinating body.[30]

The Donee Group: Process and Product

Given the close connection to Treasury and the anticipation of a continuing commission of some kind, it was not surprising that rather than marking a sharp end of the commission's influence, December 2, 1975 actually initiated a transition to another level of activity. In the next eighteen months, the research papers were to be published by the Treasury Department, and continued efforts were made to enact some of the recommendations in the report. For some commission members particular effort centered on the issue of the national commission on nonprofits, but the line between that effort and the establishment of a government advisory committee was not always sharp. The new pluralism of the group also came into conflict with narrower views of tax policy and philanthropy.

In the previous chapter it was already noted that after the initial debate of Bittker and Surrey (January 1974), the Filer Commission as a whole became relatively inactive in the absence of a legislative crisis and with apparently only a sometime-attentive Chairman.[31] For almost a year the principal activity was taking place at the periphery: commissioning and review of research papers, discussions with consultants or the "Advisory Committee," and initial considerations of fund raising.[32] Then, about the time of the publication of Pablo Eisenberg's article in the *Grantsmanship Center News* (January 1975), the commission appeared to reawaken, and for a while monthly meetings were held on carefully delineated tax and regulatory issues.

It is not clear that Eisenberg's article was the actual cause of the Filer Commission's renewed energy, but certainly the event made a difference in what happened subsequently. Characteristically, after the article came to his attention, Leonard Silverstein called Eisenberg, expressed anger over its content, and arranged a meeting with Eisenberg. At that meeting Eisenberg was asked if he could pull together some representatives of the "public interest/social action groups," and he accepted the offer with alacrity.[33] By March 6 the "public interest groups" convened in Washington, with Norton Kiritz, editor of the *Grantsmanship Center News* and director of the progressive Grantsmanship Center (Los Angeles) and Charles Halpern, an activist attorney, among those present. Subsequently Halpern and Kiritz were invited as observers to the March meeting of the commission (Chicago, March 10–11) and in connection with that meeting they met with Filer and a small group of commissioners.

In his reasoned plea for cooperative efforts between the two groups, Kiritz gave his own credentials and reminded the group that it was in danger of repeating the mistakes that foundations had made in 1969. Kiritz stressed the importance of the commission's reaching the broader constituencies of philanthropy and he urged inclusion of recipient organizations (the donees) in commission deliberations.[34] The arguments presented must have been persuasive, because Filer and Silverstein set up a meeting of the new group with representatives of the commission in Washington on April 3. Then at its subsequent meeting of April 7–8, after an effective presentation by Pablo Eisenberg, and with the active support of Chairman Filer, the commission passed a resolution for "additional research consultation" by the group of public interest/social action and voluntary organizations.[35] Thereafter a staff person for the group was also located within the office of Silverstein's law firm to insure that there would be appropriate communication between the two groups.

Matters now became more complicated as the commission's proposed agenda began to be punctuated by the dedicated energies of what was in effect an opposition group. Indeed, it could be argued that bringing such a group essentially within the commission's boundaries was a mistake. However, it appears that some commissioners, and John Filer himself, recognized the validity of the arguments being made about changes in American society; it also seems that some of JDR's staff, and even JDR, welcomed the fresh air that the new group could bring to the commission's deliberations.[36] By this time Porter McKeever had joined JDR's personal staff officially, and he was essentially the "point man" for JDR's philanthropic issues; Elizabeth McCormack worked with McKeever but was now also involved with the Rockefeller Brothers Fund. As it turned out, apparently John Filer and Burt Knauft viewed the new directions favorably, and JDR and McKeever also seemed open to the excitement that was generated; moreover, Rockefeller reportedly had confidence in Pablo Eisenberg.[37] This was important because personal accountability meant a great deal to JDR.

Although some commissioners (and staff) might not have been enthusiastic about the idea, initially there seems to have been no serious objection to working with what became known as the Donee Group or to giving them a small amount of financial support. Since the commission was in the process of raising over two million dollars, an allowance of about $50,000 to the donees hardly seemed alarming, and since the staff for the Donee Group was to consist of one person located in Silverstein's offices, their existence probably was not viewed as threatening.[38] Furthermore, these were changing times, with emerging pressures for diversity. Indeed, a significant outside source (which was in fact cited by Kiritz) presented another reason for enlarging the field of action: Vance Hartke, Chairman of the Subcommittee on Foundations of the Senate Finance Committee, had gone on record in February with the following statement:

> The Filer Commission should be completing its work in June. In the time that is remaining, I hope that its distinguished members and staff will reach out to a broader spectrum of the population for information and support assistance. Just as in any field of interest, there is an established group of experts who are called upon time after time for their advice and knowledge. The Commission has done an excellent job of harnessing these people for its work, but it cannot afford to neglect a whole wealth of as yet untapped talent which can lend a new and equally valuable perspective to the field of philanthropy.[39]

Thereafter matters did not turn out exactly as planned. To begin with, the staff person chosen to work in Silverstein's office (apparently by Eisenberg) was Ted Jacobs, whose previous position had been with Ralph Nader. His style could not have been more different from Silverstein's or the traditional and legal atmosphere of the Silverstein and Mullens law firm. Inevitably there were continued tensions in the office, and these seem to have escalated after Ted Jacobs chaired a meeting of representatives of the "public interest, social action and voluntary organizations" at the end of April. Although he was still referred to as "the director of the Commission's Ad Hoc Donee Group" in June 1975,[40] he had already accepted another job. In the end a final Donee Group Report was actually written by Jim Abernathy, a young man with a far less confrontational manner, but who nonetheless wrote a highly controversial report.

In the period from April through the summer of 1975, as final drafts of the Filer Commission Report were circulating among the commissioners, the "social action" group began to meet with increasing intensity.[41] An official commission meeting for review of their report and recommendations was not scheduled until June, but copies of chapter drafts were available before then. In any case the Donee Group had observers at the April and May meetings of the commission, so they were aware of the substance of the discussions—even though the report itself was being written outside of the full group, by Wade Greene and the subcommittee. In this period, on June 16, 1975, the "Interim Report of the Donee Group to the Commission on Private Philanthropy and Public Needs" was submitted. Presumably this was in the context of the proposed review of the Filer Commission Report scheduled for June 16–17, 1975. As agreed upon with the commission, the Interim Donee Report dealt with some of the value issues being ignored in the Filer Commission discussions,[42] and did not yet contain a set of recommendations of its own. Instead the report critiqued the Filer Commission Report and deliberations, and made suggestions for further action on the part of the commission. In response to a major omission in Filer Commission considerations, the Donee Group urged the establishment of a "Task Force on Public Needs" for studying questions related to the critical issue of "Who Benefits?"[43]

After the Donee Group's interim report was presented, at the end of June 1975, a large conference and open discussion of commission issues was held in California.[44] According to the *Grantsmanship Center News,* this conference was organized by the Southern California Citizens Task Force on Private Philanthropy and Public Needs, "a voluntary ad hoc committee of primarily Donee Representatives from the Los Angeles area." The meeting was open to members of the donee community on the West Coast who had not been previously included in commission deliberations, and it was cosponsored by the Filer Commission and the Donee Group. Representatives of many different kinds of recipient groups participated, and the process differed greatly from the way that the commission typically conducted business. Altogether over 100 people attended; eleven commissioners were present, and Burt Knauft (presumably in lieu of John Filer) as well as Gabe Rudney had significant roles in the events.[45] Consideration of the issues included elaborate procedures for voting on various options related to recommendations of the Filer Commission, and questions and ballots were available by mail through the *Grantsmanship Center News.*[46]

The discussion in Los Angeles was lively, with some interesting surprises. As reported in the *Grantsmanship Center News* later, donee groups at the Conference proved to be as conservative as Filer Commission members on at least one issue: in their voting, they supported continuation of the existing law regarding deductibility of appreciated gifts to charity at full current value. These were after all recipient organizations (including some representatives of small cultural and educational institutions), and therefore they might also have an interest in protecting incentives for giving (even if such incentives provided disproportional tax benefits for the rich). However, it also seems that the wording of that issue may have been confusing to people who were not experts in tax policy.[47] Notably, despite a luncheon speech by commissioner Graciela

Olivarez in favor of a permanent commission on philanthropy and a positive vote on the idea, in the *Grantsmanship Center News* article, Norton Kiritz expressed his own skepticism about the role of such a commission, until after the present (Filer) commission had proved itself.

Now, in the summer following the conference, the Donee Group began work in earnest on a report of their own, while the Filer Commission subgroup struggled with drafts of their report and recommendations. In addition, members of the commission's Advisory Committee seem to have discussed the possibility of writing another separate, more technical tax report and recommendations.[48] Meanwhile, based on the understanding that the Donee Group had the blessings of the commission, and that their concerns were to be considered, it might have been expected that their issues would be fully incorporated in the final report of the commission. If that was the expectation, it did not come to pass. Only some of their suggested changes were made in the summer of 1975, and these were reflected in a few brief references to needy populations and pluralism in *Giving in America.*

The response to donee concerns in the Filer Commission report was evidently not satisfactory to the Donee Group. Their own separate final report would incorporate more progressive views and would not reflect the votes of the West Coast participants concerning appreciated value of gifts. It also took a strong stand on establishing a permanent public commission, and on public regulation. The tone and substance of the Donee Group Report certainly caused some consternation among the more conservative members of the commission and staff concerned with technical tax issues and political feasibility. Meanwhile Elizabeth McCormack and Porter McKeever apparently worried that the Filer Commission Report would be so bland that it would have no impact— or possibly that it might be upstaged by the more dramatic recommendations of the Donee Group, some of which raised concerns for wealthy donors and even possibly for Rockefeller-related institutions. Urgent discussions were held with JDR, and he was asked to speak with Filer directly.[49] The problem, however, was not easily resolved. In the end, after further negotiations, the Filer Commission Report was slightly modified, with dissenting comments added. But in addition the Donee Group Report, *Private Philanthropy: Vital and Innovative or Passive and Irrelevant,* was both printed separately and also included in the final compendium of Research Papers (1977), along with other papers written by members of the Donee Group.[50] This insured that there would at least be some representation of diverse views on philanthropic issues and social needs in the commission's documents.

As a whole the Donee Group actually supported many of the recommendations in the Filer Commission Report.[51] However, in their larger total of 28 recommendations there were also some that differed radically from the commission's position. Among the more startling were the following: (1) taxing all appreciation on donated property (although phasing this in over time); (2) " . . . removal of all audit and oversight functions from the I.R.S."; (3) a recommendation for a "permanent, standing committee in the House and Senate" with oversight responsibility "over any permanent regulatory or oversight agency and power to review any legislation affecting the nonprofit sector"; and (4) a recommendation for a 6 percent payout rate (plus more if there were extra gains in the assets of a foundation). These recommendations undoubtedly came from strong feelings and a pure heart, but they were unlikely to have been politically acceptable.[52] Indeed, even including this report (*cum* recommendations) in the compendium of *Research Papers* apparently was controversial.[53]

New Groups Emergence and Commission Continuance, 1976–1977

As the Rockefeller group wished, and unlike the situation with the Peterson Commission, the Filer Commission Report was released before deliberations were completed on a new tax reform act. Thus there was still work to be done, and it made sense that activity continue in the form of a follow-up committee. Indeed, on December 22 (1975) JDR 3rd met with a personal acquaintance, Robert Goheen, now President of the Council on Foundations, to discuss follow-up to the commission, and on the 24th, some JDR staff, including McKeever, Harr, and McNerney, met over the same issue.[54] Meanwhile another possible complication was arising and at a meeting in "Nelson's apartment in New York" the brothers discussed "developments in Washington" and Nelson Rockefeller's relationship to them.[55] On January 13, two days after the meeting in Nelson's apartment, there was a meeting with JDR staff, to discuss next steps for the Filer Commission "follow-up." "[I]t was agreed that a small committee should be brought into being . . . consisting mainly of Filer Commission people and that the committee should work closely with a Treasury Department Task Force on the subject and also should encourage the interest of the Ways and Means Committee in the follow-up." In addition to Elizabeth McCormack and Leonard Silverstein, William Ruder, a public relations consultant for JDR, was present, which suggests particular concern about JDR's image and role as commission activities were being assessed.[56]

After the first of the year, commission follow-up activity increased in intensity, even while there was mixed reception in the press. On January 6 an op-ed piece in the *New York Times* assessed the Filer Commission Report, criticizing the commission for being too affiliated with the charitable establishment.

The author urged the Donee and Filer groups to "seek workable accommoda-tions."[57] Meanwhile, with Secretary Simon's encouragement, inside the Treas-ury Department, officials were beginning review of the Filer Commission rec-ommendations with regard to feasibility and implementation. On the outside John Filer asked Walter McNerney to head a follow-up committee, and in early March McNerney wrote to a small group of commissioners about participating in an "ad hoc working group to provide continuity between the commission's report and the possible formation of a permanent body." Letters of invitation were sent to Douglas Dillon, Walter Haas, Herbert Longnecker, Philip Klutz-nick, Elizabeth McCormack, and Alan Pifer.[58] By this time the Donee Group had already been incorporated and had received its first financial support from JDR 3rd as well as John Filer.[59]

The first official meeting of the Filer follow-up committee was held on March 30. Committee members in attendance (McNerney [Chair], Longnecker, Pifer, and McCormack) were outnumbered by staff, who included Porter Mc-Keever, Howard Bolton, Burt Knauft, Leonard Silverstein, and Stuart Lewis.[60] Although not present, Eleanor Holmes Norton (a black woman who was the respected chairman of the New York City Commission on Human Rights) was listed as a committee member. The discussion centered around the follow-up items mentioned in JDR's January 13 diary entry, but also included other im-portant matters. The first item involved proposals by the National Council on Philanthropy (NCOP), the Coalition for the Public Good, and the "Section 501(c)(3)" group, which evidently caused some concern. Although not dis-cussed explicitly in the minutes, Bayard Ewing had in fact been involved in bringing these organizations together and in articulating their opposition to the notion of a public commission. A second item suggested that commission staff would keep in touch with the National Committee for Responsive Philan-thropy; and a third item referred to distribution of the report and the research papers. Also discussed was the commission's budgetary deficit as of March 31, 1976.[61]

In the following months there were so many spinoff-group meetings with slightly different members present, and with government officials or without them, that it seems to have been difficult even for participants to keep matters of auspices and content straight.[62] Although by then Gabriel Rudney had re-turned to the Treasury Department, the Filer follow-up core group remained the same. In this period generally commission-related activity could be charac-terized as consisting of several basic elements: first, the commission follow-up committee, headed by Walter McNerney; second, the Donee Group itself, now incorporated formally as the National Committee on Responsive Philanthropy

(NCRP); third, activity in regard to publication of the *Research Papers;* fourth, internal review by Treasury staff of the Filer Commission Report; and finally, efforts by Leonard Silverstein to maintain a close liaison with Treasury officials around various structural issues and tax policy.

Also during this time, on a separate but related tack, Yale University President Kingman Brewster, with the help of law professor John Simon, for more than eighteen months had been moving in the direction of securing a place at Yale for future research on the nonprofit sector. By July 1976 their efforts were progressing well, and they had succeeded in obtaining a small planning grant from JDR for development of a nonprofit research center.[63] Meanwhile, the earlier existing private philanthropic groups, including the National Council on Philanthropy, the Coalition for the Public Good, and the 501(c)(3) group, had in a sense returned to the earlier vision of the late 1960s for a private nonprofit sector coordinating group. They were stepping up efforts to strengthen self-advocacy and data collecting functions from within the nonprofit sector, and were soon to form another organization, the Coalition of Voluntary Sector Organizations, which would be known as CONVO.[64]

The new Donee Group organization (NCRP) had already been formalized, and the specific "trade" groups of nonprofit organizations were coalescing, but at this time the Filer Commission group was still struggling to create an effective identity. In connection with this process, meetings of the follow-up group continued during the spring of 1976, while Silverstein and some others worked "informally, but closely" with representatives of the IRS and Treasury.[65] At the follow-up committee meeting in May, consideration was given to the "criteria for the permanent bodies being proposed within government and the private sector." The follow-up group was apparently also still expecting to present their proposals to a commission meeting "under the Chairmanship of John Filer."[66]

While the various groups were solidifying their various purposes, debate on a proposed tax bill was continuing. The bill had not yet gone to the Joint Senate-House Conference for final resolution, and Secretary of the Treasury Simon remained interested in the commission's recommendations. In reviewing the Filer Commission Report, David A. Lefeve, Special Assistant to the Secretary for Consumer Affairs, cited the value of "the collection and compendium of data" and "the suggestions for improving the philanthropic process," but came up with a mixed evaluation of the recommendations.[67] Noting that this was a time of inflation, he argued against both of the commission recommendations for increasing the charitable deduction. Lefeve liked most of the recommendations for greater accountability, had no objection to the recommendation concerning a flat 5 percent payout rate by foundations (and lower rate for other endowed tax-exempt organizations), and was willing to consider an audit fee of 2 percent (to replace the 4 percent audit tax). He firmly opposed liberalizing lobbying restrictions and the establishment of a Congressionally authorized national commission, and argued for a totally private sector organization instead. Lefeve also asked for the establishment of an interagency task force to consider the Filer Commission work more fully.

This assessment could not have been satisfactory to either JDR 3rd or the commission, and Silverstein continued his efforts with Treasury. Consideration was now given to setting up within the Treasury Department an Office of the Nonprofit Sector, to be headed by an Assistant Secretary of the Treasury.[68] Pros and cons on this proposal were discussed by Porter McKeever in a memorandum to JDR 3rd concerning his forthcoming meeting with Treasury Secretary Simon.[69] McKeever explicitly noted the "debate . . . within Treasury on the idea of an Office of the Non Profit Sector," possibly connected to an advisory committee defined by statute.[70] In this connection it apparently now seemed advisable to bring together the various groups of nonprofit organizations that had been meeting separately.

A combined meeting of these separate but overlapping groups was held on June 11, 1976. Grounds for cooperation were sought, but feelings seem to have run high. In addition to ideological differences, the groups apparently came to a near-collision over a discussion of financial support and fund raising. This meeting included representatives of "Ewing's group" of private sector organizations, Donee Group representatives, and Filer Commissioners. Philip Klutznick, an ardent supporter and still dedicated fund raiser for the Filer Commission, expressed his concern later over the direction taken with regard to the Donee Group:

> I am fearful that this division [in regard to sympathy for the outsider and "new and sometimes engaging causes"] which was far deeper in the Commission than we permitted ourselves to admit may become a factor that will discourage positive advancements of the Filer Commission endeavor. . . . I do not feel that aid and comfort to the "donee group" will serve the purpose of avoiding more extensive reforms, nevertheless, I do feel that a substantial minority is entitled to be treated with respect to their concerns.[71]

A subsequent letter from Douglas Dillon was even more stern in assessing the Donee Group as opposed "to our support of philanthropy as it presently exists in the United States." However, Dillon recognized that future meetings with the Treasury Department might necessitate the different groups working together.[72]

Over the summer activity continued both inside of government and out.

Yale continued its fund raising efforts with foundations, while the new National Committee for Responsive Philanthropy also was initiating its own activities. Meanwhile Leonard Silverstein continued acting as Executive Director of the commission, and in August he sent the follow-up committee material on the Treasury reaction to the Filer Commission Recommendations along with an Agenda for a Meeting with Treasury.[73] Also included was a recent memorandum from David Lefeve to Deputy Secretary Dixon, who now stated that he could "support 14 out of the 19 Commission recommendations." The five recommendations which Lefeve could not support were the two related to increasing the charitable deduction, the recommendation for an independent foundation category, the permanent "quasi-governmental" commission on the nonprofit sector, and the requirement for larger organizations to hold annual meetings—which he believed was a matter of "exhortation." Lefeve also noted that "Walter McNerney and Leonard Silverstein have gone . . . further in proposing that an assistant secretary position be established in the Treasury to supervise the nonprofit sector" (which he said would be costly and was not in the original proposal).[74]

Nonetheless, Silverstein (who was both skillful and persistent) had apparently discussed some proposals with the IRS and Treasury, who had found them satisfactory "on an informal basis." Among these proposals was the establishment of what was now called "the Advisory Commission to the Secretary of the Treasury." Other proposals suggested were an Office of Exempt Organization Analysis and a Division of Solicitation within the Office of the Assistant Commissioner (Pensions and Exempt Organizations).[75] In any case, by mid-September, Lefeve was gone and a new assistant (John Walker) was "assigned to work with Commission concerns."[76]

In the fall, on October 4, 1976, President Ford signed the Tax Reform Act of 1976 (PL 94-4555), a month before the national election. The Senate had finally approved the House Bill (HR 106125), but with many modifications which made it more friendly to supporters of philanthropy; thereafter the bill had moved fairly rapidly through the Conference Committee. Although few of the Filer Commission's recommendations had been enacted in the 1976 tax law, advocates for the sector had succeeded in important ways; they had ensured the maintenance of an essentially favorable status quo with regard to taxes on gifts of appreciated property and the charitable deduction. Rules about estate and gift taxes were modified, but charitable trusts were not attacked. In addition, the new law incorporated greater clarity and more permissive limits regarding lobbying activity by public charities, and increased maximum amounts of permissible deductions (to 60 percent of income). The Act also fixed the mandatory payout rate of foundations at 5 percent, replacing the 1969 Tax Reform Act requirement of 6 percent.[77]

A New Ball Game

On January 6, 1977, after some compromises on the part of Rudney and Silverstein, a first meeting was finally held of the officially constituted "Treasury Advisory Committee on Private Philanthropy and Public Needs." Committee membership reflected ideological diversity, with representatives from three different groups—the Filer follow-up committee, the Ewing group, and the social action organizations.[78] It was chaired by Douglas Dillon, and included George Romney, Walter McNerney, Marion Fremont-Smith, William Aramony (Chief Executive Officer of the United Way of America), as well as Pablo Eisenberg and other social activists. Although Jimmy Carter had already won the election and a new Democratic administration would be taking office, at the meeting William Simon announced that the Committee had the approval of Treasury Secretary–Designate Michael S. Blumenthal. Despite this auspicious beginning, it was not long before the group appeared to be in serious trouble with the new administration.

By March 15 the newspapers reported that Blumenthal had reduced the number of Treasury Department Advisory Committees from 27 to 11, and that he was "still reviewing the functions of three committees." One of the committees under review was the Advisory Committee on Private Philanthropy and Public Needs.[79] It was noted that three criteria "established by the President" were being used to evaluate the committees; these were: "compelling need," "diversity of viewpoints," and "public access and participation." Final recommendations were to be made to the President by April 15. Soon thereafter JDR wrote to Stuart Eizenstat, a special assistant to President Carter, requesting a meeting with him.[80] Later in July Porter McKeever, always concerned about appropriate roles for JDR 3rd, wrote a letter to Bill Ruder about corporate philanthropy, which also seems to indicate renewed involvement in this matter for JDR 3rd.[81]

In the meantime, the reported Advisory Committee met with representatives of the Treasury and the IRS on April 7, in a massive group meeting that seemed to meet the President's criteria but was nevertheless unsuccessful.[82] By April 11 a headline in the *Washington Star* proclaimed "Advisory Panel's Future May Be Past," and by April 27 Silverstein had received a negative letter from Blumenthal about the possibility of continuing the group.[83] However, Blumenthal suggested that the administration (particularly Laurence Woodworth, who now held a post within Treasury) valued Silverstein's advice and would help with "reconstituting the Committee" as an informal "private organization" with whom they could work.

Toward the end of June, McNerney, Eisenberg, and David Rogers (of the Johnson Foundation) met with members of the administration, including Eizenstat and representatives of Treasury and the Office of Management and Budget. After a conference call with the group later, McKeever reported to JDR 3rd that "the meeting went well," but that the administration only wanted informal arrangements. Furthermore, in what could have been interpreted ominously, a tax reform bill "that would deal with appreciated property, the standard deduction and other issues of great interest to the nonprofit community" was to be sent to Capitol Hill at the end of September. McKeever also referred to a possible meeting "of the Blumenthal/Filer people," noting that the "composition of the group remains a problem."[84]

In effect the "Blumenthal Committee" (as they apparently referred to the Treasury advisory group) had been dissolved by Blumenthal, but nevertheless in August the group (with some change of composition) seems to have participated in a Conference on Philanthropy in Washington, and later, using the name "Advisory Committee on Private Philanthropy and Public Needs," met with Carter administration officials again.[85] At this meeting Eizenstat definitively dismissed any idea of a Treasury advisory committee and suggested instead that the group might be able to help the administration in its search for solutions to the urban crisis. Eizenstat indicated that if they had any ideas on this issue, the President would welcome them. But that of course was not the role of the Filer Commission Committee, and although McNerney promised to look into the urban issue, there seemed little reason to be optimistic about the Committee's continuance.[86]

Still, with Gabe Rudney's assistance, another meeting of the advisory group was held in October. However by now the likelihood of realizing a Filer-related formal advisory group to Treasury was coming to an end. Even if, as Secretary of Treasury Blumenthal had suggested, particular individual attorneys and tax experts would continue to have some access to Treasury officials, the possibility of a unified and formal advisory group working with government was essentially gone. The private umbrella group of voluntary sector (recipient) organizations, led by CONVO, was being energized with considerable involvement of some former Filer Commission members and staff from the United Way of America; it was also clear that these individuals represented more traditional groups. At the same time, the activist National Committee for Responsive Philanthropy was accelerating its critique of the elitist foundations as well as of the previously sacred United Way, whose leadership was dominant in the other group.[87]

Nevertheless, although the battle lines had been drawn, it was still almost a year before the somewhat parallel, but clearly more visionary, concept of a permanent national commission on philanthropy was dealt its final blow. This happened when John D. Rockefeller 3rd was killed in a car accident on July 10, 1978. With his death the idea of a national commission lost its most powerful supporter and no longer seemed to be viable.

11

Lessons from the Past
and Issues for the Future

Congress and its tax writing committees have done an irresponsible job of
monitoring the tax expenditure budget. Measures must be put in place that
will assure oversight and accountability. Currently, almost all of the tax
expenditure budget is permanent. The tax committees are under less
pressure than any other Congressional committees to take their
oversight seriously.

—Common Cause, 1978, quoted in *The Great American Tax Revolt*, 1979

Legacies and Descendants

At the end of the 1970s, and after the death of JDR 3rd, efforts to create a
quasi-governmental oversight organization for the voluntary sector were
replaced by the development of a private-nonprofit coordinating mechanism.
Many groups had a stake in the outcome, but two of them—the Coalition of
Voluntary Organizations (CONVO) and the National Council on Philanthropy
(NCOP)—had the greatest interest in bringing it about. CONVO was only three
years old, while NCOP had a longer, proud history, but by late 1978 both of
these organizations lacked a full-time executive director and were uncertain
about their future direction.[1] Leaders of NCOP and CONVO arranged with
Brian O'Connell, National Director of the Mental Health Association and well
established in the nonprofit field, to carry out a feasibility study of options for
collaboration. When this study recommended merging NCOP and CONVO
into a new organization, O'Connell was asked to serve as the executive for both
organizations while an organizing committee worked out implementation plans
for their merger. By late December 1979 the two organizations had agreed to
the reorganization plan, and O'Connell became the first Executive Director of
the emergent entity.[2]

On March 5, 1980, with considerable media attention and an inaugural address by John Gardner (one of the instigators of the merger), 234 people and the press attended a charter meeting of the new organization, now named IN-DEPENDENT SECTOR.[3] The mission of Independent Sector incorporated elements originally included in discussions of the quasi-public commission proposed by the Filer Commission, such as data collection and research, as well as "protection" of the nonprofit sector. Moreover, it encompassed both public charities and "private" foundations in one organization. But the new organization was clearly delineated as non-governmental, with no official connection either to Congress or the national administration (President or Treasury Department). And with the more permissive lobbying rules proposed under the 1976 Tax Reform Act, Independent Sector could also position itself as an educational organization with advocacy activity.[4] In any case, as Independent Sector was created, the Filer Commission went out of business officially and its certificate of incorporation was withdrawn.[5] Despite what has been called the "great tax revolt of 1978" and the words of Common Cause quoted above, no new mechanism was established to monitor tax expenditures—or to ensure formal oversight of the activities of charitable organizations.[6]

By the early 1980s when a new Republican administration was settled in Washington, the idea of a permanent (and unified) public—or even quasi-public—charity commission was barely a memory. In its place, instead, were two organizations that represented very different views of the roles of philanthropy; the first was the activist, and controversial, National Committee for Responsive Philanthropy (NCRP); the second was the newer Independent Sector, the main-line organization which essentially rose out of the ashes of the Filer Commission and would attempt to keep alive its commitment to promotion of the nonprofit sector. Among other related organizations were the National Charities Information Bureau and the Philanthropic Advisory Service of the Better Business Bureau, which provided reports on charitable organizations and set their own standards for the sector.[7]

Both Independent Sector and NCRP were voluntary sector-membership organizations in the national capital and both were concerned with the condition of the third sector. Moreover, they both used the tools of research and information dissemination as primary means of carrying out their mission. Nonetheless, it could hardly be said that Independent Sector and NCRP worked together, and in fact their activities had a distinctly different focus and style. The outside critic role of NCRP placed it at the progressive end of the political spectrum, and helped to keep it small in size; the inclusive role chosen by Independent Sector shaped it as a more moderate, middle-of-the road organization, courting the support of a wide range of practitioners and researchers even while it increased the scope of its advocacy efforts. In effect in this period both organizations continued to bear the strong imprint of their origins and the diverse viewpoints of their founders.[8]

In keeping with its mission, Independent Sector held its first major research conference in 1983, ten years after the creation of the Filer Commission, and (perhaps not entirely by coincidence) at a time when significant tax legislation was again under consideration in Congress. The conference theme was "Since the Filer Commission . . . "; its focus was on the state of nonprofit sector research and the development of the third sector in the decade after the Filer Commission was created. The breadth of topics covered, and the number of practitioners and scholars from various disciplines at the conference, testified to one of the accomplishments of the Filer Commission: the awakening of interest in a field of studies centering on what was now—largely as a result of the Filer Commission and of the persistent efforts of John D. Rockefeller 3rd—more clearly identified as a separate sector of American life.

Among the key papers delivered at the Independent Sector conference was one about the Filer Commission by E. B. Knauft, John Filer's staff representative to the commission.[9] Given his personal investment in it, it was not surprising that Knauft took a positive view of the commission's efforts and their impact on public policy. However, it was not a totally euphoric assessment.[10] In his paper Knauft presented a descriptive assessment of Filer Commission achievements at the ten-year mark, including the research papers and recommendations. Knauft noted the value of the 91 research papers and the involvement of the Donee Group, and reviewed the fate of the 19 recommendations of the commission specifically; he concluded that there was some degree of positive outcome for at least 13.

In a subsequent article in *Foundation News,*[11] Knauft reiterated the point that by 1984 six of the more "quantifiable" recommendations had been realized, including: allowing non-itemizers to deduct their charitable contributions separately from their standard deduction; reducing the 4 percent excise tax to a 2 percent amount that more closely represented the true audit costs; a flat payout rate of 5 percent (rather than the higher 6 percent amount, and adjustable rates, carried over from the 1969 Tax Act); insuring that larger public charities (excluding churches) make their annual reports available; protection of the right of nonprofit organizations to lobby around legislative issues; and the continuation of the deduction for property gifts at appreciated value. Knauft also suggested that the commission might "take some credit" for maintaining the status quo with regard to charitable bequest deductions, exclusion of charitable deductions from the minimum tax provision, and continuation of IRS oversight of tax-exempt organizations. He noted that achievement of several more exhortative recommendations (i.e., corporate contributions goals, public meetings for philanthropic organizations, and diversity of staff and volunteers) could not be measured, but indicated that they had received more attention since the Filer Commission Report. Although Knauft did not attempt to prove that subsequent policy successes were direct results of commission activities, he suggested they could be viewed as eventual outcomes of commission efforts. In addition Knauft considered the creation of Independent Sector to be a realization in "modified form" of another recommendation—establishment of the quasi-public commission.[12] However, since the modifications in structure and function from the original proposal represented significant differences, this conclusion is debatable.

In his assessment, Knauft, like Pablo Eisenberg in another conference paper, reported that the Filer Commission had failed to come to grips with some larger questions referred to in its own case statement—notably, the role of the third sector in meeting human needs and its relationship to the other two institutional sectors of American life. Both Eisenberg and Knauft believed there was more work to be done,[13] but there were differences in emphasis in their two papers. Eisenberg presented a critique of Filer Commission research, stressing that it had not addressed Donee Group concerns about accessibility for diverse groups, equity in funding, and accountability, and he argued that a future research agenda was needed in these areas. Knauft also concluded that more research on critical issues was needed, but elaborated more on optional mechanisms for doing this (e.g., through Independent Sector or by formation of another group).[14]

Two Commissions in Comparison

Although Knauft mentioned the Peterson Commission, most of the papers at the 1983 Research Forum ignored the earlier commission, probably in part because Peterson's positions on the high payout rate and other matters were not popular.[15] Nonetheless, analysis of the Peterson and Filer Commissions from a longer distance reveals strong similarities as well as differences. Similarities are readily apparent; both commissions were private organizations and both were initiated by JDR 3rd. To some extent they each commanded attention from Congress and the Treasury Department but their appointees (some of whom were public officials) were not officially authorized by either the President or Congress.[16] (In comparison, however, the Filer Commission suffered more from presidential tribulations—Nixon problems—and change-over in administrations, from Ford to Carter.)[17] Both commissions were focused on tax policy and philanthropy; both were obsessed, and correctly so, with the lack of available information (data) about the voluntary, nonprofit sector. Both commissions were also headed by businessmen who previously had little connection with philanthropic activity; despite this, neither had much real success in developing greater corporate participation in philanthropy.

Both commissions were expected to deal with tax law and related philanthropic issues—but in each case, their "take" on some issues was not totally acceptable to groups that might have been assumed to support their efforts. Indeed, for both commissions there was some ambiguity about the nature of their constituency. Because of their origins and subsequent practices the connection to the Rockefeller office was always a factor, but this connection did not necessarily insure the support of the rest of the foundation community. On some issues, such as the charitable deduction for appreciated property, the two foundations took somewhat different positions. The Peterson Commission discussed the issue but abstained from making a recommendation. On the other hand, the Filer Commission supported the deduction for full value of appreciated property, but with modifications to prevent personal gain. Other suggestions, such as the Peterson Commission's proposed high payout rate, were problematic for foundations such as Kellogg or Lilly whose assets were dominated by company stocks. In contrast, discussion of the issues of responsible lobbying and political activity were probably welcomed by many charitable organizations; the Peterson Commission report reflected a time of enormous Congressional tension around political activity by foundations,[18] while the Filer Commission report specifically distinguished foundations from other nonprofit organizations in this matter. Finally, in their recommendations for more data, more public information, and additional regulation on self-dealing transactions, both commissions proposed a degree of accountability and public regulation that was not acceptable to all of their foundation brethren. This was particularly evident in the lack of widespread support for the permanent public (or even quasi-public) national commission proposed by both commissions (although with different nomenclature).

There were also significant differences between the two commissions. As the argument in previous chapters has demonstrated, the Filer Commission initially enjoyed a closer relationship with government, and particularly with the Treasury Department, than did the Peterson Commission. This enabled it to carry out a larger publication agenda, and certainly accounts for much of its greater credibility in later years. Moreover, the commission's longer time span, together with its decision to incorporate as a 501(c)(3) organization, enabled it to profit from more effective fund raising efforts,[19] and to produce a more significant body of research—both qualitatively and quantitatively—than its predecessor. In addition, the fund raising effort had another particular impact

on the Filer Commission. As a result of bringing in other foundations and charities as financial supporters, the Filer Commission developed a more articulated
constituency for its deliberations.[20] Because of its timing, the Peterson Commission had run a rescue mission as the dam was breaking, while the Filer Commission, from a greater distance, and in a time of greatly decreased value in the
stock market, was able to critique some of the provisions of the tax act of 1969
that foundations found onerous, like the high payout rate. It could also rein-
force some of the more progressive recommendations made by the Peterson
Commission (e.g., more open disclosure by foundations as well as greater internal diversity).

Overall, the quality of leadership of the two commissions was considerably different. Peterson was evidently a more forceful leader than Filer, and JDR
was clearly impressed with the way Peterson had taken hold of his task.[21] The
Filer Commission on the other hand seemed at times to lack leadership and a
sure identity—qualities Peterson maintained by his strong personality and operating style. Although staff were important in both organizations, Rockefeller
staff certainly played a more active role in final negotiations around the Filer
Commission Report. There was also significant difference in the impact of the
written output of the two commissions—since the Peterson Report was published after passage of the 1969 Tax Act it was considered a "lame duck" document, whereas the Filer materials had a recognized potential for influencing
future decisions.

JDR might have been disappointed about the timing of the Peterson Commission's deliberations, but he seemed to be more disappointed with the final
product of the Filer Commission, and with its inability to realize a brillliant
conclusion. Although Peterson was limited by time, his efforts apparently helped
defeat some of the draconian measures proposed against foundations (their
mandated demise) and helped protect the charitable deduction. The Filer Commission, despite its apparent opportunity, had less dramatic impact on tax policy, and did not succeed in unifying the disparate groups in the charitable
world (including the foundations and the 501(c)(3) group). But in the end it left
behind a significant legacy—with effects that were not realized until after JDR's
death.

Since they did not actually enjoy full government sponsorship, personal
influence was a critical factor for both commissions. However, the Filer Commission came closer to functioning as an advisory group to the Treasury Department, with the help of expert staff—Leonard Silverstein and Gabriel Rudney. Indeed, the value of this special relationship with Treasury officials became
evident when the Carter administration decided against continuing a formal
advisory status for the follow-up group and ignored the commission's recom-

mendation of a permanent oversight body for philanthropy. Altogether, given the indeterminate status of the two commissions, their achievements were greater than might have been anticipated. And, even though the status of both commissions was rooted in Rockefeller networking, power, and prestige, their credibility (particularly for the Filer Commission) was also greatly enhanced by judicious use of experts in the field of philanthropy and tax law. Experts counted—here as with Congressionally authorized commissions. Still all their recommendations were not implemented. External events presented obstacles that not even well connected experts, and persistence, could surmount.[22]

Considerable attention has been given to the Filer Commission's legacy of a sense of identity for practitioners and scholars of the third sector.[23] Despite its own rocky history, ultimately the deliberate output of research papers about the sector distinguished the heritage of the Filer Commission from that of the Peterson Commission. Another notable difference between the two commissions was an almost serendipitous outgrowth of the Filer Commission—it fostered activism and diversity by in effect giving birth to a social reform organization, the National Committee for Responsive Philanthropy (NCRP). In the next two decades, NCRP became a beacon in the emergent alternative fund raising movement, arguing for a more open work place for fund raising, and urging reforms in the United Way system of organized charity.

The Peterson and Filer Commissions were formed in a watershed period for social change, when American populism was a strong phenomenon and formal institutions in American society (and elsewhere) were undergoing critical reappraisal—even by those who most benefitted from them.[24] As noted in previous chapters, the attack on foundations at the end of the 1960s was propelled as much by general antagonism toward rich people who escaped taxes and intense fear of the concentration of power of the eastern establishment as it was by an abstract interest in tax reform. In those years there was almost constant concern about specific abuses in the stewardship exercised over the "public" use of private money held by foundations. Public questioning of institutions, including the nonprofit charitable sector, continued through the early 1970s, and was related to Congressional consideration of tax reforms. But still in this period charitable nonprofits were able to mobilize their political forces to avert the severe decree.

The 1976 Tax Reform Act unified separate transfer taxes on estates and gifts into one transfer tax, and included a modest tightening of the time required to insure use of capital gains tax provisions. But it lowered the mandated payout rate for foundations to a fixed 5 percent of income (or of assets if that amount were higher) rather than being a variable rate—which at that time was 6.75 percent. The Tax Reform Act also contained a "lobbying expenditures test" which was meant to clarify and liberalize the rules concerning lobbying.[25] As a whole, even though the tax expenditure concept was already connected to the federal budget, the 1976 Act was not hostile to philanthropy, and the non-profit sector was generally treated favorably by Congress.

Changes in the Reagan Era

With the election of President Ronald Reagan (1980) and the dominance of a new conservative ideology in Washington the picture became more mud-died.[26] Reagan preached a philosophy of smaller government and more volun-tarism, and he established a Task Force on Private Sector Initiatives in this vein. Nevertheless, his administration was responsible for a continuing reduction of federal funds for many nonprofit organizations, and particularly for the human services (other than mandated health care payments).[27] Apparently the admini-stration expected private contributions to make up for the decrease in federally funded programs, but in any case the President wanted fewer government pro-grams. In addition, the administration evidently wanted to ensure that nonprofit activity meant services—not political action. Indeed, by 1983 the lobbying ability of nonprofit organizations was attacked directly in an administration circular that caused considerable alarm. If not corrected, OMB Circular A-22 would have greatly curtailed lobbying activities by nonprofits that received government funding, even including using copying machines for printing such materials if any government funds were used to pay for the machines.[28]

President Reagan implemented his view of supply-side economics early in his administration, and so the Economic Recovery Tax Act of 1981 greatly re-duced income taxes for the rich. The Act also increased the estate and gift amounts which could be excluded from taxes, with the suggestion that by 1997 over 99 percent of all estates would no longer be subject to federal estate taxes.[29] On the other hand, the same Act also included one of the suggestions of the Filer Commission. This provision allowed a direct charitable donation for non-itemizers (individuals who took the standard deduction). The deduction was fixed by percentage to a small amount, but it provided some tax relief gen-erally to givers in lower income brackets.[30]

Lowering income tax rates for the rich (to a maximum of 50 percent in the top bracket) was justified by Reagan's belief in supply-side economics and the idea that the money made available would fuel the economy; as a side benefit it would also increase funds available for charitable giving. Thus this situation illuminated one of the paradoxes of charitable contributions and tax policy. Lowering taxes on the incomes of the rich is likely to diminish their incentive for charitable giving, since it reduces the value of their charitable deductions; but there is much less certainty about the incentive that the deductions provide for lower income individuals. Still, after the tax act of 1981 went into effect, giving by "live" individuals seems to have increased slightly, while total giving, from bequests, corporations, and foundations, declined somewhat in the recessionary climate of 1982.[31] By 1984, with a soaring federal budget deficit, and in the face of an election, the President backtracked; income taxes were raised slightly, and the reduction in estate and gift taxes was delayed. In the legislation that year a change was also made which allowed donors to foundations to have the same tax deduction for the market value of appreciated stock and bonds as other 501(c)(3) charitable organizations.[32]

After Reagan's landslide reelection, and with the help of Democrats in Congress, major tax reform became a salient issue. Even with continued negotiations between Congress and the administration, the Tax Reform Act of 1986 embodied major simplifications and reforms; however, some changes did not last, and before long it was necessary to refer to 1986 Code provisions *as revised.* In its initial sweep the 1986 Act incorporated provisions that threatened to undermine broader participation in giving. One of these was the mandated expiration of the charitable deduction for non-itemizers, the democratizing provision of the 1986 Tax Act. Although designed to be revenue neutral, the Act lowered income tax rates across the board, increased the standard deduction for non-itemizers, and effectively eliminated their additional charitable deductions. At the same time, it eliminated the full benefit for deductions from gifts of appreciated tangible property to public charities.[33]

Reviews of the 1986 tax code were mixed, and some parts, like not allowing deduction of the full appreciated value on charitable gifts of tangible property, were modified by subsequent law.[34] As expected, after the Act went into effect contributions declined as a percentage of taxpayers' adjusted gross incomes.[35] Still, despite administration rhetoric and the presumed support of Congress for the third sector, government revenues were not increased to meet increased costs; nor were decreases in government funding replaced by private contributions.[36] Consequently, in that period many nonprofit organizations began intensifying efforts to make up for declining government support by more marketing, fees, and product sales, leading to greater commercialism of the sector, and new concerns about its future.[37]

* * *

Directions for the Future: Issues for Today and Tomorrow

As the 21st century opens, the American third sector appears to be at another crossroads. Unanswered questions raised by the Filer Commission, and even more by the Donee Group, have in effect come back to haunt the sector, and with a new and current twist. Some close observers have suggested that the nonprofit sector is in a state of crisis.[38] Remarkably they are raising this alarm while the American notion of a civil society, built on voluntary association, is being exported throughout the world and American scholars are proclaiming its value.[39]

Arguably it is sensible to discount some of the rhetoric about the degree of imminent crisis facing the voluntary sector, which is, after all, alive and growing. The numbers of 501(c)(3) and 501(c)(4) organizations on the Master File of the Internal Revenue Service continued to rise in the 1990s,[40] and the amount of contributions nationwide generally remained a constant percentage of the total Gross Domestic Product (hovering around 1.8 percent) as well as increasing in actual dollars to a reported high of $174.52 billion (1998). Partly as a result of a strongly rising stock market, the increase in giving as a whole in 1998 was estimated to be 10.7 percent more than the preceding year (or an increase of 9.0 percent in inflation-adjusted dollars).[41] The sector was enjoying a new level of recognition, with an unprecedented number of academic centers devoted to the study and teaching of one or more aspects of philanthropy, fund raising, voluntarism, and nonprofit management, as well as attention from the media—although this was, regrettably, often negative.[42] Furthermore, specialized organizations were encouraging or carrying out extensive research in the field of nonprofit studies: these included the Aspen Institute (Nonprofit Research Fund), Independent Sector, and the Urban Institute; and there were at least two significant scholarly groups that produced journals dedicated to the third sector—the Association for Research on Nonprofit Organizations and Voluntary Action, ARNOVA (*Nonprofit and Voluntary Sector Quarterly*) and the International Society for Third Sector Research, ISTR (*Voluntas*).

By the late 1900s the phenomenal rise in the stock market had contributed to a marked increase in individual giving, and resulted in augmented assets for foundations specifically. Under the 5 percent payout requirement this greatly increased the minimum amounts foundations had to distribute to recipients. In addition, in this period economists were reporting that an estimated amount of $10 trillion (or more) of intergenerational wealth would be transferred in the next decade.[43] Even if only a portion of that amount were to go to charity, the turn of the century was likely to present extraordinary philanthropic opportunities. Moreover, in the 1990s a new brand of self-made millionaire, reminiscent of some of the "robber barons" of the late 19th century, began to donate enormous amounts of money for particular purposes, like the large gift to the United Nations by Ted Turner, the media mogul, or the contributions of the high-tech wizard Bill Gates. And their actions resulted in renewed attention to the potential power of individual big givers.[44]

Numbers, of course, do not tell the whole story, and at the end of 1999 there still remained grounds for uneasiness about the future of the nonprofit sector. And, unlike the Patman years, this time problems do not center only on the foundation community but related more generally in the larger group of public charities that were relatively untouched by the attacks of the 1960s. Critical questions—left unanswered by the Filer Commission—are being raised again about the role of charitable organizations in American life, and the way they function. Major issues facing the third sector at the beginning of the 21st century will be considered next in light of the experiences of the Filer and Peterson Commissions, with some concluding thoughts about the future.

Charitable Deductions

In the late 1990s the charitable deduction remained intact despite the roller coaster ride to which Congress intermittently subjects philanthropy. Even with a number of serious challenges and technical changes, the principle of tax preferences for charitable deductions was still embedded in the federal tax code, and continued to favor givers at the high end of the income scale. Although recent laws (1996) had in effect reduced estate and gift taxes generally, these taxes were not eliminated and remained a factor in determining charitable bequests.[45] But gifts of appreciated property remained (as they had been in the past) problematic, when the IRS rule allowing donors to deduct the full fair market value of stocks donated to private foundations was about to expire (June 30, 1998). This provision had been extended for short periods since 1994, and the Council on Foundations and Independent Sector continued lobbying; in October 1998 they were successful in making this a permanent provision of our tax law.[46] In addition, the concept of charitable deductions for non-itemizers, which seemed abandoned in the late 1980s—when increases in the standard deduction were firmly established as public policy—was revived in 1998. However, despite renewed efforts directed at passing such legislation, which would in effect spread tax benefits to lower-income givers, by the end of 1999 this change in the law had not been implemented.[47]

On the whole, in the late 1990s mechanisms for philanthropic giving were very much in place and the economy was strong—nonetheless, many nonprofit organizations were scrambling for money, particularly those that provide human services. Generally, in an anti–big government, pro–private enterprise environment, nonprofit entrepreneurialism was being widely encouraged. And in the 1990s the picture was still murky: giving had after all been relatively flat for most of the 1990s before the stock market rise; one study showed that between 1982 and 1992 contributions dropped from 15 percent of the budgets of nonprofit organizations to around 11 percent.[48] Although giving rose considerably toward the end of the 1990s, it was not certain if the amounts would be enough to change entrepreneurial modes of behavior—nor was it sure anyone wanted to do so. One practitioner probably expressed the sentiments of many nonprofit managers when he stated candidly: "Philanthropy has failed us."[49]

Declining Public Funding and New Entrepreneurialism

Before the 20th century drew to a close, sluggishness in philanthropic giving, and particularly corporate giving—together with decreases in available federal funding—had resulted in greatly increased commercial activity in the nonprofit sector. Moreover, nonprofit entrepreneurialism meshed well with the generally conservative climate in the country. Thus the new commercialism extended across a range of nonprofit organizations, and affected art museums, universities, hospitals, and social service organizations. Reductions of federal funding in the 1980s had turned into a pattern of decreased federal funds for the activities of many nonprofit organizations, with concomitantly more competition for grants, direct purchase, third party payments, and other available subsidies. Uncertainty became trauma when in the mid-1990s draconian cuts in federal funds for human services were proposed by conservative Republicans and Congressman Newt Gingrich; they threatened to reduce funding for "programs of interest to the nonprofit sector" by an estimated cumulative amount of $268.3 by the year 2002.[50] Although the worst fears were not realized, appropriations for fiscal year 1996 alone were $23 billion less than appropriations for fiscal year 1995.[51]

The nonprofit sector fiscal crisis that Peterson anticipated for the 1970s— with pressures on public revenues and declining philanthropic contributions— seemed to be an even more likely occurrence during most of the 1990s, as federal cutbacks were being continually discussed. But, in a direction that neither the Peterson nor the Filer Commissions had really anticipated, nonprofit commercialism moved in to fill the void. This, however, exacerbated the situation in other respects; it resulted in growing attacks on the tax exemptions of nonprofit organizations at the local and state level. For, as entrepreneurial activity on the part of nonprofits accelerated, local and state governments began to question the actual nonprofit character of these organizations and the reasons why they did not pay local taxes. Nonprofit organizations increasingly faced possible revocation of their exemption from local property or sales taxes, as state and local governments, now hard pressed to meet their own mandated responsibilities, looked for additional revenues from local organizations.[52] In turn, these challenges to local tax exemptions for charitable organizations encouraged development of new statewide nonprofit associations. Such groups were being created to protect the fiscal condition of tax-exempt organizations as well as to increase advocacy efforts of the third sector in a time when the states were becoming increasingly important in the policy game.

Purposes of the Sector: Lobbying and Diversity

Over the years many explanations have been given for the added value of the third sector. It is not possible to recapitulate all of them here;[53] but there can be little doubt that a fundamental aspect of democracy, and of the concept of civil society embedded within democracy, is a respect for diversity with a concomitant protection of ideological difference.

As we have seen, a significant legacy of the Filer Commission was recognition of the need for diversity in the foundation world and encouragement of a Donee Group, which represented newly emergent activist recipient groups. Many of these groups grew out of the civil rights activism of the previous decade and had enjoyed some degree of government support in those years. The Filer Commission's attention to the Donee Group helped the activist causes associated with it gain a sense of identity and greater visibility in the media and in the national area. Thereafter, despite the conservatism of the Reagan era, these groups continued to grow in number and activities, and in the 1980s additional progressive funding sources also emerged. Thus in the 1980s, with the encouragement of NCRP, an alternative fund raising movement developed. This movement increasingly included progressive private foundations as well as public fund raising "charities" outside of the United Way umbrella. There were population-focused groups such as the Black United Fund, Latino and Asian American funds, as well as funds for women, the disabled, and lesbian and gay individuals; there were also groups focused on the environment, and on the needs of low-income people. However, as a whole, these social change groups remained seriously underfunded, and they received only a small portion of total foundation grants in the 1990s. Indeed, the 1998 Report of the American Assembly reflected concern about this, and recommended that more philanthropic dollars go to serious community problems, including the needs of poor people.

As already noted in earlier chapters, protection for diverse viewpoints is a critical aspect of voluntary association, and it includes freedom to advocate in the marketplace of ideas, as well as in the halls of Congress. But this kind of advocacy can be weakened by demands for commercial success and practices that suggest caution in relation to controversy—which may be one of the reasons for diminished grassroots activism in relation to the welfare crises of the mid-1990s.[54] In 1995, along with attacks on welfare programs and social reform activities, there was also, once again, a direct Congressional effort to pass legislation that would muzzle advocacy efforts and lobbying by nonprofit organizations. These efforts were led by Republican Congressmen Ernest Istook (Oklahoma), David McIntosh (Indiana), and Robert Ehrlich (Maryland). Although the original measure was defeated, a modified Lobbying Disclosure Bill and other anti-lobbying proposals remained under consideration in Congress in the next few years.[55] The lesson for advocates of social reform was evident— eternal vigilance is needed to protect freedoms of voluntary association even in a democratic society.

Accountability

In the early 1990s attention turned again to the question of accountability in the nonprofit sector, but unlike 1969, this time the focus was on the entire universe of charitable organizations, and not primarily on foundations. The demand for greater accountability, with additional concern now about "public charities," accelerated after a series of abuses of the stewardship function of charities were discovered and given wide coverage in the media. Among the problems exposed were the improper actions of the national executive of the United Way of America and the treasurer of the national Episcopal Church.[56] Misbehavior in the sector more broadly was also the subject of an extensive three-part series by reporters in the *Philadelphia Inquirer* (1993), later published in book form.[57]

Media attention set off alarms for the general public and Congress, and as a result hearings were held in the Oversight Subcommittee of the House Ways and Means Committee in 1993. The next year the Department of Treasury proposed legislation to insure more adequate oversight of public charities.[58] This legislation, known as the Taxpayer Bill of Rights 2, was signed into law by President Clinton on July 30, 1996. It included a section (Section 1311) containing "intermediate sanctions" rules for public charities, which mandated penalties for individuals ("disqualified persons") connected with the charity if they engaged in "excess benefit transactions"; such transactions incorporated the private inurement concept embedded in prior legislative rules. The prohibition with regard to private inurement as legislated also included 501(c)(4), social welfare, organizations.[59] The rules would enable the IRS to impose sanctions on individuals related to public charities and social welfare organizations in a manner similar to those which had become applicable to foundations under the 1969 Tax Reform Act. Previously the penalty available for such transactions was the withdrawal of the tax-exempt status permitted the organization as a whole.

This had not been effective because it was too excessive and did not "hurt" any particular individuals involved. H.R. 2337 also included requirements directing public charities and other exempt organizations to increase the availability and public accessibility of Form 990 and related materials (including applications for exemption, Form 1023) to the general public. Monitoring responsibility for these new requirements would remain with the IRS.

In a sense, this might have foreclosed further discussion about who is responsible for oversight and protection of the sector and the public interest. But the matter was not so simple. For during the same period that the Taxpayer Bill of Rights was being implemented, the IRS itself became the subject of Congressional hearings. Although most of the attention was on IRS abuse of individual taxpayers, review of IRS capacity more broadly was also a matter of concern. And now in addition the IRS would have to assume additional responsibilities under the "intermediate sanctions" provisions of 1996, even though it had been described as lacking staff capability for the work that it was already mandated to do, and staff performance level remained an issue.[60]

Where Do We Go from Here?

At the dawning of the 21st century the nonprofit sector is undoubtedly in a period of transition. Circumstances may not be as dramatic as they were in 1969, but arguably the stakes could be just as high. Although the worst of the "crisis" facing the sector may have passed—for example, the Istook proposals concerning lobbying—the political climate in which nonprofits are currently operating remains threatening and the question of financial soundness continues.[61] In reviewing the issues facing the sector, several stand out as having immediate saliency:

First, there has actually not been any comprehensive in-depth assessment of the consequences of growing nonprofit entrepreneurialism. Such an assessment would have to deal with both theoretical issues and concrete experience, including analysis of "hard" data in the various subparts of the nonprofit sector, as well as consideration of fundamental values of American society. Certainly no systematic study has been made of the general impact of commercial and profit-making activities on clients and communities, even though there has been some recent interest in placing parts of the third sector—notably the health and hospital system—"outside" the domain of the charitable sector. This idea derives some theoretical justification from Henry Hansmann's distinction between "fee based" and donative organizations[62] and had been considered even in Congressional deliberations around the Tax Reform Act of 1969. However, the issue of inurement affects other parts of the charitable third sector as well (e.g., museums, universities, and United Ways) and criticisms of the salaries of chief executives of such large "charities"—however unjustified by fact—remained a concern at the end of the 20th century.

A second major issue in the late 1990s relates to proposals for restructuring our tax system. Neo-conservatives have challenged the basic validity of the U.S. tax code as it currently exists, and in the 104th Congress actually initiated legislation to replace our complex system with a more simplified tax structure, or a "flat tax"; it was also raised by would-be presidential candidates in the fall of 1999. In its most extreme form the proposed flat tax would do away with all deductions and tax preferences, and would eliminate the tax deduction for charitable gifts; other more moderate versions do allow for charitable tax deductions. In any case, despite the claims of its proponents, there is little evidence that the proposed flat tax in any form is more democratic, or just, than the existing tax system (with all its warts).[63]

A third underlying issue has to do with continued blurring of the sectors, and even more recently increased diminution of the line between church and state. Secular and religious organizations have always flourished side by side in the voluntary sector, but with regard to public subsidies and contracts for public purposes, limitations have been placed on the use of faith-based organizations. As part of the blurring of the sectors, in the Personal Responsibility Act of 1996 this demarcation line was removed for some services under "charitable choice."

Although the issues facing the sector have been discussed separately, they are in fact strongly interrelated. Moreover, many additional current issues, like those of the past, emerge out of ambivalent American attitudes toward the structure of philanthropy and its perceived elitism. But they also reflect an underlying cynicism about nonprofit activity supported by government, together with increasing demands for greater accountability in this growing sector of American life. Paradoxically, concerns in this regard threaten the principal underpinning of the third sector—trust. Support for the sector through tax policy depends upon the belief that philanthropy (in its broadest meaning) practices honorable stewardship in the use of money—money some define as "public"—but which can, possibly with equal justification (and apologies to Stanley Surrey) be defined as private money. The fundamental point here seems to be that whether defined as private or public, philanthropic contributions do enjoy tax benefits that are justified in our tax code because these funds are presumed to be dedicated to public purposes. Therefore accountability has to be seen as the critical means to assuring that public purposes are in fact realized. But if excessive emphasis is put on procedures of accountability then the fundamental aspect of trust in regard to other valued qualities of the sector—independence, flexibility, creativity—would seem to be in jeopardy.

This paradox—the need for public accountability in the realm of "private" contributions and voluntarism—creates the specter of excessive government oversight of charitable organizations, and raises the same fears among advocates of the third sector that their business allies have of government regulation. That fear helps to explain why the voluntary sector did not generally support the permanent public commission proposal of the Filer Commission in 1975, even when it might have been possible to achieve. It also explains why in 1998 leaders of the sector still opposed creating another public regulatory body for charities similar to that of the Charity Commission for England and Wales.[64] Indeed concern about the vital role of the third sector was evident in a number of recent ad hoc commissions and groups created to consider its future (e.g., the Armey Commission and the American Assembly of 1998) as well as in scholarly discussions. In light of concerted efforts by conservative groups to control the public agenda, and to use private, philanthropic means to do so,[65] there evidently remains need for even more in-depth exploration of ways to protect both the public interest and the array of voluntary activities that are essential to an American civil society.

The Future and the Past (Some Concluding Thoughts)

As the 21st century begins, it is still appropriate to question whether the IRS really has capacity for adequate oversight of the third sector. This is so in light of new controls which are being placed on that agency, and even though there is an expected restructuring of the IRS which will result in the creation of a new "Tax Exempt and Government Entities Division" to be in operation by January 2000. Given the past problematic performance of the IRS, however, the question persists: Do we need to create a new permanent national body to provide oversight and policy continuity for the third sector and to ensure judiciousness in safeguarding its institutions? We recognize that this is in fact no longer a small, informal sector, although it encompasses many small grassroots entities as well as large institutions. The third sector now employs millions of people, receives hundreds of billions of dollars in revenues, and has enormous resources that need to be safeguarded. Thus the question of protecting the public interest in philanthropic activity is significant for our whole society.

Philanthropic leaders have suggested that this country does not need an independent oversight body over charity—or perhaps we are simply not yet ready for it. But the question at the very least demands more, and more dispassionate, consideration. Such an oversight body was in essence the radical notion proposed by some members of the Filer Commission twenty-five years ago, and it bears reconsideration today. I suggest therefore that it is now time to create a "temporary" quasi-public commission, with responsibility for reviewing the question of a permanent oversight body for the third sector, and with full consideration of the ramifications (costs and benefits) of doing so. In addition to coming to a resolution on this long term issue, the temporary body could deliberate other questions left unanswered by the Donee Group and the Filer Commission about the sector's role in meeting human needs and the relationships among the sectors in a three-sector society. Questions about these relationships seem to be even more salient at a time when the income gap between the very rich and the poorest in our country has grown exponentially and the extent of poverty in the bottom income group cannot be denied.

An initial quasi-private commission would be time-limited, but should at least take two years for its deliberations. Preferably, it should be formed as a true presidential commission, with bipartisan support, and with a commitment to some protection from political pressure. If a presidential commission is not possible, then the commission could be formed in the Filer Commission tradition, with loose ties to government, and powerful private supporters. The commission would include representatives from government, business, philanthropy, and the public, and could undertake a serious assessment of the role of the three institutional sectors in meeting human needs; it would be concerned with "public" charities as well as "private foundations."[66] In a world where communication is global, but core institutions remain locally based, the issue becomes ever more complex. But the new millennium presents an opportune occasion to have such a philosophical discussion, and the time is now.

Appendix A

On Commissions

Every administrator since the inception of the United States has utilized
advisory groups. Every branch of our Government turns to advisory
Committees for aid or recommendations.
—Forty-third Report by the Committee on Government Operations,
U.S. House of Representatives, 1970

One way of viewing policy formulation is to consider it as a kind of discourse; this suggests that words or names will have an impact on policy development.[1] Following this line of reasoning, we would presume that in the two organizations under study here the term "commission" was selected with some degree of consciousness by their initiators. Rockefeller himself was particular about the words he used, and characteristically revised drafts of his speeches and manuscripts with his staff until he felt that the words chosen actually reflected his views.[2] JDR could also be influenced by his advisors, and names could be changed as new entities were being developed. In at least one of the two cases in this book—the Filer Commission—the final name evidently evolved along with a modification of functions that the commission would serve.[3]

Within the relatively short space of five years, from 1968 to 1973, John D. Rockefeller 3rd, private but prominent citizen, created two bodies which were expected to influence public policy. Since the word "commission" was incorporated in the final name of both of them, we may hypothesize that it had significance for JDR and other stakeholders involved in these events. And in fact this was a time in American history when commissions were much in vogue, and a vast number of national advisory commissions were being created, including the Commission on Population Growth and the American Future (1970) for which John D. Rockefeller 3rd served as Chairman.[4] Nevertheless, authors writing about the Filer and Peterson commissions have generally not paid special attention to the implications of their titles for delineating a particular public role.[5]

Despite past omissions in this regard, the repetition of the word "commission" as a theme of the two commissions raises questions about why it was used for what were essentially privately created organizations. What kind of intent and general meaning did the term convey at the time that the two commissions were initiated? And what was the subsequent significance—if any—of such a choice? In this Appendix we will follow this line of inquiry, exploring the concept of "commission" in its historical context, as a background for understanding its significance at the time of the Peterson and Filer commissions.

What Is a Commission?

Both historically and in current usage the term "commission" encompasses a complex, diverse variety of organizational types, such as advisory bodies, committees, investigatory and regulatory agencies, and task forces. Some of these usages are overlapping or have reference to organizations with similar core functions and purposes under different names. Usually, "commission" connotes some sort of public function, although organizations under private auspices also create policy and study commissions. In general, commissions may be analyzed in their historical context, or topically and comparatively,[6] by such characteristics as auspices, structure (including degree of permanence), and major function or purpose.

In his landmark article in *The International Encyclopedia of Social Sciences,* published around the time of the Peterson Commission, Harvey Mansfield noted that the term "commission" covers a range of meanings from the official document which confers an official appointment, such as a captain's commission, to the subject of his interest, which was "an official agency or institution headed by a collegial body of commissioners." Mansfield then chose to confine his discussion to this last usage, excluding the "unofficial bodies (often self-constituted) that call themselves commissions and that may . . . perform some more or less analogous functions in the larger political system or society."[7] At first glance it might seem that Mansfield's delineation of commissions as official bodies would exclude one or both of the commissions under study here. However, his distinction actually highlights a major question to be asked about the Peterson and Filer commissions. Indeed the degree to which these commissions were imbued with a quasi-public or official status ultimately turns out to be central to an analysis of the way that the commissions functioned, and also has implications for understanding public policy formulation more broadly.

European Antecedents

The term "commissioner" emerged in the late 15th century in reference to individuals charged by royal commission with responsibility for assessments (under Henry VII). However, commissions existed in early Christian Europe and elsewhere before that time, and at least one form of commission was utilized by the Romans. As far back as the Roman Republic, the Roman Senate appointed small groups of prestigious representatives, called *legati,* to carry out oversight missions in the provinces that were under Roman military control.[8] These groups (usually consisting of five people) carried out an investigatory function and were expected to make a report to the Senate upon their return. Furthermore, use of administrative and investigatory bodies continued after the fall of the Roman Empire. By the early middle ages Catholic popes were already sending out commissions for administration of canon law, and in Tudor England later (15th century) Thomas More headed a papal-authorized commission that searched for Lutheran books.[9]

Commissions have been used in eastern Europe (Russia) and elsewhere, but the American use of commissions for governmental purposes has probably been most influenced by the historical development of commissions in Great Britain. In the 16th century the crown named commissioners for hearings and determination about private property disputes,[10] and Parliament also passed acts creating such bodies to regulate charitable efforts. At the end of that century the Charitable Uses Act of 1597 established the first charity commissioners (known as roving commissioners) with (delegated) power to investigate fraudulent activity in regard to charitable trusts. Although the Act was repealed, its provisions were largely reintroduced through the 1601 Charitable Uses Act and in later laws of Parliament.[11] In 1643 the administration of excise laws was also given to commissioners, who had authority to punish violations.[12]

In the reform era of the early 1800s commissions of inquiry proliferated, and about 160 of various kinds were reportedly established between 1800 and 1850. Indeed there was so much use of commissions in this period that criticism was raised about "government by commission."[13] Although it is considered to have had a somewhat different character from most of the other commissions of this time, a notable charity commission (the Brougham Commission) was also established in 1818 to investigate and regulate charitable activity. Its mandate was extended twice, and it remained active for almost twenty years, when further renewal efforts failed. However, in 1853 legislation resulted in the permanent establishment of the Charity Commission for England and Wales (1860).[14]

Despite public criticism, use of official commissions with a variety of oversight and investigatory authority continued in 20th-century Britain. Moreover, the practice was institutionalized in regard to voluntarism and charitable activity. Thus in another reform era at the turn of the century a commission which had a particular impact on the future role of philanthropy was created. The Royal Commission on the Poor Laws and Relief of Distress (1905–1909) was given the charge of analyzing the relationship between voluntary charitable aid and public relief. This commission issued a majority report stating that while both were necessary, state aid should be given in such a manner that it would clearly be "less agreeable" than voluntary aid. A minority report written by the Fabian reformer Beatrice Webb (with George Lansbury), however, argued to the contrary for a relationship between state and voluntary aid in which the state would provide basic supports, supplemented by more particularist, special voluntary services (described as an "extension ladder" model).[15] Essentially it was the Webb view that influenced the paradigm of the strong British welfare state that developed after World War II and lasted until the Conservative government election in 1979.[16] Meanwhile the Charity Commission continued to function even in the heady days of the 1960s. However, in the next decade new questions began to be raised about charitable accountability and attention again focused on the role of the Charity Commission.[17]

In Great Britain today commissions with a variety of purposes are still used, and they may be distinguished according to function or origins by royal, statutory, or departmental appointment. However, it is the statutory British Charity Commission that played a role in the thinking of some critical actors involved with the Peterson and Filer commissions, and which had particular implications for the Filer Commission.

Commissions in American Life

Use of commissions in America can be traced back to Colonial times, but really only became a major feature of government in the 20th century. Among the many forms of American commissions that have since been utilized are: municipal commissions; specialized agencies of government that are titled commissions (i.e., county commissions of mental health); individual commissioners who are public agency or departmental heads (for example, the Commissioner of Internal Revenue of the United States); and an assortment of permanent regulatory commissions including the ICC (Interstate Commerce Commission), the FTC (Federal Trade Commission), and the SEC (Securities and Exchange Commission), as well as temporary investigatory commissions and short-term issue-oriented advisory commissions.[18] Given this diversity, it is not surprising that there is no generally accepted, complete historical compendium of commissions in American life.[19] However, there are some apparent benchmarks with regard to both permanent agencies and temporary advisory commissions.[20]

The first American Presidential advisory commission is generally considered to be the one sent by George Washington to forestall rebellion by the Pennsylvania Farmers in the Whiskey Rebellion (1794). Although one author, Thomas Wolanin, claims that this was not a true commission but an operational group of "conciliators and negotiators," the point is arguable.[21] This commission was not established by statute and may not have been in that sense a "lawful commission" but it certainly had a Presidential mandate for investigation.[22] In the early 18th century Presidents Van Buren and Jackson also appointed commissioners for fact finding. In 1842, however, the issue of authority for Presidential commissions was raised by Congress after President John Tyler's appointment in 1841 of "a nonstatutory commission to investigate the affairs of the New York Customs House."[23] The fact that such questions were raised by Congress suggests the importance already attached to this power of the executive branch of government and the issue of legislative (Congressional) authority.

The major development of quasi-judicial, regulatory commissions in the United States began with the creation of state-related railway commissions. The federal government adopted this practice, starting with the ICC in 1887 and continuing into the 20th century with the creation of other national regulatory commissions, such as the FTC and the SEC. Because they are intended to be permanent, and may exist at many levels, these agencies form a distinct category of administrative bodies, separate from the large group of ad hoc national advisory commissions which form the primary context for our analysis of the two Rockefeller-initiated commissions. However, these permanent administrative commissions are a recognized feature of American government, and they have also been the subject of investigations into governmental efficiency and reorganization, starting with the inquiry by Congress under Van Buren, and including the considerable review of government bodies in the decades after World War II.

Extensive use of ad hoc advisory commissions in 20th century America is undoubtedly related to governmental growth in this period.[24] But commission usage appears also to be related to reform ideologies that emerge in periods of social change. Thus, not surprisingly, Theodore Roosevelt has been dubbed the "Father of [American] Presidential Commissions," a title that seems merited by virtue of his creation of a number of broad-visioned, national policy–oriented commissions. These include the Commission on Public Lands (1903–40), the Commission on Inland Waterways (1908–9), the Commission on Country Life (1908–9), and the Commission on National Conservation (1908). Two others, the Commission on Economy and Efficiency (1910–13) and the United States Commission on Industrial Relations (1912–1915), were initiated during the Presidency of William Howard Taft. The Commission on Industrial Relations warrants additional attention in our story because it had special significance for the Rockefellers, and it established new patterns and continuing directions for the family. For that reason, the Commission on Industrial Relations (also known as the Walsh Commission because of its chairman, Frank P. Walsh) is considered more specifically in chapter 2.

National Advisory Commissions: From Wilson to Nixon

The U.S. Commission on Industrial Relations has not received much attention in recent studies of national advisory commissions and is most often discussed as part of the history of the Rockefeller family and the Rockefeller Foundation.[25] In fact, the story of the Walsh Commission illustrates some institutional dilemmas involved in the use of national advisory commissions in modern times. Among these are: (1) the commission was created by Congress, but members were appointed by the President; (2) in some ways it paralleled work that was being done (or could be done) by a Congressional committee; (3) it was supposed to deliver an independent report, and therefore the President was in effect supposed to maintain a hands-off stance in regard to its deliberations; (4) it was time limited and therefore once its work was done, its findings, including written reports, were "orphans" without "parental" advocates to see that there was a follow-up to any of its policy recommendations.[26] In addition it suffered a serious problem, not necessarily shared by all commissions, of strong disagreement among its members, and consequent lack of a unified outcome.

Despite these limitations, the commission focused attention on industrial abuses and the power of the rich, and, more specifically, helped redirect Rockefeller family efforts in regard to their foundation and their business affairs. So arguably, in spite of the powerful political and economic forces against it, the Walsh Commission had succeeded in bringing about some degree of public awareness of critical issues. Nevertheless (and like many later commissions), it did not result in major new public policies or enactment of significant national legislation.

In the period after World War I until the end of World War II, Presidential use of ad hoc national advisory commissions increased gradually until the 1960s, when their numbers expanded exponentially. However, there appears to be a blip in the screen in the 1930s. Grover Cleveland, Herbert Hoover, and even Harry Truman considered commissions useful, but a reading of Wolanin and Flitner (among other recent authors) would suggest that Franklin Roosevelt did not, since they do not discuss his administration.[27] Roosevelt created an alphabet soup of organizations, including the NLRB (National Labor Relations Board) and the SEC (Securities Exchange Commission), on a permanent basis, and used individual "counselors," but apparently he created few groups which satisfied Flitner's and Wolanin's definitions of independent advisory commissions. Roosevelt did establish a large number of ad hoc committees to consider legislative issues, including the notable Committee on Economic Security, which laid the foundation for the Social Security Act of 1935.[28] But these committees were not generally authorized by Congress, their members were largely public officials, and they were considerably influenced by Presidential mandates.

Given the association of commissions with both increased government and reform ideologies, the lack of Congressionally authorized advisory commissions might seem paradoxical in the expansive, change-oriented New Deal administration. However, a review of the characteristics of the Walsh Commission suggests why a President who was committed to strong program direction and success through powerbroking methods would prefer to keep closer control of policy oriented bodies. The urgency of the economic crisis facing the country also presented a situation very different from that of the Progressive era, and in addition, a truly independent commission did not fit the driving personal style of President Franklin Roosevelt.[29]

In a later reform era another President, John F. Kennedy, seemed to take a more positive view of the role of independent advisory groups (even though labeled here with the more generic name of "committee"). In Executive Order 11007 (February 26, 1962) Kennedy recognized the need for standards in the use of advisory groups, but also noted that departments and agencies of government "frequently make use of advisory committees," and furthermore that "the information, advice and recommendations obtained through advisory committees are beneficial to the government." What is particularly interesting for the story of the Peterson and Filer commissions is the definition then given for advisory committees:

> a) The term "advisory committee" means any committee, board, commission, council, conference, panel, task force, or other similar group, or any subcommittee or other subgroup thereof, that is formed by a department or agency of the Government in the interest of obtaining advice or recommendations, or for any other purpose, and that is not composed wholly of officers or employees of the Government. The term also includes any committee, board, commission, council, conference, panel, task force, or other similar group, or any subcommittee or other subgroup thereof, that is *not formed by a department or agency* (emphasis added), but only during any period when it is being utilized by a department or agency in the same manner as a government-formed advisory committee.
>
> b) The term "industry advisory committee" means an advisory committee composed predominantly of members of representatives of a single industry or group of related industries, or of any subdivision of a single industry made on a geographic, service or product use.[30]

All such advisory groups were now also required to terminate in two years, unless otherwise fixed by law or a department or agency of the government determined explicitly (in writing) that their continuation was in the "public interest." In general, somewhat more demanding standards were imposed on industry advisory committees; for example, in addition to the generally required minutes of all meetings, they were expected to keep complete transcripts of their proceedings.

In March 1964 another, more restrictive, directive was issued concerning the use of advisory bodies. OMB Circular A-63, issued in the administration of President Johnson, included a section on nomenclature, in which it indicated the need to "achieve uniformity within the executive branch" in regard to types of committees. It also stated that in order to avoid confusion with independent agencies of the executive branch "The terms commission, council or board . . . should be reserved for committees established by legislation." In addition, ad hoc groups were to have titles that gave a "clear indication of their temporary status."[31]

Even with these proposals, governmental use of advisory groups increased in the next ten years. In particular, Presidential commissions assumed more importance as crisis-oriented commissions were created around controversial events or issues. Their existence was not without problems. In fact, two of the most controversial commissions, the National Advisory Commission on Civil Disorders (the Kerner Commission, 1968) and the National Commission on Obscenity and Pornography (1970), issued reports that were not accepted by Presidents Johnson and Nixon, respectively.[32]

In an age of expanding knowledge and an almost insatiable desire for expertise, the well-known Presidential commissions were only the tip of a great iceberg. The large number and variety of advisory groups acknowledged in Kennedy's 1962 Executive Order continued to increase throughout government, in connection with the executive branch, administrative agencies, and the Congress. This phenomenon led to a growing Congressional concern about the nature of their public accountability as well as their cost.

Thus in August 1969 a special subcommittee of the House Committee on Governmental Operations undertook a "comprehensive review of advisory bodies within the Federal Government." On December 9, 1970 this subcommittee issued its report to the Committee of the Whole House on the State of the Union. The report, entitled *The Role and Effectiveness of Federal Advisory Committees,* expressed concern about the role of inter-agency committees and other advisory groups in what was now termed "the fifth branch of government," separate from the constitutionally established executive, legislative, and judicial branches, and what was considered a fourth group of regulatory boards with administrative, judicial, and executive functions.[33] The report concluded that the earlier Kennedy Executive Order and the OMB circular on advisory committees had not gone far enough in establishing standards, and furthermore that their provisions had not been adequately implemented. It identified the need for more regulation and control over advisory groups as "agents of government," and among its final recommendations was the following:

> The Congress should spell out in public law the philosophy behind and need for advisory bodies and definitely establish policy and administrative criteria for their use at all levels of government.[34]

Two years later, in the interim between the end of the Peterson Commission and the initiation of the work of the Filer Commission, Public Law 92-463—the Federal Advisory Committee Act—was passed on October 6, 1972. The Act reflected the extensive hearings and discussions of the House Committee on Governmental Operations as well as those of the Subcommittee on Administrative Practice and Procedure of the Senate Judiciary Committee (May, June, July 1971). Passage of the Federal Advisory Act seemed to indicate resolution of the historical question about a president's right to appoint commissions, and suggested that "in the contemporary era, advisory bodies have become a fact of life, even a necessity."

Among the major features of the Act were: (1) its emphasis on uniform standards regulating establishment and functioning of advisory committees; (2) the suggestion that the public should be kept informed about such bodies; (3) the requirement that legislation establishing such committees will define purpose and insure balanced points of view in its membership; (4) elaboration of the responsibilities of any advisory commission for issuing a public report to be forwarded to the President and by the President to the Congress; (5) budgetary accountability for such commissions in the Office of Management and Budget; and (6) mandated filing of copies of reports and related materials in the Library of Congress.

Implications of the contents of this Act for the subsequent development of the Filer Commission were certainly understood by the attorneys who worked with John D. Rockefeller 3rd, and undoubtedly influenced the structure and functioning of that commission. But many of the Congressional questions which led to the passage of this Act were already emerging during the time of the Peterson Commission, and were therefore also part of the context in which that commission's activities were conducted.

Appendix B

Biographical Notes on Commission Members and Staff, Peterson Commission

Chairman

PETER G. PETERSON, Chairman and Chief Executive Officer, Bell and Howell Company, Chicago

Members

J. PAUL AUSTIN, Chairman, President, and Chief Executive Officer, The Coca-Cola Company, Atlanta

DANIEL BELL, Professor of Sociology, Harvard University; author; Chairman, Commission on the Year 2000 of the American Academy of Arts and Sciences; member, President's Commission on Technology, Automation, and Economic Progress

DANIEL P. BRYANT, Chairman and Chief Executive Officer, Bekins Van and Storage Company, Los Angeles; lawyer; Director and Past President, Los Angeles Area Chamber of Commerce

JAMES CHAMBERS, President and Publisher, *Dallas Times-Herald;* author

SHELDON S. COHEN. Cohen and Uretz; former Commissioner of Internal Revenue, U.S. Department of Treasury

THOMAS B. CURTIS, Vice-president and General Counsel, Encyclopedia Britannica; former U.S. Representative from Second Congressional District, Missouri, and member of House Ways and Means Committee, Joint Economic Committee

PAUL A. FREUND, Professor, Harvard University Law School; expert in constitutional law; author; editor-in-chief of multivolume *History of the Supreme Court,* now in preparation, commissioned by U.S. Congress; Past President, American Academy of Arts and Sciences

MARTIN FRIEDMAN, Director, Walker Art Center, Minneapolis; American Fine Arts Commissioner, Sao Paulo Bienal; member, National Collection of Fine Arts Commission; author and lecturer on contemporary international art

PATRICIA ROBERTS HARRIS, Strasser, Spiegelberg, Fried, Frank, and Kampelman; member, National Commission on the Causes and Prevention of Violence; former Dean and Professor, Howard University Law School; former U.S. Ambassador to Luxembourg

A. LEON HIGGINBOTHAM, JR., U.S. District Court Judge, Eastern District of Pennsylvania; Vice-chairman, National Commission on the Causes and Prevention of Violence; former commissioner, Federal Trade Commission; member, White House Conference to Fulfill These Rights; member, Commission on Reform of U.S. Criminal Law

LANE KIRKLAND, Secretary-Treasurer, American Federation of Labor and Congress of Industrial Organizations

PHILIP R. LEE, M.D., Chancellor, University of California, San Francisco; former Assistant Secretary, U.S. Department of Health, Education, and Welfare

EDWARD H. LEVI, President, University of Chicago; former law professor, Dean of the Law School; past member, White House Task Force of Education, White House Central Group in Domestic Affairs; author

FRANKLIN A. LONG, Director for Program on Science, Technology, and Society, Cornell University; former member, President's Science Advisory Committee; former assistant director, U.S. Arms Control and Disarmament Agency

A. S. "MIKE" MONRONEY, Consultant, Aviation and Transportation; former U.S. Senator and U.S. Representative from Oklahoma; former chairman, Senate Post Office and Civil Service Committee, and member, Senate Appropriations Committee

Executive Director

EVERETT L. HOLLIS, Partner, Mayer, Brown, and Platt, Chicago; former General Counsel, Atomic Energy Commission

Associate Director

FRITZ HEIMANN, Associate Corporate Counsel, General Electric Company

Associate Director

WALTER J. BLUM, Professor, University of Chicago Law School

Assistant Director

WILLIAM A. WEINBERG, Associate, Mayer, Brown, Platt, Chicago

Assistant Director

JOHN R. LABOVITZ, J.D., University of Chicago Law School, 1969

Chairman, Finance Committee

HERMON DUNLAP SMITH, Chairman, Finance Committee, Marlennan Corporation

Source: Peterson Commission Report, 1970

Appendix C

13. Ben W. Heineman—Chairman, Chicago and North Western Railway Company
14. Julius Stratton—Chairman of the Board, The Ford Foundation
15. McGeorge Bundy—President, The Ford Foundation
16. Whitney Young—President, The National Urban League
17. Whitney North Seymour—Counsel, Council on Library Resources and the International Legal Center

VI. Restrictive Effects on the Development of Philanthropy and Operation of Foundations Including Effects of "Expenditure Responsibility" and Heavy Penalty on Trustees

18. James Killian—Chairman, Board of Trustees of Massachusetts Institute of Technology
19. Dana Creel—President, Rockefeller Brothers Fund
20. Dr. Jonas Salk—Director, the Salk Institute for Biological Studies
21. John J. McCloy—Milbank, Tweed, Hadley, and McCloy

Source: Press Release, September 9, 1969, by the Foundation Center (RAC, RFA, RG4, NAR Personal Projects: Foundations, 72, Folder: 672)

Appendix D

Table of Contents
Peterson Commission Report

Appendix E

Members of the Filer Commission

Chairman
JOHN H. FILER, Chairman, Aetna Life & Casualty, Hartford, Conn.; Director, Hartford Institute of Criminal and Social Justice

Executive Director
LEONARD L. SILVERSTEIN, Silverstein and Mullens, Washington, D.C.; Director, National Symphony Orchestra Association

WILLIAM H. BOWEN, President, Commercial National Bank, Little Rock, Ark.; Director, Arkansas Association of Private Colleges

LESTER CROWN, President, Material Service Corporation, Chicago; Trustee, Northwestern University

C. DOUGLAS DILLON, Chairman, U.S. & Foreign Securities Corp., New York; President, Metropolitan Museum of Art

EDWIN D. ETHERINGTON, Former President, Wesleyan University, New York; Trustee, Alfred P. Sloan Foundation

BAYARD EWING, Tillinghast, Collins & Graham, Providence, R.I.; Vice Chairman, United Way of America

FRANCES TARLTON FARENTHOLD, Houston; Past Chairperson, National Women's Political Caucus

MAX M. FISHER, Chairman, United Brands Company, Boston; Honorary Chairman, United Foundations

The Most Rev. RAYMOND J. GALLAGHER, Bishop of Lafayette-in-Indiana, Lafayette, Ind.

EARL G. GRAVES, Publisher, Black Enterprise, New York; Commissioner, Boy Scouts of America

PAUL R. HAAS, President and Chairman, Corpus Christi Oil & Gas Company, Corpus Christi, Tex.; Trustee, Paul and Mary Haas Foundation

WALTER A. HAAS, JR., Chairman, Levi Strauss & Company, San Francisco; Trustee, Ford Foundation

PHILIP M. KLUTZNICK, Klutznick Investments, Chicago; Chairman, Research and Policy Committee and Trustee, Committee for Economic Development

RALPH LAZARUS, Chairman, Federated Department Stores, Inc., Cincinnati; Former National Chairman, United Way of America

HERBERT E. LONGENECKER, President Emeritus, Tulane University, New Orleans; Director, United Student Aid Funds

ELIZABETH J. MCCORMACK, Special Assistant to the President, Rockefeller Brothers Fund, Inc., New York

WALTER J. MCNERNEY, President, Blue Cross Association, Chicago

WILLIAM H. MORTON, New York, Trustee, Dartmouth College

JOHN M. MUSSER, President and Director, General Service Foundation, St. Paul, Minn.

JON O. NEWMAN, Judge, U.S. District Court, Hartford, Conn.; Chairman, Hartford Institute of Criminal and Social Justice

GRACIELA OLIVAREZ, State Planning Officer, New Mexico State Planning Office, Santa Fe; Director, Council on Foundations, Inc.

ALAN PIFER, President, Carnegie Corporation of New York, New York

GEORGE ROMNEY, Chairman, National Center for Voluntary Action, Washington, D.C.

WILLIAM MATSON ROTH, Regent, University of California, San Francisco; Chairman, San Francisco Museum of Art

ALTHEA T. L. SIMMONS, Director for Education Programs, NAACP Special Contribution Fund, New York

The Rev. LEON H. SULLIVAN, Pastor, Zion Baptist Church, Philadelphia

DAVID B. TRUMAN, President, Mount Holyoke College, South Hadley, Mass.

Source: Filer Commission Report, 1975, Appendix II

Appendix F

Filer Commission Consultants and Advisors

Consultants

HOWARD A. BOLTON, Milbank, Tweed, Hadley & McCloy, New York

WADE GREENE, writer and editor; editor and principal writer of the commission's report

WALDEMAR A. NIELSEN, Director of Program on Problems of American Pluralism, Aspen Institute for Humanistic Studies

STANLEY S. SURREY, Jeremiah Smith Professor of Law, Harvard University Law School

ADAM YARMOLINSKY, Ralph Waldo Emerson University Professor, University of Massachusetts

PAUL N. YLVISAKER, Dean, Graduate School of Education, Harvard University

Special Consultants

JAMES W. ABERNATHY, Director of Research, Grantsmanship Center

MARTIN S. FELDSTEIN, Professor of Economics, Harvard University

THEODORE J. JACOBS, Former Director, Center for Study of Responsive Law

PORTER MCKEEVER, Associate, John D. Rockefeller 3rd

RALPH L. NELSON, Professor of Economics, Queens College, City University of New York

JOHN J. SCHWARTZ, President, American Association of Fund-Raising Counsel

SALLY J. SHROYER, New York

CARLTON E. SPITZER, Vice President, T. J. Ross & Associates, Washington, D.C.

Advisory Committee

KENNETH I. ALBRECHT, Assistant Vice President, Corporate Affairs, Equitable Life Assurance Society of the U.S., New York

WILLIAM D. ANDREWS, Harvard University Law School

THOMAS R. ASHER, Executive Director, Study of Political Influence, Washington, D.C.

R. PALMER BAKER, JR., Lord, Day & Lord, New York

Msgr. GENO BARONI, The National Center for Urban Ethnic Affairs, Washington, D.C.

KIRK R. BATZER, Coopers & Lybrand, New York

EDMUND C. BENNETT, Tillinghast, Collins & Graham, Providence, R.I.

PHILIP BERNSTEIN, Executive Vice President, Council of Jewish Federations and Welfare Funds, Inc., New York

RICHARD M. BIRD, Institute of Policy Analysis, University of Toronto

BORIS I. BITTKER, Yale University Law School

ROBERT J. BLENDON, Vice President for Planning and Development, Robert Wood Johnson Foundation, Princeton, N.J.

WALTER J. BLUM, University of Chicago Law School, Chicago

HENRY M. BOETINGER, Director of Corporate Planning, American Telephone & Telegraph, New York

MICHAEL J. BOSKIN, Department of Economics, Stanford University

BLAIR T. BOWER, North Arlington, Virginia

GERARD M. BRANNON, Department of Economics, Georgetown University

GEORGE F. BREAK, Department of Economics, University of California, Berkeley

ROBERT H. BREMNER, Department of History, Ohio State University

HENRY R. BRETT, Corporate Contributions Counselor, Standard Oil Company of California, San Francisco

SARAH C. CAREY, Cladouhas and Brashares, Washington, D.C.

EARL F. CHEIT, Associate Director, Carnegie Council on Policy Studies in Higher Education, Berkeley, Calif.

CARL C. CLARK, Commission for the Advancement of Public Interest Organizations, Washington, D.C.

BICE CLEMOW, Editor, West Hartford, Conn.

EDWIN S. COHEN, University of Virginia Law School

SHELDON S. COHEN, Cohen and Uretz, Washington, D.C.

WILBUR J. COHEN, Dean, School of Education, University of Michigan, Ann Arbor

MARVIN K. COLLIE, Vinson, Elkins, Searls, Connally & Smith, Houston, Texas

FRED R. CRAWFORD, Department of Humanities, Emory University, Atlanta

CHARLES W. DAVIS, Hopkins, Sutter, Owen, Mulroy & Davis, Chicago

DELFORD W. EDENS, Haskins & Sells, New York

DONALD A. ERICKSON, Department of Education, Simon-Fraser University, Burnaby, B.C.

MARION R. FREMONT-SMITH, Choate, Hall & Stewart, Boston

F. DANIEL FROST, Gibson, Dunn & Crutcher, Los Angeles

DAVID GINSBURG, Ginsburg, Feldman and Bress, Washington, D.C.

ROBERT F. GOHEEN, Chairman, Council on Foundations, Inc., New York

S. PETER GOLDBERG, Council of Jewish Federations and Welfare Funds, Inc., New York

ARTHUR JACK GRIMES, American Institute of Biological Sciences, Arlington, Va.

MALVERN J. GROSS, Price Waterhouse & Co., Washington, D.C.

CHARLES R. HALPERN, Executive Director, Council for Public Interest Law, Washington, D.C.

JAMES F. HARRIS, The Conference Board, New York

C. LOWELL HARRISS, Department of Economics, Columbia University

CARYL P. HASKINS, Former President, Carnegie Institution of Washington, Washington, D.C.

ROBERT W. HEARN, Association of Black Foundation Executives, New York

FRITZ F. HEIMANN, General Electric Company, New York

WILLIAM G. HERBSTER, Senior Vice President, First National City Bank, New York

CAROLINE HIGHTOWER, Editor and writer, New York

THOMAS D. HINTON, Executive for Finance and Administration, United States Catholic Conference, Washington, D.C.

HARRY R. HORROW, Pillsbury, Madison & Sutro, San Francisco

JAMES T. HOSEY, Vice President and Executive Director, U.S. Steel Foundation, Pittsburgh

JOHN B. HUFFAKER, Pepper, Hamilton & Scheetz, Philadelphia

HANS H. JENNY, Vice President, Wooster College, Wooster, Ohio

DOUGLAS W. JOHNSON, Office of Research, Evaluation and Planning, National Council of Churches, New York

JANET KOCH, Writer, New York

MICHAEL S. KOLEDA, Director, Center for Health Policy Studies, National Planning Association, Washington, D.C.

ALBERT H. KRAMER, National Citizens Committee for Broadcasting, Washington, D.C.

THEODORE A. KURZ, Debevoise, Plimpton, Lyons & Gates, New York

ROBERT L. LAMBORN, Executive Director, Council for American Private Education, Washington, D.C.

ERIC LARRABEE, Former Executive Director, New York State Council on the Arts, New York

HARRY K. MANSFIELD, Ropes & Gray, Boston

LEE R. MARKS, Ginsburg, Feldman and Bress, Washington, D.C.

JANE H. MAVITY, New York

PAUL R. MCDANIEL, Boston College School of Law

PETER G. MEEK, Ridgewood, N.J.

MILTON MOSCOWITZ, Senior Editor, Business and Society Review, New York

Rev. ROBERT V. MONTICELLO, Associate General Secretary, United States Catholic Conference, Washington, D.C.

PHILLIP W. MOORE, Easton, Md.

JAMES N. MORGAN, Survey Research Center, University of Michigan

ROBERT H. MULREANY, DeForest & Duer, New York

JOHN HOLT MYERS, Williams, Myers and Quiggle, Washington, D.C.

MICHAEL K. NEWTON, President, Associated Council of the Arts, New York

JOHN S. NOLAN, Miller & Chevalier, Washington, D.C.

JOSEPH M. PAUL, Assistant Chief, Charitable Foundations Section, Office of the Attorney General, State of Ohio, Columbus

JOSEPH A. PERLMAN, The Brookings Institution, Washington, D.C.

JOHN P. PERSONS, Patterson, Belknap & Webb, New York

PETER J. PETKAS, Director, Southern Governmental Monitoring Project, Atlanta

TIMOTHY J. RACEK, Arthur Andersen & Co., New York

THOMAS W. RICHARDS, National Trust for Historic Preservation, Washington, D.C.

HAROLD ROSER, Manager, Community Development Programs, Exxon Corporation, New York

ALVIN L. SCHORR, Community Service Society of New York, New York

JOHN F. SHANNON, Assistant Director, Advisory Commission on Intergovernmental Relations, Washington, D.C.

IRA SILVERMAN, Executive Director, Institute for Jewish Policy Planning and Research, Washington, D.C.

JOHN G. SIMON, Yale University Law School

DAVID HORTON SMITH, Department of Sociology, Boston College

DONALD R. SPUEHLER, O'Melveny & Myers, Los Angeles

J. JOHN STEVENSON, Chief, Charitable Foundations Section, Office of the Attorney General, State of Ohio, Columbus

LAWRENCE M. STONE, School of Law, University of California, Berkeley

NORMAN A. SUGARMAN, Baker, Hostetler & Patterson, Cleveland

EMIL M. SUNLEY, JR., The Brookings Institution, Washington, D.C.

WAYNE E. THOMPSON, Senior Vice President, Dayton-Hudson Corporation, Minneapolis

T. NICOLAUS TIDEMAN, Department of Economics, Virginia Polytechnic Institute and State University, Blacksburg, Va.

THOMAS A. TROYER, Caplin & Drysdale, Washington, D.C.

MARY JEAN TULLY, President, NOW Legal Defense and Education Fund, New York

JOHN H. VANDENBERG, Assistant to Council of the Twelve, Salt Lake City

THOMAS VASQUEZ, Financial Economist, U.S. Department of the Treasury, Washington, D.C.

JOSEPH L. VIGILANTE, Dean, School of Social Work, Adelphi University, Garden City, N.Y.

RICHARD E. WAGNER, Center for Study of Public Choice, Virginia Polytechnic Institute and State University, Blacksburg, Va.

JOHN A. WALLACE, King & Spalding, Atlanta

VICTOR WEINGARTEN, President, Institute of Public Affairs, Inc., New York

BURTON A. WEISBROD, Department of Economics, University of Wisconsin, Madison, Wis.

DAVID WESTFALL, Harvard University Law School

A.M. WIGGINS, JR., Reed Smith Shaw & McClay, Pittsburgh

AARON WILDAVSKY, Dean, Graduate School of Public Policy, University of California, Berkeley

LAURENS WILLIAMS (Deceased), Sutherland, Asbill & Brennan, Washington, D.C.

ELLEN WINSTON, Raleigh, N.C.

BERNARD WOLFMAN, Center for Advanced Study in the Behavioral Sciences, Stanford, Calif.

RAUL YZAGUIRRE, Executive Director, National Council of La Raza, Washington, D.C.

Source: Giving in America, 1975, Appendix III

Appendix G

Recommendations of the Filer Commission

Broadening the Base of Philanthropy

Extending and Amplifying the Deduction

Recommendations

1. That to increase inducements for charitable giving, all taxpayers who take the standard deduction should also be permitted to deduct charitable contributions as an additional, itemized deduction.
2. That an additional inducement to charitable giving should be provided to low- and middle-income taxpayers. Toward this end, the Commission proposes that a "double deduction" be instituted for families with incomes of less than $15,000 a year; they would be allowed to deduct twice what they give in computing their income taxes. For those families with incomes between $15,000 and $30,000, the Commission proposes a deduction of 150 percent of their giving.

Minimum Tax

Recommendation

That income deducted for charitable giving should be excluded from any minimum tax provision.

Appreciated Property

Recommendation

That the appreciated property allowance within the charitable deduction be basically retained but amended to eliminate any possibility of personal financial gain through tax-deductible charitable giving.

Charitable Bequests

Recommendation

That the charitable bequest deduction be retained in its present form.

Corporate Giving

Recommendation

That corporations set as a minimum goal, to be reached no later than 1980, the giving to charitable purposes of 2 percent of pre-tax net income. Moreover, the Commission believes that the national commission proposed in this report should consider as a priority concern additional measures to stimulate corporate giving.

Improving the Philanthropic Process

Accountability

Recommendations

1. That all larger tax-exempt charitable organizations except churches and church affiliates be required to prepare and make readily available detailed annual reports on their finances, programs and priorities.
2. That larger grant-making organizations be required to hold annual public meetings to discuss their programs, priorities and contributions.
3. That the present 4 percent "audit" tax on private foundations be repealed and replaced by a fee on all private foundations based on the total actual costs of auditing them.
4. That the Internal Revenue Service continue to be the principal agency responsible for the oversight of tax-exempt organizations.

Accessibility

Recommendations

1. That the duplication of legal responsibility for proper expenditure of foundation grants, now imposed on both foundations and recipients, be eliminated and that recipient organizations be made primarily responsible for their expenditures.
2. That tax-exempt organizations, particularly funding organizations, recognize an obligation to be responsive to changing viewpoints and emerging needs and that they take steps such as broadening their boards and staffs to insure that they are responsive.
3. That a new category of "independent" foundation be established by law. Such organizations would enjoy the tax benefits of public charities in return for diminished influence on the foundation's board by

the foundation's benefactor or by his or her family or business associates.

Minimizing Personal or Institutional Self-benefitting

Recommendations

1. That all tax-exempt organizations be required by law to maintain "arms-length" business relationships with profit-making organizations or activities in which any member of the organization's staff, any board member or any major contributor has a substantial financial interest, either directly or through his or her family.
2. That to discourage unnecessary accumulation of income, a flat payout rate of 5 percent of principal be fixed by Congress for private foundations and a lower rate for other endowed tax-exempt organizations.
3. That a system of federal regulation be established for interstate charitable solicitations and that intrastate solicitations be more effectively regulated by state governments.
4. That as a federal enforcement tool against abuses by tax-exempt organizations, and to protect these organizations themselves, sanctions appropriate to the abuses should be enacted as well as forms of administrative or judicial review of the principal existing sanction-revocation of an organization's exempt status.

Influencing Legislation

Recommendation

That nonprofit organizations, other than foundations, be allowed the same freedoms to attempt to influence legislation as are business corporations and trade associations, that toward this end Congress remove the current limitation on such activity by charitable groups eligible to receive tax-deductible gifts.

A Permanent Commission

Recommendation

That a permanent national commission on the nonprofit sector be established by Congress.

Source: Table of Contents, Filer Commission Report, 1970

Notes

1. Introduction

1. Since in this book I will primarily be discussing one Rockefeller—John D. 3rd—to avoid awkward redundancy I will generally refer to Mr. Rockefeller by a variety of shorter names, including JDR 3rd or simply Rockefeller. If I need to make a distinction between John D. Rockefeller 3rd and one of the other Rockefellers I will use appropriate terms to distinguish them, as for example the first John D. Rockefeller, John D. Rockefeller, Jr. ("Junior"), or Nelson Rockefeller.

2. Both men were corporate executives when they were selected as Chairmen. At the time he assumed leadership of the Commission on Foundations and Private Philanthropy, Peter ("Pete") Peterson was Chairman and Chief Executive Officer of Bell and Howell in Chicago. John Filer was Chairman and Chief Executive Office of Aetna Life and Casualty in Hartford, Connecticut. How they were selected will be discussed in later chapters.

3. Most estimates for the number of existing nonprofit organizations come from the Master File of Tax-Exempt Organizations of the U.S. Internal Revenue Service (IRS). In 1997, there were 1,232,214 organizations in the IRS Master File of which more than one half (or 692,524) were defined as charitable (including religious, social welfare, educational, literary, scientific and other public benefit purposes) under the Internal Revenue Code, section 501(c)(3). The actual number, however, is generally considered to be larger than indicated by the list, because organizations with recent annual revenues of under $25,000 and most religious organizations (churches, synagogues, mosques) do not have to register.

4. Alexis de Tocqueville, *Democracy in America* (1835), translated by G. Lawrence (New York: Anchor Books, 1969), Vol. 2, chapter 5, p. 513.

5. For discussion of these views, see for example John Ensor Harr and Peter J. Johnson, *The Rockefeller Century: Three Generations of America's Greatest Family* (New York: Charles Scribner's Sons, 1988); Richard Hofstadter, *The Age of Reform: From Bryan to FDR* (New York: Vintage Books, 1955), pp. 186–214; and Ben B. Seligman, *The Potentates: Business and Businessmen in American History* (New York: Dial Press), 1971). Hofstadter points out that one of the famous attacks on the Rockefeller interests and Standard Oil in the late 1890s was written by Ida Tarbell for *McClure's* Magazine (one of the "muckraking journals"), and that Ms. Tarbell claimed it was somewhat accidental.

6. These lines from a poem by John Boyle O'Reilly called "In Bohemia" (1886) are cited in June Axinn and Herman Levin, *Social Welfare: A History of the American Response to Need,* 2nd ed. (New York: Longman, 1982), p. 327, n. 50.

7. Eleanor L. Brilliant, *The United Way: Dilemmas of Organized Charity* (New York: Columbia University Press, 1990). For a discussion of this view at an earlier point of time see also Roy Lubove, *The Professional Altruist: The Emergence of Social Work as a Career* (New York: Atheneum, 1969), chapter 7.

8. Eleanor L. Brilliant, "Voluntarism," in *Encyclopedia of Social Work,* 19th ed. (Washington, D.C.: NASW Press, 1995), pp. 2469–2482; Kathleen McCarthy, Virginia A. Hodgkinson, and Russy D. Sumariwalla, *The Nonprofit Sector in the Global Community: Voices from Many Nations* (San Francisco: Jossey-Bass, 1992); Ann McKinstry Mciou and Birgit Lindsnaes, eds., *The Role of Voluntary Organizations in Emerging Democracies: Experience and Strate-*

gies in Eastern and Central Europe and in South Africa (Denmark: Danish Centre for Human Rights, 1993); Daniel Siegel and Jenny Yancey, *The Rebirth of Civil Society: The Development of the Nonprofit Sector in East Central Europe and the Role of Western Assistance* (New York: Rockefeller Fund, 1992).

9. This is certainly so even though we recognize the importance of some form of voluntary action or philanthropic activity in many other places around the world, and of course notably in England, whose Poor Laws of 1601 are credited for much of our legal delineation of charitable purposes and trusts.

10. The terms third, nonprofit, voluntary, and not-for-profit sector are generally used interchangeably by most authors, and I will do the same. Although the term "independent sector" is sometimes used, it has a more normative or specific definition. See Brilliant, "Voluntarism," and Virginia A. Hodgkinson, Murray S. Weitzman, et al., *Nonprofit Almanac, 1992– 1993: Dimensions of the Voluntary Sector* (San Francisco: Jossey-Bass, 1992).

11. For expert discussion of the legal definitions of tax-exempt organizations generally, see Bruce R. Hopkins, *The Law of Tax-Exempt Organizations* (New York: John Wiley & Sons, 1992); this book also includes a thorough consideration of the way that 501(c)(3) organizations have been specifically delineated in American law.

12. Although earlier efforts had been made to establish a federal income tax in the 19th century, it was not until the passage of the Sixteenth Amendment to the Constitution that the income tax was finally considered constitutional; immediately thereafter it was incorporated in the Tariff Act of 1913. With America's entry into the First World War income taxes were increased significantly, and at the same time, in what was to become an established pattern, the War Revenue Act of 1917 made contributions to charitable organizations deductible from taxable income (War Revenue Act of 1917, Sec. 1202 (2), 40 Stat 300, 330). See discussions in Hopkins, *Law of Tax-Exempt Organizations,* pp. 98–99; Sheldon Pollack, *The Failure of U.S. Tax Policy: Revenue and Politics* (University Park: Pennsylvania State University Press, 1996), pp. 45–56; and Paul E. Treusch and Norman A. Sugarman, *Tax-Exempt Charitable Organizations* (Philadelphia: American Law Institute, 1979), p. 5.

13. Burton A. Weisbrod, *The Nonprofit Economy* (Cambridge, Mass.: Harvard University Press, 1988), pp. 62–63. Weisbrod notes that in 1967 there were 309,000 organizations designated as tax exempt by the IRS, and the number tripled in less than twenty years to almost 900,000. In the same period, the number of charitable 501(c)(3) organizations also increased dramatically from 138,000 in 1969 to 366,000 in 1985 (an increase of over 160 percent).

14. Extensive discussion of various social science models of policy making can be found in Thomas R. Dye, *Understanding Public Policy,* 7th ed. (Englewood Cliffs: Prentice Hall, 1992).

15. See Ferdinand Lundberg, *The Rich and the Super-Rich: A Study in the Power of Money Today* (New York: Lyle Stuart, Inc., 1968); and Joseph C. Goulden, *The Money Givers: An Example of the Myths and Realities of Foundation Philanthropy in America* (New York: Random House, 1971). See also the slightly later book, G. William Domhoff, *The Powers That Be: Processes of Ruling Class Domination in America* (New York: Vintage Books, 1978).

16. This view was developed by Robert A. Dahl and other pluralists. See Dahl, *A Preface to Democratic Theory* (Chicago: University of Chicago Press, 1967), and his earlier seminal study of an American community, Dahl, *Who Governs? Democracy and Power in an American City* (New Haven: Yale University Press, 1961). The theory has been criticized as not reflecting the reality of American life. Among early critics of the actual nature of pluralism, see Henry S. Kariel, *The Decline of American Pluralism* (Stanford, Calif.: Stanford University Press, 1961). Many political sociologists have however never accepted the idea of pluralism, see for example Arthur Kornhauser, ed., *Problems of Power in American Democracy* (Detroit: Wayne State University Press, 1957), and the more recent argument in G. William Domhoff, *Who Rules America Now? A View for the '80s* (New York: Simon & Schuster, 1983).

17. Benjamin R. Barber, *Strong Democracy: Participatory Politics for a New Age* (Berke-

ley: University of California Press, 1984); Marvin E. Olson, *Participatory Pluralism: Political Participation and Influence in the United States and Sweden* (Chicago: Nelson-Hall, 1982).

18. This point is discussed throughout this book. See also Guy Beneviste, *The Politics of Expertise,* 2nd ed. (San Francisco: Boyd and Frazier Publishing, 1977).

19. In his discussion of incrementalism in *Understanding Public Policy,* Dye generally includes incrementalism in the same context as other models such as interest group or elite policy making, rather than distinguishing between the nature of the policy made and who participates. However, incrementalism is really a different kind of approach—consisting of small degrees of change—as contrasted with comprehensive sudden change. Although incrementalism is a separate concept, empirically it is generally associated with diffused decision making, and input from many groups.

20. See for example the classic article by Charles E. Lindblom, "The Science of Muddling Through" in *Public Administration Review,* Vol.19 (Spring 1959), pp. 79–88; David Braybrooke and Charles E. Lindblom, *A Strategy of Decision-Making* (New York: The Free Press of Glencoe, 1963); Aaron Wildavsky, "Budgets as Compromises among Social Orders" in Michael J. Boskin and Aaron Wildavsky, eds., *The Federal Budget and Politics* (San Francisco: Jossey-Bass, 1982); and Wildavsky, *The New Politics of the Budgetary Process,* 2nd ed. (New York: Harper Collins, 1992).

21. See for example Stuart Nagel, *Policy Evaluation: Making Optimum Decisions* (New York: Praeger, 1982); Edith Stokey and Richard Zechauser, *A Primer for Policy Analysis* (New York: W. W. Norton, 1978); and David L. Weimer and Aidan R. Vining, *Policy Analysis: Concepts and Practices,* 2nd ed. (Englewood Cliffs, N.J.: Prentice-Hall, 1992).

22. See the discussion of the highly touted (and later discarded) complex Planning, Program, Budgeting System (PPBS) in government decision-making in Wildavsky, *The New Politics of the Budgetary Process.*

23. The interaction of such groups is discussed in Lundberg, *The Rich and the Super-Rich,* and in G. William Domhoff, *State Autonomy or Class Dominance? Case Studies on Policy Making in America* (New York: Aldine de Gruyter, 1996).

2. Point and Counterpoint

1. Legislation creating the commission was enacted by Congress under a Republican President, William Howard Taft, but was implemented under a Democratic President, Woodrow Wilson. The Chairman of the commission, Frank P. Walsh, was a trial lawyer from Missouri, and not a U.S. Senator, although he is called a Senator in F. Emerson Andrews, *Foundation Watcher* (Lancaster, Pa.: Franklin and Marshall College Press, 1973), p. 161; other writers also mistakenly use this title. A history of this commission can be found in *Age of Industrial Violence 1910–1915: The Activities and Findings of the United States Commission on Industrial Relations,* by Graham Adams, Jr. (New York: Columbia University Press, 1966). Harr and Johnson discuss the events of this period somewhat differently in *The Rockefeller Century,* pp. 125–149.

2. Selig Perlman, *A History of Trade Unionism in the United States* (New York: Augustus M. Kelley, 1950), p. 228. See also "Report of Basil M. Manly," Director of Research and Investigation, *Final Report of the Commission on Industrial Relations* (U.S. Commission on Industrial Relations: Washington, D.C., 1915), p. 8.

3. See "$1,000,000 Limit on Big Fortunes," *New York Times,* August 23, 1915, p. 16; and "Industrial Board Winds up Its Work," *New York Times,* August 1, 1915, p. 11, in which the amount of $500,000 is given for the cost of the commission. The composition of the commission is also discussed in Adams, *Age of Industrial Violence,* pp. 54–71. It is worth noting also that the power to subpoena witnesses is not automatically given to ad hoc public advisory commissions or even to all special or select committees of the Congress. Interview with David Linowes, Scarsdale, New York, June 19, 1996.

4. Views of Rep. James F. Byrnes of South Carolina, U.S. House of Representatives, 63rd Cong., 3rd Sess. (Doc. No. 1630), *Report on the Colorado Strike Resolution Made under House Resolution 387,* March 2, 1915, p. 45.

5. Adams, *Age of Industrial Violence,* pp. 161–168.

6. For more detail about this incident from two different viewpoints, see Peter Collier and David Horowitz, *The Rockefellers: An American Dynasty* (New York: Holt, Rinehart & Winston, 1976), pp. 109–133, and Harr and Johnson, *The Rockefeller Century,* pp. 125–142. Original papers, telegrams, and miscellaneous items relating to this incident can also be found in files in the RCA, RFA, RG2, Business Interests, Box 23. In December 1914 the President also appointed a three-man commission after federal troops had not succeeded in bringing peace to the area. Letter from the President of the United States Transmitting *Report of the Colorado Coal Commission on the Labor Difficulties in the Coal Fields of Colorado During the Years 1914–1915,* March 8, 1916, in U.S. House of Representatives, 64th Cong., 1st Sess. (Document No. 859), *Labor Difficulties in the Coal Fields of Colorado.*

7. In this regard JDR Jr. stated that "the conduct of the business is in the hands of the officers" and in response to questioning about the violence toward employees said that he would stand by the "great principle" (in effect that the UMW would not represent company employees in negotiations). Testimony by John D. Rockefeller, Jr., Hearings of the U.S. House of Representatives, 63rd Cong., 2nd Sess., *Labor Difficulties in the Coal Fields of Colorado,* Part I (February 9,10,11, and 12, 1914), pp. 2841–2900. Rockefeller testified that "I have only such stock as qualifies me as a director. . . . I am one of my father's representatives in the case of this and other of his personal investments," and he states among other things that his father's holdings in the CFI consist of 40 percent of the common stock and 40 percent of the preferred stock.

8. Adams, *Age of Industrial Violence,* pp. 161–168.

9. See Collier and Horowitz, *The Rockefellers,* pp. 116–119; and Harr and Johnson, *The Rockefeller Century,* pp. 128–145.

10. "Manly Report," pp. 23–33, 116–126.

11. "Asks Confiscation of Great Fortunes," *New York Times,* August 18, 1915, p. 1: "The Confiscator Chairman," Editorial, *New York Times,* August 19, 1915, p. 8. See also Collier and Horowitz, *The Rockefellers,* p. 125.

12. Collier and Horowitz, *The Rockefellers,* pp. 126–133; Harr and Johnson, *The Rockefeller Century,* p. 141.

13. See Adams, *Age of Industrial Violence,* pp. 221–223.

14. "Manly Report," pp. 116–121. Although the exact terminology refers to "non-profit-making" bodies, the context of the discussion makes it evident that the primary focus is on the foundations.

15. There is a certain irony in this recommendation, for in fact, a few years before (1908), John D. Senior had tried unsuccessfully to get a Congressional Charter for the Rockefeller Foundation. See Harr and Johnson, *The Rockefeller Century,* p. 83.

16. "Manly Report," pp. 125–126.

17. Marion Fremont-Smith, *Foundations and Government: State and Federal Law and Supervision* (New York: Russell Sage Foundation, 1965), pp. 51–52. This also was the period when philanthropic leaders became more self-conscious about their roles, and one of them wrote a series of books on philanthropic giving and foundations. See for example F. Emerson Andrews, *Philanthropic Giving* (New York: Russell Sage Foundation, 1950); Andrews, *Corporate Giving* (New York: Russell Sage Foundation, 1952).

18. See James T. Patterson, *Grand Expectations: The United States, 1941–1971* (New York: Oxford University Press, 1996).

19. John D. Morris, "Foundations Face Inquiry by House," *New York Times,* July 2, 1951. The Committee that was subsequently formed was referred to by various names, including the Cox Committee, but apparently was formally named "Select Committee to Investigate

and Study Educational and Philanthropic Foundations and Other Comparable Organizations Which Are Exempt from Federal Income Taxation." In the published hearings, *Tax-Exempt Foundations,* the name appears in a shorter form as Select Committee to Investigate Tax-Exempt Foundations and Comparable Organizations (November 15, 19, 20, 21, 24, 25, December 2, 3, 5, 8, 9 10, 11, 15, 17, 22, 23, and 30, 1952), U.S. House of Representatives, 82nd Cong., 2nd Sess. (Washington, D.C.: GPO, 1953). I will generally use an even briefer name, "Select Committee to Investigate Foundations and Comparable Organizations," or, more simply, the Cox Committee.

20. F. E. Andrews, *Foundation Watcher,* and Andrews, *Patman and Foundations: Review and Assessment* (New York: The Foundation Center, 1968 [Occasional Papers: Number Three]), pp. 2–5. See also Fremont-Smith, *Foundations and Government,* pp. 356–365. Cox died on December 24, 1952 before his committee's final report was issued, and Representative Brooks Hays (Arkansas) took over. However, the final report notes that a draft was submitted to Cox before he died. The impact of these committee hearings on the Rockefellers is discussed in John Ensor Harr and Peter J. Johnson, *The Rockefeller Conscience: An American Family in Public and Private* (New York: Charles Scribner's Sons, 1991), pp. 92–97.

21. U.S. House of Representatives, *Final Report of the Select Committee to Investigate and Study Educational and Philanthropic Foundations and Other Comparable Organizations Which Are Exempt from Federal Income Taxation,* 82nd Congress, 2nd Sess., House Report 2514, 1953 (Washington, D.C.: GPO, 1953), p. 8.

22. The fact that Reece got less than half the funding he asked for ($50,000 instead of the requested $125,000) suggests that there may not have been great enthusiasm for his undertaking. Figures cited in letter to JDR 3 from Dean Rusk, August 6, 1953, with *Congressional Record* of July 27, 1953 attached (RFA, RG5, JDR 3rd, Rockefeller Foundation, Misc. 1952–55, Box 31, Folder: Reece Committee).

23. Gunnar Myrdal, *An American Dilemma: The Negro Problem and Modern Democracy* (New York: Harper and Brothers, 1944).

24. Alfred Charles Kinsey, Wardell Baxter Pomeroy, and Clyde Eugene Martin, *Sexual Behavior in the Human Male* (Philadelphia, Pa.: W. B. Saunders, 1948). Reece's reaction is discussed in Alvin Moscow, *The Rockefeller Inheritance* (Garden City, New York, 1977), p. 148.

25. F. Emerson Andrews, *Philanthropic Foundations* (New York: Russell Sage Foundation, 1956), p. 346.

26. William J. Ballinger, "Leftward Ho: The Report of the Reece Committee on Foundations," in *Human Events,* Vol. 12 (9), February 26, 1955.

27. The attacks also drew to a close around the time that McCarthy and McCarthyism were being discredited. For a recent review of this period see Patterson, *Grand Expectations,* pp. 165–206.

28. U.S. House of Representatives, *Report of the Special Committee to Investigate Tax-Exempt Foundations and Comparable Organizations* (the Reece Committee), 83rd Congress, 2nd Sess., House Report 2681 (Washington, D.C.: GPO, 1954). For later discussions of this position from the opposite (liberal) side of the political spectrum, see Edward H. Berman, *The Influence of the Carnegie, Ford and Rockefeller Foundations on American Foreign Policy: The Ideology of Philanthropy* (Albany: State University of New York Press, 1983); G. William Domhoff, *Who Rules America?* (Englewood Cliffs, N.J.: Prentice-Hall, 1967); Domhoff, *State Autonomy or Class Dominance?* pp. 26–45; Myer Kutz, *Rockefeller Power: America's Chosen Family* (New York: Simon and Schuster, 1974; and Lundberg, *The Rich and the Super-Rich.*

29. From 1940 to 1949, an estimated 1,638 new foundations were created, from 1950 to 1959, another 2,839 were added (prior to 1940 there appear to have been under 1,000 known to be in existence). The figures are found in Irving Louis Horowitz and Ruth Leonora Horowitz, "Tax-Exempt Foundations: Their Effects on National Policy," *Science,* Vol. 168 (April 1970), pp. 220–228, Table 1, where it is indicated that they are based on Treasury Department tabulations of foundations having at least $100,000 assets in 1962, and therefore that were in-

cluded in the 1962 *Directory* of the Foundation Library Center. Although the Cox Committee reported that they could not determine the exact number of foundations in existence at the time of their report, nonetheless they estimated the number of those with permanent endowments of over $50,000 to be around 1,000, and also suggested that there was a mushrooming of smaller family-type foundations. See *Final Report of the Select Committee to Investigate Foundations and Comparable Organizations,* pp. 2–3.

30. "The present tax laws governing the transfer and inheritance of property are bringing upon the Nation an avalanche of tax-free foundations whose assets are based on corporation securities.

"This means that within a relatively short period of time a problem which may now appear to be a small one could grow to gigantic and dangerous proportions. . . .

"Nor is it hard to envision the tremendous influence in educational and civic projects, that could be wielded by the handful of men to whom the spending of these funds would be entrusted." From the typescript, *Congressional Record,* Special Committee to Investigate Tax-Exempt Foundations (Reece Committee), April 23, 1953, pp. 3776–3777 in RAC, Rockefeller Foundation, Box 31, Folder: Reece Committee.

31. For example, Professor Owen Lattimore, of Johns Hopkins, who was also associated with one of the prestigious institutions formerly funded by the Rockefeller Foundation (Institute for Pacific Relations, the "IPR"). The story of these hearings is told in some detail in Harr and Johnson, *The Rockefeller Conscience,* pp. 92–97.

32. House Resolution 561, creating the Cox Committee, 82nd Congress, 2nd Session, April 4, 1952. Cited in *Final Report of the Select Committee to Investigate Foundations and Comparable Organizations,* p. 2.

33. Revenue Act of 1943, Section 117, House Report 871, 78th Cong., 1st Sess., pp. 24–25. Cited and discussed in Laurens Williams and Donald V. Moorehead, "An Analysis of the Federal Tax Distinctions between Public and Private Charitable Organizations" (1975), in Commission on Private Philanthropy and Public Needs, *Research Papers* (Washington, D.C.: U.S. Department of Treasury, 1977, Volume IV, Part I), p. 2101.

34. *Final Report of the Select Committee to Investigate Foundations and Comparable Organizations,* p. 6.

35. Revenue Act of 1950, sec. 341, later Int. Rev. Code of 1954, Sec. 6033. Cited in Fremont-Smith, *Foundations and Government,* p. 360.

36. *Final Report of the Select Committee to Investigate Foundations and Comparable Organizations,* pp. 6 and 13.

37. James J. McGovern, "Tax Exemption Provisions of Subchapter F," *Tax Lawyer,* 29, 523, cited in David L. Gies, J. Steven Ott, and Jay M. Shafritz, *The Nonprofit Organization: Essential Readings* (Pacific Grove, Calif.: Brooks-Cole Publishing, 1990), p. 126. See also Hopkins, *Law of Tax-Exempt Organizations,* pp. 6–8.

38. Fremont-Smith, *Foundations and Government.* Hopkins makes a distinction between the concept of "nonprofit organization" which he considers mostly a matter of state law, and the concept of "tax-exempt organization" which he considers principally a matter of federal tax law, Hopkins, *Law of Tax-Exempt Organizations,* p. 3.

39. For a period of about 100 years after the American Revolution, states in our country rejected the British precedent of charitable trusts and turned instead to corporate law for establishing charitable entities in our country. Charitable trusts are again being widely used, but most foundations, like other charities, are still formed under the laws of corporations (although they may also be the beneficiary of charitable trusts). See John P. Persons, John J. Osburn, Jr., and Charles F. Feldman (1976), "Criteria for Exemption under Section 501(c)(3)," in Commission on Private Philanthropy and Public Needs, *Research Papers* (Washington, D.C.: U.S. Department of Treasury, 1977, Volume IV, Part I), pp. 1909–2043. Basic principles of state laws on charitable trusts and charitable organizations (as of the mid 1960s) are analyzed in detail in Fremont-Smith, *Foundations and Government.*

40. I want to thank Donald W. Kramer, an attorney (with Montgomery, McCracken, and Rhoads) who specializes in nonprofit law, for his cautionary reminder about different treatment levels and kinds of tax benefits for charitable organizations in the various states.

41. According to Persons, Osborn, and Feldman, "federal income statutes in force briefly during and after the Civil War applied only to certain specified classes of business corporations, such as railroads, canal companies, and banks." Therefore any corporation not named was not taxed, and "no exemption provisions were needed to relieve charitable organizations from such taxes." Persons, Osborn, and Feldman, "Criteria for Exemption," p. 1993, n. 110. The income tax provision was written into the national Wilson-Gorman Tariff Act of 1894.

42. Revenue Act of 1913, Ch.16, 38 Stat. 114 (1913). It should be noted however that a federal tax on legacies was instituted in 1898 (without any exemptions) and that an exemption from this tax for charitable purposes was initially enacted in 1901. See Persons, Osborn, and Feldman, "Criteria for Exemption," p. 1925.

43. Hopkins, citing McGovern, "Tax Exemption Provisions of Subchapter F," points out that prior to 1894 it was not necessary to exclude, by name, any particular organizations from taxes because until that time "tax 'exemption' existed by statutory omission." It was only when the Tariff Act of 1894 placed a flat two percent on corporate income that Congress was forced to define the appropriate subjects for tax exemption. Hopkins, *Law of Tax-Exempt Organizations*, p. 7. The 1894 Act stated expressly that these taxes did not apply "to any corporation or association organized or operated exclusively for religious, educational, or charitable purposes, no part of the net income of which inures to the benefit of any private stockholder or individual." 28 Stat. 556 (1984), cited in Fremont-Smith, *Foundations and Government*, pp. 64–65.

44. Cited in Hopkins, *Law of Tax-Exempt Organizations*, p. 71. Note however that these uses have been interpreted more as a listing (or enumeration) of possible charitable uses, than a true definition—thus allowing British law (and later American law as well) latitude in making decisions in specific cases. Note also that although this list in some respects has remarkable currency today (allowing for some language difficulties), we would probably consider many of the activities listed more properly the subject of public, i.e., governmental obligations.

45. 36 Stat. 11 (1909).

46. Williams and Moorehead, "An Analysis of the Federal Tax Distinctions between Public and Private Charitable Organizations," p. 2100; Fremont-Smith, *Foundations and Government*, pp. 64–65.

47. See Hopkins, *Law of Tax-Exempt Organizations*, pp. 77–84 and pp. 123–127; and Persons, Osborn, and Feldman, "Criteria for Exemption," pp. 1909–1950. In the spring of 1996 the idea of giving differential tax treatment to charitable organizations that focus on helping the poor emerged in Congress, "The Debate over Dole's Tax Credit," in *Chronicle of Philanthropy*, Vol. 8 (17), June 13, 1996, p. 9.

48. *Commissioners of Income Tax v. Pemsel*, quoted in Persons, Osborn, and Feldman, "Criteria for Exemption," p. 1914, but widely discussed elsewhere as well in reference to the definition of charity. Hopkins also notes that *Pemsel* is cited frequently by the U.S. Supreme Court, see Hopkins, *Law of Tax-Exempt Organizations*, p. 71. The concept of "charitable trusts" used by McNaughten reflects the more general use of the charitable trust by the British as compared with our organizational form in the United States, and goes back to Elizabethan times and the practices embedded in the *Preamble* cited above (n.33).

49. It is claimed that the formation of foundations or charitable organizations by Carnegie, Rockefeller, and other early millionaires was not motivated by benefits from charitable tax deductions because they created (or wished to create) foundations prior to the establishment of the federal income tax. See for example Statement of J. George Harrar, Alan Pifer, and David Freeman, in *Foundations and the Tax Bill: Testimony on Title I of the Tax Reform Act of 1969, Submitted by Witnesses Appearing before the United States Senate Finance Committee, October 1969* (New York: Foundation Center, 1969), pp. 53–71. However, this argu-

ment is misleading and can be challenged on several grounds: first, the foundations were established with gifts of corporate stocks that would have otherwise been subject to taxation under the Corporation Excise Law of 1909; second, in the early 1900s Theodore Roosevelt was renewing trust busting activities, and in 1911 the Court decided against Standard Oil of New Jersey (a major business of the Rockefellers); and third, charitable gifts had been exempted from legacy taxes in 1901 (see note 42 above). Thus there were many reasons why charitable foundations controlled by corporate owners might be a desirable location for their stocks and bonds.

50. Section 5 (a) of Public Law No. 271 (64th Congress), the Revenue Act of 1916, was headed "Deductions Allowed" and contained eight paragraphs describing these deductions. However, the charitable deduction was not in fact realized until the 1916 Act was amended by Public Law No. 50 (65th Congress). In the Law (P.L. 50) passed on October 3, 1917 Section 1202 (2) contained the following additional paragraph to add to Section 5 (a) of the 1916 Revenue Act:

> Ninth. Contributions or gifts actually made within the year to corporations or associations organized and operated exclusively for religious, charitable, scientific or educational purposes, or to societies for the prevention of cruelty to children or animals, no part of the net income of which inures to the benefit of any private stockholder or individual, to an amount not in access of fifteen per centum of the taxpayer's taxable net income as computed without the benefit of this paragraph. Such contributions or gifts shall be allowed as deductions only if verified under rules and regulations prescribed by the Commissioner of Internal Revenue, with the approval of the Secretary of the Treasury.

I want to thank Martin D. Ginsburg (Fried, Frank, Harris, Shriver and Jacobson in Washington, D.C.) for helping to clarify the exact origins of the charitable tax deduction and for providing the quotation above.

51. Indeed, this is why the 4 percent "excise" tax later inserted in the Tax Reform Act of 1969 was considered such a serious threat to the principle of tax immunities that foundations had always enjoyed. See chapter 6.

52. Williams and Moorehead, "An Analysis of Federal Distinctions."

53. 40 Stat. 1057 (1918).

54. Revenue Act of 1932 (now Section 2522 of the IRC). See Lawrence Stone, "Federal Tax Support for Charities and Other Exempt Organizations" (1968), statement submitted to House of Representatives, Committee on Ways and Means, U.S. Cong., 91st Cong., 1st Sess. Hearings on Tax Reform, Part 1, pp. 155–206.

55. D. H. McLean, Jr., "Legislative History of Deductions for Charitable Contributions" (manuscript), May 20, 1963, p. 1 (RAC, GF, RG3, Box 379). See also E. C. Lashbrooke, *Tax Exempt Organizations* (Westport, Conn.: Quorum Books, 1985).

56. For more in-depth discussions of the rationale for the nonprofit sector (that is, for the existence of a "third," tax-exempt sector, including largely charitable organizations), see James Douglas, *Why Charity? The Case for a Third Sector* (Beverly Hills, Calif.: Sage Publications, 1983); Henry Hansmann, "Economic Theories of Nonprofit Organizations," in Walter W. Powell, ed., *The Nonprofit Sector: A Research Handbook* (New Haven, Conn.: Yale University Press, 1987), pp. 27–42; Lester M. Salamon, "Partners in Public Service: The Scope and Theory of Government-Nonprofit Relations" in Powell, ed., *The Nonprofit Sector,* pp. 99–117; and Burton A. Weisbrod, *The Voluntary Non-profit Sector: An Economic Analysis* (Lexington, Mass.: D. C. Heath, 1988). A summary of these arguments can also be found in Brilliant, "Voluntarism," pp. 2469–2482.

57. Ways and Means Committee Report, H.R. Rep. No. 1860, 75th Cong., 3rd Sess. (1938), p. 20, cited in McLean, "Legislative History," pp. 2–3. The "Legislative History" was

apparently prepared for JDR 3rd in connection with his discussion groups on philanthropy and 501[c][3] organizations.

58. However, restrictions were loosened the following year. The Revenue Act of 1939 expanded the provision again by allowing deductions for contributions to donees organized in U.S. possessions and territories. McLean, "Legislative History."

59. Revenue Act of 1935, Ch. 829, Sect. 102 (c), 49, Stat 1016 (1935), as cited in Marion R. Fremont-Smith, *Philanthropy and the Business Corporation* (New York: Russell Sage Foundation, 1972), pp. 13–14. For more discussion of this issue see Brilliant, *The United Way*, p. 26; Scott M. Cutlip, *Fund Raising in the United States: Its Role in America's Philanthropy* (New Brunswick, N.J.: Rutgers University Press, 1965); and Morrell Heald, *The Social Responsibility of Business: Company and Community, 1900–1960* (Cleveland, Ohio: The Press of Case Western Reserve University, 1970).

60. Fremont Smith, *Foundations and Government*, pp. 170–171.

61. Fremont-Smith, *Foundations and Government;* see also Persons, Osborn, and Feldman, "Criteria for Exemption," p. 1981.

62. C. F. Mueller Co., T.C. 922 (1950) reversed, 190 F. 2nd 120 (3d Cir. 1951), cited in note 1 in Fremont-Smith, *Foundations and Government*, p. 171. In a second footnote on the same page is cited the contradictory case of *Trinidad v. Sagrada Orden de Predicadores*, 263 U.S. 578 (1924); *Commissioner of Internal Revenue v. Orton*, 173 F. 2nd 483 (6th Cir. 1949).

63. This reason seems to have been given both by the House Ways and Means Committee and the Senate Finance Committee. Both reports are cited and the Senate report is quoted in Persons, Osborn, and Feldman, "Criteria for Exemption," p. 1981. On p. 2019, n. 571 gives the full citation to the House report, H.R. Rep. No. 2319, 81st Cong., 2nd Sess. (1950); and n. 571 locates the Senate quotation as Senate Rep. No. 2375, 81st Cong., 2nd Sess. (1950), pp. 483, 504–505.

64. Andrews, *Foundation Watcher*, p. 224.

65. Fremont-Smith, *Foundations and Government*, p. 175. For a later discussion, see Andrews, *Foundation Watcher*, pp. 224–225.

66. Andrews, *Foundation Watcher*, p. 249. According to Persons, Osborn, and Feldman, 1950 marks the beginning of a new phase in federal tax policy regarding charitable organizations: "For the first time, Statutory Rules were enacted to deal with business activities of various charities and with certain areas of abuse, including self-dealing, imprudent investments, and unreasonable accumulation of income." See Persons, Osborn, and Feldman, "Criteria for Exemption," p. 1925.

67. For one of the most comprehensive discussions of the 501(c)(3) category, see Hopkins, *Law of Tax-Exempt Organizations*. Analysis of the importance of this category (and subcategories within it) is a major part of the rest of this book.

68. John G. Simon, in Powell, ed., *The Nonprofit Sector*, p. 69, suggests that although this differentiation really starts then, it does not become full blown until the 1969 Tax Reform Act.

69. Int. Rev. Code of 1954, sec. 170 (b).

70. The earlier Revenue Act of 1934 also had placed some limitations on the political activities of tax-exempt organizations, Persons, Osborn, and Feldman, "Criteria for Exemption," p. 1925. This issue, which is recurrent and significant, will be discussed more fully in the next two chapters. However, it is worth noting here that Fremont-Smith argues generally that "the tax laws are being relied on to police activities in a manner for which they are not suited" and this dictum certainly seems applicable here (Fremont-Smith, *Foundations and Government*), p. 189.

3. Leading to Reform

1. Congressman Wright Patman, "A Fresh Look at Tax-Exempt Foundations," in *Congressional Record*, House, 87th Cong., 1st Sess., Vol. 107, No. 73, May 1961, pp. 6560–6562.

2. Andrews, *Foundation Watcher,* pp. 244ff.

3. Since this was a time of transition, it is not surprising that questions about American life and an optimistic reform spirit coexisted. See Patterson, *Grand Expectations,* chapter 11. Patterson emphasizes continuity in the optimistic spirit. For a somewhat different view see Allen J. Matusow, T*he Unraveling of America: A History of Liberalism in the 1960s* (New York: Harper and Row, 1984).

4. See Patterson, *Grand Expectations,* generally for a fascinating discussion of this period. I have borrowed the descriptive phrase for this period from the title of this seminal book.

5. The reference here is to another seminal book about the 1920s—Clarke A. Chambers, *The Seedtime of Reform: American Social Service and Social Action 1918–1933* (Minneapolis: University of Minnesota Press, 1963).

6. In the waning days of his administration, for example, Eisenhower became concerned about future direction for the country and created a Commission on National Goals. At the same time the civil rights movement was emerging after the decision of *Brown v. Board of Education* (1954) and the Civil Rights Act of 1957. All opinion was of course not unanimous. John K. Galbraith's controversial book, *The Affluent Society,* suggested that poverty was not a major issue, but also gave the message that consumerism might have gone far enough, and the country's resources should be used for building significant social infrastructures. See also James T. Patterson, *America's Struggle against Poverty 1900–1985* (Cambridge, Mass.: Harvard University Press, 1986), pp. 78–125.

7. See Herbert Stein, *The Fiscal Revolution in America,* rev. ed. (Washington, D.C.: AEI Press, 1990). For discussion of tax policy and tax inequities, see Philip M. Stern, *The Great Treasury Raid* (New York: Random House, 1964). Stern's argument is on the whole based on an earlier, somewhat more conceptual, discussion of these issues by Louis Eisenstein, *The Ideologies of Taxation* (New York: Ronald Press, 1961), p. 8.

8. See Stein, *Fiscal Revolution in America,* chapters 12 and 13. A much drier review of tax policy in this period is provided in *Congress and the Nation,* Vol. 1 (1945–64), pp. 397–427 (published by Congressional Quarterly Inc., Washington, D.C., 1965).

9. See for example Stanley M. Surrey, "The Congress and the Tax Lobbyist—How Special Tax Provisions Get Enacted," *Harvard Law Review,* Vol. 70 (1957), pp. 1145–1147. Surrey's views are also discussed extensively in Eisenstein, *Ideologies of Taxation.*

10. See "Opposition Rises to Naming Surrey to Treasury Post," *Wall Street Journal,* January 16, 1961, p. 7, and "Byrd Gets Assurances Dillon Will Have Final Say in Treasury," *Wall Street Journal,* April 13, 1981, p. 3.

11. This is well documented in memoranda (and entries from the JDR Diaries) in the Rockefeller Center Archives; some will be cited specifically below with reference to particular events. See also Eleanor Brilliant, "Looking Backward to Look Forward: The Filer Commission in Perspective," in *Toward a Stronger Voluntary Sector: "The Filer Commission" and the State of Philanthropy* (Proceedings of the National Board of Visitors of the Indiana University Center of Philanthropy, New York, December 8, 1995), Indianapolis: Indiana University Center on Philanthropy, 1996, pp. 7–28.

12. In general authors writing about philanthropy since Patman's outbreak have trouble coming to grips with his role, and some give it relatively little attention, as for example Merrimon Cuninggim, *Private Money and Public Service: The Role of Foundations in American Society* (New York: McGraw-Hill, 1972). One of the most complete discussions of Patman's activities through 1964 is given in Fremont-Smith, *Foundations and Government.* For a more personal discussion see Waldemar A. Nielsen, *The Endangered Sector* (New York: Columbia University Press, 1979). Andrews, writing contemporaneously, attempted to assess Patman's activities, but given his position in the foundation world he was naturally critical of many of Patman's significant recommendations in *Patman and Foundations.* He also discussed Patman extensively in *Foundation Watcher.*

13. These outbreaks (discussed above in chapter 2) fit neatly into the model of conflict between the finpols (the financial elite) and the pubpols (the political powers) as delineated by Lundberg in *The Rich and the Super-Rich.*

14. Concern about accumulated assets of tax-exempt organizations resulted in statutory provisions regarding unreasonable accumulation of income (in amount or duration) added by the Joint Conference Committee of the House and Senate in 1950. Testimony of Bertrand M. Harding, Acting Commissioner, Internal Revenue Service, at *Hearings on Tax Exempt Foundations: Their Impact on Small Business* before Subcommittee 1 of the House Committee on Small Business, August 10, 1964, p. 130.

15. Eisenstein, *The Ideologies of Taxation,* was written in 1961, Stern's *The Great Treasury Raid* by 1964. Stanley Surrey, Harvard Law School professor and later Treasury official, had already written several articles including the oft-cited "The Congress and the Tax Lobbyist—How Special Tax Provisions Get Enacted." Among other discussions, the economist Joseph A. Pechman had also written "Erosion of the Individual Income Tax," *National Tax Journal,* Vol. 10 (1), 1957.

16. See discussion above, chapter 2. This point was still considered generally true through the early 1990s as indicated in Hopkins, *Law of Tax-Exempt Organizations.* It is also not surprising that this point was mentioned frequently to JDR, as for example in material prepared by D. H. McLean, Jr., "Legislative History of Deduction for Charitable Contributions," May 20, 1963 (RAC, RFA, RG3, Box 370, Folder: Charitable Deduction Contributions).

17. *Congress and the Nation,* 12, p. 397.

18. Stern, *The Great Treasury Raid;* and Surrey, "The Congress and the Tax Lobby."

19. A review of the 1953 Hearings on *General Tax Revision* (2916 pages in all) reveals a litany of testimony from an enormous range of interest groups, including business groups, tax-exempt organizations, associations of all kinds, and estate planners–tax lawyers, each pleading for special privileges and protection under the Tax Code. See *General Revenue Revision,* Hearings before the Committee on Ways and Means, U.S. House of Representatives, 83rd Cong., 1st Sess., June 16, 17, 18, 23; July 8, 9, 14, 15, 16, 21; July 22, 23, 28, 29, 30, 31; and August, 3, 4, 5, 6, 10, 11, 12, 13, 14, 1953. Some of the exemptions enacted in the decade of 1948–1958 might arguably be considered good social policy, such as the marriage deduction, child care deductions, or income splitting arrangements. Nonetheless as a whole they provided far greater benefits for the rich. See Stern, *The Great Treasury Raid,* and the already noted criticisms by Surrey of the whole concept of tax incentives.

20. A technical adjustment in the manner of figuring the unlimited charitable deduction was also made in the Technical Changes Act of 1958.

21. See Stern, *The Great Treasury Raid;* and Eisenstein, *The Ideologies of Taxation,* chapter 6.

22. For most individuals the top limit on deductions for charitable contributions was 30 percent of their income. However, an unlimited charitable deduction was granted to those individuals who for a long period gave over 90 percent of their income to charitable causes. This enabled a few very rich individuals to reduce taxable income sufficiently so that they paid no income tax at all. The 1954 Internal Revenue Code revisions reduced the required qualifying period for the unlimited deduction from 10 years to 8 years. A document prepared for the Rockefellers in 1963 estimated the revenue loss from this provision to be $25 million for fiscal year 1955. D. H. McLean, Jr., "Legislative History of Deductions for Charitable Contributions," May 20, 1963 (RAC, GF, RG3, Box 370, Folder: Charitable Deductions). The amount of $25 million is given in *Congress and the Nation,* 12, p. 417, referring to the loss from increasing the maximum deduction to 30 percent for specified institutions (e.g., schools, hospitals, churches). Other sources reported the total "loss" of revenues from all charitable deductions as much higher, and constantly increasing: $2.3 billion in 1950; $2.5 billion in 1953; and an estimated $8.4 billion by 1963. See Stern, *The Great Treasury Raid,* p. 223.

23. Among the chief exponents of pluralism was Robert A. Dahl, who described its workings in an urban setting (New Haven) in *Who Governs?* For a discussion of its workings on the national level see David B. Truman, *The Governmental Process* (New York: Alfred A. Knopf, 1961). For an early critique of pluralism see Theodore J. Lowi, *The End of Liberalism: Ideology, Policy and the Crisis of Public Authority* (New York: W. W. Norton, 1969).

24. See Peter Bachrach, ed. *Political Elites in a Democracy* (New York: Atherton, 1971); Robert L. Holbert, *Tax Law and Political Access: The Bias of Pluralism Revisited* (Beverly Hills, Calif.: Sage Publications, 1975; Lowi, *The End of Liberalism;* Grant McConnell, *Private Power and American Democracy* (New York: Alfred A. Knopf, 1966); and of course Lundberg, *The Rich and the Super-Rich.* However, pluralism and the related notion of interest group liberalism continue to have appeal as conceptualizations of our society, since they are in keeping with the basic notion of democracy. See for example also Robert A. Dahl, *Democracy in the United States: Promise and Performance* (Chicago: Rand-McNally, 1972), and numerous recent writings on the "civil society."

25. The staff head, Dean Rusk, was tapped for Secretary of State, and two influential Board members were called to be part of the administration—Chester Bowles was nominated for Secretary of State and Douglas Dillon was named Secretary of the Treasury. The term "raided" comes from Waldemar A. Nielsen, *The Big Foundations* (New York: Columbia University Press, 1972).

26. It must be emphasized however that there was (and is) considerable question about the exact numbers of foundations in this period. Numbers given here were among those frequently used in the 1960s; they come from "Tax-Free Funds Come under Fire," *U.S. News and World Report,* Vol. 66 (March 3, 1969, pp. 84–85, and are based on figures from the Foundation Library Center at that time and also in Irving Louis Horowitz and Ruth Leonora Horowitz, "Tax-Exempt Foundations: Their Effects on National Policy," *Science,* Vol. 168 (April 1970), pp. 220–228. These authors, using figures from the 1964 Treasury Department Survey of Private Foundations, cite an overall number of 14,865 foundations for 1962 (Table 2, p. 222). More conservative figures for the 1960s are now given by the Foundation Center both in terms of numbers of foundations that were added annually, and—based on currently existing foundations—absolute numbers in existence at that time. Their figures however are based only on those foundations with assets of $1,000,000 or more (or that made grants totaling over $100,000 annually); therefore many smaller foundations are not counted. See *Foundation Giving: Yearbook of Facts and Figures on Private, Corporate and Community Foundations* (New York: The Foundation Center, 1992, pp. 20–24).

27. Fremont-Smith, *Foundations and Government,* p. 354. Fremont-Smith cited these discussions as proving that the House Ways and Means Committee's interest in tax problems was not confined only to years in which major tax revisions were being proposed.

28. Lundberg, *The Rich and the Super-Rich,* pp. 160–162.

29. For more details of this process, see Harr and Johnson, *The Rockefeller Conscience,* chapters 13 and 14. Despite the fact that their books (*The Rockefeller Conscience* and *The Rockefeller Century* [1988]) were written with family consent, on the whole Harr and Johnson present an even-handed historical view of Rockefeller family activities which only slightly downplays problematic issues.

30. See Kutz, *Rockefeller Power,* chapter 1, on the "The Making of Rockefeller Power." An insider's view of the history is given in Raymond B. Fosdick, *The Story of the Rockefeller Foundation* (New Brunswick, N.J.: Transaction Publishers, 1989; originally published in 1952). See also Harr and Johnson, *The Rockefeller Century,* for a well documented recent discussion of these events. A less friendly view is given in Peter Collier and David Hurwitz, *The Rockefeller Family* (New York: Basic Books, 1976).

31. According to John Ensor Harr and Peter J. Johnson, sister "Babs" was not involved in the original establishment of the RBF, but was later on the Board. In any case, Junior approved

of the founding of the RBF and gave a large gift through the "1952 Trusts" created for the brothers. These trusts were created with shares of New Jersey Standard Oil and Standard Oil of California which were in turn given over to the RBF in a signed agreement on May 21, 1952. After Junior's death in 1960, the RBF received another large contribution from his estate. See Harr and Johnson, *The Rockefeller Century*, pp. 601–602. See also Harr and Johnson, *The Rockefeller Conscience*, pp. 213–214, 519–520.

32. Lundberg, *The Rich and the Super-Rich*, p. 662.

33. Harr and Johnson, *The Rockefeller Conscience*, pp. 184–197; and Nielsen, *The Big Foundations*, pp. 65–66. JDR also had ideas for the Rockefeller Foundation which faced resistance in the early 1960s.

34. Memorandum of Dean William C. Warren, "Re: Unlimited Charitable Deduction" to the Honorable Russell B. Long, June 22, 1968, concerning problems of the 1964 Tax Act and needed rulings by Treasury (RAC, JDR 3rd, Conf., Box 14, Folder: Philanthropy, McCloy, Dillon Committee).

35. Harr and Johnson, *The Rockefeller Conscience*, p. 185.

36. However, in the musical chairs manner typical of the Rockefellers, Nelson then became President of the RBF (1955). See Harr and Johnson, *The Rockefeller Century*, p. 519.

37. The Rockefeller office will be discussed further in chapters 5 and 6. However, matters there were certainly complicated by the brothers' personalities and the variety of Rockefeller enterprises. For a suggestion of these complexities see Harr and Johnson, *The Rockefeller Conscience*, pp. 482–541.

38. Harr and Johnson, *The Rockefeller Conscience*, chapter 12.

39. Harr and Johnson, *The Rockefeller Conscience*, p. 274.

40. John J. Schwartz, *Modern American Philanthropy: A Personal Account* (New York: John Wiley, 1994), pp. 71–73; Waldemar A. Nielsen, *The Golden Donors: A New Anatomy of the Great Foundation* (New York: Truman Talley Books, 1985), p. 30.

41. The Ford Foundation Seminar is mentioned in Andrews, *Foundation Watcher*. By 1955, New York University had already held its Second Biennial Conference on Charitable Foundations, as cited in Fremont-Smith, *Foundations and Government*, p. 122, n. 8.

42. Dean Rusk, from "Building a Professional Staff," in *Proceedings of the New York University Biennial Conference on Charitable Foundations*, ed. Henry Sellin (New York: Matthew Bender, 1965), pp. 178–179, cited in Fremont-Smith, *Foundations and Government*.

43. Among those concerned was Congressman Wilbur D. Mills, who had already expressed this for the general public in his article, "Are You a Pet or a Patsy?" *Life*, Vol. 47 (21), November 23, 1959. In an editorial on page 2 of the same issue of *Life*, the authors call the mixed-up tax situation "one of the most controversial subjects today." Another presumably reliable source suggested that the number of wealthy individuals who paid no tax on their income rose from four in 1955 to seventeen in 1961; income sheltered through gifts to family foundations certainly was significant in this development. Source of numbers about the wealthy who pay no taxes, see *Congress and the Nation*, 12, p. 401; similar numbers were used by Treasury Secretary Dillon in his appearance before the Patman Committee in 1964.

44. These memoranda are in RAC, RFA, RG5, JDR 3rd Papers, Box 8, Folder: Taxes— Unlimited Deduction for Charitable Contributions, 1959–64. They include Memorandum from F. Roberts Blair to Laurance Rockefeller, "Recent Proposed Federal Legislation on Unlimited Deduction for Charitable Deduction," October 1, 1959; Memorandum from F. Roberts Blair to Mr. John D. Rockefeller 3rd, "Unlimited Charitable Deduction—H.R. 6779 *Re Averaging of 2 Years*" [*sic*] and Memorandum (in letter format) from F. Roberts Blair, "Federal Income Tax—Unlimited Charitable Deduction *Possible 1960 Legislation re 2 Year Averaging*" [*sic*], August 1, 1960. There are also other memoranda (in the same folder cited above) from Blair concerning JDR's specific qualification for the unlimited charitable deduction, as for example a Memorandum from F. Roberts Blair and John P. Hodgkins to Mr. John D. Rockefeller

3rd, October 16, 1961, "Federal Income Tax-Estimate *re* [*sic*] Qualification for Unlimited Deduction *of Charitable Contributions*," in which they make recommendations about contributions that would ensure his qualification.

45. Letter from Miss Dick, Secretary to Secretary Byrd, to Mr. John D. Rockefeller III [*sic*], May 5, 1960 (RAC, RFA, RG5, JDR 3rd Papers, 8, Folder: Taxes: Unlimited Deductions on Charitable Contributions 1959–1964).

46. Cited in Memorandum (in the form of a letter) from F. Roberts Blair to Mr. John D. Rockefeller 3rd, "Federal Income Tax—Unlimited Charitable Deduction *Possible 1960 Legislation re 2 Year Averaging*," August 1, 1960 (RAC, RFA, RG5, JDR 3rd Papers, 8, Folder: Taxes—Unlimited Charitable Deduction 1959–64).

47. Memorandum from F. Roberts Blair to Mr. John D. Rockefeller, "Unlimited Deduction Averaging Proposal *H.R. 6352*" [*sic*], April 27, 1961 with attachments of lists of members of Congressional Tax Committees and of the Outdoor Recreation Resource Review Commission (RAC, RFA, RG5, JDR 3rd Papers, 8, Folder: Taxes—Unlimited Deduction for Charitable Contributions 1959–64).

48. Memorandum to John D. Rockefeller 3rd from F. Roberts Blair, February 15, 1962, "Charitable Contributions—Inclusion of Museums, Libraries and Performing Arts Institutions in the 30% Category" (with copies to John E. Lockwood and Donald H. McLean, Jr.). The editorial in the *New York Times,* February 15, 1962, came out for broadening of the extra charitable deduction "to embrace Lincoln Center and other nonprofit institutions that qualify as educational and not only in the performing arts" (RAC, RFA, RG5, JDR 3rd Papers, 8, Folder: Taxes—Unlimited Deduction on Charitable Contributions 1959–1964).

49. Memorandum to JDR 3rd from DHMcL Jr [McLean], September 21, 1961 (no title) (RAC, RFA, RG5, JDR 3rd Papers, 8, Folder: Taxes—Unlimited Deduction on Charitable Contributions 1959–64).

50. For one example, Brother Winthrop had already moved to Arkansas (mid-1950s) and was beginning to get active in state politics by this time; Arkansas was of course Wilbur Mills's home state. But in addition, the way these committees operated might have made this a tough discussion to hold.

51. Congressman Curtis, *Congressional Record,* House, April 1, 1968, pp. 2406–2407; also Congressman Conte who was a member of Patman's committee stated, "Mr. Speaker, in my 10 years as a Members of this House I have never before been involved in a procedure like this, and I must confess that I just do not understand it at all," *Congressional Record,* House, April 1, 1968, pp. 2406–2407. Both citations come from Andrews, *Patman and Foundations,* pp. 51 and 52 respectively.

52. For example, prior to the issuance of the first interim report findings were published in the *Congressional Record.* "An Immediate Move Toward a Foundation Tax Exemption Would Serve the Best Interest of the Nation" was printed on July 23, 1962 and "Assets of Foundations Have Reached Massive Proportions" was printed the following August 20. See Andrews, *Patman and Foundations.*

53. Manning Pattillo, "Foreword" to Andrews, *Patman and Foundations.*

54. See Fremont-Smith, *Foundations and Government,* pp. 372–373; also note 67 below.

55. Andrews, *Patman and Foundations.* See especially pp. 54–55.

56. *Tax-Exempt Foundations and Charitable Trusts: Their Impact on Our Economy,* Second Installment, Subcommittee Chairman's Report to Subcommittee No. 1, Select Committee on Small Business, House of Representatives, 88th Congress (Washington, D.C.: GPO, October 16, 1963).

57. *Tax-Exempt Foundations: Their Impact on Small Business.* Hearings Before Subcommittee No. 1 of the Select Committee on Small Business, House of Representatives, 90th Cong., 1st Sess. (Washington, D.C.: GPO, 1967).

58. This was even admitted by a foundation partisan. See Andrews, *Patman and Foundations,* pp. 54–55. However, later in Andrews, *Foundation Watcher,* he refers to the more "scientific survey" of the IRS—a survey which included a far smaller sample of foundations than Patman's survey which in December 1962 numbered 534 organizations (although, as it turned out, at least one, the Foundation Library Center, was not a foundation). (*Foundation Watcher,* pp. 245–247).

59. Letter of Transmittal, *Tax-Exempt Foundations and Charitable Trusts: Their Impact on Our Economy,* First Interim Report, Subcommittee Chairman's Report to Subcommittee No. 1, Select Committee on Small Business, House of Representatives, 87th Congress (December 31, 1962).

60. Andrews, *Foundation Watcher,* pp. 251–252. Given Congressional concern about accumulation of assets by foundations, this mistake, which listed $91 million in accumulated income for one year, rather than as excess in disbursements (a negative figure) could have caused problems for the Rockefellers.

61. Letter from Chauncey Belknap (Patterson, Belknap and Webb) to John D. Rockefeller 3rd, November 2, 1964 (RAC, GF, JDR 3rd, 370, Folder: Philanthropy/JDR 3rd).

62. Stein, *Fiscal Revolution in America,* pp. 408–414.

63. *Congress and the Nation,* I, p. 398.

64. Mills speech introducing the 1964 Tax Bill in Congress, from the U.S. Congress, House, *Congressional Record,* 88th Congress, 1st Sess., 1963, Vol. 109, Pt.13, pp. 17908–9, cited in Stein, *Fiscal Revolution in America,* p. 450.

65. The definition of an operating foundation was essentially "one which devotes substantially more than one-half of its assets directly to the active conduct of the exempt charitable activities," as quoted from "Statement by Congressman Mills on February 25, 1964 in the House Relating to the Unlimited Charitable Deduction (p. 3428 of the Congressional Record" [*sic*], attachment to Memorandum to JDR 3rd from Don H. McLean, Jr., April 7, 1964 (RAC, GF, RG3, Box 370, Folder: Philanthropy, JDR 3rd).

66. Matusow, *The Unraveling of America,* pp. 56–59.

67. Federal Register, December 29, 1962; cited in Fremont Smith, *Foundations and Government,* p. 388. Thereafter the IRS could show to the public everything on the 990–A but the "non-public" portion, which includes the itemized list of contributions received. Also the forms were no longer available only in local district offices but could be seen at the national office of the IRS. In addition, greater disclosure of gifts of income and principal were to be made by the organizations. See also "Recent Changes in Tax Forms Filed by Foundations: Form 990–A (Annual Information Return), Exhibit 51, *Tax-Exempt Foundations,* Hearings before the Subcommittee on Foundations, Select Committee on Small Business, 1964, pp. 411–412.

68. Included also were lawyers, accountants, and a professor. The group met five times with Assistant Treasury Secretary Surrey, the tax legislative counsel and others from Treasury and the IRS. Testimony of the Honorable Douglas Dillon, Secretary of the Treasury, in *Tax-Exempt Foundations,* Hearings of Subcommittee No. 1 of the Select Committee on Banking and Small Business, July 21, 1964, p. 7.

69. Andrews, *Foundation Watcher.* In 1968 the Foundation Library Center changed its name to the Foundation Center. In subsequent chapters, I will generally use the name Foundation Center.

70. "Letter of Transmittal," *Tax-Exempt Foundations and Charitable Trusts: Their Impact on Our Economy,* Second Installment, Subcommittee Chairman's Report to Subcommittee No. 1, Select Committee on Small Business, House of Representatives, 88th Congress (October 16, 1963).

71. Subcommittee Report, Second Installment, p. 8.

72. *Tax-Exempt Foundations,* Hearings before Subcommittee No. 1 of the Select Committee on Small Business, September 1, 1964, pp. 273–274.

73. U.S. Treasury Department, *Report on Private Foundations* (Washington, D.C.: GPO, 1965), p. 2–5.

74. Andrews, *Foundation Watcher,* 1973, pp. 247–252.

4. The Gathering Storm

1. "United States Tax Policy" in *Congress and the Nation 1945–1964,* 12 (Washington, D.C.: Congressional Quarterly Inc., 1965), p. 399. See also Stein, *Fiscal Revolution in America,* pp. 451–453.

2. In doing this Kennedy veered from what had become accepted liberal economic dogma and employed a modified form of Keynesian doctrine. In 1962 the country had a mild recession, and therefore, in line with the argument of the British economist Maynard Keynes, in a time of depression, the government should have created demand for industrial products by increasing its own spending. For related discussions of Keynes see Stein, *Fiscal Revolution in America,* pp.131–168, and for the application of the new "American" form of Keynesian doctrine in this period, pp. 379–384. See also Patterson, *Grand Expectations.*

3. Kennedy seemed initially to have favored the idea of tax reform, but the tax legislation of 1962–63 hardly embodied real reforms. Kennedy's State of the Union message in 1963 in this regard is quoted in Pollack: "I am concerned that the enactment of tax reductions and tax reform overshadowed all of the domestic problems in the country." See Pollack, *The Failure of U.S. Tax Policy,* p. 73. Kennedy might have been ambivalent about "tax reform," as suggested by Witte, who notes that the terms "equity" or loophole did not appear in Kennedy's *1963 Economic Report of the President.* See Witte, *Politics and Development of the Federal Income Tax,* p. 159.

4. Stein, *Fiscal Revolution in America,* pp. 422–440.

5. Stein, *Fiscal Revolution in America,* pp. 405–450; Witte, *Politics and Development of the Federal Income Tax,* pp. 159–165.

6. Mills's strategies are discussed at length in John F. Manley, *The Politics of Finance: The House Committee on Ways and Means* (Boston: Little, Brown, 1970), pp. 101–142.

7. Wilbur D. Mills, "Remarks before the House on the Revenue Act of 1964," typed manuscript attached to Memo to JDR 3rd from DHMcL Jr [McLean], April 7, 1964 (RAC, GF, RG3, 370, Folder: Philanthropy JDR 3rd).

8. The Revenue Act of 1964 (P.L. 88, 272, 78 Stat.197). See also Sheldon Pollock, *The Failure of U.S. Tax Policy.* However, in his discussion of this Act, Witte (Table 8.1, p. 164) uses a total revenue loss of $11.3 billion for 1965, which includes losses from reduced corporate payments.

9. Patterson, *Grand Expectations,* pp. 466–467.

10. "Opposition Rises to Naming Surrey to Treasury Post," *Wall Street Journal,* January 16, 1961, p. 7. See also discussion in chapter 4 above.

11. Byrd Gets Assurance Dillon Will Have Final Tax Say in Treasury," *Wall Street Journal,* April 13, 1961, p. 3.

12. For a contemporary discussion of the relationship between politicians and patricians in the power structures of our country in the 1960s, see Lundberg, *The Rich and the Super-Rich.*

13. The series of memos from tax lawyers to JDR and Laurance Rockefeller is discussed in chapter 3. Note also that in a Memorandum to JDR 3rd from DHMcL Jr, on April 14, 1964 concerning the philanthropy program, Don McLean, one of JDR's staff, explicitly noted that the Rockefeller lawyer (from the firm of Milbank, Tweed) could use his own contact person to reach the "Advisory Group on Foundations organized by Treasury." He also noted that JDR could be "in touch" through his "own connections" (Memo in RAC, GF, RG3, Box 370, Folder: Philanthropy JDR 3rd).

14. Some key Rockefeller holdings in 1960 were listed in Wright Patman's "Letter of

Transmittal," *Tax-Exempt Foundations and Charitable Trusts: Their Impact on Our Economy,* First Installment (Patman Report), December 31, 1962 (Washington, D.C.: GPO, 1962). See discussion below in this chapter.

15. Harr and Johnson, *The Rockefeller Conscience,* p. 240.

16. U.S. House of Representatives, Hearings before the Select Committee on Small Business, Subcommittee 1, *Tax Exempt Foundations: Their Impact on Small Business,* 88th Cong., 2nd Sess. (Washington, D.C.: GPO, 1964) (hereafter also referred to as Patman Committee 1964 Hearings).

17. After much maneuvering and with help from Bill Moyers and Lady Bird Johnson, JDR did succeed in getting some attention from Johnson concerning the problem of population and it was mentioned in the State of the Union Address given by the President on January 4, 1965. For more details on JDR's efforts after Johnson's 1964 election, see Harr and Johnson, *The Rockefeller Conscience,* pp. 168–179.

18. Harr and Johnson, *The Rockefeller Century,* p. 558.

19. *National Party Platforms,* Vol. 2, 1960–1976, compiled by Donald Bruce Johnson (Urbana: University of Illinois Press, 1978), p. 598.

20. The *Life* magazine article by Wilbur Mills written in 1959 spoke angrily against tax abuses but did not explicitly refer to charitable deductions or foundation abuses. See Mills, "Are You a Pet or a Patsy?" p. 51.

21. Fremont-Smith, *Foundations and Government,* pp. 401–406.

22. Arnold H. Lubasch, "$10 Billion Given to Charity in U.S.: Questionable Philanthropies Collect Estimated Total of $300 Million a Year," *New York Times,* December 13, 1964.

23. See Cuninggim, *Private Money and Public Service,* pp. 190–215.

24. The reasons for this will become more apparent below. Although Harr and Johnson suggest that the brothers had on the whole relatively little contact, a close reading of *The Rockefeller Conscience* suggests considerable interrelationships around business and the settling of personal or philanthropic matters, such as Colonial Williamsburg or the estate at Pocantico Hills; Patman's argument suggested issues related to the connection between stock holdings and Rockefeller philanthropies. In Lundberg, *The Rich and the Super-Rich,* the argument is developed that the interweaving of family activities and politics increases the family's power.

25. JDR 3rd, 1964 Diary, Monday February 3, 1964 (RAC, RG5, JDR 3rd Diaries), p. 8.

26. "John D. Rockefeller 3rd as Spokesman for Private Philanthropy," typed document, dated 11/14/65, with no named author, but with attached letter from Earl Newsome to Don H. McLean, Jr., November 18, 1963 (RAC, GF, RG3, Box 370, Folder: Philanthropy JDR 3rd), p. 1.

27. Memorandum to JDR 3rd from DHMcL Jr Re Philanthropy Program, April 14, 1964 (to which the earlier Newcome materials were attached in the archives) (RAC, GF, RG3, Box 370, Folder: Philanthropy JDR 3rd, p. 1).

28. DHMcL Jr., Memorandum, *Philanthropy Program,* April 14, 1964, p. 2.

29. This group, formed in 1963, seems to be the same group referred to in F. E. Andrews, *Foundation Watcher,* p. 247.

30. The passages quoted are from the "Text of Address by John D. Rockefeller 3rd, Delivered at the Inaugural Dinner of the Federation of Jewish Philanthropies of New York: A Fresh Look at Philanthropy in Our Changing World." Marked "For Release: Monday October 5, 1964" (RAC, GF, Box 370, Folder: Philanthropy JDR 3rd), p. 1.

31. JDR 3rd, 1964 Diary, January 6, 1964 (cont.) (RAC, RG5, JDR 3rd Diaries), p. 2.

32. Letter from Chauncey Belknap to JDR 3rd, November 2, 1964 (RAC, GF, JDR 3rd, Box 370, Folder: Philanthropy JDR 3rd).

33. Harr and Johnson, *The Rockefeller Conscience,* p. 163.

34. Memorandum from Raymond Lamontagne, "Proposed Association of Foundations," November 18, 1964, with accompanying letter of November 20, 1964 from Lamontagne to Gardner (RAC, Box GF, RG3, 370, Folder: JDR 3rd).

35. Telephone call from JDR to Don McLean, February 1964 (RAC, JDR 3rd, Telephone Diaries, Book 27). In his diary JDR used "Joint Committee on Taxation," which seems to be an informal name for the Joint Committee on Internal Revenue Taxation, the important committee which set policies directives for the House and Senate on finance-related bills of the administration.

36. For detailed discussion of the interactions between these Committees, and the specific function of the Joint Committee, see Manley, *The Politics of Finance.*

37. Mills, "Remarks before the House on the Revenue Act of 1964."

38. In the RAC files, this document is attached to a memorandum from Ray Lamontagne, who recaps the major points briefly and then recommends that Belknap might be asked to discuss his proposals with John Lockwood, one of the key Rockefeller lawyers. It is interesting to note here that Lamontagne also suggests that "It might be advisable to encourage some communication between the lawyers representing the RF and Mr. Lockwood on this general question of the legal status of foundations." This seems to hint at some communication problems in family matters (which in fact was confirmed by interviews with staff members of this period). See Memorandum from Raymond A. Lamontagne to Mr. John D. Rockefeller 3rd, December 23, 1964 on the subject of *Mr. Belknap's letter of December 21, 1964* with attachments: letter from Chauncey Belknap to JDR (December 21, 1964, and memorandum, "Proposals for New York State Legislation to Enforce Fiduciary Obligations of Trustees of Charitable Foundations and Trusts," December 21, 1964, as written by Chauncey Belknap, Thomas Thacher, and John N. Irwin II of the firm of Patterson, Belknap & Webb),(RAC, GF, RG3, Box 370, Folder: Philanthropy, JDR 3rd).

39. Andrews, *Patman and Foundations,* p. 26.

40. Patman Committee, *Tax-Exempt Foundations,* 1964 Hearings.

41. Andrews, *Patman and Foundations,* p. 27. My account of the Patman Committee Hearings of 1964 follows generally the description given by Andrews, but is verified as well by a direct reading of the Patman Hearings (1964), cited with complete reference in note 16 above.

42. Andrews, *Patman and Foundations,* p. 29.

43. Patman Committee, *Tax-Exempt Foundations,* 1964 Hearings, p. 182. See also Andrews, *Patman and Foundations,* p. 31.

44. Patman Committee, *Tax-Exempt Foundations.* 1964 Hearings, p. 274. Also quoted in Andrews, *Patman and Foundations,* p. 33.

45. A newspaper article suggests the tone and intent of the exchange, "Fowler in Clash Over Foundations," *New York Times,* November 16, 1967, p. 80. The article indicates that Patman told Fowler "that for the last 26 years the Treasury had only a regulation—not a law— that tax exemption foundations file annual information returns about their activities."

46. Statement of Sheldon S. Cohen, Commissioner of Internal Revenue, before Subcommittee No.1 on Foundations of the House Select Committee on Small Business, U.S. Cong., *Tax-Exempt Foundations: Their Impact on Small Business,* Hearings, November 16, 1967 (Washington, D.C.: GPO, 1967), pp. 235–275.

47. Andrews, *Patman and Foundations,* pp. 39–45. However, one respondent well versed in the ways of Washington informed me that it was fairly common practice when matters came up in public hearings to suggest that they were already under investigation (and then presumably to start the investigation thereafter).

48. Indeed, JDR himself created his own foundation during this period, the JDR 3rd Fund (1963).

49. "Tax-free Funds Come Under Fire," *U.S. News and World Report,* Vol. 66 (March 3, 1969), pp. 84–85. See also Andrews, *Foundation Watcher,* pp. 252–254.

50. Discussion of the reasons for the increase in numbers can be found in Brilliant, *The United Way,* pp. 40–46; and Brilliant, "Voluntarism," pp. 2473–2475. For discussions of voluntary action and nonprofit organizations in this era from different viewpoints, see also Peter

Marris and Martin Rein, *Dilemmas of Social Reform: Poverty and Community Action in the United States* (New York: Atherton Press, 1967), and Jennifer R. Wolch, *The Shadow State: Government and Voluntary Sector in Transition* (New York: The Foundation Center). A definitive source for the rising number of nonprofits in this period and the ready approvals given by the IRS is Weisbrod, *The Nonprofit Economy*, pp. 62–65.

51. Statement of the Honorable Wright Patman before the House Committee on Ways and Means, U.S. Cong., *Hearings on the Tax Reform Act*, 91st Cong., 1st Sess., Vol. 1, February 18, 1969 (Washington, D.C.: GPO, 1969), pp. 12–79.

5. In Whose Interest?

1. "Tax-Exempt Foundations," in *1965 Congressional Quarterly Almanac*, Vol. 21 (Washington, D.C.: Congressional Quarterly Service, 1965), pp. 846–847.

2. *Written Statements by Interested Individuals and Organizations on Treasury Department Report on Private Foundations*, Submitted to Committee on Ways and Means, U.S. House of Representatives, February 2, 1965, 89th Cong., 1st Sess., Volumes I and II (Washington, D.C.: GPO, 1965).

3. "Major Tax Bills Move Slowly," in Section on "Economic Policy: Tax Policy—1968 Chronology" in *Congress and the Nation*, Vol. 2, 1965–1968 (Washington, D.C.: Congressional Quarterly Service, 1969, p. 171.

4. Witte, *Politics and Development of the Federal Income Tax*, p. 165.

5. P.L. 89–809. See also "Economic Policy" in *Congress and the Nation*, Vol. 2, 1965–1968 p. 149.

6. Witte, *Politics and Development of the Federal Income Tax*, p. 166.

7. Even the surtax bill was actually coupled with another bill that concerned social security benefits.

8. For discussions of this period from different vantage-points, see Eleanor L. Brilliant, "Private or Public: A Model of Ambiguities," *Social Service Review*, Vol. 47 (3), September 1973; Patterson, *Grand Expectations*, pp. 442–592; Marris and Rein, *Dilemmas of Social Reform;* Murray L. Weidenbaum, *The Modern Public Sector: New Ways of Doing the Government's Business* (New York: Basic Books, 1969); and Wolch, *The Shadow State*, pp. 52–56.

9. The growth in numbers of voluntary sector organizations in this period is discussed in Weisbrod, *The Nonprofit Economy*, pp. 62–64. For discussion of the change in voluntary sector-government relations in that period, see also Ralph M. Kramer and Bart Grossman, "Contracting for Social Services: Process Management and Resource Dependencies," *Social Service Review*, Vol. 61 (1), pp. 32–55; Salamon, "Partners in Public Service" in Powell, ed., *The Nonprofit Sector*, pp. 99–117; K. R. Wedel, A. J. Katz, and A. Weick, eds., *Social Services by Government Contract: A Policy Analysis* (New York: Praeger, 1979).

10. According to *Congress and the Nation*, the surtax was coupled with a spending cutback in a maneuver by Senator Williams in the Senate, with at least the knowledge (if not encouragement) of Wilbur Mills. *Congress and the Nation*, Vol. 2, p. 170. See also Witte, *Politics and Development of the Federal Income Tax*, p. 166.

11. According to one contemporary source: "No one has suggested that any of the three foundations which Mr. Johnson had a hand in forming has indulged in . . . abuses" (of the type cited by Treasury and Congress in early 1969). Nevertheless the same source notes that the sale of the publishing rights to Johnson's memoirs had just been arranged by the Lyndon B. Johnson Public Affairs Foundation, and was expected to realize an estimated $1.5 million or more. "Tax-Free Foundations: Study Starts in Congress," *U.S. News and World Report*, Vol. 66, February 10, 1969, pp. 81–82. In considering the inaction concerning foundation tax reforms that had prevailed during the Johnson administration, it is also worth noting that according to Lundberg, an old college roommate of the President, Robert L. Phinney, became a top staff member of the IRS in 1967. See Lundberg, *The Rich and the Super-Rich*, p. 555.

12. According to Andrews, "It was reported that Mr. Wilbur Mills had indicated that many of the activities of the Patman Committee had little to do with small business and were the prerogatives of his own tax-writing Ways and Means Committee." In Andrews, *Patman and Foundations,* p. 32. For the opinion that Patman had been "under wraps" until Johnson left office, see Robert Sherrill, "'The Last of the Great Populists' Takes on the Foundations, the Banks, the Federal Reserve, the Treasury," *New York Times Magazine,* pp. 24–25ff., March 16, 1969.

13. The CIA actually seems to have enlisted the help of the IRS to draw up counter-measures against *Ramparts* after the journal published charges that the National Student Association had been serving as a CIA front. See Wolch, *The Shadow State,* p. 67. For discussion of this incident in regard to the Patman Hearings, see also chapter 4 above. In addition, several respondents suggested to me that the CIA was used by members of the Kennedy administration also to pursue extreme right wing organizations. In any case, on March 29 the IRS "confirmed that it had revoked the tax-exempt status of the Life Line Foundation, which was operated by ultra-conservative multimillionaire Texas oilman H. L. Hunt . . . on the grounds that its activities were of a political rather than an educational nature." *Congressional Quarterly Almanac,* 89th Cong., 1st Sess., Vol. 19, p. 847. Interestingly, when Andrews was President of the Foundation Library Center (previous name of the Foundation Center), in reporting on a Russell Sage Foundation study he dismissed CIA grants channeled through foundations as "insignificant"; see Gene Currivan, "Foundations Gave $1.2 Billion in 1966," *New York Times,* May 31, 1967.

14. The 501(c)(3) classification of the Sierra Club was revoked in December 1966, although negotiations with the IRS and litigation around it continued for several years more. The Sierra Club story is discussed in Holbert, *Tax Law and Political Access,* pp. 31–44. According to Sheldon Cohen, the Sierra Club activities could not be ignored because of their high visibility in newspaper ads. Telephone interview with Sheldon Cohen, former IRS official, January 15, 1997.

15. See for example Alan Pifer (Acting President of Carnegie Corporation), "Statement of Carnegie Corporation of New York," October 22, 1965, in Committee on Ways and Means, *Written Statements by Interested Individuals and Organizations on Treasury Foundation Report,* pp. 151–153.

16. See "Statement of the Rockefeller Foundation Regarding Treasury Department Report on Private Foundations, by J. G. Harrar, President" and "Statement of the Rockefeller Bros. Fund, Inc [sic] by Dana S. Creel, Director, with a Supplementary Statement by William Warren," in Committee on Ways and Means, *Written Statements . . . on Treasury Report,* 12, pp. 432–436 and Vol. 2, pp. 735–758. Harrar's statement was also a point by point response to the Treasury Report's six main recommendations.

17. The latter organization was loosely connected with the United Fund movement nationwide primarily for evaluations of beneficiary or service delivering (recipient) organizations. The National Council on Philanthropy was a "combined" organization of donors and recipient organizations.

18. A National Association of Foundations also presented a response to the Treasury Report, but its strong tone did not seem entirely congruent with the generally more moderate responses of individual foundations who responded.

19. The President signed an international statement on the issue, but did not create the commission which Rockefeller had hoped for. For the story of JDR's efforts to get Johnson's attention on population issues, see Harr and Johnson, *The Rockefeller Conscience,* pp. 158–179.

20. Harr and Johnson, *The Rockefeller Conscience,* pp. 148–150.

21. Memorandum by William Warren, "Unlimited Charitable Deduction," revised June 11, 1968, attached to letter from John D. Rockefeller 3rd to Wilbur Mills, January 12, 1968 (RAC, RF, RG3, Box 368, Folder: Phil.: Committee on F. and P.P.).

22. The federal government's deficit for fiscal year 1967–1968 of $25.4 billion was cited as part of written material submitted to the Committee on Ways and Means, by T. Willard

Hunter, Section VI, "Recommendations" from his study "The Tax Climate for Philanthropy," in Hearings before the U.S. House of Representatives, Committee on Ways and Means, *Tax Reform, 1969*, 91st Cong., 1st Sess., Part 4 (February 26, 1969), p. 1513 (hereafter referred to as Committee on Ways and Means, *Hearings on Tax Reform, 1969*). Willard was testifying as Executive Vice-President of the Association of Independent Colleges of Southern California.

23. Stanley S. Surrey and Paul R. McDaniel, *Tax Expenditures* (Cambridge, Mass.: Harvard University Press, 1983), p. 2. For a more detailed description of the development of Treasury's analysis of tax expenditures see Stanley S. Surrey, *Pathways to Tax Reform: The Concept of Tax Expenditures* (Cambridge, Mass.: Harvard University Press, 1973). It should also be noted that the Treasury Report of 1965 had already utilized the idea of tax preferences, stating that "The Internal Revenue Code provides very significant preferential treatment for philanthropic organizations. Not only does it exempt such organizations from income tax . . . but it grants income, gift and estate tax deduction to persons contributing to them."

24. Fremont-Smith, *Foundations and Government Supervision*.

25. Memorandum to Mr. John D. Rockefeller 3rd from John E. Lockwood, Subject: Treasury Proposals on Foundations, February 2, 1967 (RAC, RF, JDR 3rd. Conf., 14, Folder: Discussions in Washington Re: Philanthropy, 1967).

26. JDR Diary, February 8, 1967 (RAC, RFA, JDR 3rd Diaries).

27. JDR Diary, September 20,1967. Actually these diary entries were found in a folder entitled: "Philanthropy: McCloy Dillon Committee" where they had been grouped together as "Minutes of 67–68 Meetings in Washington" (RAC, RFA, JDR Confidential, Box 14). John Lockwood was the senior legal counsel of the family, and was affiliated with Milbank, Tweed and McCloy; Howard Bolton, was a family attorney with Milbank, Tweed, McCloy; J. Richardson Dilworth served as head of the family office and was also the family's investment manager; Dana Creel was by now President of the Rockefeller Brothers Fund; and Douglass was counsel to the governor. The reference to the governor in this entry is interesting—this must surely have been JDR's brother, Nelson Rockefeller.

28. JDR 3rd Diary, October 12, 1967 (RAC, RFA, JDR 3rd Diaries).

29. JDR 3rd Diary, May 9, 1968 (RAC, RFA, JDR 3rd Diaries).

30. JDR 3rd Diary, June 20, 1968. In a subsequent letter to Long, moreover, Rockefeller reports on the meeting of the small group (mentioning Dillon and McCloy); and he also encloses a memorandum to Senator Long from Warren concerning proposed Congressional amendments affecting the charitable deduction. In that memorandum Warren makes the point that JDR believes that individuals electing the unlimited deduction should "nevertheless be required to pay a tax of say 10 to 15% of his taxable income." This memorandum also discusses the fact that the Treasury Department has not yet issued any regulations to clarify the 1964 amendments (as modified by Ways and Means) concerning the status of certain private operating charities such as Colonial Williamsburg and that it requires the action of the Senate Finance Committee to help alleviate an oppressive situation. Letter to the Honorable Russell B. Long from John D. Rockefeller 3rd, June 25, 1968, with attachment of Memorandum from Dean William C. Warren to The Honorable Russell B. Long, Subject: Unlimited Charitable Deductions, dated June 22, 1968 (RAC, JDR 3rd, Conf., Box 14, Folder: Philanthropy: McCloy, Dillon Committee).The Memorandum to Long seems to be essentially the same as that sent to Wilbur Mills six months earlier.

31. JDR 3rd Diary, September 12, 1968 (RAC, RFA, JDR 3rd Diaries).

32. Record of September 12, 1968 Meeting of *Informal Philanthropy Committee* (RAC, RFA, JDR 3rd Conf., Box 14, Folder: McCloy/Dillon Committee).

33. *Treasury Department Report on Private Foundations,* Submitted to Committee on Ways and Means, Committee on Ways and Means, U.S. House of Representatives, February 2, 1965, 89th Cong., 1st Sess. (Washington, D.C.: GPO, 1965), p. 22.

34. Memorandum to Mr. John Rockefeller 3rd from Datus C. Smith, Jr., September 6, 1968, Subject: Philanthropy Discussion, with attached memorandum to Smith from Russell A.

Phillips, Jr., on the Subject: *Discussion Outline re Conference on Philanthropy*, dated September 5, 1968, and in which he suggested that the outline [which was attached] might be distributed to the "strategy group." Smith suggested in his memo to JDR that the Phillips memo was too "procedural" for "the present stage of our thinking." He apparently preferred to continue with a few broader topics concerning the role of private philanthropy and abuses of public policy by private philanthropies (as given on p. 3 of the Phillips outline). In this context it is interesting to note a Memorandum from Datus C. Smith Jr. to JDR 3rd, dated 28 June 1968, in which he suggested that JDR look at a Proposal from John K. Everett, President of the New School for Social Research, dated June 26, 1968, which was for a "special project to study the problems and potentialities of private philanthropy in the United States" (RAC, RF, RG3, JDR. Conf., Box 14, Folder: McCloy/Dillon Committee).

35. Memorandum, September 24, 1968 to Messrs. C. Douglas Dillon, John J. McCloy, Alan Pifer, Oscar M. Ruebhausen, Frederick Sheffield, Julius Stratton, William Warren, Dana S. Creel, John E. Lockwood, Russell A. Phillips, Jr., and Datus C. Smith, Jr. from John D. Rockefeller 3rd, Subject: Informal Committee on Philanthropy with attached "Notes for Meeting of Informal Committee on Philanthropy to be held on September 30, 1968 in the Conference Room, Room 5600, 30 Rockefeller Plaza" (the Rockefeller Offices) (RAC, RF, JDR 3rd, Conf., Box 14, Folder: Phil.: McCloy/Dillon Committee).

36. Record of October 14, 1968 Meeting of Informal Committee on Philanthropy (RAC, RF, JDR 3rd. Conf., Box 14, Folder: Phil: McCloy/Dillon Committee).

37. Russell A. Phillips, Jr. and Dana S. Creel, *Draft Prospectus for Line of Inquiry for Proposed Commission on Philanthropy* (underlined in original) attached to Memo from Valerie Hinge to Dillon, McCloy, Pifer, Ruebhausen, Sheffield, Stratton, Warren, Creel, Lockwood, Philips amd Smith, October 10, 1968. The memo states, that "Mr. Rockefeller thought you might like to see the attached draft statement" which was to be considered at the meeting (RAC, RF, JDR 3rd Conf., Box 14, Folder: Phil.: McCloy/Dillon Committee).

38. "DRAFT" (no title), December 4, 1968, attached to Memorandum from Datus C. Smith, Jr. to John D. Rockefeller 3rd, December 6, 1968. (RAC, RF, JDR 3rd Conf., Box 14, Folder: Phil: McCloy/Dillon Committee).

39. The reference to the *New York Times* comes from a statement by an educator who was concerned about Ford's education-related activities. See Daniel Tanner, Professor of Education, Rutgers University, in Committee on Ways and Means, *Hearings on Tax Reform, 1969*, Part 2, February 21, 1969, p. 785.

40. Figure for the national debt comes from Hunter, "The Tax Climate for Philanthropies" in *Hearings on Tax Reform*, Part 4, p. 1513. The figure of $20.3 billion is cited for total foundation assets (from a study by the Foundation Center) in Fred M. Hechinger, "U.S. Foundation Assets Peak $20.3 Billion, Report Says," *New York Times*, April 4, 1967.

41. Requirement included in H.R. 15414–P.L. 90–364 and signed into law June 28, 1968 by President Johnson. See "Economic Policy," *Congress and the Nation*, Vol. 2 (1965–1968), p. 174.

42. Johnson after all not only created his own foundations and donated his private papers as he was going out of office, but was also connected to a number of rich Texans and their oil interests. See also Lundberg, *The Rich and the Super-Rich*, for a discussion of Johnson's holdings and his foundations, pp. 555–556.

43. Barr's statement is frequently cited as one of the major galvanizers for the 1969 Tax Reform Hearings. See Statement of Mortimer Caplin, Washington, D.C., in Committee on Ways and Means, *Hearings on Tax Reform, 1969*, Part 5, February 28, p. 1773; and Nielsen, *The Big Foundations*, p. 9.

44. JDR seems to have first offered the position to Bill Moyers who turned it down. See letter from Rockefeller to Bill Moyers, February 3, 1969 (RAC, RF, JDR 3rd Conf. Files, Box 14, Folder: Comm. on Private Philanthropy). In addition to being a businessman and the Chief Executive Officer of Bell and Howell, Peterson's credentials included his relationship to Sena-

tor Charles Percy (who had personally handpicked him as his successor at Bell and Howell). Since Percy's daughter had married JDR's son Jay, this in a sense provided credibility for Rockefeller in accepting Percy's enthusiastic recommendation of Peterson for the chairmanship.

45. Record of March 4, 1969, Meeting of *Informal Committee on Philanthropy* [*sic*] (RAC, RF, JDR 3rd Conf. Files, Box 14, Folder: Comm. on Private Philanthropy). Present at the meeting were Rockefeller, McCloy, Peterson, Pifer, Reubheusen, Stratton, Warren, Creel, Lockwood, Smith, Phillips, and Donal C. O'Brien (a new attendee, who was an attorney with Milbank, Tweed, Hadley and McCloy).

46. The amount spent was somewhat more than Peterson estimated, although in the end, the commission had a surplus. See chapter 7 below.

47. Patricia Harris was a professor of law at Howard University, a former dean, and also former Ambassador to Luxembourg; Father Hesburgh was president of the University of Notre Dame, and a well-known Catholic educator; Robert Lovett was former Secretary of Defense; John J. McCloy was an attorney with Milbank, Tweed, a banker, and a "world figure"; Bill Moyers was the publisher of *Newsday,* and also a former member of the Kennedy administration: Cyrus R. Vance was a former Deputy Secretary of Defense; Douglas Dillon was former Secretary of the Treasury. The group was somewhat mixed in age, and Harris had the additional status of being a minority group member and female.

48. Peterson reserved the right to select the members of the commission and the staff; he evidently considered this so important that it is referred to in the first chapter of the report. See Commission on Foundations and Private Philanthropy, *Foundations, Private Giving, and Public Policy: Report and Recommendations of the Commission on Foundations and Private Philanthropy* (Chicago: University of Chicago Press, 1970), p. 3. Hereafter this is also referred to as the Peterson Commission Report.

49. M. A. Farber, "Role of Foundations Faces Major Study," *New York Times,* April 1969, p. 1. "13 to Study Role of Foundations," *New York Times,* April 20, 1969, p. 51. (It may be a measure of the power of the Rockefeller name that the press release from JDR's office was front page news, while the Peterson release was covered further back in the paper.)

50. For list of commission members and staff, see Appendix B.

51. Peterson Commission Report, p. 3.

52. See Peterson Commission, "Operating Plan," Draft, 5/13/69, and Minutes of the Peterson Commission, May 21–22, 1969 (IUPUI, Box 5,1).

53. A copy of a Registration Statement—Charitable Organization for the Commission on Foundations and Private Philanthropy is in the File at IUPUI (Box 8,1), with a letter from the Attorney General of the State of Illinois, May 14, 1969, acknowledging receipt of the Statement. However, it is certain that the commission did not apply for tax-exempt status as a 501(c)(3) organization, see Minutes of the Meeting of the Peterson Commission, May 21 and May 22, 1969 (IUPUI, Box 5,1).

54. Papers for incorporation of the commission as a 501(c)(3) organization are in the Peterson Commission Archives but do not appear to have been filed (IUPUI, Box 8,3). It is not clear on whose advice Peterson decided not to file as a tax-exempt organization; however, many of Peterson's and the commission's activities could easily be construed as lobbying and in that case might well have been in violation of already existing IRS regulations prohibiting substantial political/lobbying activity by 501(c)(3) organizations. These were the same regulations under which the Sierra Club lost its tax-exempt status, and Sheldon Cohen, who was on the commission, would have certainly been painfully aware of this fact. See Holbert, *Tax Law and Political Access,* pp. 31–44.

55. Letter from John D. Rockefeller 3rd to Peter Peterson, May 16, 1969, written in response to the revised statement that Peterson had sent him (RAC, RF, JDR 3rd, Conf., Box 14, Folder: Comm. on Private Philanthropy).

56. Also note that one of the October meetings was held just before Peterson testified before the Senate Finance Committee.

57. Peterson Commission, "Operating Plan," Draft, 5/13/69 (IUPUI, Box 4,1).

58. These presentations were given respectively by Manning Pattillo, President of the Foundation Center; David F. Freeman, President, Council of Foundations; and Robert N. Kreidler, Executive Vice President, Sloan Foundation. Freeman in his discussion pointed out that historically all Congressional investigations of foundations, including the current one, had "occurred in times of national unease." "Summary of Commission Meeting," Friday, June 27, and Saturday, June 28 (IUPUI, Box 5,2).

59. For an example of some of the feeling in Congress about foundation support for political activities, see the exchange with McGeorge Bundy during his testimony before the Committee on Ways and Means. "Statement of McGeorge Bundy, President, Ford Foundation, Accompanied by Mitchell Sviridoff, Vice President, and David Ginsburg, Counsel," *Hearings on Tax Reform, 1969*, Part 1, February 20, 1969, pp. 354–431. Also discussed in Nielsen, *The Big Foundations*, pp. 10–11. It should be noted also that Ford grants to eight prominent members of the staff of the late Senator Robert F. Kennedy had been reported in the newspapers (including the *Washington Post*) and this also was questioned by Congressman John W. Byrnes (Wisconsin) during Bundy's testimony before the Ways and Means Committee (pp. 372–375).

60. See for example letter from Robert C. Stephenson, Executive Director, The Ohio State University Research Foundation, 23 May 1969, to Peter Peterson in which he states that "university-connected foundations may introduce an element of "static" to your study of philanthropic foundations." More directly concerned is the letter to John Labovitz (commission staff) from Philips W. Goodell, Director of Marketing Research, Bell and Howell Company, discussing the fact that "we have a very poor response from labor leaders." Another letter written to Peterson on October 22, 1969 from Market Facts, Inc., a research group that carried out a major survey for the commission, complains that "our problems in serving you effectively have been caused by last minute, substantive changes as outlined in [the] letter of October 13, 1969" (IUPUI, Box 1,5).

61. The other subjects to be covered were, in order: Tax Treatment of Charitable Contributions, Other Deductions, Minimum and Maximum Income Tax on Individuals, Tax Treatment of the Elderly, Deferred Executive Compensation, Income Averaging, Taxation of Single Persons, Capital Gains, Foreign Tax Credit, Multiple Trusts, Tax Treatment of Business Income, Tax Treatment of State and Municipal Bonds, Possible Revisions of Tax Provisions Relating to Corporate Mergers, Estate and Gift Taxes, and Treatment of Tax Depreciation by Regulatory Agencies. It should be evident that many of these provisions, in addition to charitable contributions, would have been matters of great concern to wealthy individuals and those involved in foundation activities. For example, although our story focuses primarily on foundations and charitable contributions, decisions about estate and gift taxes were of particular concern also to both the Rockefellers specifically and the larger nonprofit world (beneficiaries and foundations). See "Subject Matter of Hearing," in Committee on Ways and Means, Press Release No. 2, U.S. House of Representatives, Wednesday, January 29, 1969, *Tax Reform, 1969*, Hearings before the Committee on Ways and Means, House of Representatives, 91st Cong., 1st Sess., Part 1 of 15 (Washington, D.C.: GPO, 1969), pp. 5–10.

62. Committee on Ways and Means, *Hearings on Tax Reform, 1969*, Part I, February 18, 1969, pp. 12–78. See also chapter 5 above.

63. For example, items covered on other days, and not delineated under tax-exempt organizations, include "Tax Treatment of Charitable Deductions," in Part 5 of *Hearings* of the Ways and Means Committee (March 3, 1969), pp. 1800–1838. And although discussed separately, this subject certainly had implications for philanthropic organizations and foundations.

64. Committee on Ways and Means, *Hearings on Tax Reform, 1969*, Parts 1, 2, 3 and 4.

65. Committee on Ways and Means, *Hearings on Tax Reform, 1969*, Part 1, February 18,1969, pp. 19–20. The problem was that the assets of such foundations were largely in the stock of one company (such as that of Eli Lilly) and also that the foundation owned a large

share of the outstanding company stock. This was one of the issues raised in the 1965 Treasury Report and by Patman, and was to be an area for proposed reform in the new tax bill.

66. Statement of McGeorge Bundy before the Committee on Ways and Means, *Hearings on Tax Reform, 1969,* February 20, 1969, pp. 427–428.

67. Walsh, "Foundations Under Fire in Congress." *Science,* Vol. 163, February 28, 1969, p. 913.

68. A close reading of McGeorge Bundy's testimony suggests an acerbic interchange between him and several committee members, e.g., Representatives George Bush (Texas) and Martha Griffiths (Michigan) but for different reasons, that is politics (Bush) and finances (Griffiths). See Bush testimony before the Committee on Ways and Means, *Hearings on Tax Reform, 1969,* Part 1, February 20, 1969, pp. 379–404. In addition, an article in the *New York Times* made the point that Mr. Bundy "drew fire" in his appearance before the House Ways and Means Committee in February, and that some foundation leaders perceived him as a "red rag." This problem is also referred to in discussions in the Peterson Commission with Bundy, and also without him, for example by Bernard Wolfman, at the commission meeting in the morning of August 16, 1969. Wolfman, who was present during Bundy's Congressional testimony, reported: "you could see the change in the attitudes of the . . . Ways and Means Committee as a result of Bundy, not only what occurred in the Ford Foundation, but his arrogance to the Committee." See Transcripts of the Peterson Commission, August 16, 1969, 9:15 A.M., pp. 417–418 (IUPUI, Box 6,5).

69. Statement of John D. Rockefeller 3rd before the Ways and Means Committee, *Hearings on Tax Reform, 1969,* Part 5, February 27, 1969, p. 1567. Also reported in Nielsen, *The Big Foundations,* pp. 12–13.

70. Letter from John D. Rockefeller 3rd to Wilbur Mills, April 21, 1969, in which JDR says: "I would like to separately mention the unlimited charitable deduction. . . . On further consideration, I believe that even though any reduction in the unlimited deduction will come out of the pocket of charity, and not the donor, this deduction should not be available beyond 80 percent of one's adjusted gross income."

71. Fred Zimmerman, "*Changing the Rules:* Many in Congress Ready To Tax All Foundations, Curb Their Operations," *Wall Street Journal,* February 28, 1969, p. 1. While Nielsen seems to think (incorrectly) that JDR's reference to paying some income tax was almost accidental, he does suggest that Rockefeller added fuel to the fire, see *The Big Foundations,* p. 12. In an interview with one of JDR's staff, I was told that JDR did deliberately make this statement; also several respondents indicated that Rockefeller liked to shake things up!

72. This distinction, resisted by the foundations, is already signaled in the language of the Treasury Report of 1965, see *Treasury Report on Private Foundations,* February 2, 1969.

73. Reference to Peterson's presentation to Treasury is found in the transcript of the August 16 meeting of the Peterson Commission. In this same meeting moreover, one of the consultant-experts who is present (Mitchell Rogovin) suggests to commission members that "you people are not doing anything about the Finance Committee, I gather and this . . . [is] one of the greatest mistakes possible." See Transcript of the Meeting of August 16, 1969, 9:15 A.M. session, p. 418, and pp. 469–70 (IUPUI, Box 6,5).

74. U.S. Senate, Committee on Finance, *Tax Reform Act of 1969, H.R. 13270: Technical Memorandum of Treasury Position,* 91st Cong., 1st Sess., September 30, 1969 (Washington, D.C. GPO, 1969).

75. This was apparently facilitated by JDR's connections to Mills, who was after all a Congressman from the same state where brother Win was Governor, as well as to Charles Percy in the Senate, father-in-law of JDR's son Jay. But in addition, Sheldon Cohen was on the commission, and he certainly still had connections in Treasury and the Joint Committee on Internal Revenue Taxation.

76. Peterson's suggestion in his testimony for a required payout rate of 7–8 percent evi-

dently was disturbing to most foundation leaders, and was mentioned to the author (in 1996) by one knowledgeable respondent who is connected to the foundation world. For indication of the attention paid by the commission to beneficiary institutions such as those connected with the 501(c)(3) Group, see numerous letters in the IUPUI-Peterson Archives, such as Letter to Everett L. Hollis from Robert D. Calkins, Vice Chancellor of California, Santa Cruz, July 17, 1969; Letter from Edwin L Crosby, M.D., Director, American Hospital Association to William A. Wineberg, November 14, 1969; Letter to Peter Peterson from Bayless Manning, Dean, Stanford Law School, September 16, 1969; Letter to Everett L. Hollis, from James S. Coles, President, Research Corporation, New York, June 9, 1969; and Letter from Everett L. Hollis to Mr. Carl Kaysen, Director, Institute for Advanced Study, Princeton (IUPUI, Box 1,2–7).

77. M. A. Farber, "Foundation Tax Plan Is Attacked," *New York Times,* November 21, 1969.

78. *Foundations and the Tax Bill: Testimony on Title I of the Tax Reform Act of 1969 Submitted by Witnesses Appearing before the United States Senate Finance Committee, October 1969* (New York: Foundation Center, 1969).

79. M. A. Farber, "Agency to Police Foundations Is Being Formed by 3 Groups," *New York Times,* September 9, 1969, p. 1.

6. Law and Regulation

1. John Walsh, "Tax Reform: House Bill Holds Penalties for Foundations," *Science,* Vol. 165 (August 15, 1976), pp. 678–79. See also Thomas Parrish, "The Foundation: A Special American Institution," in Fritz F. Heimann, ed., *The Future of Foundations* (Englewood Cliffs, N.J.: Prentice-Hall, 1973), p. 38.

2. Eileen Shanahan, "Tax Reform Plan Seeks Fairer Levy on Income in U.S.," *New York Times,* February 2, 1969, p. 1.

3. See JDR 3rd Diaries, April 3, 1969 for record of one meeting with Woodworth. See also Harr and Johnson, *The Rockefeller Conscience,* pp. 293–294.

4. In any case, a number of respondents as well as written sources acknowledge the debt of the 1969 Treasury proposals to those of the 1965 Treasury Report on Foundations. The reputed haste of putting together the proposals was also challenged in the commission meetings by one of the experts brought in, Bernard Wolfman, Professor, University of Pennsylvania Law School, Transcript of the panel discussion before the Peterson Commission, August 16, 1969, 9:15 A.M. session (IUPUI, Box 6,2).

5. Two pages of errata on blue sheets in the front of the printed volume might have suggested haste, but at least one authoritative source rejected this notion. See Errata list, *Tax Reform Studies and Proposals,* U.S. Treasury Department (Joint Publication of the Committee on Ways and Means of the U.S. House of Representatives and the Finance Committee of the U.S. Senate) 91st Cong., 1st Sess. (Washington, D.C.: GPO, 1969).

6. A brief explanation of the "orphan" situation is given by Stanley Surrey in note 1 to chapter 6 in *Pathways to Tax Reform,* p. 175.

7. Letter from Joseph W. Barr, Secretary of the Treasury to Hon. David M. Kennedy, Secretary-Designate of the Treasury, January 17, 1969 in Treasury Department, *Tax Reform Studies and Proposals,* p. v. In Barr's letter he notes that attached to the "studies and proposals regarding tax reform" are some additional background materials regarding "particular industries" that were not completed by Secretary Fowler prior to his leaving the Treasury Department.

8. See Letter from Wilbur D. Mills, Chairman, Committee on Ways and Means, House of Representatives, and Russell B. Long, Chairman, Committee on Finance, U.S. Senate to Hon. David M. Kennedy, Secretary of the Treasury, January 29, 1969; and Letter from David M. Kennedy, Secretary of the Treasury to the Hon. Wilbur D. Mills, Chairman, Committee on

Ways and Means, House of Representatives, January 30, 1969, in Treasury Department, *Tax Reform Studies and Proposals*, p. iii.

9. "Statement of the Honorable Henry H. Fowler, Secretary of the Treasury, for the Congress of the United States, on the Tax Reform Program" in U.S. Treasury Department, *Tax Reform Studies and Proposals*, Part 1, pp. 3, 7.

10. This was apparently considered to be one of the provisions most likely to be rejected by Congress. See Shanahan, "Tax Reform Plan Seeks Fairer Levy . . . "

11. In these initial 1969 Treasury proposals the "schedule of rates for the minimum tax would be graduated from 7 to 35 percent" but it was to be calculated in such a way that it "would have the effect of placing a [maximum] 50 percent ceiling on the amount of an individual's total income which may be excluded from tax." "General Description of Proposals," in Treasury Department, *Tax Reform Studies and Proposals*, Part 1, pp. 14.

12. "[T]he proposed reform program will go a long way toward making the tax system more fair and equitable by removing tax abuses and defects . . . " in Treasury Department, *Tax Reform Studies and Proposals*, p. 45. For a statement of Surrey's philosophy in this regard, and on the difference between basic tax structure (fundamental rates) and incentives or preferences with special purposes (which Surrey considered as tax expenditures) see Surrey, *Pathways to Tax Reform*, and in particular, pp. 176–178.

13. This was widely recognized. See for example "Foundations Feel Heat of Tax Reform," *Business Week*, March 8, 1969, pp. 72ff; I. Mothner, "Bill to Kill Foundations," *Look*, Vol. 33 (December 16, 1969), p. 83. Reference to the vast stock holdings of foundations were in Patman's opening Statement at the Hearings on Tax Reform before the House Ways and Means Committee on February 18, 1969 (*Hearings on Tax Reform*, Vol. 1, pp. 12–24); they had already been discussed extensively in Ferdinand Lundberg, *The Rich and the Super-Rich*, and are referred to in contemporary journals, for example in Jeffrey Hart, "The New Class War," *National Review*, Vol. 21 (September 9, 1969), pp. 896–899. Peter Peterson was however to argue against restrictions on stock holdings by foundations in his testimony before the Senate Finance Committee, which is discussed below in this chapter.

14. U.S. Treasury Department, "Summary of Tax Reform Proposals," in *Tax Reform, 1969*, Hearings before the Committee on Ways and Means, U.S. House of Representatives, 91st Cong., 1st Sess. (Part 14–15), Tuesday, April 22, 1969 (Washington, D.C.: GPO, 1969), p. 5105.

15. President Richard Nixon, "Special Message to the Congress on Reform of the Federal Tax System," April 21, 1969, in *Public Papers of the Presidents of the United States, Richard Nixon 1969* (Washington, D.C.: GPO, 1970), pp. 310–313.

16. A good discussion of tax shelters and other tax protections (also referred to as loopholes) can be found in Surrey, *Pathways to Tax Reform*, chapter 3, "Operational Aspects of Tax Expenditures: Tax Deferral and Tax Shelters," which discusses such devices as accelerated depreciation and oil depletion allowances. Outgoing Treasury Secretary Joseph Barr apparently used the term "expenditures" in estimating revenue losses in his testimony before the Joint Economic Committee of the Congress, January 17, 1969, as cited in Lester A. Sobel, ed., *The Great American Tax Revolt* (New York: Facts on File, 1979), p. 11, and of course, the term was used frequently in the Hearings of the Ways and Means Committee and the Senate Finance Committee in connection with the passage of the Tax Reform Act of 1969. For a discussion of some nuances in the concept of expenditures see Pollack, *The Failure of U.S. Tax Policy*, p. 17. Outrage at the idea of "loopholes" is expressed by many authors in the 1960s, including Lundberg in *The Rich and the Super-Rich*, as well in a more specifically tax oriented book by Stern, *The Great Treasury Raid*.

17. The House Bill specifically provided that "private foundations are to be forbidden to spend money for lobbying, electioneering (including voter registration drives), grants to individuals (unless there are assurances that the grants are made on an objective basis)," and also

specifically referred to denial of "expenses incurred in connection with grass root campaigns or other attempts to . . . encourage the public to contact members of a legislative body [concerning] . . . legislation." There were some exceptions, such as voter registration carried on by nonpartisan organizations or five or more states, making available nonpartisan analysis and research to legislators, and also communications "regarding possible decisions which might affect the existence of the private foundation, its powers and duties, its tax-exempt status, or the deduction of contributions to foundations" (so long as the latter communications were not via grass roots lobbying). Also "improper expenditures were to be subject to tax." From U.S. House of Representatives, Committee on Ways and Means, *Tax Reform Act of 1969*, 91st Cong., 1st Sess., House Rept. 91–413 (Washington, D.C.: GPO, 1969), pp. 31–35.

18. Reference to Section 101(a) of the Bill, and 509(a) of the Internal Revenue Code. Explanation of this definition is given in *Tax Reform Act of 1969*, Report of the Committee on Ways and Means, pp. 40–41.

19. As discussed above in chapter 5, the idea of an operating foundation was important to the Rockefellers because of Colonial Williamsburg and possibly other involvements, including Lincoln Center. The definition of operating foundation proposed by the House, defined in Section 101(b) of the bill and to be new Section 4942 of the Code, was an organization "eligible to receive qualifying distributions from other private foundations (but otherwise subject to the limitations imposed upon private foundations)," "an organization substantially all of the income of which is expended directly for the active conduct of its exempt purposes or functions . . . provided that either (1) substantially more than half its assets are devoted to such activities" or (2) substantially all of the non-endowment support it received came from 5 independent exempt organizations and the general public (the degree of additional specificity in qualifications for operating foundations strongly suggests that the idea is tailored to some particular foundations). The description comes from *Tax Reform Act of 1969*, Report of the Committee on Ways and Means, p. 42.

20. This would become part of Sec 170(e) of the U.S. tax code; see "Legislative History: Conference Report No. 91-782," Title II, Subtitle A(3)(1), in *United States Code, Congressional and Administrative News,* 91st Cong., 1st Sess., 1969, Vol. 2, p. 2408.

21. Not all museums and universities are public charities; they may of course also be governmental or even operating foundations.

22. See "Statements and Recommendations of the Department of Treasury" in *Tax Reform Act of 1969*, Hearings before the Committee on Finance, U.S. Senate, 91st Cong., 1st Sess., Part 1, September 4 and 5, 1969 (Washington, D.C.: GPO, 1969), p. 47. Among the most active groups testifying in the Senate in relation to H.R. 13270 were the universities and institutions of higher education and research, and this issue was one that concerned them greatly. See regarding gifts of appreciated property "Statement of Lincoln Gordon, President, the John Hopkins University on Behalf of the American Universities, Summary," in *Tax Reform Act of 1969*, Hearings before the Committee on Finance, U.S. Senate, 91st Cong., 1st Sess., Part 6, October 7, 1969, pp. 5699–5700.

23. For a lucid, if somewhat simplified—and very gossipy—discussion of the Tax Reform Act's proposals concerning capital gains tax, and taxation of appreciated property in relation to charitable contributions, see Edwin S. Cohen, *A Lawyer's Life: Deep in the Heart of Taxes* (Arlington, Va.: Tax Analysts, 1994), pp. 367–381.

24. Statement of Peter G. Peterson, Chairman of the Board and President, Bell & Howell Corp. Chicago, Ill., Chairman, Commission on Foundations and Private Philanthropy, in Hearings before the Committee on Finance, U.S. Senate, 91st Cong., 1st Sess., *Tax Reform Act of 1969*, Part 6, October 22, 1969 (Washington, D.C.: GPO, 1969), pp. 6101–6103.

25. Peterson testimony before the Senate Finance Committee, *Tax Reform Act of 1969*, Part 6, p. 6099.

26. See Hearings before the Finance Committee, U.S. Senate, 91st Cong., 1st Sess., *Im-*

proper Payments by Private Foundations to Government Officials, S. 2075, June 4, 1969 (Washington, D.C.: GPO, 1969), Section 505 describing improper transactions, and Sec. 5 (d) defining government officials to include those who held any government office "within the preceding two year period."

27. April 14, 1969 Workplan of the Peterson Commission, as cited in Peterson testimony before the Senate Finance Committee, *Tax Reform Act of 1969,* Part 6, p. 6121.

28. Peterson testimony before the Senate Finance Committee, *Tax Reform Act of 1969,* Part 6, p. 6121.

29. Statement of Hon. Charles H. Percy, U.S. Senator from the State of Illinois, Hearings before the Committee on Finance, U.S. Senate, 91st Cong., 1st Sess., *Tax Reform Act of 1969,* Part 6, October 7, 1969, pp. 5798–5799.

30. H.R. 13275, introduced September 10, 1969, by Congressman Wright Patman.

31. Transcript of the Peterson Commission, Meeting of September 6, 1969, 9:15 A.M., pp. 54–60 (IUPUI, Box 7,5).

32. A complex formula was developed from the original concept of a mandated minimum tax in order to insure that some tax preferences were not counted twice. For example, if individuals did not pay taxes on income from municipal or state bonds, then giving them away to charity should not result in a deduction from their taxable income. An explanation of the concept is given initially in Treasury Department, *Tax Reform Studies and Proposals,* pp. 145–152. Its elaboration in the House Bill is explained complete with illustrative formulas in *Tax Reform Act of 1969* (Report of the Committee on Ways and Means . . . to accompany H.R. 13270), pp. 72–86. It should be noted also that part of this discussion involved controversial changes, including phasing in taxes on formerly tax-exempt interest on State and local bonds as well as recapturing taxes for long-term capital gains (pp. 78–79).

33. Senator Albert Gore, testifying before the Senate Finance Committee, *Tax Reform Act of 1969,* October 22, 1969, Part 6, p. 6057.

34. Eileen Shanahan, "Bill Would Limit Foundations Life," *New York Times,* October 28, 1969; also "Tax Exempt Organizations" in *Congressional Quarterly* (June 11, 1971), p. 1256 which describes a meeting which had been held (November 28, 1969) to defeat the 40-year Amendment by a group of foundation officials with Senator Walter Mondale (Democrat from Minnesota). In fact, Senator Mondale became one of the sponsors of an amendment to kill the 40-year limitation.

35. Interview with Senator Charles Percy, Washington, D.C., 1996; the lack of a constituency is also referred to in Harr and Johnson, *The Rockefeller Conscience* (1991), p. 297; in H. Thomas James, "Perspectives on Internal Functioning of Foundations" and also in Parrish, "The Foundation: A Special American Institution," in *The Future of Foundations,* pp. 213–214. In the same volume, however, John Labovitz, former staff member of the Peterson Commission, writes, "It may not be too far-fetched to suggest that the current provision [against influencing legislation] reflects Congressional irritation at foundations and their grantees and that its basic purpose was simply to keep them away from Capitol Hill."

36. Among the reforms emphasized in Nixon's "Special Message" were reductions in tax preferences, and the idea of a "minimum income tax"; the idea of a "low income allowance" for persons in poverty; help to workers who change jobs; and repeal of the 7 percent investment tax credit. However the President also mentioned that "exempt organizations, including private foundations would come under much stricter surveillance" and that rules affecting charitable deductions would be tightened "but only to screen out the unreasonable . . . not . . . those which help legitimate charities. . . . " From "Special Message to the Congress on Reform of the Federal Tax System. April 21, 1969" in *Public Papers of the Presidents of the United States: Richard Nixon 1969* (Washington, D.C.: GPO, 1970), pp. 310–313.

37. Letter from Edwin L. Crosby, M.D., Director of the American Hospital Association, to William A. Wineberg, November 14, 1969. Crosby thanks Wineberg for sending him "your

testimony on private philanthropy" and continues, "I thought you did an extremely good job. How did Pete Peterson do in presenting it?" (IUPUI, Box 1,4).

38. Peterson testimony before the Senate Finance Committee, *Tax Reform Act of 1969*, Part 6, pp. 6053–6182.

39. Peterson testimony before the Senate Finance Committee, *Tax Reform Act of 1969*, Part 6, pp. 6122–6174 (for printed document); much of the same material is also presented in the final Peterson Commission Report, *Foundations, Private Giving, and Public Policy: Report and Recommendations of the Commission on Foundations and Private Philanthropy* (Chicago: University of Chicago Press, 1970).

40. Peterson Commission Report, pp. 83–84.

41. That is, 38 percent of the foundations with assets of over $100 million responded "yes" when asked whether they had supported projects in the previous three years that "had been considered controversial or particularly unpopular." The report points out that these foundations are few in number but "far more important from the standpoint of expenditures" than smaller ones and then goes on to show that again the large foundations are far more likely to make grants they consider innovative. See Peterson Report, pp. 84–85.

42. Discussion around Peterson testimony before the Senate Finance Committee, *Tax Reform Act of 1969*, Part 6, p. 6115. The Senator's compliment about performance clearly refers to Peterson's argument about the need to improve investment performance—return on investments—of foundations, and his recommendation that they should have a higher payout rate related to higher earnings from assets.

43. However, the role of political affiliation in these proceedings cannot be ignored. Both Long and Gore were Democrats, after all, while Peterson was an almost prototypical Republican.

44. Although it is hard to read the tone of the interchange between Gore and Peterson only from the printed document, these remarks by Gore suggest impatience with Peterson's delineating of the expertise (and political connections) of commission members: "Mr. Chairman, I suggest we accept the validity and authenticity of the organization and get to the substance of the presentation." Senate Finance Committee, *Tax Reform Act of 1969*, Part 6, p. 6054.

45. See Peterson testimony before the Senate Finance Committee, *Tax Reform Act of 1969*, Part 6, p. 6118. He referred to their 30, 40, or 50 percent payout rate, but of course those organizations (now called United Way) would certainly have claimed to be giving away a far greater percentage of the moneys they raised since they were designed essentially to be pass-through organizations, taking off only a small percentage for administrative overhead). See Brilliant, *The United Way*.

46. Peterson testimony before the Senate Finance Committee, *Tax Reform Act of 1969*, Part 6, p. 6078.

47. Peterson testimony before the Senate Finance Committee, *Tax Reform Act of 1969*, Part 6, pp. 6067–75. During this part of his testimony Peterson was suggesting that one of the primary disincentives for big givers in the House Bill was the proposed tax on "appreciated property" given to charity.

48. Peterson testimony before the Senate Finance Committee, *Tax Reform Act of 1969*, Part 6, pp. 6084–85.

49. "While we are not in a position to make firm recommendations, we have serious questions about the adequacy of the Internal Revenue Service (IRS) as the sole federal agency regulating foundations. The problem is almost certainly more fundamental than that IRS has not been adequately staffed to deal with foundations." *Tentative Staff Position on Regulatory Provisions Affecting Foundations* (dated) 9/4/69 (unpublished document, IUPUI, Box 4,3).

50. Peterson testimony before the Senate Finance Committee, *Tax Reform Act of 1969*, Part 6, pp. 6113–14.

51. Letter from Peter G. Peterson to William Wineberg and John Labovitz, January 12, 1970, in which he states, "I believe it is fair to say that our December draft was not sufficiently critical of foundations. It tended to be laudatory when actually I feel a more accurate appraisal is that a handful have made distinctive contributions and the vast majority engage in an 'over the transom' method, very much like most individuals do."

52. Letter from John D. Rockefeller 3rd to Congressman Wilbur Mills, June 13, 1969, in which he refers to Mills's statement of May 27 and says that it is "most distressing to me to think of this potential for about-face of the Congress in regard to philanthropy." In a response from Mills to JDR 3rd on June 19, 1969, Mills is partially mollifying but notes that there is greater demand for tax reform now than in previous years. Letters in RAC, RFA, RG5, JDR 3rd Papers, Series 3, Box 62, Folder: 399. (This refers to the new classification system for JDR 3rd material.)

53. Accelerated appreciation was of great interest to corporations, banks, and holders of real estate, and therefore certainly to the Rockefeller family. The question of how capital gains would be calculated affected both corporations and individuals, and also would be likely to have an impact on charitable contributions. Both issues were discussed extensively during this period; for discussion of the provisions in the House Bill, see *Tax Reform Act of 1969*, Report of the Committee on Ways and Means, House of Representatives, 91st Cong., 1st Sess., August 2, 1969 (Washington, D.C.: U.S. Government Office, 1969), pp. 131–166; the Treasury view under Nixon, see *Tax Reform Act of 1969 H.R. 13270: Technical Memorandum of Treasury Position*, Committee on Finance, U.S. Senate (Washington, D.C.: GPO, 1969), pp. 95–112; they are also discussed (as a subset of tax shelters) in Surrey, *Pathways to Tax Reform*, pp. 100–119, and from a more irate point of view in Stern, *The Great Treasury Raid*.

54. This was, it will be recalled, the justification for creating the Foundation Coordinated Testimony Group.

55. Discussion of the Gore Amendment in Proceedings and Debate of the 91st Congress, *U.S. Congressional Record—Senate,* Vol. 115–Part 28, pp. 37199–37204. The record also suggests that during this discussion there was difficulty in getting a quorum (see p. 37199).

56. In the end the vote was 69 for the Mondale amendment to eliminate "the 40-year rule"; 18 against; 17 "pairs" and 11 not voting or indicating present. Here however the foundations did mobilize specifically to help sponsor a counter-amendment. Reference to the meeting of selected foundations with Senator Walter Mondale to defeat the 40-year amendment is in *Congressional Quarterly* (June 11, 1971), pp. 1251–1256. See comments on the Mondale-Percy-Curtis-Hollis amendment by Senator Percy, in the *U.S. Congressional Record-Senate,* Proceedings and Debates of the 91st Cong., 1st Sess., Vol. 115, Part 28, p. 37201. See also the account in Cuninggim, *Private Money and Public Service,* p. 194.

57. See Manley, *The Politics of Finance.*

58. Actually Javits expressed some concern that the agreement to take his amendment to conference might be counterproductive, but Senator Long assured him that he would take it seriously. Javits agreed to a major tradeoff at the request of Senator Tower (Texas) to divide his amendment into two parts for the Senate vote: the first part concerning the recommendation for the commission, and the second part dealing with audit fees and other substantive matters. Javits said that if the first vote carried (on the commission) he would withdraw the others "because we then would have a commission" which would be concerned "with the whole field." Remarks by Javits in *Congressional Record—Senate,* Dec. 5, 1969, Vol. 115, Part 28, p. 37208. The amendment was apparently agreed to without a roll call vote (p. 37212).

59. See discussion in connection with the testimony of John D. Rockefeller before the Senate Finance Committee, *Hearings on the Tax Reform Act of 1969,* Part 3, September 17, 1969, p. 2010.

60. Although several respondents reported that the needs of foundations were not a high priority in Congress, it would appear also that doing away with them entirely was too radical

a proposal. One key respondent who worked with the Senator suggested that he did not really expect to prevail on this issue.

61. At least according to two respondents, John R. Labovitz, staff of the commission, and John Simon, Professor of Law at Yale University and scholar of the history of tax policy and philanthropy. However, the Peterson Commission is generally not well known outside of the inner circle of scholars and persons connected to the philanthropic world, and moreover, at least one well-known philanthropy follower, Waldemar Nielsen, has taken the position that the most important recommendation of the Peterson Commission was the one concerning the permanent advisory body.

62. Sec. 101(l)(3) of the Tax Reform Act of 1969. The amount which must be paid out is the greater of the adjusted net income or 6 percent of the assets (using the figure proposed in a Senate amendment) but the 6 percent amount was to be phased in gradually. "Legislative History: Conference Report No. 91–782 on the Tax Reform Act of 1969, Statement of the Managers on the Part of the House," *United States Code: Congressional and Administrative News,* 91st Cong., 1st Sess., 1969, Vol. 2, p. 2395.

63. Levon C. Register and David E. Gormanous, "Private Foundations and the Tax Reform Act of 1969," in *Taxes,* Vol. 48, May 1970, pp. 283–291. The significance of these dates will become apparent as our story unfolds below.

64. Legislative History of the Tax Reform Act of 1969, Conference Report No. 91–782, U.S. Code, pp. 2490–2491. In making this reference to the Barr remarks, Senator Long uses the statistic that 154 rich individuals paid no income tax, and 21 individuals with income over $1 million paid no taxes.

65. Sobel, *ed., The Great American Tax Revolt,* p. 12. See also "Legislative History of the Tax Reform Act, 1969" and "Tax Policy," *Congress and the Nation 1969–1972,* Vol. 3, pp. 78–85.

66. Register and Gormanous, "Private Foundations and the Tax Reform Act of 1969," p. 283.

67. Cohen, *A Lawyer's Life,* pp. 412–413.

68. "Tax Policy," *Congress and the Nation,* Vol. 3, p. 80; Witte, *Politics and Development of the Federal Income Tax,* p. 174; and with special reference to foundations, Cuninggim, *Private Money and Public Service,* p. 194; Parrish, "The Foundation: A Special American Institution," in *The Future of Foundations,* pp. 38–39.

69. Edwin Cohen in *A Lawyer's Life* takes credit for framing this phrase during the passage of the bill (p. 417); however, it appears to have been used earlier; see Jeffrey Hart, "The New Class War," *National Review,* September 9, 1969, Vol. 21, p. 921.

7. The Peterson Commission

1. P.L. 91–172. The Act was signed into law by President Nixon on December 30, 1969.

2. The reader may recognize the source of this slightly distorted version of a line from a poem by T. S. Eliot, *The Hollow Men I,* "This is the way the world ends/Not with a bang but a whimper." Actually there was a press conference and press coverage in May 1970 when the final report was "issued"; but the publication of the book occurred six months later. The issuance of the 300-page document is reported in M. A. Farber, "Lag in Private Giving Forecast: Panel Calls for Tax Incentives," *New York Times,* May 10, 1970, p. 50.

3. One apparent skeptic connected with the commission questioned whether the whole 1969 Tax Reform Act was in the end worth the fuss. See John Labovitz, "1969 Tax Reforms Reconsidered," in Heimann, ed., *The Future of Foundations,* p. 130. This suggestion also reflects his comments about the timing of the Peterson Commission Report. Telephone interview with John Labovitz, July 1997.

4. The entire history of attacks on foundations since 1913 suggests that this is an impor-

tant distinction to the public. It has consistently been foundations and not recipient groups or operating charities that have been attacked by Congressional leaders and important Congressional committees or commissions. See also Stanley Surrey's remarks in discussion with the Peterson Committee, where he questions "Why not just hand dollars directly to the Orchestra—let them get the income? . . . What purpose does [a] foundation serve?" Peterson Commission Transcript of August 15, 1969 (IUPUI, Box 6,3).

5. In this regard see Fritz F. Heimann, "Foundations and Government: Perspectives for the Future" in Heimann, ed., *The Future of Foundations*, p. 264. Heimann suggests that JDR was in fact initially unable to get the Rockefeller Foundation interested in population until the subject became much less controversial. The story of JDR's efforts to get Presidents Johnson and Nixon involved in population is told in Harr and Johnson, *The Rockefeller Conscience*, pp. 168–79, and 395–422.

6. Hearings in the House were scheduled to begin on February 18, 1969, but the process had begun in January when Treasury reports and studies that were to become the basis of the bill were presented to the Secretary of the Treasury in the new Nixon administration, David M. Kennedy; he in turn passed them to the Committee on Ways and Means with a letter of transmittal on January 30, 1969. See *Tax Reform Studies and Proposals: U.S. Treasury Department*, Joint Publication of the Committee on Ways and Means, U.S. House of Representatives, and the Finance Committee of the U.S. Senate, 91st Cong., 1st Sess., February 5, 1969, Part 1 (Washington, D.C.: GPO), p. iii.

7. Although this has not been widely discussed in the literature on Patman, there are evident parallels between Patman's charges of excessive tax avoidance by powerful elite foundations and Surrey's concern about tax privileges awarded to those institutions and their donors. See also Patman's citation to Surrey (and statement of agreement with the quote) in his testimony before the Ways and Means Committee, "Stanley S. Surrey . . . is reported to have said in a speech on February 23, 1967: 'The present resort of tax and business planners to the creation of a private foundation to hold the stock of a business enterprise so as to perpetuate the control of that enterprise is a complete distortion of the policies and philanthropic motivations that underlie the tax benefits granted charitable contributions and charitable institutions.' " In *Tax Reform, 1969*, Hearings before the Committee on Ways and Means, House of Representatives, 91st Cong., 1st Sess., Part 1 (Washington, D.C.: GPO, 1969), p. 19.

8. The reader will also recall that the notion of tax expenditures had been introduced already in Treasury's 1968 report on the Federal Budget.

9. Draft, National Commission on Philanthropic Foundations Proposed Scope Outline, 4/14/69 (IUPUI, Box 1,9). Also note that the sentence referring to the commission's belief that there was extensive available data is found in the typed copy of this draft, but is crossed out (although no date is given for the deletion).

10. For starters, Commissioner Edward Levi was the President of the University of Chicago and Commissioner Philip Lee was Chancellor of the University of California, San Francisco. Altogether six out of 15 members of the commission (not counting Peterson) were either professors or high level administrators in academic settings. In addition Peterson was a Trustee of the University of Chicago, the Rockefeller family had an historical interest in that University, and Jay Rockefeller had recently joined its Board of Trustees. However, it should be noted that one member of the commission staff (in a personal interview with the author) verified specifically what memoranda in the archives suggest—that Ed Levi was "intellectually pure" in his approach to the issues before the committee. That however does not eliminate the possibility that others were not so disinterested as Levi, or that Peterson was responsive to those whom he considered to be part of his own constituency.

11. A memorandum to the staff from Peterson, dated August 18, 1970, states that most of the book is at the press, and a "major effort" is being made "to get financial support" for its preparation . . . and widespread dissemination." In the Preface to the Commission Report,

Peterson also states that "At the time of this writing, Mr. [Herman "Dutch"] Smith is still basically trying to persuade donors . . . that they should help reduce the impressive deficit of the Commission." Peterson Report, p. xviii.

12. Peterson testimony before the Senate Finance Committee, *Tax Reform Act of 1969*, Part 6. See also letter of August 11, 1969 to Peterson from Daniel F. Bryant suggesting that the commission modify their position about soliciting funds from foundations; a memorandum from Dana S. Creel to Governor Nelson A. Rockefeller (January 5, 1970) states "Fund-raising efforts [of the commission] have been none too successful, although about 100,000 has been raised." However, Creel also suggested that Nelson Rockefeller "stay out of this" and he would explain why to Peterson (RAC, RFA, 4, NAR Personal Projects, 69, Folder: 654). Altogether the commission archives are replete with references to the gap in funding, but silent about how the gap was covered—suggesting that possibly JDR personally supplied the money (there are particular files relating to JDR's financial contributions in the Rockefeller Archives but I was told these were still closed to researchers).

13. This point was made by Schwartz, *Modern American Philanthropy*, p. 74.

14. Peterson's concern about tax incentives is revealed in discussions with the commission. See for example Transcript of the Commission Meeting of August 15, 1969, pp. 318–319 (IUPUI, Box 6,3). Peterson emphasized this point in his statement before the Senate Finance Committee with reference to the commission's survey of large private donors (85 respondents). Peterson testimony before the Senate Finance Committee, *Tax Reform Act of 1969*, Part 6, pp. 6066–70. Tax Incentives are also referred to in relation to the Survey of Distinguished Citizens (885 returns out of a sample of 4,016 persons) in the commission report (see pp. 191–92, and p. 199). Reference to tax incentives appears with somewhat ambiguous language as part of "Recommendation to Government I" in the commission report, p.145, where it states "Incentives should be compatible with tax equity and prevention of tax avoidance."

15. Possibly this was meant to be used for continuation of the commission's efforts while a permanent group was being formed, but this cannot be demonstrated.

16. In his message to Congress, April 21, 1969 Nixon had required that a tax program be developed by Congress by the end of November 1969. Nixon asked to continue the Johnson-initiated surcharge to obtain revenues and hold down inflation while he proposed tax reform as well. See President Richard M. Nixon, "Special Message to the Congress on Reform of the Federal Tax System," April 21, 1969, in *Public Papers of the Presidents of the United States, Richard Nixon 1969* (Washington, D.C.: GPO, 1970), p. 310. See also "Tax Policy" in *Congress and the Nation*, Vol. 3, 1969–1972, p. 78.

17. These efforts are recapitulated in a document in the Rockefeller Archives, "A Summary: Negative Congressional Criticism of Foundations since the Passage of the Tax Reform Act of 1969" which also cites pages in the *Congressional Record* which cover these events. RAC, COF, Folder: "Tax Reform: General Effects."

18. There are in fact many communications in the archives about lack of funds for this purpose (see for example note 14 above). It should be also noted that in a memorandum to Peter G. Peterson, from the staff, October 31, 1969, "Status of Projects as of October 31, 1969 and Proposals for Preparation of the Commission's Final Report," the staff had explicitly said that they did not see how they could afford to distribute copies of Peterson's testimony before the Senate Committee (the preliminary report) and they recommended referring all inquiries to the GPO for copies of the text. However, material in the archives indicates that some individuals, including Stanley Surrey, did initially get copies, while others later did not. For example, Senator Abraham Ribicoff (member of the Senate Finance Committee) wrote to Peterson for a copy of the report and his request was turned down in a letter from William Wineberg on December 17, 1969, who suggests that the Senator get the reprint of Peterson's testimony from the GPO. (IUPUI, Box 1,4). Interestingly, material in the files also suggests that there were some errors deleted from Peterson's testimony before the printed text was released.

19. See "Complimentary Copy–Distribution Lists" attached to Memorandum to Messrs. Walter Blum, Fritz Heimann, Everett Hollis, John Labovitz, and William Wineberg which suggests a distribution of 2,700 copies of the report, including 50 copies to members of the administration (such as the White House and Secretary of the Treasury); 500 leading members of Congress, and appropriate Committee staff, 250 of the largest foundations (heads), 250 University Presidents, and 600 corporations.

20. See Appendix D for the complete Table of Contents.

21. Hamilton, "Philanthropy and the Economy," in Peterson Commission Report, p. 258.

22. Among over 20 letters in the "turn down" folder of the commission archives, were the following letters requesting papers: from William Wineberg to J. E. Wallace Sterling offering him $1000 for a paper (July 24, 1969); a letter from Peterson to Sir Denis William Brogan, University of Cambridge (August 8, 1969); a similar letter to Michael Crozier, Centre de Sociologie des Organizations, Paris (August 8, 1969); and a letter to Professor Charles Frankel, Columbia University (August 10, 1969). Kingman Brewster (President of Yale University) wrote Peterson stating that he had no time for an original paper (August 8, 1969); there was also a letter of refusal from John W. Gardner to Everett L. Holis (IUPUI, Box 1,3). Commission members Daniel Bell and Philip Lee also wrote letters indicating they could not produce papers (IUPUI, Box 1,7).

23. Andrews, *Foundation Watcher*, p. 256.

24. See for example the discussion below (note 39) relating to the payout that was included in the Act versus the payout that was proposed by Peterson. But note that the report did not fully adjust for the defeat of the Gore Amendment limiting the life (tax exemption years) of foundations.

25. Among those who responded was Daniel Bryant. Typed notes, dated 12/10/69, of a telephone call from Bryant indicate that he expressed great interest in the idea of a "prestigious group of citizens" who could provide reports to the President and Congress, but which should not include John Gardner (IUPUI, Box 1,7). Bryant also wrote to Peterson, with a copy to Everett Hollis, on August 11, 1969 suggesting that staff should undertake a classification of foundations. Several letters from Edward Levi suggest that he was particularly helpful, and this was confirmed in a telephone interview with John Labovitz (July 1997). See letter from Levi to Peterson, with detailed comment on a Draft (September 22, 1969), and letter from Levi to Wineberg about chapter arrangements (October 7, 1969) (IUPUI, Box 1,7). The dissents by J. Paul Austin, Chairman of the Coca Cola Company, and Lane Kirkland Treasurer of the AFL-CIO are included in the report on pp. 158–159, and 177–180 respectively.

26. Peterson Memorandum to Staff, 10/17/69; Letter of Peterson to Fritz Heimann concerning "talks with both Moskin and Daniel Robison and I hope it was helpful"; Memorandum "Random Notes," April 7, 1970 from Peterson to Messrs. Heimann, Labovitz, Wineberg, and Hyman, enclosing also material he is interested in from a book by William Rudy (IUPUI, Box 4,16). Also Peterson's earlier letter to Everett Hollis of July 9, 1969 containing a draft outline he wishes to discuss with the staff. In a personal interview with the author (July 1997) Labovitz also suggested that Peterson would jump the gun on the staff and arrange for other sources (such as those used for the surveys) when staff was not enthusiastic about a proposed line of inquiry.

27. "Wally believes that in places the prose is 'too purple' and that the draft could stand a 50% thinning out of metaphors." In typed comments received (by telephone) from Wally Blum on 4/6/70 (IUPUI, Box 4,11). These notes also suggest that Blum, who was a Professor of Law at the University, wanted less condemnation and more appreciation of the foundations in the report. Moreover, he suggested there are "dangers to foundations in getting involved in certain kinds of programs" and thought it was a mistake to recognize only one minority viewpoint in the draft. The dissenting comments from Lane Kirkland were apparently received later as indicated by correspondence from Peterson to Kirkland, June 1, 1970 (IUPUI, Box 1,9).

Blum is listed as an Associate Director of the Staff, but in the transcripts of commission meetings sounds very much like a participating commission member. For a reference to the editing of Sidney Hyman, see Peter G. Peterson, "Preface" in the Peterson Commission Report, p. xviii.

28. "Report on Survey of Distinguished Citizens" in Peterson Commission Report, pp. 217–226.

29. This is essentially the same point made by Lane Kirkland in his "Dissenting View by Lane Kirkland" in the commission report, pp. 177–178; Kirkland objects to the lack of proof for statements in the report, and the tendency to "polemics."

30. Peterson Commission Report, p. 119. This latter point is similar to the position taken by John Rockefeller in his Testimony before the Senate Finance Committee, *Tax Reform Act of 1969*, Vol. 3, September 17, 1969, pp. 2009–2011.

31. Peterson Commission Report, p. 127.

32. See the discussion about the commission's data on controversial activity in chapter 6 above.

33. Peterson Commission Report, pp. 126–146.

34. These two recommendations are highlighted respectively in the titles of chapters 17 and 20 of the commission report.

35. See Peterson Commission Report, pp. 175–176. The term "third class charities" expresses the sentiment of the report but is not actually used in it. I have borrowed it from Boris I. Bittker, "Should Foundations Be Third Class Charities?" in Heimann, ed., *The Future of Foundations*, pp. 132–162.

36. It should be noted here that the Rockefeller charities were extremely complicated: there were issues of borderline distinctions between private and operating foundations in Colonial Williamsburg and possibly Jackson Hole; the role of family members as disqualified parties (i.e., self-dealing) would relate to the Rockefeller Brothers Fund including its location on the 56th floor of 30 Rockefeller Plaza (Harr and Johnson, *The Rockefeller Conscience*, pp. 521–522); and the question of gifts of appreciated property was relevant to their gifts to foundations. See also discussion in Nielsen, *The Big Foundations*, p. 48.

37. Peterson Commission Report, pp. 160–164. It is important to remember that, although not widely publicized, the Tax Reform Act did permit lobbying by foundations when related to their own specific interests. It should also be noted that the commission's recommendations are discussed in separate chapters which focus on (1) recommendations to the foundations themselves; (2) recommendations to government concerning regulations; (3) recommendations to government concerning the new law; and (4) the recommendation for an Advisory Board on Philanthropic Policy. However, while the separation between advice to the foundations and to the government makes sense, there is overlapping content in the first three chapters and in general there is not a full separation of analysis and recommendations throughout the report—a problem Wally Blum had pointed out after reading a draft.

38. Peterson Commission Report, p. 137. A fuller discussion of this issue is given on pages 147–150, in which it is argued that in going for the higher payout figure Congress was "moving in the right direction" but that the payout rate should not be pegged to whichever is higher—foundation "income" or a percentage of assets. The report suggests that "the only correct yardstick for measuring investment performance is the *total rate of return*—the measure used by practically all mutual funds, profit sharing funds, pension funds, and other endowments. It includes interest, dividends, realized and unrealized capital gains" (emphasis in original).

39. Letter to John D. Rockefeller III from Douglas Dillon, January 6, 1970 (RAC, RFA, 3, Box 368, Folder: Phil. Comm. on Foundations and Private Philanthropy).

40. See Peterson Commission Report, particularly pp. 132–136; 139–144; and 152–156.

41. Peterson Commission Report, p. 170.

42. See letter from Peterson to George Shultz, Executive Office of the President, Director, Office of Management and Budget, November 2, 1970 (IUPUI, Box 8,4); also Memo to

Staff Commission on Foundations and Private Philanthropy, "Report on Sense of 'Philanthropy' Meeting with John Ehrlichman, George Shultz and Charley Walker on November 23 and 24, 1970" (IUPUI, Box 1,9).

43. The issue of public members on the Advisory Board is discussed in a Memorandum on December 15, 1970 to Peter G. Peterson from Everett Hollis and William Wineberg on the Subject of "Proposed Bill on 'Advisory Board on Philanthropic Policy'" (pp. 3–4), in which they suggest that the possibility of including members of Congress on the Board should be reconsidered (IUPUI, Box 1,9).

44. Peterson Commission Report, p. 182.

45. See Peterson testimony before the Senate Finance Committee, *Tax Reform Act of 1969*, Part 6, p. 6066.

46. This is discussed in Appendix A. Alan Pifer, who was involved with the Rockefeller group, certainly brought this into the American discussions based on his knowledge of the English Commission. However, Pifer's actual position in regard to the specific form (and personnel) of such a commission does not always seem to have been consistent, particularly with regard to its "publicness."

47. Fritz F. Heimann, "Introduction," in *The Future of Foundations*, p. 2.

48. Of course he may have meant it facetiously, but John Labovitz did say that "one may question whether the fuss has all been worth it." John R. Labovitz, "1969 Tax Reforms Reconsidered" in Heimann, ed., *Future of Foundations*, p. 130. However, in the same volume, another author gives credit to the Peterson Commission's advocacy of the payout requirement in securing Congressional acceptance of this as "a viable alternative" to limiting the life of foundations, Parrish, "The Foundation: A Special American Institution," in *The Future of Foundations*, p. 38.

49. This letter has already been quoted in the text above. In this Letter to John D. Rockefeller III from Douglas Dillon, January 6, 1970 (RAC, RFA, 3, Box 368, Folder: Phil. Com. on Foundations and Private Philanthropy). Dillon states:

> Now that the tax bill is law I must tell you how much the charitable world and the entire nation is in your debt. If you had not conceived the idea of the commission to study the role and operation of foundations, pushed it through to fruition and obtained Peter Peterson to head it up, I don't know where we would be today.
>
> As to foundations, while his success may not have been total, I am sure that the results would have been far, far worse if it had not been for his efforts.

John D. Rockefeller 3rd also wrote to Peter G. Peterson on December 7, 1970, stating with more enthusiasm than politeness required: "What an outstanding job I think you did as head of the Commission. The report is a major contribution. All of us related to philanthropy are much in your debt" (RAC, RFA, JDR 3rd Conf., Box 14, Folder: Com. on PP).

50. For discussion of influencing policy discourse and networking by elite and powerful individuals, see chapter 1.

51. An account of Peterson's appointment as Assistant to the President for International Economic Affairs can be found in Schwartz, *Modern American Philanthropy*, pp. 78–79. Labovitz apparently worked on the Rockefeller staff for only a few months at least partially because Rockefeller for a while lost his primary focus on the book (on philanthropy) for which Labovitz was hired. JDR returned to it later and it became *The Second American Revolution* (1973).

52. Although Patman originally suggested this might include some Rockefeller foundations, they were not cited in 1969. However Kellogg and Pew were among those specifically cited. See Labovitz, "1969 Tax Reforms Reconsidered," p. 104, and Patman's larger list in "Statement of Hon. Wright Patman, a Representative of Congress from the State of Texas and Chairman of Subcommittee on Foundations, House Select Committee on Small Business"; accompanied by H. A. Olsher, Staff Director, in *Tax Reform, 1969*, Hearings before the Com-

mittee on Ways and Means, House of Representatives, 91st Cong., 1st Sess., Part 1, February 18, 1969 (Washington, D.C.: GPO, 1969), pp. 19–20. It is also worth noting that in his testimony (on page 21) Patman specifically raises the specter of possible violations of statutes related to the Federal Trade Commission, the Securities Exchange Commission or "the Antitrust Division" which might potentially have affected the Rockefellers' multiple interests.

53. On the high payout requirement there was dissent even within the commission itself. See "Dissenting View by Commission Member J. Paul Austin, Chairman, the Coca-Cola Company, Commission Report, pp. 158–159." Labovitz also notes Kellogg and Pew's efforts to have the payout lowered in "1969 Tax Reforms Reconsidered," p. 105. Parrish also states that "the payout recommendation was opposed by some foundation spokesmen" in "The Foundation: A Special American Institution," p. 38. See also Luther Carter, "Foundations and the Tax Bill: Threat to the Private Sector," *Science,* Vol. 166, 5 December 1969, pp. 1245–11248.

54. Letter from Dana Creel, President of the Rockefeller Brothers Fund to Manning Pattillo, January 28, 1970 (RAC, RFA, JDR 3rd Conf. Files, Box 14, Folder: Commission on Private Philanthropy).

55. Schwartz, *Modern American Philanthropy,* p. 77. Schwartz also suggested that there was considerable endorsement of the idea expressed, but there is some question what this means. For example, Merrimon Cuninggim, the respected leader of the Danforth Foundation, stated only that the proposal merited "careful study." See Cuninggim, *Private Money and Public Service,* p. 224.

56. Cuninggim, *Private Money and Public Service,* p. 204.

57. Bittker, "Should Foundations Be Third Class Charities?," pp. 144–146. However it should be remembered that Patman had initiated the Hearings in the House in February 1969 with a much worse recommendation—a 20 percent tax on the gross income of foundations. Statement by Patman before the House Ways and Means Committee, February 18, 1969, in *Tax Reform, 1969,* Part 1, p. 13.

58. For example, according to Alan Pifer all that was needed "for an adequate bill are the payout requirement and the provision against self-dealing." Pifer is quoted in Luther J. Carter, "Foundations and the Tax Bill: Threat to the Private Sector," *Science,* Vol.166, p. 1248.

59. The Peterson Commission's apparent harshness toward foundations and their fiscal abuses was perhaps a response to this as well. In fact, Patman scolded David Freeman, President of the Council on Foundations and a Rockefeller friend, for not responding to the idea of mandatory controls. Eileen Shanahan, "Patman Urges Tax on All Foundations at Inquiry in House," *New York Times,* February 19, 1969, p. 1.

60. Richard E. Friedman, "Private Foundation–Government Relationships" in Heimann, ed., *The Future of Foundations,* p. 174. However, see chapters 5-7 above for discussion of the difficulty of doing this.

61. Despite court decisions and the changes in the Tax Code of 1950, this was still one of the major complaints raised by Patman, and justifies the location of his Subcommittee on Foundations under the jurisdiction of the House Select Committee on Small Business. See quotation from former Internal Revenue Commissioner Mortimer M. Caplin referring to the problem of "unfair competition" for business from tax-exempt organizations, in "Tax Free Groups Studied Again," *U.S. News and World Report,* 66 March 19, 1969, pp. 100–101.

62. This was of course a major issue in the Hearings of the House Committee on Ways and Means on Tax Reform in 1969.

63. Alan Pifer appeared to waver on the publicness of an "Organization for the Foundation Field," and at times appeared to be on the same side as Pattillo and others of the foundation field who wanted to establish some sort of nonprofit membership oversight group. See for example Pifer's letter to Peterson (May 22, 1970) about "the new committee that has been created by the Council [Foundations] and the Center [the Foundation Center] to implement the Gardner Report" (IUPUI, Box 1,4).

64. See Letter to George Schultz [*sic*] from Peter G. Peterson, November 2, 1970, in which he proposes both a task force on tax policies and incentives to charitable giving, and the Advisory Board on Philanthropic Policy, and refers to discussions with Charley Walker (another member of the Nixon administration) about these ideas. JDR also wrote Shultz a letter about the Advisory Board on Philanthropic Policy in which he mentions their brief talk about "my Population Commission." See letter from John D. Rockefeller 3rd to the Hon. George P. Shulz, July 14, 1970 (IUPUI, Box 1,9). The Commission on Population Growth and the American Future was established by P.L. 91–213 and signed into law on March 16, 1970. Lack of response by Nixon to the idea of an Advisory Board on Philanthropy is also noted in Harr and Johnson, *The Rockefeller Conscience*, p. 402.

8. After the Tax Reform Act

1. Provisions of the Act here (as elsewhere) were complex. On the one hand the maximum deduction permissible for total charitable deductions was increased (effective 1970) from 30 to 50 percent, with more complex delimiting rules applying to contributions made to private foundations, particularly in regard to procedures affecting gifts of property with appreciated value. On the other hand, the unlimited charitable deduction (for the few, like some Rockefellers, who qualified) was to be phased out by the end of 1974, since the maximum allowable charitable deduction for 1975 for the very rich would also be 50 percent. There are numerous explanations of these provisions of the Act in the Rockefeller Family Archives by the family lawyers, including a painstaking explanation by Howard Bolton, who in the early 1970s was apparently the leading tax attorney for the family, from the firm of Milbank, Tweed, Hadley and McCloy. Explanations of the various provisions of the 1969 Tax Act that affected private foundations can be found in "Private Foundations and the 1969 Tax Reform Act," by the Chairman and Staff, Council on Foundations (1975), in *Research Papers* of the Filer Commission (Washington, D.C.: U.S. Department of the Treasury, 1977), Vol. 3, pp. 1557–1662; and in even more detail (and with later updates) in Treusch and Sugarman, *Tax-Exempt Charitable Organizations*.

2. See discussion of this provision in relation to the Peterson Commission above in chapter 7. For a thorough discussion of the implications and practice of this provision of the law, Section 4942 (e), in the first few years after enactment of the Tax Reform Act, see Eugene Steurle, "Pay Out Requirements for Foundations," in Filer Commission, *Research Papers*, Vol. 3, pp. 1663–1677. The minimum annual "payout" (a required minimum distribution) was to consist of all earned income or a percentage of net worth (based on real value of assets) whichever was higher, and was to be adjustable by the Secretary of the Treasury in line with actual money rates and investment yields. The payout rate of 6 percent was to be applied in 1970 for all foundations organized after May 26, 1969; transition rules applied to those established before that date. Treasury did apparently respond to the importuning of the foundations and there was no required payout rate for the already-established foundations in 1970 and 1971. Thereafter their payout rate was to go to 4.125 percent in 1972; 4.375 percent in 1973; 5.5 percent in 1974; and finally was to "catch up" with new foundations in 1975. Steurle presents a useful chart of these figures (p. 1664); however, the reader is cautioned that he reverses the headings of the columns. In any case, it is evident that there was manipulation of dates throughout the Act, related to the requirements of specific people and after negotiations.

3. Final regulations on program-related provisions concerning lobbying and political matters were not issued until late 1972. For a discussion of the issues involved in these provisions, from a former government official who later became an attorney for the Council on Foundations, see Thomas A. Troyer, "Charities, Law-Making, and the Constitution: The Validity of Restrictions on Influencing Legislation" in *Thirty-first Annual Institute on Federal Taxation,* Reprint from the Proceedings of the New York University Thirty-first Annual Institute on Fed-

eral Taxation (New York: Matthew Bender & Co., 1973), pp. 1415–1469. There was extensive discussion of these provisions also in Hearings before the House Committee on Ways and Means on H.R. 13720, 92nd Cong., 1st Sess. (1972).

4. For the significance of this status after 1969 see Treusch and Sugarman, *Tax-Exempt Charitable Organizations,* pp. 237–241.

5. "Tax Gremlins Hit the Ford Grants," *Business Week,* January 24, 1970, p. 40. The article notes that the Ford Foundation "is deferring payments while it examines its grant making and reporting procedures. The Foundation wants to make sure its money is being given and spent for legally tax-exempt purposes." Howard Dressner, Ford Foundation Secretary, is also quoted as suggesting that the law might give a much "more conservative cast" to philanthropic efforts. But it should be noted that the COF "collection" in the RAC contains folders (1970) specifically related to "Grants to Individuals" given by foundations, and these were numerous, including a list by the Danforth Foundation.

6. The author happened to be visiting a curator at the Frick in this period, who explained then that the museum might be doing this (at a time when the author in fact did not understand its full significance). The Frick actually did later request contributions and was also apparently able to qualify, in part, as a private operating foundation under the law. The museum now charges admission, perhaps also for economic reasons.

7. Council on Foundations, "Private Foundations and the 1969 Tax Reform Act" in *Research Papers,* p. 1575.

8. There are many sources for this. See for example the entry in JDR's diary for May 11, 1970, in which JDR comments on the issue of "the RBF investments being handled by the office"; JDR notes in the entry that he had brought this issue up at the last RBF Board meeting (RAC, JDR Diaries, 1970, p. 58). David Rockefeller suggested in an interview with the author that he, and possibly several other family members, thought that his brother was perhaps too cautious on these matters in the aftermath of the 1969 tax act (personal interview with David Rockefeller, June 18, 1997). However the RBF did move out of the Rockefeller family offices in Room 5600 and other efforts were begun to differentiate the various family affairs more precisely.

9. The new definitions and provisions relating to private (non-operating) foundations were contained primarily in Sections 101 and 201 of P.L. 91–1472 (the Tax Reform Act of 1969). A good brief explanation of these provisions with their new numbers under the IRC (e.g., Code Section 4940, 4941 and 4942) is found in Ernest D. Fiore and Paul E. Klein, *The Tax Reform Act of 1969* (Albany, New York: Matthew Bender, 1970). In the need for interpretation, a flood of documents was prepared by the tax experts, and disseminated by groups such as the Council on Foundations. However testimony and communications presented at the Hearings of the Subcommittee on Foundations, Finance Committee of the U.S. Senate, *Private Foundations,* 93rd Cong., 2nd Sess., May 13, 14 and June 3, 1974, suggest this was still an issue at that time. See for example the several letters to Hon. Vance Hartke, Chairman, Subcommittee on Foundations, relating to the Winterthur Museum in Wilmington, Delaware, pp. 104–107, as well as letters from the Isabella Stewart Gardner Museum (Boston, Mass.) and the Frick Collection (New York) on pp. 107–108, of the Hearings.

10. See chapter 8 above. Since the commission had not registered as a 501(c)(3) organization, and since Peterson himself was a businessman, there could not really be questions raised about any lobbying activities by Peterson personally or the commission.

11. Memorandum from Datus C. Smith, Jr. to John D. Rockefeller 3rd, March 3, 1970, on the subject of "Follow-up on Philanthropy."

Smith says: "It is my recommendation (consistent with advice from Howard Bolton and Leonard Silverstein) that we not make any moves at all, pending issuance of Treasury Regulations. Quite a number of the problems—even the relatively high-policy ones that you would discuss with the President—may look quite differently, according to what the regulations say." Smith also suggests that "[i]t is also possible that your talk may be more useful after the Peterson Report is public" (RAC, RFA, RG5 JDR 3rd Papers, Series 3, Box: Philanthropy and Public Interests, Folder: Committee on Foundation Field). Smith was the staff person in charge of the JDR Fund and at this point a chief advisor to JDR on philanthropic matters; he was also reportedly extremely protective of JDR's persona.

12. In his diary entry of May 11, 1970 Rockefeller indicates that he had decided not to stand for reelection and had held his last Board meeting as Chairman of the Board of Directors of Rockefeller Center (May 11, 1970, JDR 3rd Diaries). In the next year he resigned from the Chairmanship of the Rockefeller Foundation. In the "Profile of John D. Rockefeller" by Geoffrey T. Hellman in *The New Yorker* (November 4, 1972, p. 52), Hellman suggests that he stepped down from leadership of both boards at 65, but there was about a year between the two resignations, and JDR was known to be punctilious about interpreting the new federal law. With regard to JDR's interest in youth, it should be noted that the voting age had just been lowered to 18; this change would go into effect by June 1971.

13. See Malcolm L. Stein, Office of Tax Legislative Council, U.S. Treasury Department, April 17, 1970, "How the New Law Will Affect Foundation Operations: A View from within the U.S. Treasury Department" ("Copy"—apparently of a speech to a meeting of the Council on Foundations, and distributed by the Council). In this speech Stein discusses issues involved in what he emphatically describes as the "transition" year.

14. In line with established practice, regulations are generally listed in the *Federal Register* for public comment. However, there were several occasions during this period when, under heavy pressure from the foundations, Treasury issued temporary guidance for the foundations. I want to thank Professor Daniel Halperin, a Treasury official in this period, for pointing this out. For an example of foundation discussion of two proposed regulations in this period, see Council on Foundations, Memorandum to Members, 71–5, March 29, 1971, "Subjects: 1) Proposed Regulations on 4% Excise Tax on Investment Income (Sect.4940) and 2) Proposed Regulations on Taxable Expenditures (Sect. 4945)" (COF, Filer Commission, Box 1, Folder: C/F Memorandum to Members 4945). The proposed regulations were published in the *Federal Register* March 20, 1971, for comment by April 19, 1971; meanwhile, though not final, they were to serve as guidelines for the tax year 1970.

15. The speech by Malcolm Stein cited above (note 13) is only one example; there are numerous explanatory documents in the Rockefeller Archives, in both the JDR 3rd Collection and the Council on Foundations, for this period. See also the papers of the Arden House Conference of November 13, 1972, in Heimann, ed. *Future of Foundations*. These papers were reportedly published with money left over from the Peterson Commission.

16. John Walsh, "Foundations: Taking Stock after the Tax Reform Bill," *Science,* 167 (March 20, 1970), p. 1598. It is conceivable that there was at least as much bravado as reality in such statements. Certainly by the time of the hearings on tax reform in 1973, when the effects of the changes of the Tax Reform Act were more evident (e.g., the high payout rate for all foundations), the economy was different, and the foundations were protesting many of the key provisions of the Act.

17. Council on Foundations, "Private Foundations . . . ," in Filer Commission, *Research Papers,* 1975, pp. 1265–1568. These figures come from a study for the American Bar Association by John R. Labovitz, "The Impact of the Private Foundation Provisions of the Tax Reform Act of 1969: Early Empirical Measurements," *Journal of Legal Studies,* Vol. 111 (1) (January 1974), pp. 63–107.

18. Quotation from "Nixon's Statement on Signing Tax Bill," *New York Times,* December 31, 1969, cited in Cuninggim, *Private Money and Public Service,* p. 212. Merrimon in fact suggests that the concerns of the foundations might have been somewhat excessive.

19. Letter of January 28, 1970 from Dana Creel to Manning Pattillo, cited in chapter 7, n. 54.

20. The existence of the new committee was reported to JDR by Datus Smith, in a memo about the "New Philanthropy Committee," February 19, 1970, in which he states, "I believe

the impetus came largely from Dana Creel and Alan Pifer, and I think reflected some disillusionment with both Manning Pattillo's and David Freeman's organizations" (RAC, RFA, RG5 JDR 3rd., Series 3 Home and Office Philanthropy and Public Interest, Folder: Committee on the Foundation Field). Affiliations of the members were listed as follows: Cuninggim, Danforth Foundation; Heckman, Hill Family Foundation; Norton, Cleveland Foundation; and Don Price, Harvard University. But of course they also had connections to the COF, the Foundation Center, and NCOP.

21. In his memo of February 19, 1970 to JDR (cited in note 20 above) Datus Smith suggests that "On their specific request I have refrained from telling Peterson about this committee, as they want first word of it to go to Pete from John Gardner."

22. *Report of the Committee on the Foundation Field,* April 15, 1970, John W. Gardner, Chairman, Merrimon Cuninggim, Vice Chairman. Unpublished paper, marked in pen: Confidential (RFA, RGA 5 JDR 3rd papers, Series 3 Philanthropy and the Public Interest, Folder: Committee on the Foundation Field, 1969–1970).

23. See Brilliant, *The United Way.*

24. The influence of the 501(c)(3) group is argued in Schwartz, *Modern American Philanthropy,* pp. 59–73.

25. This was certainly true of JDR who was an initiator and major supporter of the Asia Society, as well as an active alumni of Princeton; his wife and various other members of the Rockefeller family, including Nelson, were deeply involved in the Museum of Modern Art. Other examples of mixed interests are also noted in Harr and Johnson, *The Rockefeller Conscience.*

26. Peterson came from Chicago, and prior to becoming Chairman of the Peterson Commission had little contact with New Yorkers or eastern elite groups. Note also that there were few staff or commission members who could be described as connected to the eastern establishment.

27. Letter from Alan Pifer to Peter Peterson, May 22, 1970 (IUPUI, Box 1,4). Although in the letter Pifer refers to the chapter "on Organization for the Foundation Field" he is clearly referring to the chapter that deals with the Advisory Board on Philanthropic Policy. In any case, for whatever reason, the letter glosses over differences in the conceptualization of the proposed organizations.

28. Jack Schwartz, in an interview with the author (New York City, October 16, 1992), suggested that John Gardner would not have wanted a quasi-public organization, as did Gardner himself in a telephone interview (August 25, 1995). Subsequent events bear this out. Moreover, in the book he wrote about two years after the events described, *Private Money and Public Service,* Cuninggim, who was a member of the Gardner Committee, was still saying only that the Peterson idea for an Advisory Board on Philanthropic Policy was worthy of consideration.

29. Possibly this was another reason for delaying publication of the report.

30. A brief history of the founding of the Coalition for Public Good, as it came to be called, is given in Schwartz, *Modern American Philanthropy,* pp. 90–93. Schwartz was a participant in the events and he reports that the Coalition grew out of the efforts of a "Program for Philanthropy" initiated by his organization (the American Association for Fund-Raising Counsel) and its President, J. O. Newberry. However, when the Coalition was established more formally in late 1971, it was chaired by Bayard Ewing, who had just completed a term as President of United Way of America, and it was staffed by John S. Glaser, a Vice President of the national United Way.

31. Thomas C. Reeves, "Introduction" in *Foundations under Fire,* Thomas C. Reeves, ed. (Ithaca: Cornell University Press, 1970), p. 35. Of course, "excessive" assets were precisely the problem to be addressed by the high payout requirements of the Tax Reform Act.

32. M. A. Farber, "Foundations Find Tax Act Acceptable," *New York Times,* January 10, 1970, p. 69.

33. Parrish, "The Foundation: A Special American Institution," in *The Future of Foundations*, p. 38. Parrish was also a staff member of the Peterson Commission.

34. Cuninggim's opinions were undoubtedly expressed several months apart; however, in addition to reflecting some rhetorical content, they are given in different contexts. For the more dour view that "the era of good feeling seems to be over," see Cuninggim, *Private Money and Public Service*, p. 1.

35. Labovitz, "1969 Tax Reforms Reconsidered" in *The Future of Foundations*, p. 144. Labovitz suggested also that the tax on investment income (4 percent) was particularly atrocious.

36. John Simon, Statement before the Senate Subcommittee on Foundations, Committee on Finance, U.S. Senate, 93rd Cong., 1st Sess., October 1 and 2, 1973, Hearings on *Private Foundations*.

37. M. A. Farber, "Foundations Find '69 Tax Reform Not as Harmful as Feared," *New York Times*, May 9, 1972, p. 32.

38. Testimony of John Simon before the Subcommittee on Finances of the Senate Finance Committee, October 1973. Cited in the COF Study, "Private Foundations and the Tax Reform Act," in the Filer Commission, *Research Papers*, p. 1575.

39. John R. Labovitz, "The Impact of Private Foundation Provisions of the Tax Reform Act of 1969: Early Empirical Measurement," *Journal of Legal Studies*, Vol. 3 (1) (January 1974), pp. 61–106.

40. Ralph L. Nelson, "Private Giving in the American Economy, 1960–1972," in Filer Commission, *Research Papers* (Washington, D.C.: U.S. Department of the Treasury, 1975), p. 121.

41. "Remarks of the Honorable Edwin S. Cohen, Under Secretary of the Treasury," at Arden House, November 13, 1972 (RAC, COF, Filer Commission, Box 1, Folder: "Tax Effects: General").

42. Farber, "Foundations Find '69 Tax Reform Act Not as Harmful as Feared," *New York Times*, May 9, 1972, p. 32. Source for the data was given as the American Association of Fund-Raising Counsel (AAFRC).

43. See Council on Foundations, "Private Foundations and the 1969 Tax Reform Act," and Norman Sugarman, "Community Foundations" in Filer Commission, *Research Papers*, pp. 1557–1678, and pp. 1689–1722; also, Labovitz, "The Impact of Private Foundation Provisions of the Tax Reform Act," *Journal of Legal Studies*, January 1974, pp. 78–80. Labovitz also discusses other aspects of the Act which will be considered below in connection with the Filer Commission's work.

44. Cited in Parrish, "The Foundation: A Special American Institution," in *The Future of Foundations*, p. 38. In interviews with foundation officials for his study of "The Impact of Private Foundation Provisions of the Tax Reform Act of 1969," Labovitz found substantially the same reaction to many regulations (*Journal of Legal Studies*, pp. 76–77). However, in the same article, Labovitz also describes the deleterious effect and "anguish" caused foundation officials by uncertainty about interpretations of regulations.

45. Heimann stated also that "Congress does not need to be shielded from foundation-financed lobbying. Every other interest group is busy lobbying." As an attorney for General Electric, he was certainly well aware of the extent to which businesses lobbied Washington. See Heimann, "Foundations and Government: Perspectives for the Future," in Heimann, ed., *The Future of Foundations*, p. 166.

46. Press Release, Internal Revenue Service, Washington D.C., October 9, 1970, attached to Memorandum to Members [of the Council on Foundations] from David F. Freeman, "Treasury Temporarily Suspends Exemption Rulings of' Public Interest Law Firms and Other Similar Organizations," October 16, 1970 (RAC, COF, Filer Commission, Box 5, Folder: Political Activity). See also the account in Holbert, *Tax Law and Political Access*, pp. 44–49.

47. One example is cited in F. Emerson Andrews, in "Philanthropy in the United States:

History and Structure," in John J. Corson and Harry V. Hodson, eds., *Philanthropy in the 70s: An Anglo-American Discussion: A Report on the Anglo-America Conference on the Role of Philanthropy in the 1970s,* Ditchley Park, England, April 28 to May 1, 1972 (New York: Council on Foundations, 1973). Andrews reported that "Early in December 1971, a group of Episcopal Clergyman and Lawyers issued a report expressing the view that the Nixon administration, through the Internal Revenue Service, has adopted a policy of 'intimidation' of groups, including churches, that disagree with its policies on such issues as the Vietnam War and Civil Rights." In fact, in 1969 the IRS had already refused to grant the National Resources Council and the Project on Corporate Responsibility charitable status "on the grounds that their activities were not charitable." This was also reputedly part of the administration's desire to curb the formation of more critical advocacy groups according to J. C. Jenkins, "Nonprofit Organizations and Policy Advocacy," in Powell, ed., *The Nonprofit Sector,* p. 302, cited in Wolch, *The Shadow State,* p. 65.

48. Cuninggim, *Private Money and Public Service,* p. 97.

49. RAC, COF, Filer Commission, Box 5, Folder: Lobbying Re 1969 Tax Act.

50. This is evident in the COF/Filer Commission files for this period. These files in the Rockefeller Archive Center reveal a constant flow of communications between attorneys in Washington, the COF, and their members concerning these issues (see RAC, COF, Filer Commission, Box 5).

51. Nixon named Max C. Fisher (from Detroit, and formerly connected with the Department of Housing and Urban Development) to be chair of the Center; but this organization was certainly not intended to fill the role suggested for a new advisory Board/Commission on Philanthropy.

52. For a more in-depth discussion of the nature of the criticism against the role of advisory groups in our government, see Appendix A. However, the release of this report helps to explain why Peterson might have gone into a meeting with officials in the administration that month expecting to discuss an advisory group on philanthropy, and come out with a different kind of job offer.

53. William J. Baumol, "Enlightened Self-interest and Corporate Philanthropy," Peterson Commission Report, pp. 262–277.

54. See Memorandum from Datus C. Smith, Jr. to Mr. John D. Rockefeller 3rd, August 20, 1970, in which Smith writes: "In pursuit of Burke Marshall's idea of stimulating creation of a "Corporate Commission" in somewhat the same way in which you brought the Peterson Commission into being, I have been urging Dick Dilworth to suggest a name for your consideration. . . . " He mentions the name Ernest C. Arbuckle, board chairman of Wells Fargo Bank International Corporation. However, Datus Smith and JDR also met for lunch with John Gardner on March 12 to discuss the new Committee on the Foundation Field. JDR reported that "We agreed that it should be high level and not just confined to professional people, but . . . have representatives both on the donor and the recipient side . . . there might well be a lower level professional group in addition." JDR also added that "Gardner is such a fine person that it is a pleasure to do business with him." I am inclined to agree with Peter Hall that the Rockefeller relationship with Gardner was more cordial in appearance than in reality. See Peter Dobkin Hall, *Inventing the Nonprofit Sector and Other Essays on Philanthropy, Voluntarism, and Nonprofit Organizations* (Baltimore, Md.: Johns Hopkins University Press, 1992), p. 78.

55. This point was made frequently in discussions of that period. See for example John Simon, "Foundations and Public Controversy: An Affirmative View," in American Assembly, *The Future of Foundations,* p. 73. See also Thomas A. Troyer, "Charities, Law Making and the Constitution" in New York University, *Proceedings,* pp. 1415–1469.

56. Several respondents reported this. Perhaps an example of this is suggested in the words of JDR himself. He reports that in the late afternoon of February 5, "Messrs Smith, Barrett and I went to see Mr. Emilio Collado (Executive Vice President of Standard Oil of New Jersey).

. . . Had a good but not too conclusive talk with him concerning the corporate responsibility in relation to social problems." JDR 3rd Diaries 1970, pp. 13–14. The lack of business support for the Peterson Commission is more demonstrable. In a letter to Datus Smith, October 21, 1970, "Dutch" Smith lists the total contributions ($91,900) and the total number of contributors (67). However he also notes that they had 101 "regrets" (turndowns); of these only 4 were from individuals, and 10 were from banks; the rest—87—were from corporations. Attachment to letter from Herman D. Smith to Datus Smith, October 21, 1969 (RAC, RFA, RG5, JDR 3rd, Series 3, Office and Home Papers, Folder: Commission on Foundations 1970–71).

57. This too was complicated. David Rockefeller was certainly interested in philanthropy; he served as chair of the RBF during this period and met with Wilbur Mills and other Congressional leaders without John. See for example Letter to Wilbur Mills from David Rockefeller, July 25, 1969 (RAC, RFA, RG3, Box 368, Folder: Phil. Committee on Foundations and Private Philanthropy). However David (as Chairman of Chase Manhattan) had other matters to attend to. In any case, it was John's role to take on the leadership in philanthropic matters publicly, and his staff was supposed to insure this.

58. Entry of Tuesday, April 28, 1970 in JDR 3rd Diaries, 1970, p. 39. The presence of Leonard Silverstein is particularly significant in light of his position later as staff director of the Filer Commission. See below, chapter 9.

59. Woodworth did note that Congress was discussing "whether or not some restriction on charitable giving should be incorporated into the law affecting estates." This would obviously be a subject of some importance to the Rockefellers and other donors with large estates, as well as to the charitable "field." The JDR diaries do not mention another event of some importance to the foundations, which was Patman's "mortgage money bill" that would have made the foundations become the mandated financial backer of high risk (low income, inner city) mortgages. But in a letter to Peterson of May 22, 1970, Alan Pifer noted, "We got to work promptly after your call and as you probably know, it was defeated yesterday in the Banking and Currency Committee (IUPUI, Box 1,4).

60. JDR 3rd Diary, April 30, 1970. While in Washington, JDR also stopped by to see others, including Senator Robert C. Byrd of West Virginia, about his new population commission.

61. Memorandum to the Foundation Lawyer's Group, From the Drafting Committee, June 17, 1971, discussing materials relating to proposed regulations under Section 507, 4940, and 4976, in preparation for a meeting "to be held at the office of Silverstein and Mullens, June 22, 1971" (COF, Filer Commission, Box 4, J4940–FLG).

62. In his diary entry for Tuesday October 26,1971 (RAC, RFA, JDR 3rd Diaries, Box 3, 1971, p. 111), JDR records that he had breakfast at the Metropolitan Club with Woodworth, and adds: "*Had asked to see him to talk further about the general status of philanthropy in the Washington picture. He indicated that the situation was calm* but with *two* or three changes brewing—one *being cutting the pay-out requirement from 6% to 5%* and spreading it over a longer period. *Another was making it possible for non-profit agencies to appear before Government bodies* on behalf of Legislative change. Toward the end of our talk, Mr. Woodworth suggested the possibility of bringing together a small group from the foundation field to meet informally, say twice a year, with him and some of his key people, and possibly a similar group from the Treasury, with the purpose of discussing problems and ideas relating to philanthropy. . . . Told him that I was appreciative of his suggestions and like the idea" (emphasis in original).

63. JDR Diary, October 3, 1971 (emphasis in original). It may be only coincidence but the use of the term "private initiative" does echo the title of the group being formed in Washington with United Way leadership around the same time—the "Coalition for Public Good Through Private Initiatives." See note 30 above. The term was also used in a document of the earlier Committee of the Foundation Center, NCOP, and COF, "A Program of Self-Policing by Philanthropic Foundations," August 25, 1969.

64. Patman's report on the 15 largest foundations had been in the works for more than a year, and had received newspaper attention already that spring, but it was noted as "in production" in "Tax-Exempt Organizations," *Congressional Quarterly,* June 1, 1971, p. 1256.

65. Nixon of course ran again for President and won; during the early stages of the campaign, Mills appeared to be a possible Democratic candidate, but subsequently he withdrew his candidacy. Accordingly, variations on the themes of tax reform were indicated in newspapers during this period. See for example Eileen Shanahan, "Mills Cites Drop in Tax Avoidance But Agrees to Prod Nixon for New Reform Plans," *New York Times,* February 8, 1972; Shanahan, "An Administration Slide Show Attacks the Idea of Tax Reform," *New York Times,* April 24, 1972; and Shanahan, "Nixon and Mills Expected to Delay on Tax Reform, *New York Times,* November 30, 1972.

66. Shanahan, "Nixon and Mills Expected to Delay on Tax Reform, *New York Times,* November 30, 1972, p. 1.

67. "Mills Sees House Passing 'Major' Tax Bill in '73, but Extra Revenue Should Be Small," *Wall Street Journal,* December 6, 1972.

68. In a letter to Wilbur Mills, November 1, 1972, JDR suggested the possibility of establishing a "small study group of individuals to study the incentive question in regard to philanthropy and to . . . report to you. . . . " Mills responded quickly and positively on November 8, 1972, in a letter stating that if JDR would organize such a committee "he would look forward "to studying the report of such a group." He also suggested that "the group could work with Laurence Woodworth if it wants to have some . . . contact with the Committee . . . " (RAC, RFA, JDR 3rd, Box 14, Folder: Commission on Philanthropy). It should also be recalled that establishing a "Committee on Tax Incentives" was recommended in the Peterson Report. In his diary entry of January 9, 1973, JDR noted discussion of a committee on "the question of tax incentives" (to philanthropy) which he had with Peter Peterson, who suggested he see William Simon, the new Deputy Secretary of the Treasury.

69. "Mills Suggests Eliminating Some Tax Preferences," *Wall Street Journal,* February 6, 1973.

70. The point about the erosion of the concept of tax exemption was a serious one. However, the amount of money paid in taxes might be considered an expenditure and therefore included as part of the payout amount, so that it would not necessarily be an additional loss to the foundation.

71. Brilliant, "Looking Backward to Look Forward."

9. The Filer Commission in Action

1. Interview with John Filer, in Hartford, Connecticut, October 13, 1992.

2. JDR diary entries reveal that Filer was not the first person approached for the position. At the time when the commission had been first discussed, and it was referred to as the Committee to Study Tax Incentives, JDR and his advisors (Howard Bolton, Leonard Silverstein, and Datus Smith) met with businessman William Matson Roth (March 12, 1973) and Roth agreed to undertake the chairmanship if other responsibilities did not intervene. (Although he did not serve as chairman, Roth did serve as a commission member.) Even before Roth, the former Governor of Pennsylvania, William Scranton, had apparently been considered for the Chairman's position (RAC, JDR 3rd Diaries, February 12, 1973 and March 12, 1973). It was Porter McKeever who had spoken with Bayless Manning about Filer. Despite years at Stanford Law School in California, Manning was part of the "eastern establishment," and he was a member of the Aetna Board of Directors. Manning indicated that the only reservation he could think of was that Filer had been in his present job "barely a year and might be reluctant to take on an outside assignment of major dimensions." He was uncertain about Filer's political affiliation but thought he might be Republican (this casualness is a little hard to take at face value given the political climate the commission was to operate in). Memorandum from Porter

McKeever to Howard A. Bolton and Leonard Silverstein, Subject: John H. Filer, July 16, 1973 (RAC, RF, JDR 3rd Conf., Box 14, Folder: Commission on Philanthropy).

3. At this time there was probably a closer connection between such institutions and their communities. But even twenty years later, when I was in his office in Hartford, John Filer looked out the window and commented sadly about the condition of the area around him (interview with John Filer, October 13, 1992).

4. Memorandum from Porter McKeever to Howard A. Bolton and Leonard Silverstein, Subject: John H. Filer, July 16, 1973 (RAC, RF, JDR 3rd Conf., Box 14, Folder: Commission on Philanthropy).

5. Knauft called himself "Burt" and that is how I will generally refer to him.

6. Holbert, *Tax Law and Political Access*, pp. 52–61.

7. From *Press Release* (September 25, 1973) included in *Private Foundations*, Hearings before the Subcommittee on Foundations of the Committee on Finance, U.S. Senate, 93rd Cong., 1st Sess. October 1–2, 1973, p. 3.

8. In 1974 the 6 percent payout rate would be mandated for all foundations. For an example of concern about Congressional proposals on limiting charitable deductibility, see ACPRA "TAX INFORMATION SERIES," January 20, 1973, which refers to discussions in the Ways and Means Committee, and particularly a bill, H.R. 1040, introduced by Representative James Corman (Democrat, California). See also discussion in chapter 9 above.

9. See for example the discussion between Robert Freeman (Council on Foundations) and the Chairman, Senator Vance Hartke, in *Private Foundations*, Hearings before the Subcommittee of the U.S. Senate Committee on Finance, October 1 and 2, 1973, p. 99–100. It is worth noting that Vance Hartke was from Indiana, a state where the influence of the Lilly Endowment was certainly significant.

10. *Private Foundations*, Hearings before the Subcommittee of the U.S. Senate, October 1 and 2, 1973. At these hearings foundation leaders could of course appear on their own behalf, and were invited to do so. The illustrious group that took part in the panels included Merrimon Cuninggim and Howard Dressner (representing the Ford Foundation), Landrum Bolling (Lilly Endowment), David Freeman and Robert Goheen (Council on Foundations), Russell Mawby (Kellogg Foundation), and John Simon (Taconic Foundation). Alan Pifer (Carnegie Corporation) also appeared. It should be noted also that during these hearings many of the panelists (including Marion Fremont-Smith, Alan Pifer, and Sheldon Cohen) spoke directly to the issue of creating a national charity commission in the English mode.

11. See chapter 8 above.

12. Reviews of the transcripts and minutes of meetings suggest that all three were above-average in participation. Judge Newman was cited by several respondents as having played a key role in the deliberations, and even in the writing of the commission report.

13. Fisher had already been given a position in the Nixon administration. Fisher was a big contributor to the Republican party and he would also later argue strongly for the conservative point of view on the commission. Leonard Silverstein said that it was the President's idea to put Fisher on the commission. Interview with Silverstein, December 8, 1992, Washington D.C.

14. In my interview with John Filer (Hartford, October 13, 1993), Filer said that a friend had offered him advice about chairing a commission, and that the friend started with "the Commission should not attempt to be representative." Filer suggested that he had been given that advice too late.

15. A list of commission members is given in Appendix E.

16. A list of commission members, dated September 9, 1974, names 31 members, counting John Filer, and including all the "final" women on the commission (but not Marian Whitman). Thus there had been some additional dropouts before the final report (IUPUI, Box 28,4).

17. The point about the lack of women's involvement was later made explicitly by commissioners Frances T. Farenthold, Graciela Olivarez, and Althea T. L. Simmons. See *Giving in*

America, p. 197. A perusal of the list of consultants and advisory committee members also indicates that there were few individuals of color on the commission. See Appendix F.

18. Porter McKeever was now assuming the responsibilities for primary staff support to JDR on philanthropic matters. This was the position formerly filled by Datus Smith, who was retiring.

19. The minutes of the meeting indicate that "invited guests and staff of the commission were also present" but there is no indication of who else beside Silverstein was in this category. However, the following commission members were listed as attendees: John Filer, Bayard Ewing, Max Fisher, Earl Graves, Paul Haas, Philip Klutznick, Ralph Lazarus, Elizabeth McCormack, Walter McNerney, John Musser, Jon Newman, and David Truman. CPPPN, Minutes of the Meeting of October 3, 1973 (IUPUI, Box 29,3).

20. CPPPN, "Minutes of the First Meeting," October 31, 1973, p. 2 (IUPUI, Box 28,5).

21. By not covering the entire tax-exempt universe the commission would be able to focus on philanthropic and tax areas related to charitable giving. And at the same time the commission could presumably avoid involvement in sensitive and controversial issues being raised in Congress and elsewhere concerning the tax-exemption of trade associations—501(c)(6)—and other categories of overtly political 501(c) organizations. In fact on August 1, 1973 the IRS had already indicated "that it planned to tax political parties and fund raising committees for income derived from stocks given as political contributions." See Sobel, ed., *The Great American Tax Revolt,* p. 33.

22. The Minutes state that in addressing the commission, Simon "affirmed the high degree of Treasury's interest in the commission's efforts and the Treasury's willingness to make its facilities (to the extent consistent with budget and disclosure problems) fully available to the commission and its staff," CPPPN, Minutes of the Meeting of October 31, 1973, p. 9 (IUPUI, Box 29,3).

23. Although Treasury was considered a supporter of the commission, that was not necessarily true for the IRS. As had been the case in the 1960s, and as subsequent events were to demonstrate now, even though it was part of the Treasury Department, the IRS frequently seemed to act as though it were independent of Treasury. Moreover, in Filer Commission meetings later, there were problems indicated about IRS cooperation with their study, as well as more general criticism of IRS oversight role of the field of philanthropy. The Michigan Survey, also referred to as the Morgan study because of its director, became the paper "Results from Two National Surveys of Philanthropic Activity," by James N. Morgan, Richard F. Dye, and Judith H. Hybels, and was published in the *Research Papers* of the Filer Commission, Vol. 1, pp. 157–324.

24. This is laid out in a Memorandum from Conrad Teitel, attorney, to the 501(c)(3) group on "Tax Reform," February 6, 1973, in which he discusses the first day of tax reform hearings (panel discussions) in the House Ways and Means Committee. He suggests that because the idea was put forth by Mills (and in an unrelated context) it was significant. Teitel notes, "Under current law there are unlimited estate and gift tax charitable deductions. If a limit is placed on the gift tax charitable contribution deduction, a donor could actually have to pay a gift tax on a lifetime charitable gift. And if a limit is placed on the estate tax charitable deduction, charitable bequests would often be substantially decreased because the bequest would be diminished by estate taxes." (RAC, COF, Filer Commission, Box 1, Folder: Tax Effects/Tax Reform [Hearings], 1973.)

25. David Rockefeller was reported as being "interested to learn about" Martin Feldstein's study and he gave $5,000 toward its cost (Memorandum from Richard E. Salomon to David F. Freeman, President of the Council on Foundations, Inc., December 27, 1973 (RAC, RFA, RG3, Box 369, Folder: Phil: Phil-COF). Feldstein's studies on this subject turned out to provide evidence of the importance of the tax incentive as an inducement to charity, particularly in the higher income brackets.

26. Minutes of the First Meeting, October 31, 1973. The packet sent to the commission-

ers subsequently probably included a "Summary of the Report and Recommendations of the 'Peterson' Commission on Foundations and Private Philanthropy" since this file document, with the heading "Commission on Private Philanthropy and Public Needs" was dated December, 1973 (IUPUI, Box 29,3).

27. The reference of course is to the words of Robert Burns in the poem *To a Mouse*. Burns said it somewhat differently, using his own poetic vernacular:

The best laid schemes o' mice and men
Gang aft a-gley.

28. Several respondents said they remembered meetings of the research committee at the time of "plenary sessions" of the commission. The files also include an agenda for a meeting in September (no date) at which there would be a heavy (two-day) discussion of research. However, there are minutes of a meeting of the Research Committee, February 18, 1974, which listed as present, Walter McNerney, chairman, Elizabeth McCormack, member, and John Musser, alternate member. Named as "also present" were John Filer, Leonard Silverstein, "and the following staff and invited consultants," Paul Ylvisaker, James Morgan, Howard Bolton, Gabriel Rudney, E. B. Knauft, and Robert E. Falb (IUPUI, Box 29,3). There are also minutes of an Advisory Committee Meeting on January 9, 1975.

29. Evidence for the meeting of September 19–20, 1974 is based on a Memorandum to Commission Members from Leonard L. Silverstein, Subject: Philosophical Discussion, dated September 12, 1974 (IUPUI, Box 41,4. Evidence that there may have been several "plenary" sessions in that period comes from a Memorandum by Leonard Silverstein to Commission Members on October 17, 1974 in which he refers to the "October 10 meeting in Chicago" at which "Chairman Filer announced future Commission meeting dates" (IUPUI, Box 29,3). These dates include November 11 (evening) and November 12 at United Way Headquarters (Alexandria, Virginia). In the memo, Silverstein mentions other meetings for which there are transcribed records: January 13 (evening) and January 14, at O'Hare International Airport (Chicago); and February 6 and 7 in Denver, Colorado. There appear to be no other records of either the October or the November meetings in the Rockefeller Archives or the IUPUI Archives. However, the October meeting had already occurred when the memo was sent, and one respondent did remember attending what he referred to as a terrible meeting at United Way of America in Alexandria which (to him) was dominated by airplane noise. In fact the location of that meeting (in November) would have been very close to National Airport.

30. Mills admitted he had been drinking on October 9, 1974; Fanne Foxe gained notoriety by jumping into the Tidal Basin. The significance of the event for the workings of Congress made it not only highly "gossipy" news, but worthy of reporting widely in more staid publications. It appears, for example, in "Inside Congress," in *Congress and the Nation*, Vol. 4, 1973–1976 (Washington, D.C.: Congressional Quarterly Service, 1977), p. 764.

31. The reorganization plan is discussed in *Congress and the Nation*, Vol. 4, 1973–1976, p. 764. See also Barber Conable (with A. L. Singleton), *Congress and the Income Tax* (Norman: University of Oklahoma Press, 1989), pp. 20–23, and the analysis in Pollack, *The Failure of U.S. Tax Policy*, pp. 164–168. It is not clear whether the Rockefeller group would have preferred a more open process. However, the rule against floor amendments in the House had been a "primary target" of Common Cause and John Gardner. See "Economic Report/Capital gains laws loom as prime targets of new Ways and Means hearings on tax reform," *National Journal*, 12/2/1972, p. 1844.

32. Although the initials for this committee were actually CRP, with the pronunciation used (derogatorily) it was known as CREEP. See for example the discussion in Patterson, *Grand Expectations*, pp. 772–777.

33. According to one authoritative source, Nixon's problems with charitable deductions for his personal papers were at least partly a matter of inattention by the President and his personal attorneys to the significance of the date by which relevant provisions of the Tax Re-

form Act (regarding donations of ordinary income producing property) were to go into effect. If the President had asked to move the cut-off date for donations of such property to December 31, 1969 (from July 25, 1969) like President Johnson, he would have received a full charitable deduction for his gift of personal papers to the Nixon library. See the story as told by Edwin S. Cohen, Assistant Secretary of the Treasury for Tax Policy under President Nixon at the time. Cohen, *A Lawyer's Life,* pp. 367–381.

34. This story is told in some detail in Collier and Horowitz, *The Rockefellers,* pp. 478–479. It almost appears that the two brothers were in competition with their various commissions, but that is of course somewhat speculative. However, most authors who write about the Rockefeller brothers, including John Harr and Peter Johnson, suggest that a serious degree of tension existed between John and Nelson.

35. In *The Rockefeller Conscience* Harr and Johnson suggest that the Congressional hearings could have done far more damage, p. 512. However, Collier and Horowitz take a somewhat bleaker view of the whole process and its outcome for the family, particularly in regard to the hearings in the House; see Collier and Horowitz, *The Rockefellers,* pp. 478–501.

36. Another more local event might have influenced the delay in the spring of 1974. In March 1974 the IRS revoked a 1969 ruling that had enabled ITT to acquire the Hartford Fire Insurance Company, in what was then said to be the largest corporate takeover in history. Given the location and nature of the Hartford Company, tax matters and the IRS could well have been sensitive issues for John Filer.

37. Press Release, Commission on Private Philanthropy and Public Needs, February 27, 1974 (IUPUI, Box 27,8). The new research director was Gabriel Rudney, an economist, who would become a significant part of the Filer Commission activity.

38. See note 3 above. It is also interesting that according to Collier and Horowitz, "As late as February 11, 1974, [Nelson] Rockefeller was still defending Nixon and expecting him to stay in office." See Collier and Horowitz, *The Rockefellers,* p. 480.

39. Hopkins, *Law of Tax-Exempt Organizations,* p. 312. According to *Congress and the Nation,* the inability of Ways and Means to pass tax legislation in these years was a significant sign of weakening of the power of the committee and the chairman; if this was so that might explain why Mills had responded favorably to JDR's suggestion of an advisory committee. See "Inside Congress," *Congress and the Nation,* Vol. 4, 1973–1976.

40. A version of this story is told by one of the participants in his book, Schwartz, *Modern American Philanthropy,* and the importance of the luncheon was also mentioned by several respondents. The success of Philip Klutznick and the American Association of Fund-Raising Counsel (AAFRC) in raising over two million dollars for the commission is mentioned in Harr and Johnson, *The Rockefeller Conscience,* p. 377.

41. Interview with Burt Knauft, November 17, 1991, Washington, D.C.

42. JDR's views were probably mixed: on the one hand he certainly was aware of the importance of tax policy for charitable deductions and the Rockefeller interests; on the other hand he consistently suggested his bigger vision about the role of philanthropy and the voluntary sector in our society. This concept of a double vision emerges in many of my interviews, and is demonstrated in earlier chapters of this book. It was referred to also in my interview with John Filer. According to Knauft and other respondents, Filer held a broad view of the role of philanthropy and the direction for the commission's efforts, and this is substantiated by remarks at a meeting of the Council on Foundations, February 26, 1975, in which Filer stated:

> We set out to launch, as we styled it, "a broad range, in-depth study of philanthropy, its relationship to government, and its role in American Society." In short, we gave ourselves an undoable task. We do believe the work of the Commission will provide a comprehensive view of philanthropy and its contribution to our society.

Despite Filer's remarks and the rhetoric of the *Case Statement,* it does seem as if both Silverstein and Rudney were on the whole dedicated to keeping the commission agenda closer to the narrower, more definable issues of tax policy and philanthropy, rather than entering into an all-encompassing, more free-floating discussion of philanthropy's role in regard to social needs.

43. Titles of excerpted summaries for the indicated dates (IUPUI, Box 41,6).

44. The chairman, however, was not always John Filer; in at least two sessions David Truman or someone else chaired the meeting because Filer had personal matters that kept him away.

45. Pablo Eisenberg, "The Filer Commission: A Critical Perspective," *Grantsmanship Center News,* January/February 1975, p. 45. According to Eisenberg, the story had actually been leaked to a journalist earlier by one of the women on the commission. It should also be noted that Eisenberg was a personal friend of Wade Greene, whom he had known in college. Interview with Pablo Eisenberg, November 11, 1973. At least two respondents suggested that the whole ruckus might initially have been deliberately arranged in order to bring attention to the work of the commission, but this is unproven.

46. It is difficult to get an exact count of the papers from commission files in the IUPUI, but this figure is used by Burt Knauft in his article, "The Filer Commission Revisited," *Foundation News,* January/February 1984, pp. 12–15. See also the *Research Papers of the Commission on Private Philanthropy and Public Needs* (Washington, D.C.: U.S. Department of the Treasury, 1977), referred to as *Research Papers* of the Filer Commission throughout. The *Research Papers* were divided thematically into five volumes, but because of their size they were printed in six bound volumes.

47. According to Gabriel Rudney, Porter McKeever wanted the commission's research "to have a level of excellence that would go unchallenged." There were apparently different views on the matter of editing, but in the end it seems that Rudney made suggestions and helped some individuals to revise their work. Interview with Gabriel Rudney, Washington, D.C., May 17, 1994. There was also a Compendium editor for the research papers, Judith G. Smith, who is listed in *Giving in America.*

48. Recommendations of the Filer Commission are given in Appendix G.

49. Several respondents mentioned this, including Leonard Silverstein. It is also supported by the voluminous pages of printouts of Feldstein's econometric models that are in the IUPUI Archives (Box 31). Furthermore, four of the research papers published by the commission (1977) were either authored or co-authored by Feldstein. All the studies did not show exactly the same effects, but as a group they certainly influenced commission deliberations. See Martin S. Feldstein and Charles Clotfelter, "Tax Incentives and Charitable Contributions in the United States: A Microeconometric Analysis"; Feldstein and Amy Taylor, "The Income Tax and Charitable Contributions: Estimates and Simulations with the Treasury Tax Files"; Michael J. Boskin and Feldstein, "Effects of the Charitable Deduction on Contributions by Low-Income and Middle-Income Households: Evidence from the National Survey of Philanthropy; and Feldstein, "Charitable Bequests, Estate Taxation and Intergenerational Wealth Transfers." In addition there is a paper by Arnold Zellner, "Evaluation of Econometric Research on the Income Tax and Charitable Giving" which assesses some of Feldstein's work on price and income elasticities of individual giving (all of these papers are in Volume 3 of the *Research Papers*).

50. These papers (in Volume 1 of the *Research Papers*) may be considered illustrative of some of the more distinguished papers presenting new material on the scope of the Voluntary Sector: Ralph L. Nelson, "Private Giving in the American Economy, 1960–1972"; Gabriel G. Rudney, "The Scope of the Private Voluntary Charitable Sector"; and Burton A. Weisbrod and Stephen H. Long, "The Size of the Voluntary Nonprofit Sector: Concepts and Measures."

51. Volume 1 included a historical review of the development of voluntary associations, "Private Philanthropy and Public Needs" by historian Robert H. Bremner; there was also an illuminating exploration of the history of the charitable exemption, "Criteria for Exemptions under Section 501(c)(3) by John P. Persons, John J. Osborn, Jr., and Charles F. Feldman (Volume

4). Among the topic-specific papers were "The Charitable Foundation: Its Governance," by Lawrence M. Stone; C. Lowell Harris, "Corporate Giving: Rationale, Issues, and Opportunities" (both in Volume 3); "Alternative Approaches to Encouraging Philanthropic Activities," by Gerard M. Brannon and James Strand"; and "A Study of Federal Matching Grants for Charitable Contributions" by Paul R. McDaniel, in Volume 4. The article by David Ginsburg, Lee R. Marks, and Ronald P. Wertheim, "Federal Oversight of Private Philanthropy" in Volume 5, argued for continuing the IRS role in regard to this oversight.

52. See "Private Philanthropy and Public Affairs," by Jane H. Mavity and Paul N. Ylvisaker; "Philanthropic Activity in International Affairs" by Adam Yarmolinsky; "Some Aspects of Evolving Social Policy in Relation to Private Philanthropy" by Wilbur J. Cohen; and "A Report on the Arts" by Caroline Hightower, for Associated Councils of the Arts. These were all in Volume 2 of the *Research Papers,* along with the miscellaneous group of case studies, and some of the more controversial papers submitted by members of the Donee Group and noted below.

53. A number of close-up case studies were deliberately included in Volume 2. In addition, Rudney suggested that the important thing was that overall the research papers represented preliminary efforts in a new field, but he also recognized that there were real differences in the quality of the research and writing. Interview with Gabriel Rudney, Washington, May 17, 1994.

54. Volume 5 included comparative analyses as well as specific proposals for a new public advisory commission. See, for a thoughtful presentation on this subject, Adam Yarmolinsky and Marion R. Fremont-Smith, "Preserving the Private Voluntary Sector: A Proposal for a Public Advisory Commission on Philanthropy," *Research Papers,* Vol. 5.

55. Communications (letters and memoranda) in the Council on Foundation material in the Rockefeller Archives suggest that Robert Goheen, President of the Council on Foundations, was one of the big disseminators. For the request not to disseminate commission research, see Memorandum of January 24, 1975 from Leonard Silverstein to All [Commission] Consultants (RAC, COF, Box 3, Agency Citizen's Committee [Filer] Contact 1/75–5/75).

56. See CPPPN, Research Project Expenditures for the six months ended February 28, 1975, attachment to CPPPN, Financial Statements and Schedule, Six months ended February 28, 1975 (Unaudited), by Peat, Marwick, Mitchell & Co (IUPUI, Box 28,3).

57. In addition to the papers named, there were several that specifically addressed minority needs, including "U.S. Foundations and Minority Group Interests," submitted by the U.S. Human Resources Corporation; "Philanthropic Foundations of the U.S. and Their Responsiveness to the Special Needs, Problems, and Concerns of the Hispanic Community, 1960 Through 1971," by The National Council of La Raza (1977); and "Patterns of Ethnic and Class Discrimination in the Corporate and Philanthropic World" by Geno Baroni, Arthur Naparstek, and Karen Kollias. These papers and several others which addressed alternative needs of less powerful or more disadvantaged groups are in *Research Papers,* Vol. 2, Part II. These were among the papers not on the earlier list of "Research in Progress) of June 2, 1974 (IUPUI, Box 27,6).

58. John Filer had expected the work to be completed in a shorter time, but in any case, by then he may have wanted to devote full attention to his work at Aetna. In addition he had agreed, at the Governor's request, to chair a Committee on the Structure of State Government in his own state of Connecticut, and probably thought it was time to bring matters to closure at the Filer Commission. It is also interesting to note that in early November, about a month before the presentation of the report was made, Ford had dropped Nelson Rockefeller from the vice presidential slot on his ticket for the next election.

59. This concept is discussed above in chapter 8. See also Sobel, ed., *The Great American Tax Revolt,* pp. 45–46.

60. Several respondents mentioned this. See also Harr and Johnson, *The Rockefeller Century,* pp. 380–381, and 430.

61. This quotation is from "Comments and Dissents" in the final report, and part of the

comments of a group of women, composed of Commissioners Frances T. Farenthold, Graciela Olivarez, and Althea T. L. Simmons. See *Giving in America,* p. 197.

62. *Giving in America,* p. 201. In another separate comment (p. 210) one of the women in the group, Graciela Olivarez, also states that "Corporate giving was perhaps the one area which revealed the least amount of consensus among the Commissioners." This may have been so, but her statement may also reflect uneven participation in the meetings. Indeed, a reading of the summaries and transcripts, and interviews with many respondents, suggests that there were several areas of strong disagreement among the commissioners.

63. *Giving in America,* pp. 201–202. These comments were made jointly by the people named. However other dissenting remarks on various points in the report were also made separately by some individuals or sub-parts of this group.

64. Gabriel Rudney suggested that JDR was disappointed that the report did not include a specific recommendation for a $50 charitable tax credit. Apparently debate in the commission was acrimonious around this proposal, which would actually have benefitted more moderate-income contributors. According to Rudney, JDR was upset that Howard Bolton could not deliver agreement on this issue.

65. The idea for this is said to have come from Porter McKeever, who in effect was reported to have "saved the day."

10. Filer Commission Follow-Up

1. According to Pablo Eisenberg, Filer made a point of telling Eisenberg how pleased he was to have him involved (interview with Pablo Eisenberg, Washington, November 17, 1993). Mary Jean Tully (a NOW representative and part of the Donee Group) was also present, and she reported a similar experience to the author. Telephone interview with Mary Jean Tully, February 9, 1998).

2. The article about the commission's report by Eileen Shanahan appeared on page 16 of the *New York Times,* on December 3, 1975, although articles had appeared on the front page of the *New York Times* and the *Wall Street Journal* in late November. In this regard it is interesting that JDR had discussed the question of how much publicity to give to the report at a meeting with Porter McKeever and Howard Bolton on November 3, 1975. In his diary entry for that day, JDR states that despite disappointment with the report, they "believe it is an important step forward and therefore deserves my public support" (RAC, RFA, JDR 3rd Diaries, 1975, p. 110). According to Robert Bothwell, the story, with references to the Donee Group, was picked up and reported by newspapers across the country, after the reports were released (telephone interview with Robert Bothwell, August 7, 1998).

3. Several respondents stated that it was George Romney who jumped the gun, and he was certainly one of those who objected to its major recommendation for establishing a permanent, public national commission on philanthropy. However, there is no mention of him in articles that appeared about the commission report in the *New York Times* ("Tax Easing Urged by Charity Panel," November 24, 1975, p. 32) and the *Wall Street Journal* ("Tax Report: A Special Summary and Forecast of Federal and State Tax Developments," November 26, 1975, p. 1). Both articles stress the tax inducements arguments of the report. Since the Donee Group had threatened to hold its own press conference that day, it is possible that earlier release of information about the Filer Commission Report might in fact have been done by commission staff to ensure being first (interview with Mary Jean Tully, December 9, 1993).

4. "Tax Report," "Special Summary and Forecast of Federal and State Tax Development" in the *Wall Street Journal,* November 26, 1975, p. 1. Further evidence of Fisher's views may be found in this remark: "It is very difficult for me to substantiate taking a million dollars away [from taxes] to give a million dollars to philanthropy," CPPPN, "SUMMARY, Commission discussion of Extending Charitable Deductions to Non-Itemizers from March 10–11, 1975 meeting (Chicago)," p. 204 (IUPUI, Box 41,13).

5. In a letter to John Filer, Walter McNerney quotes the economist Ralph Nelson as

having told him that "excepting religion, philanthropy *has* been keeping pace with growth in the GNP" (emphasis in original). Letter from McNerney to Filer, June 24, 1975 (IUPUI, Box 29,4). However, while the commission report notes the special case of religious giving, it still makes the general point that giving has not been keeping pace with inflation. See *Giving in America*, p. 15.

6. The reader will recall the discussion of this in relation to the Tax Reform Act of 1969.

7. See CPPPN, "SUMMARY," Commission discussion of Appreciated Property from March 10–11, 1975 meeting (Chicago), pp. 228–305 (IUPUI, Box 42,1).

8. Among these were Elizabeth McCormack, and Jon Newman, who was reported by many respondents to be one of the most respected members of the commission. Furthermore, it has to be at least questioned whether the Rockefeller "brothers" would have welcomed opening this can of worms, because such action in Congress would raise the whole subject of tax on appreciated value, estate taxes, inter vivos gifts, and other matters which would have an impact on their personal situation. In fact it appeared that tax reformers in Congress almost succeeded (briefly) in closing the "loophole" that allowed appreciated property to escape taxation (on gain in value) at death. In light of existing capital gains rules, this could have made charitable gifts of appreciated property by living individuals comparatively more attractive from a tax standpoint than bequests of such property to heirs. The change in the tax law (and the uproar it caused before being removed) is discussed in Pollack, *The Failure of U.S. Tax Policy*, pp. 82, 123).

9. *Giving in America*, p. 151. Note that several respondents suggested that JDR 3rd had a strong interest in any taxable consideration that would affect the financial welfare of his children, including direct bequests and presumably charitable remainder trusts.

10. *Giving in America*, p. 19. This seems to refer obliquely to the consideration of various kinds of other incentives, such as tax credits or matching funds by the government, and the complications these would cause religious contributions particularly. However, the Donee Group, apparently responding to an earlier version of the Filer Commission Report (p. 128) quotes the report as saying that "inducements to giving should not be construed so as to discourage giving to current recipients." The Donee Group cites this sentence in the context of their argument about the need for more funding of progressive social change organizations like the National Welfare Rights Organization and the Mexican American Legal Defense and Educational Fund, rather than for funding of traditional institutions. Donee Group Report, "Private Philanthropy: Vital and Innovative or Passive and Irrelevant," pp. 57–61.

11. See Pollack, *Failure of U.S. Tax Policy*, pp. 81–82. That the commissioners were aware of the Congressional discussions is evident by references to Congress throughout the "Summary" transcripts that spring. In that context mention was made of an effort by Laurence Woodworth to whittle away at some part of the charitable tax deduction.

12. In 1975, Congress enacted the Earned Income Tax Credit (EITC) for the working poor, but rejected repeal of the oil depreciation allowance in the Tax Reduction Act of 1975. This may help explain why JDR suggested the tax credit proposal which Gabriel Rudney indicated that JDR wanted and which Howard Bolton could not deliver (see chapter 9 above, note 64). Although this would benefit lower-income donors, and therefore might be acceptable to Bayard Ewing for United Way reasons, it would reduce federal tax income as well as possibly raise constitutional issues. McDaniel and Surrey suggested another option—a matching gift by government for charitable gifts, but this would not do much for low income donors. See CPPPN, "Summary: Committee Discussion of Charitable Deduction Generally from February 5–7, 1975 Meeting (Denver)," pp. 166–189; and the continuation of that theme at the meeting in Chicago, "Summary: Commission Discussion of Extending Charitable Deduction to Non-Itemizers from March 10–11, 1975 . . . ," pp. 151–222 (IUPUI, Box 41,7 and 13). Paul McDaniel wrote a paper for the commission on matching grants ("Study of Federal Matching Grants for Charitable Contributions," published in *Research Papers*, Vol. 6) but since his study did not validate the tax incentive motive for giving, it was not given much play in commission discussions.

13. These recommendations clearly were less threatening in terms of legal issues or philosophy, since they were basically only incremental modifications of existing laws, in contrast with a tax credit, which would have raised questions about the public nature of private donations.

14. This despite the fact that there was some effort to reach consensus along the way. See "Minutes of Chicago Meeting—March 10 and 11" which shows an apparent attempt to summarize key consensus points to that date, but seems to be stretching matters a bit (IUPUI, Box 41,5). Also evident from the number of dissents to the CPPPN Report, *Giving in America*.

15. Once again there are references in the archives to a meeting of the Filer Commission to be held on June 16, 1975 for review of the final draft, but no evident indication of the meeting having taken place—there seem to be no records of minutes, summaries of transcripts etc.), as there are for other meetings.

16. There are numerous letters suggesting changes as well as marked-up drafts in the IUPUI Archives. See for example the Letter from Jon Newman to Leonard Silverstein, with attached "brief statement" for inclusion in the report, July 3, 1975; and the letter from Walter McNerney to John Filer, June 24, 1975, which also contains extensive suggestions—however neither refers specifically to the recommendations (IUPUI, Box 29,4). Burt Knauft and other members of the commission (including Leonard Silverstein) confirmed that most of the discussions at the end were done in small groups, and by mail or telephone.

17. See Appendix A for discussion of the elements of a successful commission. We will also return to this point in the next chapter.

18. JDR's disappointment with the final product is expressed in numerous diary entries. On August 19, he stated that the report did not seem "to have the forthrightness he [Filer] and I had agreed was essential when we first talked." JDR also stated, "I am concerned as to the usefulness and effectiveness of his approach and hence of the final product" and finally (in the same diary entry)—"I went quite far with Mr. Filer in my comments, only stopping short of telling him that if the report went through substantially as it is I could not support it." He also refers specifically to "the question of rewriting the recommendations." He makes the point again on November 3, 1975: "Messrs. McKeever and Bolton both recognize that the report falls considerably short of our hopes and expectations" (JDR 3rd Diaries, 1975, pp. 75, 75–76, and 110).

19. The summary transcripts (in the archives) indicate that these discussions generally began with presentations by experts/consultants, and included active participation of advisory committee members and consultants, and staff, in addition to commission members. The transcripts also suggest that with the exception of Elizabeth McCormack "the ladies" were often quiet, and this is verified further in interviews with key respondents.

20. These are the headings highlighted in *Giving in America,* in the Table of Contents, Part II, chapters 6, 7, and 8—where Recommendations for each heading are also given.

21. The term "hortatory" was used by E. B. Knauft later in categorizing several recommendations of the Filer Commission. See Knauft, "The Filer Commission Revisited" in *Foundation News,* January/February 1984, pp. 12–15. Since corporations under existing law could give up to 5 percent of profits this may have been one of the areas of disappointment for JDR and his staff.

22. For discussion of these issues, see above, chapters 7 through 9.

23. The idea of organizations having legitimacy derives from a brilliant conceptualization by the sociologist Talcott Parsons. See Parsons, *Structure and Process in American Society* (New York: Free Press, 1960). However, the commission seems to have largely ignored an important sense of the concept—that legitimacy derives from the valued outputs (or products) of an organization. In terms of philanthropy, that could also require analysis of the social needs being met, or answering the question: who benefits?

24. Unsympathetic attitudes were expressed by John Filer himself, who had asked at a commission meeting, "Why do we have to say anything nice about the IRS?" Silverstein's remarks in this discussion provide some insight into the way he handled such issues. First he

said, "I think one has to give them credit." and a few minutes later as the argument developed, he said less equivocally, "The final document [about an oversight agency] has been submitted to a law firm in New York for extensive study, and their judgment is to continue to use the IRS" ("Summary: Commission Discussion of Oversight Agency from March 10–11, 1975, Meeting [Chicago]," pp. 35–39 [IUPUI, Box 41,10]).

25. Marion Fremont-Smith was an attorney, whose book was discussed extensively in earlier chapters; Adam Yarmolinsky was Ralph Waldo Emerson Professor at the University of Massachusetts, and an expert in public administration and government.

26. It will be remembered that several consultants to the commission had attended "the Ditchley Conference" in England in 1972 where there had been considerable discussion of the public Charity Commission for England and Wales. And Commissioner Alan Pifer, who was head of the Carnegie Corporation, had already discussed the charity commission idea with JDR 3rd and others before the Filer Commission was established.

27. I want to thank Adam Yarmolinsky for suggesting this to me in a telephone interview on February 10, 1998.

28. See for example the various drafts of models for a permanent commission in the IUPUI Archives (Box 46,4), and the correspondence related to these drafts from Fremont-Smith and Adam Yarmolinsky. A packet of materials, "Models for a Continuing Oversight Advisory Commission on the Voluntary Sector," includes Tab B, "An Act to Establish an Advisory Commission on the Voluntary Sector" (Draft—May 9, 1975 by Fremont-Smith and Yarmolinsky, also noting that pages 4 and 11 were revised 6/9/75. Page 4 refers to members on the commission, who will be government appointees; page 11 relates to an advisory council for the commission. This means that there would be the same kind of functional split recommended by the Peterson Commission, and utilized to some extent by Leonard Silverstein in the Filer Commission.)

29. Letter from Adam Yarmolinsky to Leonard Silverstein, May 9,1975, in which he says "Copies of the current draft of the continuing organization memorandum and *statute* (emphasis mine) have gone off today from Marion Fremont-Smith's office" (IUPUI, Box 46,4). See also note 27 above.

30. On the commission, for example, Herbert Longenecker, who had been President of Tulane University, supported it reluctantly, while Alan Pifer had considered some similar idea previously. Graciela Olivarez, a member of the national board of the Council on Foundations, was in favor of a public commission, while the Reverend Raymond Gallagher, Bishop of Lafayette, Indiana, was opposed to it; so basically were Lester Crown (a trustee of Northwestern University) and Bayard Ewing—both of whom were connected to the United Way of America. See "Comments and Dissents" in *Giving in America,* p. 222 and also the discussion in "Summary: Commission Discussions of Oversight Agency from March 10–11. 1975 meeting (Chicago)," pp. 62–111. Several respondents also noted opposition from religious interests connected with the commission, although as finally designed, the primary functions of the proposed permanent commission seemed to be data collecting and public information.

31. Even JDR 3rd, who was frequently generous in his appraisals of people, expressed his disappointment. In summarizing a discussion with Porter McKeever about the report in his diary, he noted, "Filer just doesn't seem to have taken hold—given the leadership the way we had hoped" (JDR 3rd Diary, September 15, 1975, RAC, RFA, JDR 3rd Diaries).

32. It will be recalled that the advisory group was somewhat amorphous in form (see chapter 9). One respondent, Adam Yarmolinsky, remembered meeting frequently in small groups with Leonard Silverstein but didn't think those were formally constituted "Advisory Committee" meetings. Telephone interview with Yarmolinsky, February 11, 1998. However, in addition to various individuals labeled as the Advisory Committee there are minutes of at least two meetings of the Advisory Committee to the Commission, one in February 1974, and another on January 9, 1976, and apparently Silverstein used them as a sounding board on occasion.

33. According to Burt Knauft, he was instrumental in persuading Filer to meet with the social activist group; he read the Eisenberg article himself and brought it directly to the attention of Filer (telephone interview with Burt Knauft, Feb 10, 1998). Silverstein also confirmed that John Filer welcomed the idea of their participation.

34. Statement by Norton Kiritz, provided to the author by Kiritz.

35. Although the Donee Group Report gives the date as April 18, the records ("Summary" transcripts and related memoranda) in the Filer Commission Archives at IUPUI give the commission meeting dates that month as April 7–8, 1975.

36. Indeed, several respondents suggested that there were informal connections between commission staff, the Rockefeller office, and Pablo Eisenberg, as well as activist (female) members of the commission. Furthermore, Eisenberg, like JDR, was a "Princeton man."

37. By the end of December 1975, Pablo Eisenberg had already received $5,000 in support of the new social action organization, the National Committee for Responsive Philanthropy (a formal outgrowth of the Donee Group). In a letter informing him of the grant from Mr. Rockefeller, Porter McKeever notes that it is a one-time grant and represents "a strong vote of confidence in your own commitment and leadership." From the tone of the letter (and a reference to a previous telephone conversation) it appears that McKeever's role as intermediary was also significant. Letter from Porter McKeever, Associate, John D. Rockefeller 3rd to Pablo Isenberg [*sic*], December 22, 1975 (RAC, Rockefeller Associates, McKeever, Box 1, Folder: C).

38. The amount promised initially seems to have been $50,000 but in an interview with the author Pablo Eisenberg used a $60,000 figure and that is also the amount frequently cited. The financial records do not specify, but it is likely that this included an additional payment for producing the final Donee Group Report (interview with Pablo Eisenberg, Washington, D.C., November 17, 1993).

39. *Federal Register,* February 12, 1975, as cited by Norton Kiritz, "Presentation to the 'Commission on Private Philanthropy and Public Needs,'" March 10, 1975, p. 3 (a copy of this was given to the author by Norton Kiritz).

40. See "Donee Organizations Urge Change in Private Philanthropy," *Grantsmanship Center News* (July–August 1975) Vol. 2, No. 4, pp. 58–67.

41. Interview with Mary Jean Tully, New York, December 9, 1993. See also Donee Group Report, p. 51.

42. *Interim Report of the Donee Group to the Commission on Private Philanthropy and Public Needs, June 16, 1975* (photocopy of a typed ten-page report, supplied to the author by Norton Kiritz from his personal files).

43. A partial effort to deal with these questions can be found in a paper written that summer (1975) for the Donee Group and published in the commission's compendium of research papers. See Reynold Levy and Waldemar A. Nielsen, "An Agenda for the Future," in *Research Papers,* Vol. 2, Part 2, pp. 1029–1067.

44. There seem to be no actual records of another June meeting of the whole commission; the only reference in the file was to a meeting that would be held in June to discuss the full commission report but I did not find minutes or other material on the June meeting either in the commission archives at IUPUI or at the Rockefeller Archives. For papers relating to the California meeting, I am indebted to Norton Kiritz for providing me with copies of his personal file materials.

45. The information in this paragraph comes largely from "Donee Organizations Urge Change in Private Philanthropy," *Grantsmanship Center News* (July–August 1975), Vol. 2, No. 4, pp. 58–67, a copy of which was supplied by Norton Kiritz. Interestingly enough, even allowing for the passage of time, many respondents affiliated with the commission seemed to have a severe case of amnesia in reference to these events.

46. The survey was carried out and discussed in two issues of the *Grantsmanship Center News,* Vol. 2, Nos. 2 and 3.

47. Of 65 people voting, it was reported that 70 percent voted against "eliminating, limiting or phasing out" full value deductibility for gift of appreciated property, while 62 percent favored "the creation of a permanent commission to oversee private philanthropy." See *Summary Report on Community Leadership Conference on Private Philanthropy and Public Needs,* Los Angeles, California, June 30, 1975, Appendix B; also in "Donee Organizations Urge Change in Private Philanthropy," *Grantsmanship Center News* (July–August 1975), Vol. 2, No. 4, pp. 58–67.

48. See Draft "Proposal Recommendations of the Advisory Committee of the Commission on Private Philanthropy and Public Needs" (typed document in IUPUI, Box 27,8). The document begins: "A supplement to the Report of the Commission on Private Philanthropy and Public Needs is proposed." Staff is listed on page 3, as Reporters: Robert E. Falb and Stuart Lewis; Consultants: Boris Bittker or John Simon, Howard Bolton, Gabriel G. Rudney, Stanley S. Surrey, Leonard L. Silverstein, and John H. Filer (these last both ex officio); and there is an Advisory Committee list attached, as well as an indication that there would be a budget.

49. In his diary entry of Tuesday, August 19 JDR records in some detail his discussion with John Filer about the report and the necessity to rewrite its recommendations and other parts to give greater emphasis and focus. Also present (at the luncheon) were Porter McKeever, Paul Ylvisaker, Leonard Silverstein, and Wade Greene (JDR 3rd Diaries, 1975, pp. 75–76). One respondent suggested that Rockefeller's staff was particularly concerned about the impact of some proposed recommendations on the Rockefeller Brothers Fund.

50. The Donee Group Report is not included in the "Compendium of Commission Research" (to be published) as cited in *Giving in America.* This could have been an accidental omission, or, more probably, the decision to include their report in the *Research Papers* could have been reached after *Giving in America* went to press in the fall of 1975. See Appendix I: "Commission Studies" in *Giving in America,* p. 223. For a discussion of Donee Group papers see chapter 9; the paper by Levy and Nielsen (note 42 above) could also be considered Donee Group writing. See also Brilliant, "Looking Backward to Look Forward," p. 27, n. 53.

51. A detailed comparison of their recommendations is found in notes provided to the author by John Glazer, former staff member of United Way of America, and at that time William Aramony's liaison to Bayard Ewing.

52. In an interview I had with the author of the Donee Group Report, he said that in retrospect he might have written the report differently (telephone interview with Jim Abernathy, December 29, 1992). In fact, after NCRP was incorporated, there was a new document dealing differently with some of the major issues in the early report.

53. Several respondents indicated that McKeever had been instrumental in resolving some major obstacles prior to publication of the commission report. It may be that his particular contribution was not only in regard to the treatment of dissenting comments within the Filer Report itself, but also in relation to the publication of the Donee Report. Earlier discussions in regard to funding of the Donee Group did not actually indicate that the group would present its own recommendations in a separate report but suggested that the group would present to the commission a statement of values connected with their research.

54. JDR 3rd Diary, December 22 and December 24, 1975 (RAC, JDR 3rd Diaries). The presence of John Harr, the biographer-historian for JDR and the family, suggests that there were other issues on the table, probably either archival interests of the family or the personal history of JDR.

55. The reader will recall that it had been announced in November that Nelson Rockefeller was not going to be on the Ford ticket in the next election, but it is not clear whether his running for the Presidency was still under consideration. There was also some discussion of the fiscal crisis in New York City and State, which presumably would mean particular sensitivity to any question of changing the tax-free status of state and municipal bonds (which would of course make such investment less desirable). The brothers' meeting is recorded in JDR 3rd's diary on Tuesday, January 13, 1976 (JDR 3rd Diaries 1976, p. 5).

56. This seems to be another example of efforts to "frame" JDR 3rd's persona. In any case, at this time his son, Jay Rockefeller, was beginning his campaign for Governor of West Virginia, while according to the *New York Times* rumors persisted that Nelson Rockefeller was still running for President, *New York Times,* February 7, 1976, p. 22.

57. Fred M. Hechinger, "Potholes in the American Way of Giving," *New York Times,* January 6, 1976, p. 31.

58. Copy of letter from Walter McNerney to Douglas Dillon, Herbert Longenecker, Philip Klutznick, Walter Haas, Elizabeth McCormack, and Alan Pifer, March 9, 1976 (RAC, General Files, RG3, Box 369, Folder: Commission on Private Philanthropy and Private Needs/ McKeever, 1976).

59. Letter from Pablo Eisenberg to Porter McKeever, April 2, 1976 (RAC, Associates, McKeever, Box 1, Folder: C).

60. Stuart Lewis was an attorney in Silverstein's law firm.

61. "Conference Memorandum, Meeting of the Follow-Up Committee of CPPPN" [sic], March 30, 1976 (RAC, GF, RG3, Box 369, Folder: Commission on Private Philanthropy and Public Needs). The committee was also "advised of a meeting with Secretary Simon and colleagues attended by Messrs. McNerney and Silverstein on March 30, 1976" (that date may be an error, but it is the one given).

62. This seems evident in the later effort at recapitulation of the various committees in an archival document that is a combined handwritten and typed paper (with corrections), and relating to the Advisory Committee on Private Philanthropy and Public Needs. This is part of a group of file documents that includes minutes of an August 9th (1977) meeting between members of the Committee with Government Officials (in the White House); an Agenda for another meeting on October 4th, and a document that appears to be a summary review of the October 4th meeting (Advisory Committee members only) that is entitled "*Outline of the Meeting.*" Under items 1 and 2, which were presented by Mr. McNerney, it notes that the Advisory Committee began with the Filer Commission; then "put together a group that met once with Secretary Blumenthal—Treasury dismissed the group and this was then followed [by] an attempt to establish another group through Constanza and Eizenstat"—also noted is the "line between Advisory Group and Filer Commission [is] tenuous." Under Items 3 and 4, given by Mr. Silverstein, it is further added that the Blumenthal Committee was chaired by Mr. McNerney and became the present Advisory Committee (IUPUI, Box 28,5).

63. Letter from Kingman Brewster to Landrum Bolling (President, Lilly Endowment) July 10, 1976, referring to a previous meeting in Indianapolis and noting that Yale already had a small planning grant for a research center on nonprofit organizations (RAC, RFA, RG3, Box 369, Folder: Commission on Private Philanthropy and Public Needs, McKeever, 1976).

64. By July 8, 1976 CONVO had developed a statement of purpose; by March 10, 1977 bylaws were in place and CONVO had replaced the earlier Coalition for the Public Good (these dates come from material of a participant in the events, that is, from documents in John Glaser's files). See also the account of this period by Brian O'Connell (but without specific dates) in O'Connell, *Powered by Coalition: The Story of the Independent Sector* (San Francisco: Jossey-Bass, 1997), pp. 26–27.

65. "Public Report Activities of the Commission on Private Philanthropy and Public Needs," with attached list of the Interagency Task Force on the Filer Commission, dated May 10, 1976 (IUPUI, Box 31,2). Conference Memorandum: Meeting of the Follow-Up Committee of CPPPN, May 18, 1976, which refers to a May 18 meeting of the Follow-Up Committee, held at the Carnegie Corporation in New York, and to a May 13 meeting with Treasury Department Representatives. At the May 18 meeting a proposal by United Way for an ongoing organization (i.e., presumably CONVO) was also discussed.

66. "Conference Memorandum: Meeting of the Follow-Up Committee of CPPPN," May 18, 1876 (a summary record in the IUPUI, Box 31,2).

67. This paragraph is based on the Memorandum for Deputy Secretary Dixon from

David A. Lefeve, Special Assistant to the Secretary for Consumer Affairs, Subject: Evaluation of the Filer Commission Report, April 13, 1976 (IUPUI, Box 31,2).

68. Ideas for several offices related to the nonprofit sector as well as an advisory commission and a public needs institute appear in a file document in the Filer Commission Archives in Indianapolis. See Discussion Draft 5/20/76, Proposal for Permanent Bodies Concerned with Nonprofit Sector (IUPUI, Box 31,2).

69. Memorandum to John D. Rockefeller 3rd from Porter McKeever, re Supplement on Meeting with Simon, May 24, 1976 (RAC, GF, RG3, Box 369, Folder: Commission on Private Philanthropy and Public Needs, McKeever 76, # 1).

70. Quoted from McKeever Memorandum to JDR 3rd of May 24,1976 (RAC, GF, RG3, Box 369, Folder: CPPPN, McKeever, 76, #1).

71. Letter of June 29,1976 from Philip Klutznick to Bayard Ewing concerning Follow-Up Committee Meeting of June 11, 1976, in which Klutznick discusses the issue of funding for the various groups (IUPUI, Box 31,2). It should be noted that as late as July 14, 1976 Klutznick was still requesting more funding from JDR for commission related activities, in a letter giving a brief report on activities of the commission after the report, and mentioning the costs for additional research requested by the Treasury Department and other public information and staff expenses. Letter from Philip Klutznick to John D Rockefeller 3rd, July 14, 1976 (RAC, RFA, RG3, Box 369, Folder: Commission on Private Philanthropy and Public Needs).

72. Letter from Douglas Dillon to Leonard Silverstein, August 4, 1976, and acknowledging Ewing's letter (IUPUI, Box 31,2). Over the summer Kingman Brewster was also accelerating his fund raising efforts for the Yale Research program, so it appears that indeed there was increasing competition for funds in the new field which had essentially been created by the Filer Commission.

73. Memorandum to Follow-Up Committee from Leonard Silverstein, August 6, 1977 with attached agenda and other material, CPPPN, Treasury Department Meeting, August 13, 1976 (IUPUI, Box 31,2).

74. Document headed "Deputy Secretary Dixon, David A. Lefeve, Special Assistant to the Secretary for Consumer Affairs, Filer Commission Report," and stamped with the date July 14, 1976 (IUPUI, Box 31,2).

75. Memorandum from Leonard L. Silverstein to the Follow-Up Committee, September 12, 1976, with attached "Outline [for] Proposals for the Nonprofit Sector." (IUPUI, Box 31,2).

76. Memorandum from Leonard L. Silverstein to Follow-Up Committee, September 12, 1976. Attached to the memorandum was the "Outline: Proposals for the Nonprofit Sector," which included an Advisory Commission to the Secretary of the Treasury, an Office of Exempt Organization Analysis, and a Division of Solicitation.

77. The Tax Reform Act of 1976 (P.L. 94–455) in the end was a compromise version of H.R. 10612 as amended, after what was described as strong competition among "tax expenditure groups." (H.R. 10612 was the first major tax bill to pass after the concept of tax expenditures was incorporated in the federal budget submission.) In general, changes in regard to estate and gift taxes seemed to provide more incentive to charitable giving by larger estates, and more incentive for heirs to give property to charity. Some special treatment was also provided for family farms, which would have had direct benefits for some Rockefellers, including David Rockefeller's family (they raised pedigreed cows). A summation of the Act's provisions from the point of view of 501(c)(3) organizations can be found in *Focus on Federal Relations*, "Special Issue: The Tax Reform Act of 1976" (Vol. 4, No. 10), December 10, 1976 (Internal Information document of the United Way of America).

78. In an optimistic mood, on January 7, 1977 Gabriel Rudney (under Secretary of Treasury Simon's authority) issued a press release about the existence of the Treasury Advisory Group, which as now constituted certainly seemed to meet any criteria regarding diversity of

viewpoint. In addition to Douglas Dillon as Chair, members connected to the Filer Commission included Alan Pifer, George Romney, Leonard Silverstein, Walter McNerney, William Matson Roth, and Marion Fremont-Smith; Paul Ylvisaker also served; representatives of more activist groups included Vilma Martinez and Mary Gardiner Jones (National Consumers League); on the advisory group were also James Joseph, an African American who was President of the Cummins Engine Foundation, Thomas Troyer, an attorney for the Council on Foundations, and William Aramony, National Executive of the United Way of America. From News Release from the Department of the Treasury, "Treasury Secretary Announces Membership of Committee to Advise Treasury on Tax Aspects and Standards for Private Philanthropy," January 7, 1977 (Contact: Gabriel Rudney). Demonstration of continued Rockefeller interest in these activities is clear since this release is attached to a letter from Gabriel Rudney to George Taylor (Rockefeller Brothers and Associates), January 26, 1976 [*sic*], in which he thanks George Taylor for his help with the "draft release" [which] "provided the needed impetus for the January 7 release." Given the date of the attached news release, and the reference to the date January 7, the year 1976 in Rudney's letter is clearly an error at the beginning of a new year (RAC, RFA, RG 17, Associates, McKeever, Box 1, Folder: Filer Commission).

79. Department of the Treasury, News Release, "Treasury Secretary Blumenthal Cuts Advisory Committee, March 15, 1977" (Contact: Robert Nirp) (RAC, RFA, RG 17, Associates, McKeever, Box 1, Folder: Filer Commission).

80. Letter from John D. Rockefeller 3rd to Stuart R. Eizenstat, Presidential Assistant, March 1, 1977, with bcc to Jack Harr and Porter McKeever. In the letter JDR suggests possible contact with the White House about "a serious situation affecting our society today" and refers to his attached staff statement discussing "the gradual erosion of the all-important private nonprofit sector" (RAC, RF, RG 17, Associates, McKeever, Box 1, Folder: Filer Commission).

81. However, McKeever might have been about to stretch Rockefeller's limits somewhat, since several key respondents strongly suggested that working with corporate leaders was definitely not one of JDR's strengths. Letter from Porter McKeever to William Ruder, July 19, 1977 (RAC, RF, RG 17, Associates, McKeever, Box 1, Folder: Filer Commission).

82. There were 22 people on the committee, including a few women; and almost 20 members of the public attending. CPPPN, Minutes, April 7, 1977 (RAC, RF, RG 17, Associates, McKeever, Box 1, Filer Commission).

83. Urban C. Lehnen, "Advisory Panel's Future May Be Past," *Washington Star,* April 11, 1977, p. A-1.

84. Memorandum from Porter McKeever to JDR 3rd, Re Conversation with Walter McNerney, June 22, 1977 (RAC, RF, RG17, Associates, McKeever, Box 1, Folder: Filer Commission).

85. List of attendees of the Conference on the Philanthropic Center, August 9, 1977 and Agenda (IUPUI, Box 28,3). Also in the archives is a memorandum from Gabe Rudney to Walter McNerney, Porter McKeever and Leonard Silverstein, referring to an upcoming meeting (actually listed as October 6) and discussing the agenda. In the same file is the agenda for the Advisory Committee Meeting on Private Philanthropy and Public Needs, October 4, 1977, with an attached list of attendees that now includes Ken Allen, Executive Director, National Center for Voluntary Action; Bob Bothwell, Executive Director, Committee for Responsive Philanthropy; Howard Dressner, Vice President and General Counsel, Ford Foundation; Jack Moskowitz, United Way; and many key players from the Filer Commission, including Knauft, McKeever, McCormack, McNerney, Silverstein, and Rudney.

86. Several respondents repeated a now almost apocryphal story about that event—apparently the group present was incensed, and since there was a short interlude as the decision was being made, Paul Ylvisaker and Alan Pifer went into a separate room to write an immediate rebuttal. But of course, it made no difference.

87. By the early 1980s NCRP was actively involved in the efforts in Congress to open up

the United Way–dominated Combined Federal Campaign (the CFC) to new charitable groups. See Brilliant, *The United Way,* pp. 130–149 and 209–210.

11. Lessons from the Past and Issues for the Future

1. According to one participant, after JDR's death contributions to start a new "entity" in honor of JDR ($25,000 each from the JDR fund and the Rockefeller Brothers Foundation) were postponed because of the collaboration underway by CONVO and NCOP. This is discussed in Schwartz, *Modern American Philanthropy,* pp. 127–128.

2. The difficulty in forming one new combined organization was partly due to the different viewpoints of the funders (donors/philanthropists) in NCOP and the recipients (public charities) in CONVO. The story of the formation of Independent Sector is told by Brian O'Connell and John ("Jack") Schwartz, who were both active participants. However, the events described in their book remain somewhat murky. See O'Connell, *Powered by Coalition,* and Schwartz, *Modern American Philanthropy.*

3. I use capital letters here to illustrate the way that Independent Sector has preferred to write its name—in order to avoid confusion with the concept of an independent sector with which it is of course concerned. But hereafter I will use the more common style, Independent Sector, in referring to the organization. The name itself was an issue, as NCOP, in particular, did not want the word "voluntary" in the title. See O'Connell, *Powered by Coalition,* pp. 55–56.

4. In the next decade, this concept became problematic and federal implementation guidelines were delayed. In my interview with Leonard Silverstein (1993) he made the point explicitly about Independent Sector turning into an advocacy organization.

5. Although the Filer Commission was dissolved, CONVO (also located in Washington) was not. NCOP, however, apparently did go out of business formally. See O'Connell, *Powered by Coalition,* pp. 55–56.

6. And this was so despite the words of John Gardner's own organization, Common Cause, quoted at the beginning of this chapter.

7. See Schwartz, *Modern American Philanthropy,* pp.140–142. In his book Schwartz also discusses other umbrella organizations involved in the third sector such as the National Society of Fund Raising Executives (NSFRE) and the 501(c)(3) group. Evidently neither the Rockefeller group nor Congress considered the standard setting and enforcement activities of the National Charities Information Bureau or the Philanthropic Advisory Service of the Better Business Bureau to be adequate.

8. See above, chapter 10. For a discussion of the impact of founders on organizations, see Edgar H. Schein, "The Role of the Founder in Creating Organizational Culture," *Organizational Dynamics,* Summer 1983, pp. 13–28.

9. E. B. Knauft, "Functions of the Nonprofit Sector: The Place of the Filer Commission in the Scope and Activity of the Third Sector" in *Working Papers of the Spring Research Forum: Since the Filer Commission* (Independent Sector, New York, May 3, 1983, pp. 119–137.

10. For example, Knauft recognized the difficulty of the research and the fact that not all the papers had a direct impact on the related recommendations. See Knauft, "Place of the Filer Commission," pp. 124–126.

11. E. B. Knauft, "The Filer Commission Revisited," *Foundation News* (January/February 1984), pp. 12–15.

12. Knauft, "The Place of the Filer Commission," pp. 128–129. See also the discussion in Brilliant, "Looking Backward to Look Forward."

13. Pablo Eisenberg, "Accountability, Accessibility and Equity in Philanthropy: Filling the Research Gap," in *Working Papers of the Spring Research Forum: Since the Filer Commission,* pp. 139–182. This point had also been made in the paper by Reynold Levy and Waldemar Nielsen which was included in the compendium of Filer Commission research papers. See

Levy and Nielsen, "An Agenda for the Future," pp. 1029–1067. See also the discussion in Brilliant, "Looking Backward to Look Forward," p. 20-22.

14. Knauft already worked for Independent Sector by then, but in a sense he was at least opening up the possibility for consideration of another commission—an option to which the attendees apparently were not terribly responsive.

15. See discussion of this issue in chapters 5 and 6 above.

16. President Nixon apparently had considerable awareness of both commissions, including naming at least one person to be included on the Filer Commission (Max Fisher).

17. The reader will recall that as the commission ended, Nixon gave Peterson a position in his administration. Consequently Peterson personally must have attracted the attention of the President and his staff while chairing the commission.

18. Peterson Commission Report, pp. 68–69 and 162–163. Political activity by foundations became a big factor during the Congressional hearings on the 1969 Tax Reform Act. See chapters 5 and 6 above for further discussion of this issue.

19. Interview with John J. Schwartz, New York City, 1994. See also details about these efforts in Schwartz, *Modern American Philanthropy*, pp. 100–105. Schwartz highlights the role of his organization, American Association of Fund-Raising Counsel (AAFRC), and Commissioner Philip Klutznick (who also later became head of the Commerce department under Carter), but acknowledges the work of E. B. Knauft and others in raising over two million dollars for the commission.

20. It will be recalled that the Peterson Commission deliberately did not connect to the foundations for fear of being perceived as lobbying for them. At the time such lobbying seemed potentially problematic, but later tax rules were defined as specifically permitting lobbying in a group's own self-interest. However, Peterson also wanted to be independent in his recommendations and not beholden to the foundation community in any way.

21. Apparently the Nixon administration was also impressed, since the President brought Peterson into the government after the commission finished its work. In any case Filer did not get a similar reward, although in a nice twist, Treasury Secretary Blumenthal followed the path of others in and out of government, and by 1980 had become a trustee of the Rockefeller Foundation.

22. See Appendix A for discussion of the implementation problems faced even by official Presidential/Congressional commissions.

23. In a sense, the Filer Commission coalesced developments that had begun before. Thus, for example, there was already a group formed around scholarship on voluntarism, "The Association of Voluntary Action Scholars," formed in 1971 and not well known. The concept of the Third Sector was also already used by others, including Wally Nielsen, and, notably, Theodor Levitt in *The Third Sector: Tactics for a Responsive Society* (New York, AMACOM, 1973).

24. In 1998 reports were suggesting that Americans had even less faith in institutions than they did two decades before, but the late 1960s and early 1970s were characterized at the time by a distrust of all large institutions (government, business, and even philanthropic ones).

25. Implementation of the lobbying expenditures test in the 1976 Tax Reform act was delayed for many years, due to court cases and problematic regulations of the IRS. See Hopkins, *Law of Tax-Exempt Organizations*, pp. 300–326. Tax implications of the Act are considered in Sobel, ed., *The Great American Tax Revolt*, pp. 66–67, and in Gerald E. Auten, Charles T. Clotfelter, and Richard L. Schmalbeck, "Taxes and Philanthropy among the Wealthy," Working Paper No. 98–13, Office of Tax Policy Research, University of Michigan Business School, 1998.

26. For analysis of Reagan tax policy generally, see Michael J. Graet, *The Decline and Fall of the Income Tax* (New York: W. W. Norton, 1997), pp. 52–67 and 123–139.

27. For analysis of the impact of the Reagan cuts on nonprofit organizations, see Alan

Abramson and Lester M. Salamon, *The Nonprofit Sector and the New Federal Budget* (Washington, D.C.: Urban Institute Press, 1986); Salamon, "Nonprofit Organizations: The Lost Opportunity" in *The Reagan Record*, John Palmer and Isabel Sawhill, eds. (Cambridge, Mass.: Ballinger Press, 1984), pp. 31–68; and Salamon, "The Marketization of Welfare: Changing Nonprofit and For-Profit Roles in the American Welfare State," *Social Service Review*, Vol. 67, No.1, March 1993, pp. 16–39,

28. This circular had been issued twice before (1980, 1981), but its 1983 version was particularly problematic. See Office of Management and Budget "Amendments to OMB Circular A-22, "Cost Principles for Nonprofit Organizations," 1983.

29. Panel Publishers, *Analysis and Application of the 1981 Tax Law Changes (Economic Recovery Tax Act of 1981)* (Special Report, n.d.), p. 20.

30. The 1981 Tax Act, P.L. 97–34, allowed for phasing in of the charitable deduction for non-itemizers until the end of 1986 when the provision would automatically expire if not renewed. The "direct charitable deduction" was fixed at a percentage of a small amount donated to charity, starting in 1982 and 1983 as 25 percent of the first $100 and increasing in 1984 to 25 percent of the first $300. For 1985 the deduction would be 50 percent of any amount donated to charity and in 1986 the total amount donated could be deducted. Explanation from *Analysis and Application of the 1981 Tax-Law Changes [Economic Recovery Tax Act of 1981]*, Panel Publishers, 1981, p. 11.

31. The problem with determining causes of fluctuations in giving is of course that a number of variables may contribute to any effect, such as the economy, stock market prices, or the various different—even contradictory—measures in the tax act itself, such as those dealing with income tax rates, appreciated property, or estate taxes. Generally there is also an impact on giving just before changes are made in a new law (e.g., if deductions are to be less generous giving may be accelerated before the rules change and may drop right after) so the timing of changes is sensitive. Figures on giving historically are found in Ann Kaplan, ed. *Giving USA, 1997: The Annual Report on Philanthropy for the Year 1996* (New York: AAFRC Trust for Philanthropy, 1997), pp. 32–38.

32. Tax Reform Act of 1984. This Act also slightly reduced the time needed before a property became eligible for capital gains treatment of added value. In 1983 an even more notable event occurred in relation to parameter setting for charitable (501 [c][3]) organizations. In the case of *Bob Jones University v. United States* the U.S. Supreme Court ruled that "[a] private educational institution that has racially discriminatory policies cannot qualify for tax-exempt status under federal law as a charitable organization." The ruling was based on the concept that charitable organizations could not act contrary to accepted public policy, and thus could not discriminate on racial grounds. This became incorporated in federal tax law. See Hopkins, *Law of Tax-Exempt Organizations*, pp. 81–96, and the discussion in Surrey and McDaniel, *Tax Expenditures*, pp.129–132.

33. I.R.C. Sec. 170 (e) (1) (B). See also summary in *Highlights of the Tax Reform Act of 1986*, Special Report Prepared by Baker and Hostetler (Boston: Warren, Gorham and Lamont, Inc., 1986), p. 91.

34. Many groups complained, but museums were particularly affected by the removal of permissible tax deductions for the full value of donated tangible personal property, i.e., works of art. Because of the uproar, this provision was postponed, then finally revoked, effective June 30, 1992, under the Budget Reconciliation Act of 1993.

35. Apparently giving by those with "the highest capacity to give" had declined as a percentage of their adjusted gross income from 1982–1985 but declined even more precipitously following the 1986 Tax Act. See *Impact of Tax Restructuring on Tax-exempt Organizations*, A Report by Price Waterhouse LLP and Caplin & Drysdale, Chartered, April 28, 1997, pp. 4–10. This report presents a good discussion of the need to clarify the difference between total contributions (dollar amounts) and giving as a percentage of personal income. An earlier decline in the second of these was a primary concern of the Peterson and Filer commissions.

36. Schiff, *Charitable Giving and Government Policy,* pp. 1–4.

37. However, the impact of reduced government funds was different for the various sub-sectors of the third sector; thus, government health spending continued to rise in this period. See Lester M. Salamon, "The Marketization of Welfare." This article and others on this issue can be found in Salamon, *Partners in Public Service: Government-Nonprofit Relations in the Modern Welfare State* (Baltimore, Md.: Johns Hopkins University Press, 1995).

38. This is essentially the underlying theme in Lester M. Salamon, *Holding the Center: America's Nonprofit Sector at a Crossroads* (New York: Nathan Cummings Foundation, 1997). It was also the major theme of a conference of *Voluntas* (International Journal of Research on the Voluntary Sector) in London, October 1997.

39. See for example Jean Cohen and Andrew Arato, *Civil Society and Political Theory* (Cambridge, Mass.: MIT Press, 1992); Caroline Hodges Pesell, "The Interdependence of Social Justice and Civil Society" (Presidential address delivered at 66th annual meeting of the Eastern Sociological Society, Boston, Mass., March 30, 1996), *Sociological Forum,* Vol. 12, No. 2, 1997, pp. 149–172; Adam Seligman, *The Idea of Civil Society* (New York: Free Press, 1992); and Michael Walzer, "The Idea of Civil Society: A Path to Social Reconstruction," *Dissent* (Spring 1991), pp. 293–304.

40. According to Independent Sector, in 1994 there were 599,745 501(c)(3) (charitable) entities on the Master File and 501(c)(4) (social welfare) organizations (without counting the estimated 341,000 churches that would be considered as charities, but which do not have to file with the IRS). Together the 501(c)(3) and (c)(4) groups make up about two-thirds of the 1,135,598 organizations on the IRS Master File in 1994. See Table 1.2, "Number of Active Entities on Master File of Tax-Exempt Organizations 1987–1994 (Fiscal Year Ending September 30)," in Hodgkinson and Weitzman et al., *Nonprofit Almanac 1996–1997,* p. 38. The numbers have been slightly revised since then as the IRS "cleaned up" its list. A copy of Table 27 was supplied to me by the IRS in the fall of 1997 (apparently from an Information Book of the IRS) and it listed 654,186 501(c)(3) and 139,512 501(c)(4) organizations, and a total of 1,188,510 exempt organizations in 1996. By 1997, this had grown again to a total of 1,232,214 tax-exempt organizations.

41. Ann E. Kaplan, *Giving USA, 1999: Executive Summary* (AAFRC Trust for Philanthropy, 1999), p. 1.

42. In 1993 there were about 35 university-based academic centers concerned with the nonprofit sector and by 1998 there were reportedly a few more. The 1993 number comes from Independent Sector, *Nonprofit Centers and Programs Focusing on the Study of Philanthropy, Voluntarism and Nonprofit Activities* (Washington, D.C.: Author, 1993). The problems caused by constant, and instant, media attention was raised by several respondents, and emphasized as a cause of sector problems by Bennett M. Weiner, Vice President and Director, Philanthropic Advisory Service and Council of Better Business Bureaus (Arlington, Va.) (telephone interview with Mr. Weiner, June 4, 1998).

43. Robert B. Avery and Michael S. Rendell, "Estimating the Size and Distribution of 'Baby Boomers' Prospective Inheritance." I want to express my appreciation to fund raising consultant Stephen C. Nill (a partner in Mentors in Philanthropy) for sending me a copy of this unpublished study, which has been cited widely since it was released in 1993. For example, see Julie L. Nicklin, "A Historic Transfer of Wealth: College Fund Raisers Prepare for Intergenerational Shift," *Chronicle of Higher Education,* November 3, 1993, p. 10.

44. "Philanthropy in America" (Staff) in *The Economist,* May 30, 1998, pp. 19–21.

45. "Abolishing the estate tax would have reduced charitable bequests by about $3 billion out of an estimated $7 billion in 1996." This was considered significant even though such bequests were "only a small fraction of charitable giving" because the estate tax could have other potential side-effects. See Price Waterhouse and Caplin and Drysdale, *Impact of Tax Restructuring,* p. 4.

46. This provision was incorporated into P.L. 105-277, signed into law by President

Clinton on October 21, 1998. Previously, the extension of the provision had been part of the Tax Payer's Relief Act of 1997, which expired on June 20, 1998. See Memo to Selected IS Members from Joy Terrell, Associate Director, on "Action Needed to Secure Extension of Section 170(e)(5)," April 21, 1998. I want to acknowledge the assistance provided me for this section by Curtis Rumbaugh and the Public Policy Staff of Independent Sector.

47. Despite receiving bipartisan support, H.R. 2499 did not pass in the 105th Congress, but efforts continued with another bill, the Charity Giving Tax Relief Act, H.R. 1310.

48. See Table 4, "Private Giving a Share of Nonprofit Revenues," in Salamon, *Holding the Center,* p. 23.

49. Interview with Michael B. Friedman, former Executive of the Mental Health Association of Westchester, now Director, Network Development, Department of Psychiatry, Cornell Medical Center, White Plains, New York, June 7, 1998. This quote was made after the report cited above by Dickey and Marchetti, "Donations to Charity Rise 7.5%." And in any case it would take a large increment over several years to make a significant difference for most nonprofit organizations.

50. See Alan J. Abramson and Lester M. Salamon, "FY 1997 Federal Budget: Implications for the Nonprofit Sector," unpublished document, cited in Salamon, *Holding the Center,* 1997, p. 19; for a discussion of the commercialization of nonprofits, see also Salamon, "The Marketization of Welfare," in Salamon, *Partners in Public Service,* pp. 203–242. Note also that this figure would be reduced to 216.2 billion by including entitlement programs of income assistance that were projected to increase by over $52.1 billion in that period. According to Salamon, in the 1980s and early 1990s, only government support for health care continued to grow. However, with the growth of managed care in the late 1990s even this would need to be reexamined.

51. Once again advocacy activities were a big target. For example, the Legal Services Corporation took a 31 percent cut from 1995 funding and was subject to severe restrictions on the kinds of cases its lawyers could handle. Among those prohibited were class action suits, abortion cases, and challenges to welfare reform laws. "Fiscal Year 1996 Appropriations Resolved," Government Relations Update, Office of Government Relations, National Association of Social Workers, Washington, D.C., May 29, 1996.

52. Among the states that have been particularly vigilant in this regard is Pennsylvania. See reports in *Don Kramer's Nonprofit Issues* for 1998, and, for example, "Hospitals Denied Real Estate Tax Exemption," in the March 1998 issue, p. 3. Happenings in other states are also reported in Kramer's newsletter, and are frequently listed in the column "Around the States."

53. See for example James Douglas, *Why Charity? The Case for the Third Sector* (Beverly Hills, Calif.: Sage Publications, 1983); Henry B. Hansmann, "The Role of Non-profit Enterprise," *Yale Law Journal,* Vol. 89, 1980; Salamon, *Partners in Public Service*; and Weisbrod, *The Nonprofit Economy.*

54. Although there was some lobbying by organized groups, the drastic changes in welfare provisions, and the loss of the concept of entitlement in the process, really were not marked by the kind of mass protests and organizing efforts that characterized, for example, welfare organizing in the 1960s.

55. See for example "Legislative Report—Republicans again seek to limit advocacy" in *Don Kramer's Nonprofit Issues,* Vol. 8 (4), April 1998.

56. Probably the most notorious of these scandals was the case of William Aramony, CEO of the United Way of America, who was ultimately jailed for various wrongdoings. The Aramony scandal got a great deal of media attention—and was the subject of significant segments on ABC's *Nightline* and the MacNeil-Lehrer show on PBS in February 1992 after the story broke in the *Washington Post.*

57. G. M. Gaul and N. A. Borowski, *Free Ride: The Tax-Exempt Economy* (Kansas City, Mo.: Andrews and McMeel, 1994).

58. *U.S. Department of the Treasury's Proposals to Improve Compliance by Tax-Exempt*

Organizations, Hearings before the Subcommittee on Oversight of the House Committee on Ways and Means, 103rd Cong., 2nd Sess., March 16, 1994, pp. 16–26,

59. Section 1311 of H.R. 2337, which was signed into law by President Clinton on July 30, 1996. The intermediate sanction rules became part of a new section 4958 of the Internal Revenue Code, added to the Code by Section 1311 of the Act, which also expanded disclosure requirements on Form 990 that tax-exempt organizations are mandated to file annually with the IRS. Independent Sector supported the enactment of this legislation along with other watchdog groups. See "Intermediate Sanctions: Strengthening Public Trust in Charitable Organizations," an unpublished paper on this issue by Independent Sector, October 16, 1996 and their other related bulletins on this matter including Robert Boisture and Lloyd H. Mayer (Caplin and Drysdale), "*Special Report:* IRS Issues Proposed Regulations on Disclosure of Forms 990 and Exemption Applications," October 21, 1997.

60. See Richard W. Stevenson, "Review of I.R.S. Is Ordered on Eve of Agency Hearings," *New York Times,* April 28, 1998, p. A16,

61. See the documentation of issues in "The Legal and Legislative Environment 1996" in Kaplan, *Giving USA 1997,* pp. 165–174. See also Salamon, *Holding the Center* (written about the same time) in which he enumerates four crises (fiscal, political, effectiveness, and legitimacy). However, the report of the 93rd meeting of the American Assembly in 1998—which included major foundations and academic advocates of the sector, and which was planned when the crisis loomed—while recognizing that the sector faced problems, in the end still rejected the idea of extreme urgency. See Debra E. Blum, "Philanthropy Should Focus on Gap Between Rich and Poor, Report Says," *Chronicle of Philanthropy,* May 7, 1998, p. 14.

62. Henry Hansmann, "The Two Nonprofit Sectors: Fee for Service Versus Donative Organizations," in V. A. Hodgkinson, R. W. Lyman, and Associates, eds., *The Future of the Nonprofit Sector* (San Francisco: Jossey-Bass, 1989), pp. 27–42.

63. For a thorough comparison of the flat tax in several variations, see Price Waterhouse and Caplin and Drysdale, *Impact of Tax Restructuring.*

64. Joel Fleischman, from the Center of Ethics and the Law at the University of North Carolina, had great difficulty even in presenting this as a possibility for discussion at a meeting of foundation professionals and academics at the American Assembly in Los Angeles, May 1998. See Blum, "Philanthropy Should Focus on Gap Between Rich and Poor, Report Says."

65. In one of the last reports issued under Robert Bothwell's direction, in 1998 NCRP discussed the rising power of conservative foundations. However, over the years NCRP focused more on the United Way and the alternative fund movement than it did on monitoring the foundation arena. In the world of foundations, perhaps the National Association of Grantmakers, the Women's Funding Network, and other ethnically oriented groups could be considered among the current organizational venues for social change. In early 1999, a new Director was hired by NCRP and Bothwell became a Senior Fellow for Research there.

66. The Foundation Center and other foundation groups—in line with a recommendation of the Filer Commission—prefer the term "independent foundation" for most established foundations that are not dominated by family or small "insider" groups; however, the law still refers to them as private foundations.

Appendix A

1. See Louise G. White, "Policy Analysis as Discourse," *Journal of Policy Analysis and Management,* Vol. 13, No. 3 (1994) 506–525. White refers to three kinds of discourse in relation to the policy process: analytic, critical, and persuasive. All three relate to the use of commissions for policy purposes, but the concept of persuasive discourse may be particularly applicable to the purposes of the Peterson and Filer commissions.

2. See the discussion of this practice in Harr and Johnson, *The Rockefeller Conscience,* pp. 278–280, 312–316.

3. See Brilliant, "Looking Backward to Look Forward." Also see discussion above in chapters 6 and 7.

4. Rockefeller's persistence is considered one of the primary reasons for the creation of this statutory commission which was initiated by Congressional action. It should also be noted that JDR had already created a private Population Council so that he would have been well aware of differences between the Council and the proposed commission. The commission and its controversial recommendations are discussed in Charles F. Westoff, "The Commission on Population Growth and the American Future," in Mirra Komarovsky, ed., *Sociology and Public Policy: The Case of Presidential Commissions* (New York: Elsevier, 1975), pp. 43–60.

5. Significance of the quasi-public status of the commissions is at most indirectly referred to in discussions of Rockefeller philanthropic interests in Peter Dobkin Hall, *Inventing the Nonprofit Sector and Other Essays on Philanthropy, Voluntarism, and Nonprofit Organizations* (Baltimore, Md.: Johns Hopkins University Press, 1992); and only slightly more so in Harr and Johnson, *The Rockefeller Conscience*, and Nielsen, *The Big Foundations*.

6. This scheme for analysis of the term is suggested by Harvey Mansfield, "Commissions, Government" in David L. Sills, ed., *International Encyclopedia of the Social Sciences,* Vol. 3 (New York: Macmillan and Free Press, 1968), pp. 12–18.

7. Mansfield, "Commissions, Government," p. 12.

8. Personal communication with Robert Palmer, Professor of Roman History at University of Pennsylvania, March 10, 1996. One example of the use of such a group was the sending out by the Senate of ten commissioners to Macedonia and five to the Illyrians after the defeat of the Macedonians. Commissioners' functions moreover seemed to include some policy determination as well as administrative oversight of the defeated peoples. See Deodorus Siculus, *Bibliotheca Historica*, Book 31, Section 8, subsection 6 (Loeb Library edition, 1954).

9. H. W. Do, "More, Sir Thomas," in *Encyclopedia Britannica*, Vol. 14 (Chicago: William Benton Publishers), p. 832.

10. M.H.B., "Commissioner," *Encyclopedia Britannica*, Vol. 6 (1971), p. 157.

11. Justin David Smith, "The Voluntary Tradition: Philanthropy and Self-Help in Britain 1500–1945," in Smith, Colin Rochester, and Rodney Hedley, eds., in *An Introduction to the Voluntary Sector* (London: Routledge, 1995), pp. 12–13.

12. M.H.B., "Commissioner," *Encyclopedia Britannica*, Vol. 6, p. 157.

13. For an extensive discussion of the use of commissions in this period (with particular focus on the charity commission) see Richard Thompson, *The Charity Commission and the Age of Reform* (London: Routledge and Kegan Paul, 1979). See also M.H.B., "Commissioner," *Encyclopedia Britannica*, Vol. 6, p. 157. This article also uses another quote from the time, referring to commissions as "the chosen instruments of schemers and of the enemies of public liberty" (cited from J. Toulmin Smith, *Government by Commissions Illegal and Pernicious*, 1849).

14. Smith, "The Voluntary Tradition."

15. Smith, "The Voluntary Tradition," pp. 23–24.

16. This election brought in the Thatcher government which moved toward devolution of national government responsibility and increased privatization of services—using both the for-profit and not-for-profit sectors. For a discussion of the implications of this view for voluntary activity in this period see Nicholas Deakin, "The Perils of Partnership: The Voluntary Sector and the State, 1945–1992," in Smith, Rochester, and Hedley, *An Introduction to the Voluntary Sector*, 40–65.

17. See Deakin, "The Perils of Partnership"; for later questions of accountability and increases in the powers of the Charity Commission in 1992–1993, see also Colin Rochester, "Voluntary Agencies and Accountability" in Smith, Rochester and Hedley, *An Introduction to the Voluntary Sector*, pp. 190–207.

18. Commissions may even exist within larger organizations to focus attention on par-

ticular issues, and are often created for this purpose by private professional associations, among other groups.

19. See Mansfield, "Commissions, Government" for a general discussion of this problem; for a more recent comment, see David Flitner, Jr., *The Politics of Presidential Commissions: A Public Policy Perspective* (New York: Transnational Publishers, 1986), p. 4, n. 5. Post–World War II studies of national public commissions have tended either to focus on permanent regulatory/administrative commissions, or, beginning in the 1970s, on ad hoc presidential advisory commissions that may or may not have been initiated in Congress.

20. There have also been national organizations that used "commission" in their names, but which were essentially operating agencies, for example, the U.S. Sanitary Commission (a privately funded group which acted as an auxiliary to the Army Medical Corps). This commission provided supplies and materials to hospitals and medical units serving soldiers in the Civil War and was actually a private organization assisting the government's war effort. There was also the unrelated and privately initiated Rockefeller Sanitary Commission established by John Rockefeller in 1909, and which later became part of the Rockefeller Foundation. For discussion of this commission, see Fosdick, *The Story of the Rockefeller Foundation,* p. 10.

21. Thomas R. Wolanin, *Presidential Advisory Commissions: Truman to Nixon* (Madison: University of Wisconsin Press, 1975), p. 5

22. David Flitner, in *The Politics of Presidential Commissions,* suggests that this should be considered an early form of presidential commission. See Flitner, pp. 7–8.

23. An act of Congress in 1842 actually attempted to prohibit public monies being spent on statutory commissions but like later attempts at such controls, this effort also was not successful. Flitner, p. 8–9.

24. That is, growing populations and immigration, increasing industrialism, and more complex political and economic problems, led to the development of new instruments of government to deal with a changing American society.

25. The Walsh Commission, established under President Taft, had a dual heritage—Congressional establishment and Presidential appointees—but as noted above in chapter 2, in December 1915, President Wilson appointed his own three-person advisory commission to investigate the situation. The Walsh Commission does not appear in historical reviews in Flitner, *The Politics of Presidential Commissions* (1986), or Wolanin, *Presidential Advisory Commissions* (1975); but it is discussed extensively in the books by Harr and Johnson (1988), and Collier and Horowitz (1976), which deal with the Rockefeller family, and in other books dealing with the big foundations such as Nielsen, *The Big Foundations,* p. 5. The commission is discussed briefly in an earlier book that was originally published in 1945 and reissued more recently: *Presidential Commissions,* by Carl Marcy (New York: Da Capo Press, 1973).

26. Wolanin considers there are two basic facts which describe the condition in which commission recommendations exist: (1) that they are only advisory; and (2) that commission reports and recommendations are often "orphans" (his word). See Wolanin, *Presidential Advisory Commissions,* p. 157.

27. For views of the usefulness of commissions by these Presidents see Wolanin, *Presidential Advisory Commissions,* particularly pp. 11–53. For a discussion of Roosevelt's view of government and administration (including the Civil Service Commission), see Richard Polenberg, "The New Deal and Administrative Reform," in Frank P. Evans and Harold D. T. Pinckett, eds., *Research in the Administration of Public Policy* (Washington, D.C.: Howard University Press, 1975), pp. 97–104.

28. See Marcy, *Presidential Commissions,* pp. 27–28 and W. Andrew Achenbaum, *Social Security: Visions and Revisions* (New York: Cambridge University Press, 1986), pp. 18–26.

29. Roosevelt's leadership style is discussed extensively by many authors. See, for example, Arthur Schlesinger, *The Politics of Upheaval* (Boston: Houghton Mifflin, 1960).

30. "Executive Order 11007," included as Appendix A, in U.S. House of Representatives,

Committee on Government Operations, 91st Cong., 2nd Sess., *The Role and Effectiveness of Federal Advisory Committees,* Forty-third Report of the Committee on Government Operations (Washington, D.C.: GPO, 1970).

31. OMB Circular No. A-63, included as Appendix B in U.S. House of Representatives, *The Role and Effectiveness of Federal Advisory Committees* (1970). It is worth noting that concern about uncontrolled costs and lack of accountability of Presidential advisory groups, appointed without statutory (i.e., Congressional) authority, have also been articulated by several Congresses since the 19th century.

32. These commissions were considered expensive at the time; the National Commission on Obscenity and Pornography cost $1.8 million, and the Kerner Commission around $1.5 million. See U.S. House, *The Role and Effectiveness of Federal Advisory Committees* (1970), p. 12. In some respects the Commission on Population Growth and the American Future (chaired by JDR 3rd) should be added to the list of controversial commissions, because of Nixon's repudiation of its strong pro-choice recommendation. Lists of the major national advisory commissions created in these years can be found in Wolanin, *Presidential Advisory Commissions* (1975), and Flitner, *The Politics of Presidential Advisory Commissions* (1986).

33. See U.S. House, *Role and Effectiveness of Federal Advisory Committees* (1970), pp 5–6.

34. U.S. House, *Role and Effectiveness of Federal Advisory Committees* (1970), p. 20.

Index

JDR 3rd is used for John D. Rockefeller 3.

ELEANOR L. BRILLIANT is Professor of Social Work at Rutgers University where she teaches courses on social policy, management, organization theory, and women's issues. She is on the Graduate Faculty of Rutgers University and is a member of the Women's Studies Faculty. Brilliant has been on the Scholar's Advisory Council of the Indiana University Center on Philanthropy, was national Treasurer for the National Association of Social Workers, and has been Vice President for Administration/Secretary of the Association for Research on Nonprofit Organizations and Voluntary Action. Among her major publications are *The United Way: Dilemmas of Organized Charity* (1990), and *The Urban Development Corporation: Private Interests and Public Authority* (1975) which dealt with Nelson Rockefeller's interests in planning and housing development. Brilliant is completing a national study of women's funds and the Women's Funding Network.